THE INTEGRATED EARLY CHILDHOOD CURRICULUM

THE INTEGRATED EARLY CHILDHOOD CURRICULUM

Suzanne Krogh

University of Florida

McGraw-Hill Publishing Company

New York St. Louis San Francisco Auckland Bogotá
Caracas Hamburg Lisbon London Madrid Mexico
Milan Montreal New Delhi Oklahoma City
Paris San Juan São Paulo Singapore
Sydney Tokyo Toronto

This book was developed by Lane Akers, Inc.

THE INTEGRATED EARLY CHILDHOOD CURRICULUM

2 3 4 5 6 7 8 9 0 DOC DOC 9 5 4 3 2 1 0

ISBN 0-07-557053-X

This book was set in Baskerville II by the College Composition Unit in cooperation with Black Dot, Inc.
The editors were Lane Akers and Linda Richmond;
the production supervisor was Salvador Gonzales.
The cover was designed by Joseph Gillians.
R. R. Donnelley & Sons Company was printer and binder.

Chapter Opener Photo Credits
Chapter 1: Elizabeth Crews/The Image Works; Chapter 2: Elizabeth Crews/Stock, Boston; Chapter 3: Susan Lapides/Design Conceptions; Chapter 4: Elizabeth Crews; Chapter 5: Bob Kalman/The Image Works; Chapter 6: Elizabeth Crews; Chapter 7: David Strickler/Monkmeyer; Chapter 8: Elizabeth Crews/The Image Works; Chapter 9: Ulrike Welsch; Chapter 10: Dan Chidester/The Image Works; Chapter 11: Elizabeth Crews; Chapter 12: Kathy Sloan; Chapter 13: Elizabeth Crews.

Library of Congress Cataloging-in-Publication Data

Krogh, Suzanne.
    The integrated early childhood curriculum / Suzanne Krogh.
        p.   cm.
    Includes bibliographical references.
    ISBN 0-07-557053-X
    1. Early childhood education—United States—Curricula.
I. Title.
LB439.4.K76   1990
372.19—dc20   89-48908

contents

Chapter Seven: Social Studies   203

Chapter Eight: Art   235

Chapter Nine: Music and Movement   265

PART THREE   MAKING IT WORK   313

Chapter Ten: Parents   315

From its inception to the final draft, this book has been a very personal experience, one begging some explanation. Officially, work on it began when I first sat down at my typewriter and stared out the window for inspiration, but in actuality the seeds were probably planted when I was 3.

On a trip to Wisconsin, my parents and I passed a restaurant, in front of which stood a Native American dressed in the regalia of a nineteenth-century chief. I was immediately impressed by this new experience and declared with some finality, "He's two things. He's a man and he's an Indian." For years my parents loved to tell this story as proof of their eldest daughter's superior intellect. I've never had the heart to tell them what every teacher of young children has observed: Most preschoolers will, quite suddenly and without warning, make deep, philosophical-sounding statements about the most mundane issues.

My own view of the experience, however, is that it was still an important one as it may well have marked the beginning of my lifelong preference for anything that can be, or do, at least two things at once. It was inevitable in its planning that this book would have to meet that specific challenge. Thus, you are about to embark on a reading and studying experience that aspires to a meeting of two views of teaching and learning. The task in writing has been to avoid creating a book that is at cross-purposes; the goal has been to achieve a dual entity that, like the person I observed so many years ago, can be both man and Native American.

The first view the book takes is that each subject or curricular area is important in its own right. Indeed, each curriculum chapter in this book contains statements from national associations that argue for the importance of the subject area they foster and champion. The second viewpoint of the book is quite different. It takes the position that the most natural, enjoyable, and beneficial learning takes place not by studying single-subject areas but by following themes of interest. In this view, subject areas are subsumed by grander issues that incorporate them as a part of the whole.

Both these views have much to recommend them. In order to achieve a unification of the two, this book focuses both on individual subjects and suggests how to integrate subject areas into a broader, interest-based curriculum. As you will see in the curriculum chapters, this man–Indian way of looking at children's learning has support from the same associations that argue the importance of their own single subjects.

The important thing, I have concluded, is that a book—this book—should provide a global view of what children can do and learn. Then, each teacher must adapt to each situation appropriately. By incorporating both subject areas and student interests into one book, I hope I will have helped make this kind of flexibility possible for you. Read the arguments for the importance of each and every curricular subject. Then see how following young children's interests can help you weave these subjects into a meaningful whole.

In Part One we take a look at the human element in schooling: the child and the teacher. The physical-motor, social-affective, and cognitive development of children provides the foundation for all the teaching decisions we make. Thus, we begin with children. You will, no doubt, have taken courses in child development. If so, you well know that there is no one acceptable way of looking at children's growth and that research on this subject continues to go on. A book such as this cannot hope to cover every viewpoint in depth and so leaves that task to child development texts. Our purpose in Chapter One is to review each viewpoint briefly and to describe the way it relates to this book. The other side of the classroom's human equation is you, the teacher. Ways to look at yourself as a person and in relation to children are considered in Chapter Two. Practical suggestions for classroom use in fulfilling all the teacher's roles are also included in Chapter Two.

Part Two is the heart of the book: the curriculum itself. Although each subject is given its own chapter (Chapters Four through Nine), guidelines provide direction toward integration with interests. In fact, Part Two opens with Chapter Three, which provides step-by-step instructions for integrating subjects with individual interests. Different formats for creating an integrated curriculum are introduced and then reintroduced throughout the remaining chapters of this part.

Part Three is designed to take the student out of the college classroom and into the real world. Chapter Ten discusses parents and their importance in making a success of your efforts in the classroom. Chapter Eleven describes the environment, suggesting ways in which the integrated curriculum can be made most successful. Chapter Twelve discusses ways to view an entire school year, primarily in the preschool, and should help you to get your own program underway. Finally, Chapter Thirteen discusses the ever-present problem of needing to meet the requirements and expectations of school and government officials in the primary grades. This final chapter discusses ways of meeting these expectations while still making use of the curriculum integration proposed by this book.

You will find that this book is both philosophical and practical. There are a number of units and themes I hope you'll try out. My own personal favorite was designed by someone else, a teacher who was a student in my early childhood course. "Digging to China," like my own flower curriculum unit in Chapter Two, was inspired by children's needs. My hope is that after you have tried some of the ideas presented here, you will expand and adapt them to better meet your own needs and then create more ideas that are entirely your own—and your children's. If you would like to share your feelings and experiences, I look forward to hearing from you.

ACKNOWLEDGMENTS

A number of people from several generations contributed to the successful completion of this book. The children of the Benjamin Franklin International School (BFIS) in Barcelona offered feedback on many of the ideas and helped create new ones. I am grateful to the administration at BFIS for letting me use their computers in the after-school hours. Kim Stoddard of the Department of Special Education at the University of Florida provided the sections on mainstreamed children for Chapter One. Several reviewers of the manuscript provided invaluable insight: Kathryn Castle, Oklahoma State University; Rosalind Charlesworth, Louisiana State University; Marilyn Church, University of Maryland; Walter Hodges, Georgia State University; Linda Jones, University of Lethbridge; and Margaret Lay-Dopyera, Syracuse University. Lane Akers has been the best possible editor. Also I wish to express gratitude for the influence of my mother, Gertrude Lowell, who continues to demonstrate that growing and learning can last a lifetime.

Suzanne Krogh

THE INTEGRATED EARLY CHILDHOOD CURRICULUM

CHILD AND TEACHER TOGETHER

A generation ago, any child who began first grade already knowing how to read was viewed with suspicion and even alarm by the teacher. It was supposed to be understood that parents would leave such intellectual training to the schools which, presumably, knew more about what they were doing. Any alarm the teacher might have felt at greeting a child who could already read probably had two causes. First, it was thought that the parents might well have used improper, even coercive methodology to teach the child (never mind that many of these children more or less taught themselves). Second, the teacher didn't know what to do with the child since the beginning curriculum was already planned and well established.

If the school system provided kindergarten, it was viewed as a kind of prep school for first grade, but the focus was on social/emotional development more than on preparation for academics. Children were to learn to love school and each other. While kindergarten teachers did not need to share their first-grade colleagues' nervousness about advance preparation, there was still a feeling that the social milieu of the neighborhood could never quite stand up to the more carefully planned experiences of the school setting.

Nursery schools had another function, although in many ways they were similar to the kindergartens. If the first-grade teacher was the guardian angel of intellectual growth and the kindergarten teacher was overseer of social and emotional development, then it was the nursery school teacher who was responsible for children's health. Although the schools' primary mission was to provide positive play experiences for small children, emphasis was put on nurturing children physically if there was a need. Further, children were not permitted to partake in the day's events until an on-duty nurse declared them fit each day. (Remember, this was before antibiotics made the survival rates of the very young soar dramatically.)

A radical change was on the horizon at the same time, however, and in just a few years attitudes would begin to change concerning what cogni-

1

tive, affective, and physical development and experiences children brought with them on their first day of school. No longer were early readers viewed with suspicion and dismay. In fact, teachers of reading began to reproduce the relaxed atmosphere of the home right within the classroom. And once early reading was accepted it also became more expected. The benign social atmosphere of the kindergarten turned more academic. Nursery schools also began to change as some of the academic focus turned to them. For young children in nursery school or kindergarten, physical experiences were emphasized when it was learned that motor skills had more importance than previously believed.

Much of the change took place as knowledge about child development grew. New respect for what children accomplished on their own before entering school forced teachers to rethink their attitudes toward beginning students. No longer could they assume blank slate status for children's minds and social understanding. The research that led to these new attitudes continues, but there is still a wealth of information that can guide us as teachers to understand our children better.

In this section we will look at some of the history that led to today's clearer understanding of child development. Different ways of viewing cognitive, affective, and motor development will be discussed and will also be related to the stance taken by this text. It is assumed that you have previously studied theories of child development. Thus, this introductory chapter should be considered as a memory refresher. If you have not studied child development, you may find it useful to read further in the books listed at the end of the chapter.

In Chapter Two the teacher's role is considered. Being a teacher of young children is a happy but important responsibility, one that requires self-understanding as well as effective teaching methods. Both these aspects of the early childhood teacher's career are discussed, with some specific suggestions for you to try.

_____ chapter one

The Developing Child

In this chapter we look at the various ways children develop from infancy. A knowledge of these is basic to making curriculum decisions in the classroom. Although teachers cannot be expected to know the developmental stages of each and every child, a general understanding will provide much assistance when planning appropriate activities. We begin with a discussion of physical growth and motor development, continue with social and affective development and cognitive development, and conclude with a description of the integrated curriculum as it can appear in an out-of-school setting. Real-life children guide us through each of the three major components of development in this chapter. Use their stories to help you review the theories. (If you have never studied child development, it will be helpful to do more in-depth reading than this chapter offers.)

There is a special "what if?" section at the end of the discussion of each development phase in this chapter. Our question in these sections is: What if the children we have just learned about had severe problems in their development? The children featured in each of the three developmental components are normal, yet not every child you meet will be. It is helpful to know what deviations you might expect to see and to have some idea of the general directions you could take when you seek help in dealing with them.

Infant learners are remarkable. In a few short years they progress from cognitive ignorance and physical helplessness to expressive ability in at least one language, intuitive understanding of mathematical principles, political know-how for getting what they want, and skill in walking, running, climbing, maybe even somersaults. How do they achieve so much in such a short time? The answers have been sought for centuries and the closing arguments have yet to be heard. We will look at the three areas of child development and the research findings to date. Think about children you have known as you read.

MOTOR DEVELOPMENT AND PHYSICAL GROWTH AS A PART OF THE WHOLE CHILD

Although there is agreement among theorists on the existence of motor development stages, there are slightly differing models. We use the one presented by Gallahue (1982), which indicates four general phases that begin before the baby is born and end in the teen years. Each of the phases contains two or three stages. As we discuss each of these, we will visit Christi and Monica as they develop together.

Christi and Monica are two 14-year-old girls who have known each other since infancy. Although they share the same group of friends and are about evenly matched academically, their physical appearance and athletic interests diverge widely. Christi is tall, olive-skinned with dark hair, and constantly worried about her weight. Monica is blonde, a bit shorter, and wiry. Both of them love sports, but their interest and capabilities have little in common. Christi is on the swim team and loves to go for long, slow runs with her father. Monica loves to dive and is working her way through increasingly difficult levels of proficiency in judo. The roots of their physical and motor differences were observed in their infancy, and we will follow their progress as we discuss the topic of physical growth and motor development.

Before meeting them in their infancy it might be interesting to note that the girls were born just a week apart (a fact that the older Monica eventually learned to use to her advantage in many an argument). Their parents were close friends with very similar cultural upbringing and expectations for their children. The middle-class homes and the private nursery school education they provided for their children meant that environmental conditions were also similar. The one difference was that Monica was the youngest of three children and therefore had older siblings with whom she strove to keep up. Christi was her parents' first child with a younger brother born when she was 5.

Reflexive Movement Phase

It may be universally true that parents of firstborn infants are more nervous than parents who have had at least one other child. Christi's parents were no exception and found themselves staring at their new daughter's movements, wondering if she were normal. At the first opportunity, they laid their own infant next to Monica and (without telling her parents what they were about) quietly began to compare and contrast. It wasn't long before mother and father stared at each other and laughed in relief. Only then did they explain that since Christi did nothing but stare at the ceiling and wiggle her hands aimlessly they had thought perhaps something was the matter. Monica's mother laughingly admitted she had once had the same concern, and then she explained, "Most of what they do right now is just reflexes. Look." She laid a finger to the side of Monica's cheek and the infant immediately began a rooting movement as if looking for motherly nourishment.

The phase of growth that Monica's mother described begins before birth and continues until around the baby's first birthday. There are two stages within the phase: information encoding and information decoding.

Information Encoding Stage   The fetus or the newborn infant learns during this stage by involuntary reactions to stimuli. These reactions are called reflexes and the infant learns from them even though active thought is not involved.

Information Decoding Stage   By the time the infant has reached 4 months of age, voluntary movements are overtaking involuntary, for the brain has stored enough information that the infant can use it to respond to new sensory stimuli.

Examples of infant reflexes are sucking and rooting, both important for early survival. Others that have lifelong utility are sneezing, blinking, yawning, and coughing. Additionally, it is possible to observe the tiniest infant both "walk" (by holding the child upright in the air) and "swim" (by holding it in or just above water). Stepping movements will be made in the first instance and rhythmic swimming movements are observable in the second. These early reflexes do not always seem to be connected to later voluntary behavior. For example, the stepping reflex disappears at about the fifth month, long before the baby begins to actually experiment with walking. There is also a crawling reflex that can be induced by pressing on the bottom of the foot of a prone infant. Actual voluntary crawling begins at about 7 months, but by then the crawling reflex has been absent from the baby's movement repertoire for 3 or 4 months.

Nevertheless, it is believed that there is at least an indirect connection between early reflexes and later voluntary movements. Such early reflexes as stepping, crawling, or grasping with the fist are stored in the infant's brain and more than likely are used later as a basis for intentional acts.

In a normal infant, reflexes come and then go as the child's brain and neuromuscular system develop. If a reflex is missing or if the child retains it after the usual age that it disappears, or it is too strong or too weak, then there are early signs of a possible dysfunction.

Physical Growth   There is a wide variety in acceptably normal birth weights, and children who are born prematurely can catch up later if their difference is not too extreme. By the infant's fifth month, birth weight has doubled and by the end of the first year it has tripled. Much of this increase is a filling out process, because the baby's length doesn't double until about 14 months.

Rudimentary Movement Phase

Less than 7 months after Christi's parents were reassured that their daughter was normal, the two babies sat side by side on the floor surrounded by toys. Christi picked up a rubber bear and began to explore it with all her senses, while Monica did the same with a plastic rattle. Before long, Monica lost interest in the rattle and clumsily threw it to the floor where it bounced out of reach. Meanwhile, Christi turned the bear over, tasted it, then looked for a replacement before throwing the bear away. The girls continued in this behavior, Monica going through three toys for every two that Christi did. As the last toy bounced out of reach, Christi looked around, saw that there were no toys remaining, and then busied herself exploring the only other toy she could find: her own ten fingers. Monica, however, was immediately frustrated. She flopped over on her stomach and tried her best to crawl toward the nearest toys. She hadn't quite mastered the technique yet, but she wiggled one way and then the other trying to get her body closer to her goal. Meanwhile, Christi sat contentedly exploring her fingers.

The two girls were behaving quite normally, although very differently. Even at this early age the motor behaviors they exhibited portended the differences in the athletic preferences of their coming teen years. Already Christi was calm, methodical, and slower moving while Monica preferred more activity and variety within it.

Reflex Inhibition Stage   What the mothers observed during that afternoon playtime was the beginning stage of the rudimentary movement phase. This first stage begins at birth, along with the information encoding stage, and lasts until about the first birthday. Its name is the *reflex inhibition stage,* signifying that with the development of the brain it is possible for the child to reject reflexes in favor of voluntary movement. During this stage, voluntary movement is primitive, poorly integrated, and rudimentary. When Monica decided to move toward the toys, the best she could do was to flop over and grope around. Her intentions were correct, but her movements, while voluntary, lacked control.

Precontrol Stage   A second stage in this phase begins at about age 1 and continues for the next year. It is termed the *precontrol stage,* indicating that greater control as well as precision is now possible for the infant. The perceptual and motor systems begin to be better integrated, and movement abilities grow rapidly. Through repeated practice, the infant works at refining many skills begun so clumsily during the preceding year.

The acquisition and mastery of skills during the rudimentary movement phase consume many of the infant's waking hours. Some stability and basic control of the body are necessary for the movement skills they make possible. By the second month the infant should be able to lift head and chest and by the eighth month roll easily from stomach to back. Stability in sitting emerges between the sixth and eighth months, as does supported standing. By the twelfth month the child can stand alone.

As stability increases, movement abilities also grow. Between the sixth and ninth months the infant first crawls (on stomach) and then creeps (on hands and knees). Tentative steps may be taken by the carefully held 6-month-old child, but real attempts at supported walking usually begin about the ninth or tenth month. By the twelfth or thirteenth month the infant is ready to solo.

The schedules by which infants achieve their stability and motor goals depend largely on maturation, but environment can be a factor as well. Several studies done over three decades (see Gallahue, 1982) reported on the influences contributed by different settings. Infants raised in environmentally sterile institutions in which they received little physical handling or opportunity for movement suffered motor retardation. Yet Hopi Indian babies who spend the first months of their lives bound to their mothers' cradleboards suffer no ill effects. It has been hypothesized (Gallahue, 1982, p. 91) that the difference lies in the surroundings. The Hopi babies are close to their mothers and are able to enjoy the varied visual surroundings to which they are carried; the institutionalized babies have no such advantage. Further, as the months pass the Hopi infants are given increasingly long periods of physical freedom. Since most of an infant's progress is made naturally through maturation, it appears most reasonable that the function of the caregiver adult is to provide an environment that is most supportive of the infant's efforts.

Physical Growth   The child's second year continues to be a time of rapid growth although it isn't as dramatic as the first. By their second birthday, boys are about 35 inches tall and weigh about 32 pounds, while girls average about 34 inches and 31 pounds. Part of what makes babies and small children have a bodily appearance different from that of adults is the order in which growth takes place. Parts of limbs closer to the trunk of the body grow first, so that the upper arm will grow before the hand, the thigh before the foot. As the infant moves into childhood, the trunk itself begins to grow more quickly than the head, but more slowly than the limbs, while the hands and feet grow fastest of all.

Fundamental Movement Phase

This is the phase that concerns us most as early childhood educators, for it describes the motor development of children from the time they are 2 years old until they are 7. We will visit Christi and Monica during the stages of the fundamental movement phase, each time observing similarities and differences as they develop. During these years the girls attained increasingly complex use of their bodies, yet the skills they learned remained fundamental. In motor development terms this means that the skills were at a basic level and not yet ready to be completely integrated into the complex maneuvers required of true sports.

Initial Stage   One sunny summer afternoon when they were 3½ years old, the girls were taken to the pool by their fathers. They immediately and joyfully took to the water, even where it was deep. The fathers seized the opportunity and tried valiantly, but in vain,. to teach some rudimentary swimming skills. The girls happily refused to do anything but "walk" their legs and push with their hands. They got practically nowhere, but they did learn to stay afloat.

In this initial stage of the fundamental movement phase, children make their "first goal-oriented attempts at performing a fundamental skill" (Gallahue, 1982, p. 46). These attempts are uncoordinated, badly sequenced, and off the proper rhythm. By the time children are as old as Christi and Monica were in the pool, many of their goal-oriented attempts have been successful. Something as complex as true swimming, however, is beyond their capabilities. Generally, the observer can expect to see success in the development of simple skills such as walking up and down stairs, throwing a ball overhand, kicking a ball or rolling it, walking on tiptoe, building a tower of blocks, jumping in place or from a bottom step, running, and riding a tricycle (Skinner, 1979).

By the summer of the swimming pool incident, Christi and Monica had achieved every one of the skills just listed. However, Monica would spend much time trying out different ways to go up and down the stairs next to the living room, while Christi, after joining her for a few minutes of companionship, would settle on the bottom step to watch. It was becoming more and more apparent that the movement "styles" of the two girls were, and would continue to be, quite different. At the same time, the experience in the swimming pool offers a good example of the benefits of the right environment and some extra training.

Elementary Stage   Almost a year after the two girls played in the pool with their fathers, they spent a morning together at Monica's house. Although they attended different nursery schools, they had both learned the poem-chant "Five little monkeys jumping on the bed." Inspired by the raucous rhythm and the sound of their own voices, the two girls began to role-play what they had learned, using what they didn't have at school: Monica's bed. The increasing noise alerted Monica's mother to the possible need for supervision and she walked into the room just in time to see an unexpected sight. Christi was, as might be expected, happily jumping up and down in near-perfect rhythm. Monica, however, was executing a backward flip!

"Look!" she announced when she saw her mother, "I can do a somersault with no hands," and before her mother could stop her, she went sailing through the air yet again. Her mother gulped, suggested they both come to the kitchen for a snack, and made plans to put Monica in a beginning gymnastics class where she would learn to do her tricks in safety.

Again, we see differing development in the two girls, still within the range of "normal." The elementary stage of the fundamental movement phase "involves greater control and better rhythmical coordination of fundamental movements" (Gallahue, 1982, p. 46). Achieving this stage depends largely on proper maturation. Advancing beyond it often requires some instruction, practice, or at least motivation. (Yes, without one or more of these, many adults never develop some skills beyond this stage!)

Children of 4 and 5 years are typically at this stage, although some skills may be achieved earlier. The observer may note skills developing such as somersaults (usually forward and safely earthbound!), use of scissors, dressing self (tying shoes may remain a problem), catching a ball with two hands, hopping easily on one foot, roller skating, riding a junior bicycle, possibly hitting a swinging ball, and a smoother control of body activity in general (Skinner, 1979).

Mature Stage   Achieving this stage means that children, ordinarily by the age of 5, 6, or 7, can produce "mechanically efficient, coordinated, and controlled performances" (Gallahue, 1982, p. 46). Over the years, general development takes place in three areas: manipulation (both gross and fine motor), stability (both while the body is still and during movement), and locomotion (moving through space). Within the acceptable range of accomplishment there is still room for differences, as Christi and Monica demonstrate once again.

By the time they were 6, the two girls were taking swimming and diving lessons together at the local YMCA. While they were both able to keep up with their peers, the similarities stopped there. Christi loved the challenge of swimming multiple lengths of the pool, and she gladly put forth the effort it took to learn different strokes. Monica, on the other hand, did as little as possible during swimming class and would eventually have to take and pass the same Red Cross level three summers in a row. At the diving board it was different. Monica transported her monkey-on-the-bed routine to the pool and her very first dive off the board was—to everyone's amazement but her own—a back flip. Soon she was confidently attempting new tricks off the high board while Christi still had trouble going in headfirst off the low board.

While the two children each demonstrated a natural athletic ability, they were also fortunate to have parents who cared about their physical development. In the 3 years since the day the two had played with their fathers in the pool, there had been many similar opportunities as well as swimming lessons. Thus, each had reached the mature stage of this phase with little difficulty and much joy. The mature stage is a critical one to reach for children who hope to progress later into the world of sports.

The movements that characterize the fundamental movement phase are fundamental for two reasons: They are basic rather than complex, and they form the necessary foundation for future development.

Some mature skills that children should be expected to achieve include walking and running with total ease and control; jumping, hopping, galloping, sliding, leaping, and skipping with fluid motion and correct landings; climbing (ladders, etc.) with good balance and body control; and correct throwing, catching, kicking, striking, rolling, trapping, volleying, and dribbling of balls.

Physical Growth   From the beginning of this phase until the onset of puberty and adolescence, children will grow about 2 inches a year and gain an average of 5 pounds a year. Boys are just slightly heavier and taller than girls and have more muscle and bone mass. By the time children are 6 years old, their brains are almost 90 percent of their projected adult weight.

Sport-Related Movement Phase

This final phase in the development of motor abilities begins at about age 7 and continues through the high school years. "It is a period when basic locomotor, manipulation, and stability skills are progressively refined, combined, and elaborated upon in order that they may be used in increasingly demanding activities" (Gallahue, 1982, p. 46). At its most advanced stage athletes develop their most complex and specialized skills and demonstrate most strongly their preferences for specific types of sports, just as Christi and Monica did in the opening paragraphs of this chapter. The teacher of young children will, at the most, be exposed to children in the first of this phase's three stages; for that reason, it is the only stage we will discuss further.

General (or Transitional) Phase   The general stage begins at age 7 or 8 and continues through the rest of elementary school. It is a stage built on the preceding one in that children bring to it the skills they have been perfecting and are now ready to incorporate into a variety of play activities and games. For example, the many ways children learned to jump in kindergarten can now be transferred to jumping rope; kicking a ball just for the fun of it carries over into the game of kickball; the act of running applies to relay races and other games.

It is important during the early years of this sports-related phase to ensure that the many skills learned in the previous phase are not lost through too much specialization too soon. If children are exposed to a large variety of games and activities, they will know the joy of performing competently and will build a base from which they can make later decisions about competitive sports or recreational activities.

Here we visit Christi and Monica one last time as we see how they made their transition from simple, fundamental movements to their junior high school sports. Although their parents were delighted to note that both girls had athletic ability, and although they suspected that Christi would one day be a swimmer and Monica would participate in gymnastics-related sports, they made a decision to let the girls find this out for themselves. (During one conversation the fathers agreed that if the girls had been boys they probably would have more tempted to push them into the "right" sport. They also agreed that not doing so probably gave the girls an advantage.)

The result of the parental decision was that the girls had just the wide variety of experiences that motor development studies have shown to be the most beneficial. They continued their swimming and diving lessons during the summer; tried soccer and hated it; giggled their way through ballet classes; and, of course, participated in the games and sports provided in the school physical education program. It was in the sixth grade that Monica discovered judo and refused to engage in "that boring swimming" ever again. A year later Christi became a potentially very competitive swimmer and the two girls went their athletically separate ways. Throughout their developing years the girls had been fortunate to have an environment that was conducive to appropriate maturation and parents who happened to choose the most supportive ways of encouraging them.

Not all children are as fortunate. For their sakes, and for every child's sake, it is important that teachers of young children be aware of the motor development stages of their students and the ways that are most appropriate to support their progress.

Physical Growth   Because children continue to grow slowly and change their shapes minimally during the elementary grades, they have several years in which to feel at home in their bodies. This provides an opportunity to increase coordination and motor control. During these years boys and girls have similar growth patterns, although boys tend to have longer limbs and greater height, while girls are wider in hip and thigh. Because of their great similarities, boys and girls should be able to participate in most athletic activities together (Gallahue, 1982, p. 117).

What If? Motor Development and Physical Growth of the Exceptional Child

The sequence and rate of motor development for exceptional children is significantly more divergent than that of average children. For example, the rate of motor development may be much slower in a visually impaired child (Fallen & Umansky, 1985). Children with cerebral palsy may exhibit slight motor disabilities or total lack of muscular control. In addition, a child may have the motor ability but not the cognitive ability to understand a particular motor task such as jumping rope or riding a tricycle. Children of particular concern for teachers of young children are those identified as both physically delayed and mentally handicapped.

The physically delayed and mentally handicapped youngster follows a similar pattern in motor development as the typical child but at a much slower pace. The reason for this delay cannot always be identified. Factors such as prenatal care, premature birth, anoxia, and trauma after birth may affect the motor development of the child (Hallahan & Kauffman, 1988). The attitude of the child and the attitude of others toward the child also have been found to have a significant effect on the child's motivation and ability to develop motor skills.

Let's assume that of the two girls we have just discussed, Christi was identified at birth as developmentally delayed. As Christi continued her development the difference between the two girls would become more obvious. At 7 months, Monica would explore each toy without adult interference. Christi would not freely experiment with the toys unless given adult direction. The more severe the retardation or disability, the more intervention is necessary to encourage growth through play. A lack of self-initiated play by disabled children is one of the important differences between handicapped and nonhandicapped children. This lack of initiative in play is often due to deficits in skills such as visual tracking, incidental learning, and spontaneity with toys.

When most children reach the initial stage of the fundamental movement phase they can accomplish simple skills, such as throwing and kicking a ball, which set the stage for more complex skills. As a handicapped child Christi would not attempt these skills because she may not have successfully mastered the rudimentary movement skills or may not have experienced the rewarding aspects of play (Paloutzian, Hazasi, Streifel, & Edgar, 1971).

Some handicapped children will never reach the sport-related movement phase, but parents and teachers should encourage the child toward this goal. Here are some guidelines and suggestions they may find applicable.

• Provide children with normally developing role models as playmates.
• Give the child direct instruction or physical prompting to complete an activity.
• Phase out prompting as soon as the child can work without help.
• Try social reinforcement or tangible rewards for effort.
• Avoid setting unrealistic expectations, especially comparing the child to other, more normally developing children.
• Provide for play that includes cooperation between handicapped and nonhandicapped children.

Social and Affective Development as a Part of the Whole Child

When Micky was 3, he was allowed for the first time to play in the frontyard. Unlike the back, it had no fence around it, so his mother walked him around the permitted boundaries and was very explicit about the consequences of exceeding them. "I'll be here watching to be sure you're safe. If you go in the street where the cars are, I'll have to spank you." Micky appeared awestruck; he had never been spanked before.

For a while all went well as Micky played with his two favorite trucks. But eventually the lure of the curb and the street proved too great and, emitting a loud "vroom," Micky rolled a truck over the edge and onto the street. Immediately his mother pulled him back, hugged him, and explained that she loved him very much but that he would now suffer the consequences.

But Micky didn't think he should be spanked. "I forgot," he said, "that you were looking." His mother responded that he must always obey, even when she wasn't there. The spanking was a minor one, but obviously a shock to Micky, and he soon wanted to go back into the house.

His mother was a little shocked by the experience, too, and wondered why she couldn't have thought of something other than a spanking to deal with the problem. She began reading some popular books on discipline and talking with friends who didn't spank their children. Over time she began to help Micky learn to reason about behavior on his own. When there were infractions of rules or improper conduct, mother and son sat down together and talked.

To fully appreciate the outcome of this approach, we will have to move ahead 5 years. Over time, of course, Micky changed considerably, although his mother's approach to discipline did not. By the age of 8, Micky was becoming impatient with the mother-son discussions. One day, after a particularly trying one, he blurted out, "What I want to know is, why do we always have to talk about everything? Why can't you be like other mothers? They just spank their kids and get it over with. You always make me think!"

Micky at age 8 was more interested in the speedy practicality of a quick punishment than in reasoning. His case is certainly nothing out of the ordinary. Forever, no doubt, parents and educators have observed such changes in child attitude. The explanations for these age-related changes have differed over time and between philosophers, psychologists, and educators. In the discussion that follows we will look at three major ways of explaining the changes in child attitudes and behaviors such as those we saw taking place in Micky.

Psychoanalytic View

The psychoanalytic view draws from the work of Sigmund Freud (1856–1939). Foremost among those committed to this way of looking at children has been Erik Erikson (1902–   ). Although he based his research and conclusions on Freud's theories, Erikson (1963) shifted emphasis from Freud's ideas of neurotic conflict to his own observations of ego development. He then placed the concept of ego development within a societal framework. He postulated that the ego goes through eight stages on its way from birth to full maturity. The first four of these are completed by the end of elementary school. At each stage there is a central crisis that must be resolved in some way before the next stage can be approached. This crisis consists of antagonistic social-emotional forces pulling the infant, child, or adult in opposing directions. One direction is affectively positive, the other negative. If the person resolves the conflicts in a positive way, his or her emotional and social life will be more successful. In the description of the stages that follows, the ages that are given are approximate.

Stage One (Age: 0–12 months)   *Crisis: Trust vs. Mistrust:* It is the mother's responsibility to provide the infant with sufficient sensitive care so that the infant feels secure in trusting her. An indication that this stage is developing positively is the baby's ability to let its mother leave the room, confident that she will come back.

Stage Two (Age: 12 months–3 years)   *Crisis: Autonomy vs. Shame and Doubt:* As the child becomes autonomous he learns to control his use of the toilet. He needs both assurance and guidance to "protect him against meaningless and arbitrary experiences of shame and of early doubt" (Erikson, 1963, p. 252).

Stage Three (Age: 3–5 years)   *Crisis: Initiative vs. Guilt:* The child has much energy and easily forgets failures. Tasks are taken on "for the sake of being active and on the move..." (Erikson, 1963, p. 255). The child may feel guilt about some of the tasks he has in mind, particularly the desire to take the place of the same-sex parent.

Stage Four (Age: 6–12 years)   *Crisis: Industry vs. Inferiority:* Children become industrious as they increase their skills, learn diligence, and apply themselves to their tasks. These capabilities, plus the ability and willingness to work with others, are necessary for success in school. With failure, a sense of inadequacy and inferiority may emerge.

Although Erikson's proposed stages continue on through adulthood, we will stop here and see how this theory might explain Micky's behavior at the two different stages in which we observed him.

Recall that Micky was just about 3 when his first spanking took place. This timing would coincide with Erikson's stage three with its crisis of initiative vs. guilt. Micky was excited by the new opportunity to demonstrate autonomy and, despite his mother's warning, asserted his own will by driving the truck into the street. The spanking he received would have been most unpleasantly important at this age, particularly since it was administered to his bottom. "The 'behind' is the small being's dark continent, an area of the body which can be magically dominated and effectively invaded by those who would attack one's power of autonomy..." (Erikson, 1963, p. 253).

At age 8 (stage four) Micky had changed drastically in his outlook. His oedipal desires firmly suppressed, he was concerned with and interested primarily in the culture of the school. He simply wanted to get his mother's discipline out of the way and get on about his business.

Social Learning View

Rejecting the stage theories proposed by researchers such as Erikson, Albert Bandura (1963) proposed instead a social learning theory. He argued that stage theories ignore differences between people due to biological, socioeconomic, ethnic, cultural, and child-raising variables. The differences in those variables can make major differences between individual children.

At the same time, there is stability within each child. This is because the variables of family, biology, and culture are likely to remain reasonably constant during the time it takes a young child to develop the basic social learnings. So, while Erikson argues for individual change over time and stability across people at any one age, Bandura suggests the opposite: A given child matures in a line of continuity while other children may mature quite differently. The primary way children learn is by modeling those in the environment, which explains the importance of family, biology, and culture as well as the less stable variables.

Bandura's theory grew from the ideas of behaviorism. It is not without its critics (Hoffman, 1971). A primary criticism is that if we depend primarily on modeling to promote approved behavior, the expected result will be conformity, possibly good but just as likely bad.

Bandura's theory also can explain Micky's behavior. In his earliest experience, Micky initially modeled his mother's behavior. But, of course, his enthusiasm eventually overwhelmed his memory. Social learning theory would suggest that the spanking was an inappropriate corrective and that further modeling would have worked better. In Bandura's (1963) studies, children consistently modeled the aggressive behavior of adults, a finding that demonstrates the need to avoid such solutions as spanking.

Micky's mother did learn eventually that there were more effective ways to deal with Micky's behavior. Yet, after a time, even these were not working as well as they should. In social learning terms, Micky was continuing to model behavior, but by age 8 his imitative focus had transferred from his mother to his peers. As a result, he was impatient with his mother's discussion technique and eager to return to his friends.

Despite the fact that the social learning and psychoanalytic views of affective development frequently conflict with each other, it is certainly possible to accept some of each in our role as teachers. If we are aware of the crisis stage of our children, we will have a better understanding of and sympathy for the "antagonistic forces" they are coping with. Further, we need to be continually alert to the behaviors we model, for in our interactions with children they will certainly find opportunities to imitate us.

The Constructivist View

The third view of affective development may be seen as complementary to rather than in conflict with these two preceding approaches. Our starting point for a discussion of the constructivist view begins, but does not end, with the work of Jean Piaget (1896–1980). A Swiss psychologist born in the late nineteenth century, he saw merit in both psychoanalytic and behaviorist traditions. His own view was that the solution to the argument is to put them together. Biology is important and determines much of what a child can accomplish. Environment is important, too, and is acted upon by the child using the biological capabilities at his or her disposal.

Although Piaget's primary interest in child research was related to cognitive development, he did undertake studies in social and moral development in the 1920s. The results were reported in his book, *The Moral Judgment of the Child*, published in 1932. Although he was certainly aware of the emotional aspects of life, he chose to focus on the moral, viewing its development as interdependent with cognitive development. That is, in order to make a moral decision, it is necessary for one to have the cognitive structure necessary to think about the problem.

For the young child, morality can cover a broad range of issues such as rules, authority, friendship, helpfulness, respect for property, sharing, telling the truth, keeping promises, and so on. There is an underlying theme to all these issues: justice and a sense of fairness. Piaget chose to focus his research on the first issue, rules, seeing it as the childhood precursor to the issue of laws in the larger society. He selected the game of marbles as his research focus and from his observations of children playing marbles, he delineated stages of development in their understanding of rules and fairness. By extension, other issues may be included in the stages.

Stage One (Age: Preprimary)   *Heteronomy:* To be heteronomous is to be other-directed rather than self-directed. Very young children are egocentric and can't relate to rules except as they affect themselves. They will follow what authority says even if they don't understand. Discipline is arbitrary, meted out by authority figures in a nonlogical fashion. Big people can punish simply because they are big. Heteronomous children assume they know the rules of the game even when their definitions differ from those of their playmates.

Stage Two (Age: Kindergarten–Primary)   *First Transitional Stage*: Children learn about rules in a very literal sense, but their shaky knowledge of them may produce conflict with other players in a game. Because they are so literal, a rule is viewed as a law that has been handed down by some authority figure: a teacher, a parent, or even God. Thus, being right is critically important. Is it any wonder that this is the sometimes exasperating age of the tattle-tale? On the positive side, children can be observed demonstrating the beginning of real cooperative play.

Stage Three (Age: About 8–11 or 12)   *Second Transitional Stage*: Children begin to see that rules have not been created by an all-powerful authority but that they are cooperative agreements. Now, modifications of the rules become possible during a game. Moral judgments are made that focus less on the self as children learn to see others' points of view. How peers view issues becomes more important than how parents do. These two sometimes opposing influences can cause problems for the child, yet these years are important for growth in the understanding of fairness and justice.

Stage Four (Age: 11 or 12 and up)   *Autonomy:* Children have a firm understanding that rules can be changed and still provide fairness. This is a period of real cooperation and understanding of others.

Let's return one last time to Micky to see how constructivist theory might interpret his behaviors. When he was 3, Micky's attitude toward authority was that he need obey it only when it was around. That is, he acted entirely within his own interests. Further, he had no concept that the spanking was a logical outcome of his misbehavior even if his mother had explained this to him. He could only relate to what he himself wanted.

When he was 8, Micky preferred a punishment that fit the "crime" rather than the lengthier talk sessions. In constructivist theory the influence of the environment is important and in this case that meant his friends. Therefore, he was impatient to have the punishment and be done with it.

While Piaget was interested in children's moral development, he chose to devote his subsequent years of research to the study of cognitive growth. It was more than 20 years before his *Moral Judgment of the Child* was used as he had hoped it would be: as a springboard for further research on moral development by others. Lawrence Kohlberg (1976), then at the University of Chicago, explored Piaget's stages with boys between the ages of 10 and 17, further extending the stage descriptions. In the 1970s, William Damon (1977) and Robert Selman (1980), both of whom worked with Kohlberg, extended the stage descriptions even further, focusing more on early childhood and the elementary years. They studied the development of children's views of self and others, their expanding awareness of fairness, and their growth in the ability to make moral judgments.

Kohlberg, Damon, and Selman are not, by any means, the only researchers who have based their studies and theories on the games of marbles Piaget played long ago with Swiss boys. But they have been leading thinkers in an ever-expanding field of knowledge. As Piaget had hoped, his early work was used as a springboard for further research. However, despite the strength of the theories as they have been developed, a major flaw in the basic work done by both Piaget and Kohlberg has come to light, a flaw held in common with the work done by Erikson. It is the apparent bias of these researchers against the female moral structure.

What About the Girls?   The game of marbles has traditionally been played almost exclusively by boys. After Piaget had observed them developing a sense of rules, fairness, and justice, he observed girls at their games such as hopscotch or hide-and-seek. There he saw little interest in competition or "the splendid codification and complicated jurisprudence of the game of marbles" (1932, p. 77). Piaget viewed this behavior as a major strike against their developing sense of morality and justice. Kohlberg then continued the tradition by ignoring girls in his more than 25 years of research.

Carol Gilligan (1982) has taken both Piaget and Kohlberg, as well as Erikson, to task for this omission. She points out that while boys are preoccupied with resolution of disputes, legal elaboration of rules, and concepts of fairness, girls are concerned with continuing relationships, caring for others, and the avoidance of success at the expense of others. Whereas Piaget saw the female thought as defective, Gilligan regards it as simply different.

Gilligan believes that there should be a "changed understanding of human development and a more generative view of human life" (p. 174). We should consider what the consequences will be if we don't help young children avoid growing in the traditional, stereotypical male-female patterns. If teachers simply permit nature and culture to take their course with girls, they may well miss out on critical opportunities for learning teamwork, cooperation, negotiation, and leadership. Coincidentally, through the choices made in play materials, girls may miss out on the natural learning of mathematical skills. And, without some teacher intervention, boys may never adopt the qualities of caring, nurturing, valuing of relationships, or competing without damaging others.

Teachers do children a disservice by not introducing them to the best in each other. If they can encourage ever more interaction, cooperation in learning, independent decision making, and child leadership within the classroom, they will have done much toward encouraging cross-sex understanding.

What If? Social and Affective Development and the Exceptional Child

The exceptional child's developing social skills are influenced by the same variables as the average preschooler's. However, there may be others as well. Fallen & Umansky (1985) found that the lack of social skills in young handicapped children may come predominantly from the child being harshly punished or corrected, neglected, or overprotected and always receiving help. In addition, parents who treat a disability as a completely handicapping condition do not allow the exceptional child to meet his or her maximum potential.

The children whom parents and educators are most concerned about are those who disrupt the home and the classroom. If the story of Micky were retold describing him as a child with behavior problems, the outcome would be somewhat different. After Micky's mother set up the rules, Micky would immediately forget them and the consequential spanking. Micky would also forget the rule after the second, third, and fourth spankings. The mother would attempt to talk to Micky, and he might even sit and listen, but again when the situation arose Micky would do what he wanted to at the time. Since remembering would not be in his self-interest, it would also be beyond his capabilities.

As Micky got older and the mother got wearier because of the repeat events, she would try different methods of interaction with Micky. In the end, the mother would wonder why nothing worked and how her child got this way. The teachers at school would wonder why the mother didn't discipline the child.

Micky's problem could be easily determined following Erickson's theoretical basis. Micky would be described as resolving all his conflicts negatively. Thus, his emotional needs and social life are unsuccessful. An answer to Micky's problems would be to assist Micky in resolving his problems in a positive manner. Plenty of praise for small successes would help relieve him of the shame and doubt of stage two or the guilt of stage three.

Erickson's theory is not used as frequently as the social learning theory when describing children with behavior problems. The success of using modeling to teach appropriate behavior is one of the reasons for the continued use of the principles of the social learning theory (Guralnick, 1980; Peterson & Haralick, 1977). According to this theory, Micky's behavior is learned through imitating the behavior of important others such as his friends and his mother. In addition, Micky will learn that the method he chooses to interact with others gets him what he wants.

Interventions focusing on the behavioral principles of this theory and on behavior modification have resulted in changes in the behavior of children like Micky. For change to become permanent, however, the child must develop a sense of intrinsic value for the desired behavior. The constructivist viewpoint blends the external forces of the environment with the internal character of the child to assist professionals in understanding and helping the exceptional child.

Stage one of Piaget's levels of development is heteronomy. The child will usually follow the directions of the adult when the authoritarian figure is present, but as soon as the authority leaves, the child will proceed with the behavior that satisfies the child's needs. In Micky's case at age 3 he wanted to go get the car in the road and he did just that. He understood the rule but forgot it when the rule no longer satisfied his needs. This tendency on the part of young children is even stronger for exceptional children.

In stage two of development (the transitional stage) the typical child becomes rule-oriented. The exceptional child may not respond in this manner because the youngster has not developed to the same cognitive level as his or her peers. Punishment is still seen as arbitrary and nonlogical. The child with poor social skills does not understand that there is a consequence for his or her actions. In addition, the child is constantly getting "tattled on" and becoming less popular because the youngster never follows the rules. That is why special education teachers in an attempt to help their students advance to the transitional stage often ask handicapped children to "tattle" rather than to meet their own needs through fighting.

At about age 8, the average second- or third-grader can understand the relationship among rules, intentions, actions, and the results of actions. But the child with behavior problems is just beginning to "tattletale." This child alienates his or her peers because of a lack of understanding of cooperative play. The child with poor social skills cannot begin to grasp the concept of cooperation found in most youngsters at stage four (autonomy).

In Micky's case, the attitudes and behavior he demonstrated at age 3 would be seen at age 8 if he were an exceptional child. It is not that (the exceptional) Micky is trying to be difficult. Micky cognitively cannot comprehend the intricate social relationships that so many of his peers have grasped.

A parent or professional could assist Micky or any disabled child by exposing the child to those children who are successfully working through these relationships and by explaining the intricate social system that underlies them. The handicapped child will not acquire the skills through observation. Providing modeling and step-by-step guidelines for making moral decisions (external guidelines are slowly phased out), along with positive feedback, can assist the child with poor social skills to develop to the same social level as his or her peers.

COGNITIVE DEVELOPMENT AS A PART OF THE WHOLE CHILD

We now look at the ways in which children are perceived to develop cognitively. Over time, three broad categories of thought have emerged, each with a metaphorical model of the child as cognitive learner.

The first category takes the point of view that children are much like flowers. They are preprogrammed, just as plants are, to develop in a very specific way, responding as plants do to the proper amount of care. The second category regards children's minds as blank slates. Learning takes place largely because of what the environment contributes. Thus, the slate is written on as people, places, and events become a part of the child's life. The third category takes the position that children are builders of their own intellects. They begin with their own biological entities that interact with the environment, resulting in a self-created intellectual structure.

As a teacher of young children, your approach to educating them will depend to a great extent on whether you view children as unfolding flowers, blank slates, or self builders—or perhaps a little of each. In the next three sections we explore the histories and arguments for each of the categories.

The Child as Unfolding Flower

In the middle of the eighteenth century, Jean Jacques Rousseau (1712–1778) inspired his countrymen with his writings on democracy. Equally revolutionary was his attitude toward the upbringing of infants and children. Rejecting many centuries of negative attitudes and ignorant treatment of children, he insisted that children should be given gentle encouragement from adults to grow in the ways nature intended them to. Using nature as his analogy, Rousseau depicted the human being as a plant whose growth could only be impeded by the wrong training or confinement.

> When set free, the plant retains the bent forced upon it; but the sap has not changed its first direction and any new growth the plant makes returns to the vertical. It is the same with human inclinations (Rousseau, 1956, 1762, p. 12).

Today we might not agree with some of Rousseau's ideas about nature. He believed, for example, that nature's way is to "torment children" below the age of 8 with assorted ills that only the most fit can survive. And we probably would dismiss some of his methods for promoting survival, such as the ice-cold bath. Yet, despite his less than modern understanding of human physiology, Rousseau's humaneness and interest in child development have inspired educators for more than 200 years.

The man who has taken Rousseau's nativism most seriously and applied it in the most thoroughly scientific manner has been Arnold Gesell (1880–1961). His description of children's growth also refers to nature.

> Like a coral he grows by accretion, like a tree he grows by branching out. Rich experience with things, with handicrafts and group activities, is necessary for the sound development of words, ideas and attitudes (Gesell and Ilg, 1943, p. 254).

It was Gesell's view that children develop in a prescribed series of steps, each with its own corresponding approximate age. Thus, we can read books published by the Gesell Institute of Child Development with titles such as *Your Four-Year-Old: Wild and Wonderful* or *Your Six-Year-Old: Defiant but Loving*. Observations of "hundreds" of children helped Gesell and his associates determine developmental norms in children's physical and intellectual capabilities and interests. These observations led Gesell to be concerned that educators not push young children beyond their readiness for any intellectual activity. It would be better, he argued, to err on the side of waiting too long to introduce something new than to coax a child along too soon.

There is much to admire in Gesell's approach to children, particularly in these times of pressuring children to achieve too much too fast. One can almost imagine one of today's fast-track children entering a Gesell classroom and breathing an audible sigh of relief. At the same time, the lockstep definition of child development—the concept of child as tree, or flower, or accreting coral—leaves the child helpless, a mere recipient of the inevitable.

The Child as Blank Slate

Almost 300 years ago John Locke (1632–1704), the English philosopher, laid the groundwork for one of today's most prevalent ways of looking at children. His view was that at birth all babies' minds are like "white paper, void of all characters" and that it is the environment that eventually, for good or ill, writes their personalities and intelligence on this tabula rasa. Development, in this view as in the one we have just discussed, is a one-way street. In this case it is the environment that creates the child, and the child has no role in manipulating the environment. Locke discussed the importance of the environment in *Some Thoughts Concerning Education* (1693). Education, Locke said, takes place from birth and is the responsibility of both parents and teachers who should create a positive atmosphere devoid of the traditional punishments.

> Beating then, and all other sorts of slavish and corporal punishments, are not the discipline fit to be used in the education of those who would have wise, good, and ingenuous men; and therefore very rarely to be applied, and that only on great occasions, and cases of extremity (Locke, 1964, p. 35).

On the other hand, Locke had little regard for the wide use of "things that are pleasant to them" as rewards for study. Apart from material rewards and corporal punishment, Locke still believed in the need to reinforce behavior and that children would come to love academic learning if it were presented as a game rather than as drudgery. Locke saw the need to make the best of the environment but never saw this enjoyment as anything of the child's creating. Even the games he recommended were focused on the transmission of knowledge: dice with letters or numbers on them for a fun drill was one example.

Despite Locke's belief that infants' minds were blank, to be written on by the environment, he did not view all minds as created equal.

> God has stamped certain characters upon men's minds, which, like their shapes, may perhaps be a little mended; but can hardly be totally altered and transformed into the contrary (Locke, 1964, p. 43).

We might say that Locke's view in this regard was the precursor of the concept of a fixed intelligence. In coming to his conclusions, Locke relied on experience and observation, thus making his philosophy one of empiricism. His method has been repeated in this century by those who argue for a very similar view of the way young children learn.

The leader in this new avenue of research has been B. F. Skinner (1904–   ), whose empiricism mirrors, to a great extent, that of Locke. Skinner experimented first with pigeons, rats, dogs, and monkeys, later transferring his ideas to the learning of people, whom he found extraordinarily similar in their learning processes. A child as well as a pigeon will respond to stimuli in the environment. In the case of the child, the blank slate with which he or she arrives in the world is written on by adults, older children, and the influence of the general environment. Through all these various stimuli and the child's responses to them, he or she is conditioned to learn.

Reinforcement is the impetus to increased learning in this theory of behaviorism. Skinner, as well as other behaviorists, believes that the most effective reinforcement is positive. Like Locke, Skinner found that punishment

> ...did not suppress behavior as it had been supposed to do....As soon as punishment is withdrawn, the behavior bounces back...subject to aversive control in general because of its by-products. All sorts of emotions are generated which have negative side effects (Evans, 1968, p. 33).

The views of behaviorism are attractive to many in our present-day culture in which a scientific approach to most things, including education, is the approach most sought after and trusted. On the other hand, behaviorism is unpopular with those who disagree with its willingness to manipulate children to whatever ends adults deem attractive. The blank slate view, much as the unfolding flower view, is that learning is one way. The child as slate is written on, but he or she cannot erase or write back.

The Child as Builder

For one answer to the shortcomings noted in these first two sections, we now turn to a third view of children. It is this view that provides the primary underlying philosophy of this book, although you will also find elements of each of the other two.

Jean Piaget did not intend to spend his life studying children. As a child, a young man, and finally a briefly retired octogenarian, his interests lay in the mollusks that inhabited the lakes of western Switzerland. At the same time, his varied interests and broadly based intelligence led him to the exploration of other scientific fields.

After receiving his doctorate in biology, he studied and worked in France, standardizing IQ tests and interviewing children in an attempt to learn why similar ages gave similar wrong answers.

Returning to Switzerland, Piaget became director of studies at the Institute J. J. Rousseau in Geneva. His research there focused on various aspects of intellectual growth such as the concepts of space, time, number, language, logic, reasoning, and, as we have already discussed, morality. As each study evolved, so did Piaget's understanding of his early findings in Paris. There were, indeed, patterns of intellectual growth that were age-related. Further, they could be divided into several stages that were found to hold true across races and cultures. Only the ages at which a stage was acquired might differ somewhat, depending on intelligence or the environment, while the sequence of the stages never varied.

At the very heart of Piaget's theory was a view of the developing child that differed enormously from the two major views we have just discussed. Piaget did not see that children were totally preprogrammed with a schedule of development that simply required sufficient nutriment to make them bloom successfully. Neither did he believe the child was the passive recipient of all the environment had to offer. He saw merit in both these views, acknowledging that every child has genetic limitations and is influenced to a great degree by the quality of the environment. At the same time, Piaget believed that children assist in constructing their own intelligence.

The structures a child builds are psychological and differ depending on age. Structures at first are primitive and lacking in clarity or accuracy; toward adulthood they attain complexity and the adult definition of reality. In this constructivist theory of how knowledge is acquired, children build relationships in their understanding between objects, or between ideas, or between ideas and objects.

There are several key concepts in the definition of children's knowledge construction and Piaget created his own terminology to define them:

Accommodation: The child takes something totally new into the intellectual structure. It may be necessary to alter old views and look at ideas quite differently.

Assimilation: A new idea is not so revolutionary that it has to be accommodated. It can fit into previously held ideas. Assimilation is not so rigorous an exercise as accommodation. In fact, it can be defined as one kind of play. It is important to note that in actuality accommodation and assimilation take place simultaneously.

Structural changes: As children adapt their intellects by means of accommodation and assimilation, changes in the intellectual structure itself take place. Over a period of several years, identifiable stages can be observed, each one different in many ways from the previous one.

Let's take a brief look at each of the stages. Some knowledge of them is essential for teachers who wish to make competent curriculum and teaching methodology decisions. Within the four periods discussed below there are subsidiary stages with often complex refinements.

Sensorimotor Period Motor activities and the physical senses provide the primary means of learning and building the intellect in this first period. Its duration covers the first 2 years of life and begins with repetition of reflex actions such as sucking. It then moves on to coordination of some behavioral schemes to create intentional behaviors and ends with enough understanding of the world that deliberate imitative behavior and true make-believe are possible.

During this period, children take their first steps in *decentering*, or moving out of their total focus on self. As very young infants they cannot distinguish themselves from others, but by the end of the period they have no trouble comprehending this kind of separation.

Preoperational Period   As children enter preschool they also enter the preoperational period. A major development is a new ability known as *symbolic functioning*. Children can now, with no difficulty, use one thing to symbolize another. In practical terms that means they can pretend a mud pie is really for lunch or a tricycle is their father's car. It is partly because of this ability that children's language now develops at such a rapid rate. Words are abstract utterances that symbolize objects, actions, and so on that may not be present.

Of course, there is still much that the child cannot do, and it is important for teachers to be aware of these limitations. For example, when sorting objects with varying attributes, the child can focus on only one variable at a time. This inability to focus more broadly Piaget called *centration*, or centering attention on just one attribute at a time. If sorting buttons, the child may put all the red ones together and all the white in a separate pile. She won't notice, however, that they could also have been divided into a pile of large and small buttons. This same limitation keeps her from successfully ordering objects from smallest to largest or relating parts to wholes.

Appearances can be deceiving, even to adults. For the preoperational child the problem is much more pronounced. If we were to take the piles of buttons the child had made and spread them into two rows of five buttons each, she would agree that the rows were equivalent—as long as they were equally spaced. But if we then spread out the red row to cover more territory, she would believe that now there were more red buttons.

Variations of the same lack of understanding occur if the child considers liquid or mass: pouring from one shape container into another shape may make him think the amount of liquid has changed; changing the shape of a ball of clay may make him think that one has more clay in it than another of equal amount.

In language development, the children center on their own need to communicate and assume that those around them know exactly what they mean and they may respond with frustration when they don't. Although their understanding of the rules of grammar is growing, they will not yet have a grasp of the exceptions that are a common part of the most everyday speech.

While the preoperational child is advancing impressively in making sense of the world, it is obvious that much is still not understood. Her intellectual perceptions are still bound by the most salient physical attributes of the objects she manipulates, and so far she is aware only of her own view of the world, assuming that everyone sees it as she does.

Concrete Operational Period   As children move out of the preprimary years and into elementary school they become adept at performing intellectual skills that were previously beyond their reach. They become more able to classify according to more than one variable, to rank order items in logical series, to understand that amounts of mass or liquid don't change just because their shape does, and to intellectually manipulate new and more complex relationships. Linguistic communication improves as children complete their basic understanding of grammar.

Again, it is important to mention what children cannot do. Although they have a much more mature understanding of many processes and relationships, it is still based on concrete reality. True abstraction is not yet possible, and learning takes place most successfully when concrete objects are present.

Although Piaget suggested that concrete operations emerge at about 7 years of age, teachers can expect to see the first signs of development toward the end of kindergarten and sometimes before then. (In different cultures at different historical times, ages have varied, sometimes widely.)

Formal Operational Period   The term "formal operations" signifies the ability to form abstract ideas, to formulate and test hypotheses, and to think reflectively. The period can begin as early as 11 years and continues into young adulthood.

Let's briefly summarize. The position of this book is that while the views of child as unfolding flower and blank slate each have something to offer, it is the third view, that of child as builder of self, that provides the most promise as a basis for curriculum development. In part this is true because the third approach does not negate either of the other two but contains some elements of each. Further, although recent research has shown the posited developmental stages to be controversial at times, it is still possible to use Piaget's basic structure as a reference point. In addition, this view of child development lends itself to a curriculum that tries to emulate the way people learn most naturally.

THE SCHOOL OF LIFE: THE INTEGRATED CURRICULUM IN ITS NATIVE HABITAT

In this section we demonstrate the way in which self-propelled learning makes use of an integrated curriculum without self-conscious manipulation and the way in which learners quite naturally choose their own level of challenge.

To demonstrate what a learning "curriculum" looks like when it hasn't been tampered with by any but life's natural teachers, let us look at two out-of-school experiences. The first is hypothetical and may have happened to anyone reading this book. The second tells about a true learning experience that involved two small boys. In each case we see the participants constructing their own learning. As they do so, they make use of much of the school curriculum, even though they are not in school.

Experience 1: Adult Learning in the Real World

Many of us have had the experience of buying a car or accompanying a relative or friend who was buying one. This shopping adventure is usually a major learning experience that involves much of the traditional school curriculum.

A first step in the experience is usually to read the ads and descriptive brochures (language). Then there is the necessity of comparing prices, figuring interest, computing payments, and generally determining the best financial deal (mathematics). The car's specifications must be considered too: type of transmission, fuel efficiency, and size and power of engine (science). The buyer almost always has some interest in the aesthetics of the car: its color, design, and interior (art). Finally, the buyer must learn to deal with the various tactics of one or more salespeople and to present his or her case well to the lending agency (social studies).

All in all, this one experience uses all parts of the curriculum with the exception of music and physical education. (It may or may not involve drama!) That's pretty broad coverage for one learning experience, but it's not unusual. Most of the learning in our lives is along the lines of an integrated curriculum. Few, if any of us, go out of our way to confine a new experience to a math or social studies learning. We're usually not even conscious that that's what it is.

Experience 2: Children Learning in the Real World

Outside of school, children also learn in a cross-curriculum manner. As you read this story, think about the subject areas that are being learned. Think too about the developmental levels of the boys' learning behavior. You will find that Ben was a child who had moved quite fully into concrete operations while Danny was at the final stages of the preoperational period, perhaps ready in some ways to begin entering concrete operations.

Their father had helped them start the backyard fort and then had left on a business trip. Saturday morning Danny and Ben leaped out of their bunk beds ready to spend a day on further construction. It was only a few minutes before they realized that little progress, if any, could be made. During the night the temperature had dropped, it had begun to rain, and the backyard no longer appeared the inviting place to play that it had all during the school week.

The boys tried for a while to work on the fort, but the rain increased in intensity, and they finally accepted their mother's suggestion to come in and enjoy the benefits of "the great indoors." Disappointed in the way the day was turning out, the two soon fell to squabbling and complaining that there was nothing to do. Longingly they glanced at the darkened television set, knowing they had used up their weekly allotment of viewing time.

As the weather grew worse so did the boys' tempers. Finally the inevitable happened. The boys were sent to their room. For a short time angry words escaped: "Your fault!" "No it's not!" "Yes it is!" Then there was a moment of silence, a bit more bickering, more silence, a scream or two, and finally the quiet sound of two boys peacefully conversing.

Relieved that all seemed to be going well, their mother focused her energies on the Saturday cleaning. As she scrubbed the kitchen floor, 5-year-old Danny approached looking important.

"Ben says to ask you if we got anything heavy, like bricks." His mother smiled, wondering when Danny would figure out that being a gofer was not the glory trip he thought it was.

"Sure," she answered. "There are a few cement blocks in the garage. Next to the lawnmower."

One by one Danny lugged the blocks through the kitchen, down the hall, and into the bedroom. From the bedroom came the voice of his 8-year-old brother, "Can't you hurry up a little? I can't hold these things in place all day!"

Danny scurried back for his fifth trip looking concerned and slightly fatigued. At last he announced very loudly, "You want any more, you go get 'em. I'm all through!"

Ben tried his big-brother technique. "Yeah, well you're just a baby, I guess."

"No, I'm not. You just wanna boss me around all the time." In the kitchen his mother smiled. Experience, she thought, is a great teacher.

As the sound of happy industry continued, she decided it was safe to take a peek into the bedroom. "Hi, Mom!" they said in unison. "We decided to make an indoor fort. Like it?" To the casual observer the room was a disaster. The bunk bed had been pushed partway into the closet and blankets were suspended from its upper level, held in place by cement blocks. Chairs, tables, and toy box had been stacked in precarious balance to make the fort's wall.

"You've certainly been busy, haven't you?" their mother managed to say and reminded herself that they were creating, learning, and happy. The mess could always be cleaned up later.

At that moment the boys had spread paper and markers out on the floor and were making identifying signs to be taped around the room. Ben was writing the words in large letters while Danny decorated with assorted geometric figures and an occasional airplane or gun. "Mom, I'm having trouble spelling this one," Ben said. "Is it 'No girls a-l-o-u-d' or 'no girls a-l-l-o-w-e-d'?"

Interestingly, when the weather cleared up later in the afternoon, the boys refused to leave their project. The next morning when they awoke (halfway in the closet), they had to be towed forcefully to Sunday school, then happily spent the rest of the day perfecting the fort, having lost interest in the backyard version that had inspired their activity.

The Curriculum   As a center of learning, the boys' bedroom was certainly less structured than any classroom. There were no time limits or schedules, there were no pages to be covered by a certain day, no assigned seats or lines to be quiet in. And yet much learning took place. Almost the entire curriculum, in fact, was represented in some way, and each boy learned it at the level appropriate to his age.

Language   At age 5, Danny had a working knowledge of the purpose of print. He could read simple commercial signs, write his name, and recognize most of the letters of the alphabet. Once he had decorated Ben's signs, he made copies of them, complete with primitive lettering. Then, over the next 2 days he wandered the room mumbling the words to himself, occasionally tracing them with his finger or asking Ben to tell him a forgotten word. When his father came home on Friday night Danny read every word aloud, proudly and accurately.

The language learning for Ben was on a smaller scale as he was already a fluent reader. His spelling, however, was still somewhat shaky and so he asked his mother for help, as we saw. Helping Danny read the signs gave him informal reinforcement of what he had learned.

Mathematics   When building the original outdoor fort, the boys had made numerous and careful measurements, usually with the help of their father. Now, they transposed their learning indoors. While it wasn't necessary to match lengths of lumber as they had in the outdoor fort, the boys placed similar emphasis on symmetry and balance. One of Ben's activities on the second day of work was to use his mother's yardstick to measure the distance between the bunk bed and each side of the door. This was followed by painstaking movement of the bed back and forth, inch by inch, until it was placed in a perfectly centered position.

Sometime later, Danny took the same yardstick and used it to measure the length of the room. This, in Ben's eyes, had no functional meaning even after Danny announced solemnly that the room was "four sticks longs and a little bit extra." To Ben, measurement needed meaning and a goal; to Danny it was the process that was all important. In either case, a mathematics learning had taken place.

Science   At the most basic, concrete level, a number of physics learnings took place. Whether it was carrying and balancing cement blocks, draping blankets on the bed, or leaning chairs and tables against each other, the boys learned something about the way forces relate to each other.

Social Studies   As an exercise in social cooperation, an informal situation such as this offers the richest of rewards. If Danny's and Ben's mother had isolated each boy rather than sending them to their room together, the boys would never have had the opportunity to work out their own system of social interaction. Fortunately for them, she was wise enough to know that leaving them in the room together would ultimately pay off. Danny, of course, learned a lesson in assertiveness when he realized, while carrying a heavy concrete block, that he was being taken advantage of. And Ben found out that power has its limitations. In a democratic society, cooperation is essential for progress, as are limitations on power. While the boys didn't read this in a social studies text, they learned it firsthand.

Art   It might be argued that building the fort was, in itself, an art experience. From the beginning, the boys were highly aware of the aesthetic aspects of their building and worked to make it not only sturdy but visually attractive as well. Making their signs with careful lettering and decorations was one manifestation of their interest in making the structure appealing.

Child Development   By looking back to see how each boy learned something about the various curricular areas, we can see that the learning experiences were appropriate for each one of them. Neither one had to be tested to see if he were ready for a particular level of learning. He instinctively knew and followed through with the appropriate activity. This will not always be the case when people are left to direct their own learning, because there are too many factors that enter in. But when a potential learning experience is as inherently interesting as the fort-building experience was, the chances are good that all of those involved will participate to their highest capacity.

The last point does not apply only to cognitive learning, although that was the focus of our story. In their need to learn to negotiate, cooperate, and be helpful friends to each other, Danny and Ben engaged in experiences that would assist their social and affective growth. Additionally, much of the work they did was physical, particularly as they moved furniture around. No doubt much of this was done by trial and error, another learning experience. The learning in all three areas of development was, in this case, far broader than anything the boys could have learned by sitting at desks in a schoolroom for the same amount of time. They learned in a natural way, the way we all learn when left to our own devices.

Of course, it isn't always possible to replicate this kind of experience in a school setting. There are deadlines to be reached, tests to be held accountable for, schedules to be maintained. And twenty-five children can't be left alone in a room to work out their differences on a rainy day. Yet, there are many ways in which integrated learning that makes use of children's interests and which recognizes their developmental capabilities can be incorporated into the school program. Later, in Parts 2 and 3, we take an in-depth look at some ways in which this can be done. At this point, we need to consider what might happen if cognitive development does not take place as we have described it in this section.

What If? Cognitive Development and the Exceptional Child

Historically, the cognitively exceptional child was seen as a menace, and institutions were developed to protect society from the child and the child from the cruel assaults of society. This belief was illustrated in the terms chosen to describe exceptional children, terms such as "feeble-minded," "idiotic," and "insane" (Hallahan & Kauffman, 1988).

Jean Marc Itard, a French physician, was one of the first to attempt intervention with the cognitively exceptional child. In 1799 he civilized the "wild boy of Aveyron," demonstrating that with proper intervention exceptional individuals could be helped to develop more normal skills (Blackhurst & Berdine, 1981). The concept of educating the handicapped child continued to gather support in Europe and the United States through the work of Edouard Seguin and Maria Montessori. The outlook for the handicapped seemed optimistic and hopeful. Unfortunately, this did not prove to be the case, and the handicapped were relegated to institutions where only minimal custodial care was given (Blackhurst & Berdine, 1981).

Interest in the handicapped increased again after World War I and World War II because of the intellectual screening completed on all individuals in military service. The public was beginning to realize the magnitude of the numbers of individuals with mental, physical, and social handicaps. Through the Kennedy era the programs for handicapped children and adults continued to flourish.

During these years, researchers and theorists in special education highlighted the theories of behaviorism used in programs for severely handicapped individuals (Rogers, 1988). More recently, attention has been focused on the importance of play skills for young handicapped children, particularly the way these youngsters relate cognitively to Piaget's two early periods of development: the sensorimotor and preoperational periods. The importance of this recent research on play cannot be understated due to the fact that researchers have found repeatedly that handicapped children follow the same progression as nonhandicapped children in the sequence of sensorimotor learning through play (Krakow & Kopp, 1983; Mahoney, Glover, & Finger, 1981; Motti, Cicchetti, & Sroufe, 1983; Rogers, 1988; Sigman & Ungerer, 1984).

Although exceptional children progress through the same stages, they produce a different qualitative level of play, particularly in the areas of creativity and exploration (Rogers, 1988). Handicapped children exhibit more immature and repetitive play than their nonhandicapped peers. However, through modeling, the handicapped youngster's quality of play can be enhanced. Through a carefully structured social play situation, exceptional children interact with their nonhandicapped peers, and through observation and modeling they expand their own repertoire of play.

One specific technique is to match a developmentally delayed 5-year-old with a nondisabled 3-year-old (Hill & McCune-Nicolich, 1981). Developmentally delayed children often exhibit poor language skills, and symbolic play is important to encourage development (Rogers, 1988). What is important is a stimulating environment and appropriate language and social models. These models could include adults encouraging effective communication with the children through the use of expanded sentence structure. In addition, a nonhandicapped preschooler could also provide appropriate modeling to a developmentally delayed youngster by showing the exceptional student how to take turns in a classroom game.

The importance of a role model is perhaps one of the significant differences between handicapped children and their non-handicapped peers. The typical preschooler will develop cognitively without significant intervention. The handicapped peer, on the other hand, does not pick up these skills without external assistance.

Although the story of Danny and Ben could occur when one child is handicapped, the need for outside intervention would increase as the severity of the child's disability increases. The importance of children learning through a natural experience is just as beneficial for handicapped youngsters as it is for nonhandicapped children. Due to handicapping conditions, the exceptional child needs varying amounts of structure within the natural environment to reap the benefits of the natural learning situation. Let's assume that Danny is the child with a cognitive handicap. Ben may not expect him to understand some of the tasks involved in their project. This attitude often occurs when a sibling, parent, teacher, or friend does not expect the handicapped child to be able to complete the task and therefore does it for the child (Fallen & Umansky, 1985). This makes the child more disabled and often results in the self-fulfilling prophecy of "I can't." A small intervention would require that those working or playing with the child be knowledgeable of the fact that handicapped doesn't necessarily mean "can't do."

If Danny also had significant problems in social skills, he might be unable to converse with his brother to make plans for playing indoors. He would want it to stop raining and he would want it *right now!* Here, the parent would offer minor intervention by setting up guidelines for the process of problem solving. The situation is handled in a slightly more structured format with Ben providing the appropriate role model. Where a nonhandicapped child would learn the process through natural experiences, the handicapped child needs some direction.

If Danny's disability resulted in poor coordination, he might become easily frustrated because of his inability to create the bed tent. This also would require intervention on the mother's part to help Danny understand that he may have to work harder at some things but that he is still quite capable.

The natural situation is a superior learning experience for the handicapped child because it is not a contrived learning environment in which the activity is predetermined by the curriculum. The handicapped child is an important part of the success of the project and learns through observation, imitation, and trial and error. It is important for the classroom teacher to realize that the activity or lesson must be based on the child's current level of performance, not on the child's chronological age. The difference in learning for the handicapped and non-handicapped child involves varying the degree of structure and the amount of intervention.

Perhaps one of the easiest techniques for providing external assistance without significant intrusion in children's play is the use of peer tutors. A peer tutor is a child selected from within the class to assist the handicapped child when necessary. The peer tutor must demonstrate the ability to assist the handicapped child without making the child dependent on the tutor. In many situations, a successful pairing of two students is the only external intervention necessary in the "natural" learning environment.

TO DISCUSS

1   Compare your early athletic experiences with those of other students in your class. What kinds of lessons and activities were provided by parents and teachers? Did these affect the interests and capabilities you have today?

2   Discuss the strong and weak arguments for the psychoanalytic, social learning, and constructivist views of social/affective development. Determine which views are the most useful for you to adopt and adapt as you work with young children.

3   Try analyzing Ben's and Danny's experience in terms of the three theories of cognitive development. Some questions to discuss:

   a In what ways could Ben and Danny be described as unfolding flowers?

   b In what ways could Ben and Danny be described as blank slates? In what ways did the environment "write" on them?

   c In what ways could Ben and Danny be described as builders of their own intellects? Which of their actions guided their learning?

   d Can you see any places in which assimilation or accommodation probably took place?

TO DO

1   Find two children of the same age. Refer to the motor stage(s) in which you expect them to perform. Using equipment such as balls, stairs, and perhaps jump ropes, challenge them to show off whatever skills they possess. Keep the experience fun and nonthreatening. Note the skill levels of each child for each ac-

tivity. Compare them to each other as well as to the results brought back by other members of your class.

2   Observe one boy and one girl in an early childhood play setting. Write a running commentary of their social behaviors over at least 30 minutes. Then compare your findings with those of the social/affective theorists featured in this chapter.

3   Make observations of children in a nursery school, in a kindergarten, and in a primary grade. Compare and contrast your findings at each level for sex differences and behavior. Before beginning, develop a guiding list of questions based on the issues raised in this chapter.

BIBLIOGRAPHY

Bailey, E. J., & Bricker, D. (1985) Evaluation of a three-year early intervention demonstration project. *Topics in Early Childhood Special Education, 5(2):*52–65.

Bandura, A., & Walters, R. (1963) *Social learning and personality development.* New York: Holt, Rinehart & Winston.

Blackhurst, A. E., & Berdine, W. H. (1981) *An introduction to special education.* Boston: Little, Brown.

Boyd, W. (Ed.) (1963) *Jean Rousseau.* New York: Columbia University Press.

Brown, P. (1980) Fitness and play. In P. Wilkinson (Ed.), *In celebration of play.* New York: St. Martin's Press.

Corbin, C. (1980) *A textbook of motor development.* Dubuque, IA: Wm. C. Brown.

Damon, W. (1977) *The social world of the child.* San Francisco: Jossey-Bass.

Damon, W. (1983) *Social and personality development.* New York: W. W. Norton.

Erikson, E. (1963) *Childhood and society.* New York: W. W. Norton.

Evans, R. (1968) *B. F. Skinner: The man and his ideas.* New York: Dutton.

Fallen, N. H., & Umansky, W. (1985) *Young children with special needs.* Columbus, OH: Merrill.

Gallahue, D. (1982) *Understanding motor development in children.* New York: Wiley.

Gay, P. (Ed.) (1964) *John Locke on education.* Richmond, VA: William Byrd Press.

Gesell, A., & Ilg, F. (1943) *Infant and child in the culture of today.* New York: Harper & Row.

Gilligan, C. (1982) *In a different voice.* Cambridge, MA: Harvard University Press.

Guralnick, M. J. (1980) Social interactions among preschool children. *Exceptional Children, 46:*248–253.

Hallahan, D. P., & Kauffman, J. M. (1988) *Exceptional children: Introduction to special education* (4th ed.). Englewood Cliffs, NJ: Prentice-Hall.

Hanson, M. J. (1985) An analysis of the effects of early intervention services for infants and toddlers with moderate and severe handicaps. *Topics in Early Childhood Special Education, 5(2):*36–51.

Haring, N. W. (1982) *Exceptional children and youth.* Columbus, OH: Bell & Howell.

Hill, P., & McCune-Nicolich, L. (1981) Pretend play and patterns of cognition in Down's syndrome children. *Child Development, 52:*611–617.

Hoffman, M. (1971) Identification and conscience development, *Child Development, 42:*1071–1082.

Irwin, E., & Frank, M. (1977) Facilitating the play process with LD children. *Academic Therapy, 12(4):*435–443.

Jenkins, J. R., Fewell, R., & Harris, S. R. (1983) Comparison of sensory integrative therapy and motor programming. *American Journal of Mental Deficiency, 88(2):*221–224.

Kohlberg, L. (1976) Moral stages and moralizations: The cognitive-developmental approach. In T. Lickona (Ed.), *Moral development and behavior.* New York: Holt, Rinehart & Winston.

Krakow, J., & Kopp, C. (1983) The effect of developmental delay on sustained attention in young children. *Child Development, 54:*1143–1155.

Lever, J. (1976) Sex differences in the games children play. *Social Problems, 23:*478–487.

Locke, J. (1963, 1964) *John Locke on education.* New York: Teachers College, Columbia University.

Mahoney, G., Glover, A., & Finger, I. (1981) Relationship between language and sensorimotor development of Down syndrome and nonretarded children. *American Journal of Mental Deficiency, 86(1):*21–27.

Morrison, B., & Newcomer, T. (1975) Effects of directive vs. nondirective play therapy with institutionalized retarded children. *American Journal of Mental Deficiency, 79:*666–669.

Motti, F., Cicchetti, D., & Sroufe, L. A. (1983) From infant affect expression to symbolic play: The coherence of development in Down syndrome children. *Child Development, 54:*1168–1175.

Nesbitt, J., Neal, L., & Hillman, W. (1974) Recreation for exceptional children and youth. *Focus on Exceptional Children, 6(3):*1–12.

Paley, V. (1984) *Boys and girls: Superheroes in the doll corner.* Chicago: University of Chicago Press.

Paloutzian, R., Hazasi, J., Streifel, J., & Edgar, C. (1971) Promotion of positive social interaction in severely retarded young children. *American Journal of Mental Deficiency, 75:*519–524.

Peterson, N. L., & Haralick, J. G. (1977) Integration of handicapped and nonhandicapped preschoolers: An analysis of play behavior and social interaction. *Education and Training of the Mentally Retarded, 12:*235–240.

Piaget, J. (1953) Jean Piaget. In *History of psychology in autobiography.* Worcester, MA: Clark University.

Piaget, J. (1965, 1932) *The moral judgment of the child.* New York: Macmillan.

Piaget, J. (1970) *Science of education and the psychology of the child.* New York: Viking.

Rogers, S. J. (1988) Cognitive characteristics of handicapped children's play: A review. *Journal of the Division for Early Childhood, 12:*161–168.

Rousseau, J. (1956, 1762) *Emile for today.* London: William Heinemann.

Runac, M. (1985) Motor development. In N. H. Fallen & W. Umansky (Eds.), *Young children with special needs* (pp. 193–248). Columbus, OH: Merrill.

Selman, R. (1976) Social-cognitive understanding: A guide to educational and clinical practice (pp. 299–316). In T. Lickona (ed.). *Moral development and behavior.* New York: Holt, Rinehart & Winston.

Sigman, M., & Ungerer, J. (1984) Cognitive and language skills in autistic, mentally retarded and normal children. *Developmental Psychology, 20(2):*293–302.

Skinner, B. F. (1953) *Science and human behavior*. New York: Macmillan.

Skinner, B. F. (1961) *Cumulative record*. New York: Appleton-Century-Croft.

Skinner, L. (1979) *Motor development in the preschool years*. Springfield, IL: Charles C. Thomas.

Whitman, T. L., Mecurio, V., & Caponigi, J. (1970) Development of social responses in the severely retarded children. *Journal of Applied Behavior Analysis, 3:*133–138.

Zaichkowsky, L., Zaichkowsky, L. B., & Martinek, T. (1980) *Growth and development: The child and physical activity*. St. Louis: C. V. Mosby.

The Classroom Teacher

It's probably true that there are as many ways of teaching as there are teachers. Further, each of these teachers will alter his or her methods depending on changes in environment, resources, and especially children. A major task for every teacher, whether new recruit or seasoned veteran, is to continually seek methods and techniques that work. Despite the almost infinite variety that individual teachers display in organizing, planning, and so on, it is possible to make sense of and bring order to the various approaches to working with children.

This can be done by classifying the multitude of approaches into two major categories depending on how the teacher views his or her role. Throughout education history these two categories, or *models of teaching,* have existed either alternately or side by side. In the first model the teacher's role is to transmit knowledge to students. The focus in this model is on knowledge and choosing what is more important for children to learn. It is assumed that the teacher's responsibility is to choose the information wisely and then present it in the most appropriate fashion. Historically, the method for doing so has been direct instruction rather than the more free-form approaches to teaching. The rationale has frequently been that this is the most effective and efficient method for imparting predetermined knowledge.

The second model assumes that the teacher's role is to focus first on the child's needs and then on the knowledge to be imparted. This child-centered approach to teaching argues that because children are inherently different they have different intellectual and social needs as well as different learning styles. The teacher's primary task is to learn each child's needs and interests and then to guide the learning in appropriate ways. The transmission of knowledge isn't ignored, but it takes second place to the child. Historically, child-centered teaching has used direct instruction less frequently than more facilitative methods. That is, the teacher's role is to step backward more often than to step forward; to observe, aid, and coach more frequently than to lecture and to instruct. The concept that children can learn through play as well as through work is a manifestation of the child-centered philosophy.

In this chapter we take a look at the history of the two models, particularly as they apply to working with children in their early years. After comparing the two models in the real-life experience of one child, we discuss which is more appropriate most of the time for teaching the curriculum as presented in this book. Finally, we look at the various roles of the teacher in the early childhood classroom and make practical suggestions for fulfilling them successfully.

SOME EARLY HISTORY

In prehistoric times there must have been little time for or interest in indulging a child's interests in learning. The critical necessity was the transmission of survival knowledge. As civilizations emerged, the subject matter became more complex, and direct instruction was the favored method. For example, in early Egypt, young boys received the specific knowledge they needed depending on the careers their family background had determined they would follow. In China, education was valued highly and in the sixth century B.C. Confucius argued that obedience to parents and reverence for ancestors was the important underlying theme for all learning. Thus, although he also argued for the merits of creativity, the theme of obedience and reverence led to direct teaching and rote learning. Teaching in early Greece also focused on the transmission of knowledge. In Athens, early moral education was taught through storytelling, while academic subjects such as letter formation, reading, grammar, arithmetic, and drawing were taught in routine approaches to direct instruction. In Sparta, the teaching method was quite different: young boys were left to roam in packs, instructed to survive however they best could (surely one of history's more extreme examples of hands-on learning!). Yet, the transmission-of-knowledge model held here also, for there was a clearly determined goal in sending the boys out: to give them the knowledge they needed to make them effective citizen-soldiers.

The medieval centuries in Europe carried on the tradition of knowledge transmission through directive methods as monasteries and convents taught children to read, write, and copy Latin, as well as to count and use their fingers to do simple reckoning. Materials were in short supply so that much had to be learned by rote recitation.

Throughout these medieval years children were regarded as miniature, albeit defective, adults. The concept that children might be something quite different came about over a period of centuries. It was not until the seventeenth century that John Locke proposed children be treated with humaneness in their education. After Locke, the transmission-of-knowledge model remained unchanged, but it became important that the child should actually *like* learning. This did not mean that Locke recommended actual play as a way for children to learn. Far from it. But educational toys and books were encouraged while spanking was to be used as a last resort in discipline.

The knowledge to be transmitted, Locke argued, should reflect the child's and the family's needs. The educational toys about which he wrote so enthusiastically were for the upper classes. For poor children, he considered training in useful trades more important and condoned corporal punishment. Whichever class Locke was writing about, the emphasis was on the curriculum with the child to be brought to it in the most efficient way. It had not occurred to anyone yet that it was possible to do it the other way around.

In the next century, Jean Jacques Rousseau proposed that the child should lead the adult and that the subjects of the curriculum were negotiable—thus inciting an educational revolution. Rousseau's proposal countered centuries of traditional teaching— transmission of knowledge usually through direct instruction— with the concept of child-centered education. Throughout early history there had been a scattering of child-centered educationists, and Rousseau was certainly not the first to advocate humaneness in teaching or the use of concrete, hands-on lessons. What made Rousseau stand out from the others was his insistence that children would learn best by self-rule—by choosing their own learning with little or no interference from adults. Here, for the first time, we see value given to the role of play in children's lives, for if they are permitted the freedom to choose their own learning tools and methods, it is to be expected that they will choose that activity most natural to them: play.

The ideas that Locke and Rousseau presented to the western world were a culmination of centuries of thinking and also the beginning of a philosophical conflict that has yet to be resolved. Over the generations our growing awareness of the developmental needs and interests of children has been, at times, at variance with our feeling that we have important and necessary things to teach them. The difference in the views of children these two philosophical giants held lies at the base of the problem.

To Locke, the child's mind was a tabula rasa, a blank slate, simply asking to be written on by the environment. If the responsible adults in that environment took care to teach and model what was positive and to eliminate or, at least hide, the negative, the child would flourish. In Rousseau's view, the child was not born as a blank slate but as an innately good being; only the negative influences of nature, man, and things within the environment could misshape growth. He compared children to young plants that have a predetermined plan for growth and if nurtured carefully turn out as well as they should.

We discussed these ideas more fully in Chapter One. Here, our focus is on teachers' perceptions of their roles in children's learning. As teachers, do we see ourselves as Locke did, writing the most important knowledge on children's minds? Or do we prefer to follow the lead of children in our charge, fulfilling their needs and interests as we observe them? Do we view children as empty receptacles waiting eagerly for the world's knowledge to be poured into them by us? Or do we believe that children can discover much of the world on their own—even perhaps through play—with some guidance from us? If we prefer the implications of the first and third questions, then we have chosen to follow the centuries-old transmission-of-knowledge model. If the second and fourth, then our choice is the child-centered model that has emerged over the last two centuries.

Transmission of Knowledge

For countless centuries a primary concern of education was to take the greater knowledge of adults and effectively transmit it to children. For the most part that meant direct instruction in one form or another. The technology of this century has introduced new possibilities for this model of teaching and learning. B. F. Skinner, whose views of cognition were discussed in Chapter One, was a pioneer in the field.

Believing that positive reinforcement is the quickest, most efficient way to knowledge acquisition, Skinner observed that most school instruction provides delayed reinforcement, if any, and that much learning is thus lost. To supplement direct instruction Skinner advocated teaching machines. In the early 1960s, when he developed them, these machines were manually operated, child-directed affairs with built-in self-correction. Today, of course, the personal computer would serve the same function with more efficiency. Concluded Skinner, "The simple fact is that, as a mere reinforcing mechanism, the teacher is out of date.... If the teacher is to take advantage of recent advances in the study of learning, she must have the help of mechanical devices" (1961, p. 154).

To Skinner there was no question of the appropriate road to learning: he considered reinforcements for correct responses to stimuli the most efficient means of achieving the greatest education possible. Looking to what a future educational system of teaching machines might hold, Skinner eloquently stated his case:

> We are on the threshold of an exciting and revolutionary period, in which the scientific study of man will be put to work in man's best interests. Education must play its part. It must accept the fact that a sweeping revision of educational practices is possible and inevitable (1961, p. 157).

Continuing to align himself with the transmission-of-knowledge educational model, he added that when schools had begun to play their part as they should, "…we may look forward with confidence to a school system which is aware of the nature of its tasks, secure in its methods…." (1961, p. 157).

It was 1961 when Skinner wrote in such excitement of the learning revolution to come. He had, after all, updated the time-tested model of knowledge transmission through the use of modern technology. His enthusiasm has been vindicated in recent years by the development of educational software for the computer, even for very young children. Many, or most of these programs have been based on the traditional model of direct teaching, but more recent software has included attempts at involving children in directing their own learning. Although the efficiency of direct instruction through machines was at first highly attractive, it was eventually inevitable that this kind of teaching would have to take into account the powerful legacy left to education by Jean Jacques Rousseau.

Child-Centered Education

For more than 200 years educationists have been grappling with the child-centered philosophy first espoused by Rousseau. Many who took him seriously in his own generation tried—with little success—to educate in the nondirective fashion he suggested. Achieving more success was the Swiss educator, Johann Pestalozzi (1746–1827). A generation younger than Rousseau, he devoted much of his life to applying Rousseau's ideas in actual schools. Through a succession of personal problems, failed schools, and financial difficulties, Pestalozzi still managed to become known worldwide for his courageous experiment in child-centered learning.

The educational ideas that Pestalozzi bequeathed to future generations were useful and adaptable. For young children he recommended "sense-impressions" as a way to learning and he left more abstract methods for older children. He believed the teacher need not be an exalted master but someone who follows the leadings of the child. Direct instruction of knowledge could best be achieved through "object lessons," what we would call manipulative materials. Pestalozzi, with Rousseau, believed that good teachers teach children, not subject matter. Thus, from the middle of the eighteenth century to the first years of the next, the concept of child-centered education was born and nurtured.

For application at the early childhood level we can turn to Pestalozzi's German contemporary, Friedrich Froebel (1782–1852). Froebel, whose interests lay in the preprimary years, studied Rousseau and visited one of Pestalozzi's schools. The ideas of object lessons and sense perception appealed to him, and to those

Froebel added his own twist: He believed a spiritual basis underlay children's responsiveness to manipulative learning. Rejecting the stern Calvinism of his time, Froebel envisioned children as inherently good, following a divine plan that took them through discrete states of physical and mental development: infancy, early childhood, and childhood. The purpose of education was to nourish children at each stage so that they would unfold in the way of God's plan.

Froebel created manipulative toys for every stage and gave each one a spiritual purpose. For example, a baby's woolen ball would not only aid physical development but "confirm, strengthen and clear up in the mind of the child feelings and perceptions...and awaken spirit and individuality" (Shapiro, 1983, p. 23). This rather heavy expectation for metaphysical understanding on the part of small children is typical of Froebel's inconsistent understanding of children's development. Yet his discovery of children's physical, social, and cognitive stages provided a beginning for educational researchers of the future.

Putting his philosophies to work, Froebel established a school for children ages 4 to 6, intending it to be a bridge between the secure home and the demanding grammar school. The atmosphere was to be child-centered and devoted to educational play. Since the overall goal was to nurture children's physical, social, cognitive, and spiritual growth in a warm, loving setting, the name *kindergarten,* or children's garden, was coined. In practice, the child-centered ideas of Rousseau were only partially observable in Froebel's kindergarten. The school had a prescribed curriculum with set goals and predetermined materials. Play was highly structured in order to ensure children's absorption of the underlying spiritual significance.

Froebel's ideas spread to the United States in the middle of the nineteenth century, and the country's first kindergarten was actually taught in German. In Germany, Froebel had established teacher training courses and these were exported to the United States. The training in both countries was carefully prescribed, even rigid. The methodology for teaching through structured play was clearly defined. Children were allowed to experiment with the materials but only within certain limitations.

This compromise between child-centered education and knowledge transmission was the underlying approach of yet another major force in early childhood education, Maria Montessori. Born in 1870, Montessori distinguished herself early by becoming Italy's first female medical doctor. She became internationally known for her ability and caring, for her spirited defense of women's rights, and for her pioneering efforts to teach retarded children. It was her success with children that finally turned her from an assured medical career to the more risk-laden path of educational explorer.

From retarded children, Montessori moved to experimentation with normal but disadvantaged children. Although she gave credit to such influences on her thinking as the French Jean Itard and Eduoard Seguin, Montessori curiously refused to associate herself in any way with Froebel's ideas. Yet, there were many similarities between the two. She too strove to make her schools child-centered, basing her curriculum and materials on early experiments and observations of children's preferences. Like Froebel, she eventually developed materials that allowed for some exploration and experimentation but which, nevertheless, were confining and rigid. And, like Froebel, she included an underlying spiritual theme in her materials and methods. Montessori, however, had a more realistic view of what children could and could not do and understand at each stage of development (Montessori, 1967).

Montessori's ideas took hold in the United States, just as Froebel's had. Eventually, Froebel's schools and teacher training institutions disappeared entirely as his vaguely mystical approach was replaced by this century's scientifically based early education. A further concern for many educators was his very structured definition of play. As early as 1887 Anna Bryan, at her Louisville, Kentucky, teacher training school introduced innovations to make the Froebel materials more playful. Patty Smith Hill went further, permitting children to make paper dolls and furniture from them. Hill became famous in time for inventing the large, wooden building blocks that are now a part of most kindergartens and for introducing child-sized housekeeping equipment. She also instituted the concept of a free-play time (Cowe, 1982). Although Bryan, Hill, and other pioneers in early education in the United States owed much to Froebel's early work, their continued explorations into new ideas led eventually to an almost total rejection of his philosophies and methods.

Montessori's schools and training institutions also faded for a while, to reappear in the 1950s when they were perceived as a means to increase children's academic learning. Yet, whether Montessori's and Froebel's schools and training institutions have been in vogue or out, their influence has had a permanent place in early education. Many of their ideas have been incorporated so completely into education that we have forgotten their origins.

For example, in their training institutions, both of them taught their students to reject an authoritarian approach in favor of facilitation of learning. Both trained their teachers to be observers of children's behavior and to model careful use of teaching materials. Finally, these two pioneers in early education believed strongly that a teacher's job was not simply to increase cognitive knowledge but to help the development of social and moral capacities.

Despite their influence and popularity in this country, it was neither Froebel nor Montessori who had the most impact on child-centered early education, but John Dewey (1859–1952). A professor of philosophy, first at the University of Chicago and later at Columbia University, Dewey's interest in education led to a decades-long movement of *progressivism.*

Like Froebel and Montessori, Dewey was interested in educating the whole child: the physical, social, and moral as well as intellectual attributes. Unlike them, however, Dewey had no intention of creating specific learning materials. He believed that children could learn from the real world around them, and that meant using real tools for activities both in and out of the classroom. Part of introducing children to real learning was the incorporation of democracy into the classroom.

In addition, the Dewey-inspired curriculum would be integrated. Teachers could do this by blending several curricular areas into thematic units of study. Or they could focus children's learning on real-life activities that led, incidentally, to academics. (At the end of this book's curriculum chapters you will find examples of both approaches.)

Dewey was philosophically opposed to the traditional transmission-of-knowledge model of educating and stated his reasons strongly:

> Frequently it [knowledge] is treated as an end in itself, and then the goal becomes to heap it up and display it when called for....Pupils who have stored their "minds" with all kinds of material which they have never put to intellectual uses are sure to be hampered when they try to think. They have no practice in selecting what is appropriate, and no criterion to go by; everything is on the same dead static level (1966, 1916, p. 158).

Unfortunately for the progressive movement, Dewey's ideas were often stretched or misinterpreted so that the movement itself developed a bad name for a kind of education that gave children little academic rigor or intellectual challenge. By the 1950s when the Russians took an early lead in the space race, Americans took a hard look at their education system and found it lacking in rigor. The blame, to a large extent, was placed on Dewey's philosophy and on the movement it fostered.

The focus of education, including that for the early years, changed markedly during the late 1950s. Any interest in social development was replaced by academic challenge. The revival of interest in Montessori schools occurred at this time, largely because her method was seen as a way to introduce children to earlier academic learning. It is ironic to note that although Montessori and

Dewey both worked to educate the whole child, it was Montessori who was perceived as being academically oriented and Dewey as having simply social interests.

It was at this same time that Piaget's works began to be translated into English, thus adding another view of child-centered education to the list of theories, philosophies, and practices that had begun with Rousseau's naturalistic education. While Piaget's interest was in child development, not education, his observations and recommendations included approaches to classroom teaching.

In Chapter One we discussed the constructivist theory about the development of children's intellects and moral understanding. Piaget's view that children construct their own intelligence led him to reject the traditional notions of adults transmitting knowledge to children as the best way to educate. Piaget's earliest work with children in a school setting was in a Montessori school and many of his ideas about child development and education were similar to hers. As Piaget's thinking and research evolved, however, he was less inclined to support the prescribed materials of a Montessori curriculum, in part because of their close-endedness. He argued instead for open-ended materials with room for plenty of experimentation. Teacher guidance was certainly necessary, and academic rigor was important, but the focus should be on teaching children how to think on their own. Piaget's view of the teacher in this kind of setting was similar to Dewey's:

> It is obvious that the teacher as organizer remains indispensable in order to create the situations and construct the initial devices which present useful problems to the child. Secondly, he is needed to provide counter-examples that compel reflection and reconsideration of over-hasty solutions. What is desired is that the teacher cease being a lecturer, satisfied with transmitting ready-made solutions; his role should rather be that of a mentor stimulating initiative and research (1975, 1948, p. 16).

"Initiative and research" were as important and applicable to early childhood, in Piaget's view, as they were for older students.

The child-centered approach to teaching, with its roots in the writings of Rousseau, has been in conflict with the Locke-inspired transmission-of-knowledge approach from the beginning, but for teachers in the United States the issue has been strongest since the mid-1950s when Russian advantages in space forced educators to take a closer look at their education system. With some exceptions, the transmission-of-knowledge model has come away with the stamp of approval, even for very young children in nursery school. Thus, 200 years of progress in understanding how young children learn has to some extent been rejected in favor of the older, time-tested view of teaching and learning.

During this same period, England has also taken a closer look at its early education and, with some exceptions, has chosen the child-centered model. Drawing from the ideas of Piaget, Montessori, Dewey, and others, British educational leaders have developed a system that incorporates many of the ideas set forth by them. To get an idea of the differences between the British approach to child-centered teaching and the transmission-of-knowledge approach that is more common in the United States, we can look at the experience of one young child who spent his kindergarten year in his native England and the first grade in the United States.

ONE BOY, TWO SCHOOL CULTURES

Tom was 6 when his father began a year of teaching in a university in the United States. He was temporarily uprooted from his neighborhood school in England and given the opportunity to spend first grade in a very different environment. His father, an education professor, observed with some bemusement, and occasional amazement, the vast differences between the two systems of education (Bell, 1984). In writing about Tom's experiences, Bell emphasized that in both places the child thoroughly liked his teachers and worked hard to please them. For their part, the teachers in both places worked hard to care well for their students. There, however, the similarity stopped. Here are some of the comparisons he made.

Work   In England work and play were intermingled throughout the day and Tom had been unaware as to which was which. In the United States he learned that he must complete the "work" at a certain number of stations before he could go to the library or "do fun games." The materials in his British school had been varied; in the United States they were primarily worksheets.

What Did You Do in School Today?   This question in England had been answered by such responses as "butterflies" or "trees." In the United States it was more likely to be "the letter p" or "the short e sound."

Breadth of Curriculum   The curriculum in the United States was much narrower, primarily including reading and math. Gone were the science experiments, most of the art, the nature table. The room was "visually bare," a room, his father said, that "perhaps suited a curriculum pared down to basics."

Tom's Attitude   In England Tom had tried hard and had loved school. In the United States he was proud of his accomplishments in reading, but generally bored with school as a whole. Each day after school Tom "played frantically for the first hour with an enormous store of pent up energy" seemingly to obliterate the great boredom he felt throughout the day. In England Tom had come home "drained" and ready for some quiet time.

Reward System   In England this had consisted of an occasional small, gold star, with the work usually being an end in itself. In the United States Tom's father was amazed at the array of smiley faces, badges, scratch-and-sniff stickers, and so on. He also observed that in the United States there was much more competition between children, who had great concern as to what page in the reading book other children were on or how many reward tickets others had collected. In England there had been little consciousness of the academic standing of other students.

Playmates   The British school had emphasized a feeling of community among all classes. Tom's friends had come from all the grades and even included the principal. In the United States his friends were only in his own grade and he had no idea who the principal was.

The Principal   In England this had been a headteacher who "exerts her moral and social influence, but...affords a measure of real autonomy to individual teachers." The American principal was "more the senior executive, ensuring that the aspirations of the community of parents (as these were manifested in the policies of the local school board) were translated into effective and efficient actions" (Bell, 1984, p. 5).

Tom's father found communicating with the American principal much more stilted and uncomfortable and was surprised to find that his interest in meeting her was regarded as somewhat odd. In England there had always been a close relationship between administration and parents.

Teacher Power   In England the teacher had had the trust and respect of the principal and was expected to make her own decisions about the progress of her students. In the United States a child could not move up to the next level reading book without a formal test from the curriculum specialist.

Independence and Maturity   In England the children could independently choose their own work but there was also much contact with the teacher. In the United States the work was primarily the "ubiquitous worksheet," which isolated the children and, at the same time, gave them no independence through decision making.

Tom's father concluded that the American school required more social maturity from its students but less intellectual maturity. And, he added, "I think I detected the same features in the Middle school and the High schools I visited, and most certainly it characterised the University in which I taught" (Bell, 1984, p. 9).

The picture one gets from Bell's descriptions is of British schools that contain a richly varied atmosphere with children moving around throughout the day while teachers interact and observe—and of American schools with a sterile atmosphere and an emphasis on the basics so strong that it precludes other important subjects. It is tempting to argue that perhaps this great difference was due to the fact that Tom had graduated from kindergarten to first grade, yet observation of the primary grades in England would yield the same conclusions about differences.

A further contrast between the two systems relates to the emergence of reading. The expectation in British schools is that children will learn to read at different rates and that their personal schedules should be respected. It is also assumed that they *will* read eventually, whereas in the United States there is greater concern that without much direct help, children may well fail to learn to read. It should be noted, too, that there is a contrast in the way the teachers were regarded. The British teacher is viewed as one who facilitates the natural emergence of intelligence, knowledge, and skills. The teacher in Tom's American school was, instead, someone who transferred knowledge and skills to the waiting blank slates of children's minds. The British teacher is viewed as knowledgeable and able to make decisions about curriculum, materials, and children's progress. Tom's American teacher was given little leeway in making decisions and was constantly held accountable by those in authority.

It is interesting to visit elementary schools in the United States that were built during the late 1960s and 1970s. Many of them show signs of having tried to adapt the more open system of British schools. People from the education world of that time visited schools in England and came home impressed. Almost overnight walls were torn down to make more "open classrooms" and teachers were asked to teach in teams with little preparation or training. It is not surprising that the project was doomed to fail and that walls would soon be rebuilt, once again isolating teachers. (Somehow the observers of British schools for young children had failed to take careful note of the many years of planning and adaptation that had gone into the original model.)

It is one purpose of this book to provide ways in which the more open, child-centered model can be reintroduced into American schools in the early grades. It is not expected that we can be idealistic and hope for walls to be torn down again, but that some measure of richness can be returned to the sterility now all too prevalent. In other chapters we discuss the materials, the curriculum, and the physical atmosphere. Here, we will present our view of the teacher's role, or roles. In the following sections we first discuss the special attributes and attitudes needed by a teacher in this kind of classroom. This will be followed by a description of the various roles such a teacher needs to fill.

THE TEACHER AS A PERSON

The teacher in a child-centered classroom must behave and think in ways different from a teacher whose primary purpose is to transmit knowledge. In the former model, and it is the one advocated by this book, the teacher must have enough self-confidence to step back and let children share in the power. Generally speaking, it is easier and faster to be authoritarian, and authoritarianism is perhaps suitable for knowledge transmission but not for child-centered learning. With some thoughtful effort and willing experimentation, however, success is quite attainable. One major route to success is to exploit the tendency of young children to do as we do, not as we say.

Modeling

Because young children are imitative, much can be accomplished if we model what we want the children to do and become. If we want them to treat each other with courtesy and dignity, then we must do the same to them. If we yell at children, they will soon be shouting at each other. If we spank them, they will hit each other. And, while most of them will not hit or yell at us, the chances are good that they will feel helplessly resentful. On the more positive side, teachers can:

• Speak softly, or at least without yelling, even to the whole class. If children know the teacher usually has something important or interesting to say, they will stop to listen.
• Let children know sincerely when the teacher admires or appreciates something they have done. If a teacher tells them that a behavior is inappropriate, he or she should also explain why.
• Greet each child individually in the morning, making eye contact, letting each one know that he or she is welcome and special.
• Model appropriate courtesies. Unless children are allowed to sit on the tables, teachers shouldn't. Unless the snack table is set up for free use during the day, teachers should not walk around

with a cup of coffee while teaching. If children are expected to walk around, rather than through, work and play areas, then the teacher should too.

• Demonstrate polite behavior with other adults in the classroom. Children are very interested to observe adult interaction and will frequently imitate the behaviors later.

• Encourage play. Philosophical and conventional wisdom agree that play is the natural work of the child. Research, however, has shown that there are children from economically or psychologically deprived backgrounds who have little ability for play. With these children try taking a minor role in dramatic play, removing yourself after you have been able to influence the course of the play. Or playfully demonstrate some physically challenging exercises or equipment.

• Expand on these ideas as you get to know your children better. Teachers should ask themselves if what they are doing is something the children are also allowed to do, or if it is something they would like them to begin doing or to do more of.

Modeling behavior is not extraordinarily difficult because it primarily requires the teacher to decide what it is that children should do and then to demonstrate where possible. The focus, in other words, is on an exterior aspect of the teacher: behavior. A second aspect of the teacher as a person is more closely tied to the teacher's interior feelings.

Ego Involvement

Many people become teachers of young children in part because of the ego gratification and loving reinforcement that students in this age group provide. Unless carried to extremes, this motivation isn't a bad one. An early childhood classroom is usually a place where much affection passes between teachers and students. To have a truly child-centered class, however, it is necessary for teachers to keep ego involvement in check. They should expect to hear children declare that "no one" taught them to read, they just did it. They need to be glad when a child says proudly, "I tied my shoe myself!" Teachers can offer little ones a lap to sit on but should not be disappointed when children prefer to return to work on a project or go play with friends. In short, it is fine to be pleased when a child expresses affection and warmth and teachers certainly need to give it. They need to be careful, however, that they are not depriving children of the growth in independence because they, themselves, need what the children give them.

Decisions and Choices

As a person, the teacher must be willing to relinquish some hold on power and let children make many of their own choices and decisions. Some teachers who take a realistic look into their own needs may discover that they would really be happier having all the power for themselves. But in a society that strives to be a democracy, it is worth helping even very small children learn the responsibilities and rights that accompany independent decision making.

As often as possible children should be given the opportunity to choose whether they want to work alone or together. For the youngest children that may simply mean looking at a book alone in a rocking chair or playing in the housekeeping corner with three friends. In the primary years it might mean giving children a choice of working on math problems alone, with a friend, or in a small group. These choices don't have to be formally offered by the teacher each time they need to be made. If children are permitted freedom of movement during the day these choices happen quite naturally.

Making academic choices can also be done when teachers are clear about the goals they've set. Covering all material in a math book to page 59 is an unacceptably superficial goal. A teacher can, instead, note that these pages help children achieve addition skills, with sums to 5. With almost no extra labor involved, the children can be given a choice of doing the problems from the book, completing worksheets, testing each other with flash cards, or playing homemade math games. Although the children are presented with choices, they all relate to one major goal: learning sums to 5. The children are not allowed to run wild with their decision making; the choices did not include playing in the block corner or coloring.

Another time, however, it might be possible to give this extra freedom. If the teacher knows that the entire class will soon be tested on the addition facts for a countywide test, then the extent of decision making will probably be just as described. If timing is less important, then the blocks, crayons, and so on can be included with the stipulation that addition be worked on at some time before a deadline set by the teacher.

For very small children or for children who have little experience in making choices, it is better to start small to avoid overwhelming them with the many possibilities. It may be annoying to adults to see a child standing in the middle of a room stuffed with toys and games saying, "There's nothing to do." What the child may actually be saying is, "There's so much here that I can't focus." It is a good idea at the beginning of the school year to start with very few choices and only during a limited part of the day. As the teacher observes the behavior and maturity of the children, decision making can then be expanded gradually.

As we have seen, the teacher as a person needs to be someone who does not need, or overcomes the need, to be a strong authority figure. This teacher needs to be willing to relinquish some control and share in the possession of power by giving children opportunities to make their decisions and choices. The teacher as a person is warm and loving with young children and enjoys receiving warmth and love back, yet does not use children to fill his or her needs to the extent that children are deprived of their right to grow.

THE TEACHER'S ROLES

Each teacher is a juggler, trying to bring proper balance to the classroom. In the child-centered classroom the juggling is more likely to take the children's needs and interests into account than in the transmission-of-knowledge classroom. Such juggling requires that the teacher be willing to play several roles at once.

The Teacher as Facilitator

Based on the Latin root word *facilis,* meaning "easy," *facilitating* education means "making academic and social learning as easy as possible for children." It does not mean that teachers should avoid giving children challenges, but it does indicate that roadblocks should be removed whenever they seem to appear. When teachers facilitate learning they think flexibly and may choose from a variety of teaching techniques and methods.

Children are permitted by the facilitative teacher to learn in different ways about different topics depending on their own needs, interests, and preferred learning styles. They are allowed to be active in their learning rather than passive receptacles of a teacher's wisdom and knowledge. They are encouraged to think on their own, make their own decisions, and rely on their own ingenuity. It is in this context that learning through play becomes a viable choice for the teacher to make.

If teachers hope to facilitate—make easy—their children's learning, then choosing the method by which children learn most comfortably is a sensible option. "Children play in an effort to understand and master their environment. Play provides an avenue through which they can have repeated experiences which help them to master cognitive, physical, and social skills" (Butler, Gotts, & Quisenberry, 1978, p. 17). Play can take the form introduced by Patty Smith Hill earlier in the century: free play in centers devoted to such things as block building and housekeeping. Play can also be an integral part of the curriculum with academic activities chosen for their playful, experimental attributes.

The facilitative teacher can still provide direct instruction but must make a decision that determines when it is appropriate to do so. This is different from assuming direct instruction as the norm with play and independent decision making as frills to be permitted if there is extra time.

The facilitative teacher is a question asker, constantly alert to the need to pose questions that will encourage children to think about what they are doing in new and more cognitively mature ways. This teacher is just as aware that children need to ask their own questions and explore them in their own way.

The errors in knowledge, judgment, perceptions, and so on that children communicate are not seen as inadequacies by the facilitative teacher. Rather, they are viewed as the manifestations of continual growth and these should be built on. The teacher looks for the right "teachable moments" to introduce new ideas that will help a child progress.

When the facilitative teacher integrates curricular subject matter it soon becomes apparent that flexibility in teaching methods is the most effective way to teach. The integrated curriculum is one that takes children's real interests into account, thus making it possible that there will be times when direct instruction will quickly impart needed knowledge, others when exploration and play will help children decide what they need to learn next.

The Teacher as Instructor

To this point we have downplayed the instructing role of the teacher, relegating it to the transmission-of-knowledge classroom. Yet, direct instruction is appropriate when the teacher has new materials to demonstrate, a story to share, or important information to give and little time to do it in, or when she simply has information that can be given more effectively if done directly. If the decision to use direct instruction is made knowledgeably and wisely, it can often be the best teaching technique for the moment. Of prime importance when using direct instruction with young children is to avoid lecturing to them. They are rarely able to listen for long periods of time. When teachers wish to play the instructor role with young children they can do any of the following.

1. Get children's attention by displaying concrete objects. If teachers simply position themselves in the center of the room, either on a chair or on the floor, and if they have something in front of them that is new and interesting, it may not even be necessary to call the children to order. The promise of something new and interesting will act as a magnet. This technique will work even when there isn't a directly related object at hand. It is necessary only to choose something marginally connected and lay it down as a conversation starter.

2. Present new materials by using as few words as possible. A demonstration with virtually no words at all is appropriate for the youngest nursery school children, and no more than simple explanations are needed for the primary grades. Long explanations tend to distract and bore.

3. Avoid sharing lesson plans and long-range goals before engaging in a new activity. These are important for teachers to have in mind but young children frankly don't care. (Reread the last sentence of number 2!) There are other ways to let children know that a new unit or theme is about to emerge. Some examples:

- If the children chose this themselves, nothing more than casual discussion will be necessary. They are already expecting it.
- New room decor and bulletin boards are attention grabbers and state the teacher's intention without the need for explanations.
- It is possible to do two or three activities of a related nature before discussing the new theme. Children will naturally start to discuss and ask about what's happening. The teacher can then make explanations and ask for feedback in a more natural way than is provided by lecturing.
- The teacher can announce at the close of a school day that the following day something new and wonderful will be begun. It is only necessary to describe briefly what will be happening. The children will come to school eager to learn more.

4. Respect the children who "can walk and chew gum at the same time." It should not be assumed that even the most exciting concrete object or an outstanding presentation will act as a magnet to everybody. There are almost always children who stubbornly prefer to finish the project they're on. At this time, teachers should remember that finishing what one has started is a very worthwhile goal and then accommodate it. Some children really do prefer to do two things at one time, just as there are adults who feel the same way.

To make this idea work, a rule may be necessary that anyone who doesn't come to the group lesson must work in absolute silence in order to avoid causing a disturbance. It takes very little time then to say, "You've forgotten the rule about being quiet. Please come join us now."

5. Keep direct instruction short in duration. With very little children, 10 to 15 minutes is usually plenty. Primary children can last perhaps 20 to 30 minutes depending on their interest. If the topic is especially popular, as much as an hour may go by before restlessness sets in. When children are on the floor or immobilized at desks, teachers should keep in mind that they are probably moving about more than the children and therefore have less need to change activities. It is a good idea to try sitting on the floor once or twice just as the children do. It can get quite uncomfortable after a while!

The Teacher as Play Provider

Play is crucial to all phases of children's development: motor, affective, and cognitive. While this view has traditionally been accepted for children in nursery school, there has been a movement in recent years to take play away from children in kindergarten and the primary grades. Few decisions could hinder their progress more!

Children need vigorous, uninhibited play as well as fluid, gentle play in order to develop physically. If children are not encouraged to develop their motor capacities through play, they may establish patterns and habits of inactivity that will stay with them through life.

Children need time for imaginative and dramatic play to aid them in dealing with their fears and wants. "This is accomplished by playing out the event again and again, until it no longer holds any elements which upset or inhibit the child" (Weininger, 1979, p. 28). Further, this kind of play offers children the necessary opportunity to develop social skills. These are not skills that are simply nice to have if there's time after the "real" work is done. Many children today spend hours on a school bus, often with no-socializing rules. More hours are devoted to television viewing. There is less time than ever for them to learn about basic human communication and techniques for getting along with others.

Children need time to play in order to develop cognitively. Assimilation in the Piagetian sense provides a cognitive definition of play in that it is the process of playing around with accommodated ideas. Reorganizing, regrouping, rethinking, and restructuring are activities that all take place through play.

Children are naturally active and imaginative. When we stifle this part of their lives we inhibit much of their growth as well. Play is a vitally important element in any preprimary or primary classroom.

The Teacher as Manager

In a classroom structured according to the transmission-of-knowledge model, questions of management are relatively straightforward. The teacher, as the authority, may use a variety of management techniques, but they are devoted to keeping the children on task and paying attention. The management strategies in a child-centered classroom are usually more complex because the teaching and learning modes are also more complex. What works well with one group of children may fall flat with another. What works well in one kind of activity may have no relevance to another. Ideas that held the class together in October contribute to its disintegration in March. Flexibility, then, is a primary criterion for a teacher's success. The ideas that follow have been found useful, but teachers may need to adapt them to their own needs.

1. Freedom and independent decision making should be introduced gradually. For a teacher to grant such liberty at the beginning is to invite chaos. It is more effective to think of freedom as a reward for well-developed, civilized behavior—a goal to strive for rather than a gift up front.

Freedom can still be introduced from the very first day of school. A free-choice period can be provided after the teacher has had time to observe children during the early part of the day. This free period may last as little as 15 to 20 minutes for preschoolers or as much as 1 hour for primary children. An appropriate goal is a full morning or afternoon in which children are permitted to choose their own work or play. The goal may be reached as early as November or as late as mid-spring.

Similarly, children should be asked to contribute classroom rules very gradually. On the first day of school preschoolers can probably handle one or two rules, while primary children should feel comfortable with three or four. Others can be added later.

Classroom meetings are important for enhancing children's self-direction, but they should be held sparingly at first. The youngest children can meet for a few minutes in the morning to help plan the day and then again at the end of the morning to review what happened and to begin to develop a feeling of community. Older children can also meet to help plan; then they can follow up with a post-lunch meeting to evaluate the progress of the day and to make appropriate adjustments in both intellectual and social learning. For primary children, these short, daily meetings are more important at first than weekly, formal ones which can come later.

2. The work that children do should be chosen because it matters to them. One such way to induce bad behavior is to bore children with activities they can't relate to. One method for choosing well is to let the children themselves indicate what their interests are. This can, however, be carried too far in that young children have had little experience in the world and aren't aware of what other things are out there for them to learn about. Thus, it is also necessary to branch out and learn about the outside world, but still the activities can be focused in such a way that they matter to children. As one example, the teacher may note that the first-grade science book decrees that children learn about inclined planes. In order to make this learning matter to the children, it might be a good idea to ask them to bring in their favorite toy cars and trucks and then to do experiments with them on simple wood boards.

One good disciplinary technique to use with young children is to redirect their attention from one activity to another that may have more interest and meaning. But if the next activity also provides no interest, the problem will remain. The answer can usually be found by giving an unsettled child two or three choices of activities.

3. Play is a natural avenue for children's learning, but it requires some management on the part of the teacher. Decisions must be made about where to place specific materials. If the teacher notes that children are divided along gender lines in the blocks and housekeeping corners, it may be wise to move some blocks into the house and some dolls into the block piles, or to completely integrate the two centers. Further decisions need to be made about behavior. How much freedom of movement and noise can be tolerated? Rules will no doubt need to be established, as may limits on the number of children in each area. If academic learning through play is the teacher's goal, it may be a good idea to set a rule that each child must spend a minimum amount of time in each of the play/learning centers.

Some children will respond more than others to new centers in which play is the expected behavior. While there is no theoretical agreement regarding the concept that children develop through actual stages of play, it is still possible to see young children at several levels:

- Solitary play (egocentrically satisfying their own needs)
- Onlooker play (observing others but not participating)
- Parallel play (playing side by side but not with each other)
- Associative play (exchanging toys and ideas but each doing what he or she wants)
- Cooperative play (true group play; children choose group or independent activities according to mood) (Adapted from Weininger, 1979).

If play centers are chosen with these different levels all available at varying places, there will be something for everyone, making one less management problem for the teacher.

4. It is important to realize that good management in a child-centered classroom takes a lot of preplanning. In a classroom in which the teaching is primarily based on passing on knowledge, there is a moderate amount of planning followed by an intense period, lasting most of the school day, when the teacher imparts the knowledge as effectively as possible. In the child-centered classroom, the teacher must plan extensively before the children enter so that the environment is rich with activities that can be learned in a variety of ways. The teaching period is less intense overall than in the other model, so that once preparations are made, the teacher can relax a little. This time can then be used to observe children's social and academic behavior.

5. Teachers should decide how much noise and movement they can tolerate and then help children stay within that level. Despite the ideal of child-centeredness, this concept will work only if teachers feel comfortable and happy. A teacher who is a loud person with heavy movements can expect a class to be more vivid in its behavior than that of a teacher who is quiet. Here is one instance when modeling of behavior will usually go a long way toward achieving what the teacher wants.

One technique for keeping noise down is to move throughout the room talking quietly to different groups. If the entire class is becoming unruly, it may be wise to stop everything for a few minutes and call a group meeting to discuss progress. As part of the discussion the teacher can emphasize the need to be quiet so that all can work effectively.

If the teacher is busy with a small group and can't get the attention of a noisy group elsewhere, a nearby child can be sent on a mission. If this is preschool, the message may simply be that the teacher wants to see a particular child. If the children can read, the teacher can send a note to the other group asking them to work or play more quietly. Signing it with love won't hurt and may help.

A traditionally popular attention getter is flicking the overhead lights. This generally works if the teacher has good rapport with the children but even then it wears off after a while, as do most related attention getters. It works better to change these fairly frequently and almost anything on hand works well for a while: tone bell, piano chord, two rhythm sticks, a special song.

Singing, in fact, can have a broader disciplinary use. Somehow, when children are reminded of behavior rules by means of music, the threat to their self-esteem is less and they feel more willing to comply. Some specific ideas:

• To get the attention of a single child or a group the teacher sings: "Can you hear me?" to any tune. Children respond with, "I can hear you," using the same tune.

- After sending the current attention-getting signal, the teacher sings, rather than states, "It's much too noisy."
- Using any familiar tune, the teacher alters the words to fit the management situation.
- A counting song such as "Ten Little Indians" is used. The teacher sings it slowly, clearly, and quietly to get the class's attention. A game is made of children's ability to pay attention before the number 10 is reached.

Most teachers will find that the respect they show their children, the trust they demonstrate by giving them increasing freedoms, and the joyful atmosphere that comes from singing (or at least speaking with pleasantness) will go a long way toward creating and maintaining a well-managed classroom. For techniques that can be used in extreme situations, with emotionally handicapped children, or for working with unfamiliar cultures, a book on management and discipline may offer extra help. Three books with helpful suggestions for use with younger children are *Discipline and Classroom Management* by Osborn and Osborn (1981), *Practical Guide to Solving Preschool Behavior Problems* by Essa (1983), and *Elementary Classroom Management* by Charles (1983).

A major part of good classroom management is the teacher's observation of the children both individually and collectively. This observation encompasses social and intellectual behaviors and interactions. Because it is of such importance for everything that happens in the classroom, we have declared it a teacher's role in its own right.

The Teacher as Observer

For a teacher, the most delightful moments of the day are probably the times of interaction with children. Observation, on the other hand, requires that the teacher step back and melt into the wall. At the time, observation may not provide the enjoyment that active teaching does, but the long-term rewards make the effort worthwhile.

For example, the teacher may be aware that a boy who wants desperately to play in the block corner is not welcome there; with a few minutes of observation the teacher may note that he has two or three small behaviors the other children find annoying. Or a child may be having trouble with arithmetic; while observing her, the teacher may note that she pushes away the manipulatives in disdain saying, "That's baby stuff. My sister said." In either case, the teacher has been able to observe the child's problems and can then make knowledgeable plans to solve them. Observations for different purposes have different techniques. All of them have their own rewards.

Observations of Cognitive Learning   Tests, in all their formats, provide only a limited appraisal of children's cognitive development. Observation can tell the teacher which children learn best through motor activities and which prefer to snuggle immobile in a corner with a book; who prefers to work alone and who is more secure doing projects with others.

If children are permitted to read aloud to each other rather than always having them in a teacher-supervised reading group, it is possible to observe several children at one time and to make notes of specific problems to be dealt with later. Observing children working alone with arithmetic problems allows the teacher to detect their methods of thought and the efficiency of them. When children work together the teacher can observe which ones have sufficient understanding to be able to explain problems to others.

Observations of Affective Development   Studying children's social interactions and individual emotional behavior can tell the teacher much about such things as the formation of friendships, power struggles, personality difficulties, and working relationships. Within each classroom there is usually a hierarchy—subtle or overt—of social interactions. In a classroom of young children, a hierarchy may change rapidly in a short period of time, or it may develop early and remain. Through observation the teacher can actually see the hierarchies forming and be prepared to step in when it would be beneficial to do so. Within each classroom, too, there are usually a few children who have difficulty relating well to the others. Again, by observation, the teacher may find that it's possible to identify the problems and to help children correct them.

When teachers are continually involved with teaching, it is difficult to know what is really going on beneath the surface of learning the curriculum. But when the classroom is left to the children for a while, the teacher can learn a lot. There are varying theories and models of observation. The suggestions that follow are some that have been used successfully in child-centered classrooms. They are flexible and can be adapted to the teacher's specific situation.

Observation Techniques   It is important that teachers observe the whole child. That means that it is important to watch what the child says and does, and that an effort is made to understand underlying feelings and attitudes about learning, social interactions, and the self. To do these things teachers can do the following.

1. Greet all children individually when they come in each morning, perhaps shaking hands or giving a small hug. Then give another hug around the shoulders or at the base of the neck. Once a teacher knows the children even slightly, it is possible to tell who fought with his or her mother at breakfast, who didn't have enough sleep, and who is already moving into high gear. If there seems to be some general trend in feelings that day, it may be possible to alter some of the day's activities. If individual children are being watched for behavior problems, the teacher can predict what will need to be done during the day.

2. Make the first activity of the day one that can be observed easily, even if it is only for a few minutes during the settling-in time. Here observation begun at the door can be continued. Further, the teacher can sense the direction the day would take if left entirely to the children and then decide what needs to be done to alter the established plans or to follow on their new interests.

3. Face the class, with back to the wall, when working with individuals or groups. In that way the teacher can always have the grand picture of what is going on. This applies even when the teacher is talking with some children for a very few minutes. If the teacher needs to sit down at a table with a group and the only remaining chair is facing the wall, it is simple to ask one child to move.

4. During free play and work, wander the room with a clipboard on which can be written a running commentary or brief notations. It is a good idea to always use the same clipboard so that children become accustomed to it and lose interest in its purpose. When asked about it, the teacher can say, "I like to write down what's happening so that I can remember everything."

5. Get a sense of social interactions by writing as much of the children's dialogue as possible on the clipboard. Or note movements children make from one center to another. It is better to exclude any evaluative remarks or words until the data collection is complete and the teacher can look back on what happened. Words to avoid include "nastily," "arrogantly," "whining," "prissy," and so on.

6. Use the clipboard to jot down quick notes about academic progress. As the teacher listens to children read to each other, a record can be made by writing a child's initials, then phonetic mistakes or other problems. If misconceptions about math manipulatives are observed, these can be described in abbreviated terms. Children testing each other with flash cards can be observed and specific mistakes, if they are made repeatedly or if there are apparent patterns, can be jotted down.

One shorthand method is to use a number-coding system with specific materials or activities. After the child's initials, write the name of the material or activity. Then code a "1" if the activity appears to be over the child's head, a "2" if its challenge meets the child's abilities and interests, and a "3" if it is beneath the child's level.

7. Observe them as teachers. A tape recorder can be placed in an inconspicuous location when the teacher will be doing a presentation. Then the teacher can listen later to determine conversational nervous tics ("uh-huh," "like—," "ya know," etc.); preference for boys or girls; high or low achievers; the quality of voice including the appropriate enthusiasm; and success in balancing the amount of talking and listening engaged in.

8. Reflect on the day. At the end of the day it is good to take 10 minutes to jot down any observations that were missed earlier. Look over notes to determine future plans or discard others as unnecessary.

The Teacher as Evaluator

Observation is one way to evaluate what is going on. At other times, more elaborate or formal evaluation is important. The conscientious teacher will want to know if the curriculum is achieving its goals. For this a plan for evaluation will be critical.

The primary reason for teachers to evaluate children's work is to find out if they have accomplished what they set out to do. If this important step isn't taken, children may be pushed ahead before they understand what's going on, they may be held back unnecessarily, or they may simply be bored. In order to make any kind of evaluation, it is necessary that the teacher have a clear understanding of the original goals. Beginning teachers commonly make the mistake of evaluating only parts of what was done, perhaps the least important parts. Or they lose sight of the goals and purposes and evaluate whatever is most salient in children's activities. To succeed in evaluation the following steps need to be taken.

1. Before beginning a lesson or an activity, list the goals and purposes that make the experience worthwhile. What, specifically, will the children know and be able to do when it is finished?

2. During the activity, keep the goals and purposes in mind and alter them if it seems wise. Here is where evaluation can first take place, through careful observation.

3. After the activity other evaluative tools can be used, keeping in mind again the original goals and purposes. Evaluative tools might include testing of some sort, informal observation, or follow-up activities.

Unless it is necessary to determine clinically what a child's problems may be, there is generally no real reason to give a formal test to evaluate learning in the preschool years. For teachers in the primary grades, accountability is a major thrust in education today and they may feel that the burden of evaluation is already too high. There are criterion tests, norm-referenced tests, county tests, state tests, end-of-chapter tests, and on and on. Yet there is still important evaluation for the teacher to do whether in this type of situation or in a play-oriented preschool. To provide alternatives to testing, we suggest two other methods: observation and follow-up activities.

Observation as Evaluation   This is an ongoing kind of evaluation and should begin as soon as the activity begins. By observing children from the beginning, it is possible to determine if the activity needs changing, replacing, speeding up, or slowing down. Observation need not be silent and removed. It can include dialogue with children in which questions are asked and answered. Techniques discussed in the section "The Teacher as Observer" may be used when observing for evaluation.

Follow-up Activities   One of the most effective ways to evaluate an activity is to do a follow-up activity that can only be done successfully if the first activity has been learned. Some examples of how this might work include the following.

1. *Principal activity:* A trip to the supermarket (or other store) to learn how pricing is done, how cash registers are used, and how change is made.
   Follow-up activity: A center is created in class that includes goods to price and a cash register to use.

2. *Principal activity:* Several weeks of experimentation with color mixing at the easel with the purpose of letting children discover the primary, secondary, and tertiary colors.
   Follow-up activity: The easel is supplied with only the primary colors, and children are challenged to mix and name as many colors as they can.

3. *Principal activity:* The children learn to sing and recite an assortment of songs and poems.
   Follow-up activity: Parents, principal, and others are invited in to enjoy an informal program of entertainment.

Perhaps it is surprising to consider these follow-up activities as evaluative ones. Frequently, teachers simply consider such experiences as natural outcomes of the initial activities. Yet, the alert teacher can use them for evaluation, both of the activity and of the children's understanding. Such evaluation should then be used to make decisions about further experiences.

Evaluation techniques may be summarized as various forms of tests, formal and informal observations, and learning activities that provide double duty as evaluations. Using a combination of these will make evaluation less burdensome and more useful than relying simply on one format.

The Teacher as Planner

We are now ready to look at the planning that goes into direct teaching, supervised independent learning, and evaluation.

A child-centered classroom that makes use of an integrated curriculum needs planning that is knowledgeable, efficient, and well-orchestrated. At the same time, flexibility as the hours, days, weeks, and months unfold is essential, for the children may lead the learning in directions not predicted. Thus, it is important for the teacher to have broad, general goals in mind and to leave room for change.

In planning for the year it is a good idea to lay out overall themes in consecutive order, leaving room for others that will emerge as the year develops. If academic goals are required by the school or the school system, these can be listed under each theme for the appropriate time in the school year. If it is impossible to meet some goals within a particular theme, it may be a good idea to reorder the themes.

When planning for each week, it is essential to return to the overviews provided by the larger themes and units. As the class falls behind or moves more quickly ahead, the teacher can readjust activities and schedules. As new interests emerge, these can be incorporated into the schedule. If a look at weekly accomplishments indicates that the overall program for the year is being ignored, forgotten, or avoided, it will be a good idea to return to the yearly plan to determine problems and to find solutions for them.

Planning for each day is most critical at the beginning of the school year. Daily observation will inform the teacher of the needs for the next day. As the school year progresses, weekly planning becomes more important, and there is more of a flow from day to day. Within the week's grander picture, the children will even be able to help plan the day's learning or the teacher will be able to make short-term corrections.

In general, planning for child-centered learning and an integrated curriculum is less structured but no less important than planning for the transmission of knowledge. It is the overall picture that is important. The teacher needs to know which long-term and which short-term goals should be attained. The teacher needs to become continually better acquainted with the needs and interests of the children, and the teacher needs to have a clear picture of where the class is heading so that, if needed, flexible planning is possible.

This has been an overview of what planning will look like. In the final two chapters of the book we will discuss this critical subject in more detail.

The Teacher's Reflective Role

One of the most important things a teacher must do is to think about what has been happening in the classroom and then make rational choices about what should happen next. Without this kind of thoughtful decision making, teachers show their willingness to relinquish their power to outsiders and to give their children less consideration than they deserve.

Agreeing with Dewey's argument that reflective teachers need to adopt attitudes of introspection, open-mindedness, and willingness to accept responsibility for decisions and actions, Ross, Bondy, and Kyle (in press) have said, "The introspective teacher engages in thoughtful reconsideration of all that happens in a classroom with an eye toward improvement. The open-minded teacher is willing to consider new evidence (such as unexpected occurrences in a classroom or new theoretical knowledge) and willing to admit the possibility of error."

It is often difficult for beginning teachers to engage in this kind of reflection because the pressures to do what other teachers suggest, to simply follow current practices, and to rely on what they recall teachers doing with them are very strong. There are a few strategies that might prove helpful for beginning teachers to consider. First, the selection of a first job is critical. It is sometimes difficult, or even impossible, to be selective, but when it is feasible, the beginning teacher can try to choose a school in which teachers are permitted to make their own decisions about teaching methods and materials, a school in which the principal or director respects and trusts teachers as professionals.

Second, beginning teachers can keep in touch with their professors and trainers. Too often they believe that they must sink or swim on their own once graduation has taken place. Yet, continued communication is almost always welcomed by faculty who hope to see sound theories and research put into practice.

A third strategy is to observe which of the experienced teachers in the new school seem to be independent decision makers, which ones use a variety of teaching techniques, and which ones have a good knowledge of child development. These teachers will probably be quite willing to share their ideas and to provide support at critical times.

A teacher has may roles to fill, yet they are all possible. If decision making is based on thoughtful reflection and if the teacher is willing to admit mistakes and correct them, progress is certain to follow. Beginning teachers need to keep in mind that no amount of academic preparation will make them ready to deal immediately and successfully with every opportunity and problem that presents itself. Continued growth will be required in the classroom situation, and it should be welcomed rather than avoided.

TO DISCUSS

1   Discuss pressures to conform to others' teaching methods or ideas that have already taken place in student teaching experiences. Talk about ways these pressures were avoided or obeyed. How were these situations different from or the same as those that might be faced after graduation? Discuss possible techniques for dealing with such pressures, perceived or real.

TO DO

1   Plan a two-part activity in which the second acts as an evaluation of the first. Teach it in your current classroom experience and analyze it for its effectiveness as principal lesson and evaluation.
2   During a free-play or free-work situation, observe children, using any of the techniques described in "The Teacher as Observer." Note any existing problems and then make plans for correction or improvement. Discuss these with your directing teacher and implement them as feasible.

BIBLIOGRAPHY

Almy, M. (1959) *Ways of studying children*. New York: Teachers College, Columbia University.

Aries, P. (1965) *Centuries of childhood*. New York: Vintage Books.

Barth, R. (1972) *Open education and the American school*. New York: Agathon Press.

Bell, A. (1984) From butterflies to stations: Reception class to grade one. *TACTYC (Journal of Tutors of Advanced Courses for Teachers of Young Children)*, *5(1)*:1–9.

Butler, A., Gotts, E., & Quisenberry, N. (1978) *Play as development*. Columbus, OH: Merrill.

Charles, C. (1983) *Elementary classroom management*. New York: Longman.

Cowe, E. (1982) *Free play*. Springfield, IL: Charles C. Thomas.

Dewey, J. (1966, 1916) *Democracy and education*. New York: Free Press.

Essa, E. (1983) *Practical guide to solving preschool behavior problems*. Albany, NY: Delmar.

Heafford, M. (1967) *Pestalozzi: His thought and its relevance today*. New York: Barnes & Noble.

Kramer, R. (1976) *Maria Montessori*. Chicago: University of Chicago Press.

Locke, J. (1964) *John Locke on education*. (P. Gay, ed.) New York: Columbia University.

Montessori, M. (1967) *The Montessori method*. Cambridge, MA: Robert Bentley.

Osborn, D. K., & Osborn, J. (1981) *Discipline and classroom management*. Athens, GA: Education Associates.

Piaget, J. (1975, 1948) *To understand is to invent*. New York: Viking.

Ross, D., Bondy, E., & Kyle, D. (in press) *Reflective teaching in the elementary school*. New York: Macmillan.

Rousseau, J. (1963) *The Emile*. (W. Boyd, ed.) New York: Columbia University.

Shapiro, M. (1983) *Child's garden*. University Park, PA: Pennsylvania State University Press.

Skinner, B. (1961) *Cumulative record*. New York: Appleton-Century-Crofts.

Stallings, J. (1977) *Learning to look*. Belmont, CA: Wadsworth.

Weininger, O. (1979) *Play and education*. Springfield, IL: Charles C. Thomas.

part 2

THE INTEGRATED
CURRICULUM

In Chapter One we visited Danny and Ben as they learned informally at home, creating their own curriculum in a very natural way. You will recall that as the boys built their indoor fort they did not consciously set out to learn reading or math or social studies. In effect, however, that's what they did. Their interest was in building the fort, but in order to accomplish that, they needed to calculate distances, write signs, develop leadership patterns, and so on. Thus, they learned school subjects within the context of a project that had importance to them. In Chapter Three we discuss ways in which teachers can, to a great extent, replicate this natural learning within the classroom setting. It involves a type of planning that is somewhat different from the traditional approach, but it can use traditional subject matter as its base if required.

In Chapters Four through Nine each subject area of the curriculum is first treated separately and then integrated with the others. That is, language, mathematics, science, social studies, art, and music and movement are each presented as important in their own right, and then combined with the others for more natural learning. For each subject a bit of teaching/learning history is included; then an update is provided. This update includes the current views of associations dedicated to furthering the cause of each of the subject areas. (Examples of these are the National Council for the Social Studies and the National Council of Teachers of Mathematics.) As you will see, the general consensus of all these associations is that their focal subjects can frequently be taught best by integrating them with other areas of the curriculum.

At the end of each chapter you will find ideas for teaching across the curriculum, either by using informal themes or by creating more structured units. In each chapter, themes and units are provided for both preprimary and primary grades. They are intended to be practical, possibly to use now in your student teaching or to adapt later in your own classroom.

chapter three

Weaving the Web

In his book *Charlotte's Web,* E. B. White spun a tale of fantasy that pits a spider-heroine against a family of farmers who plan to "murder" and eat her friend, a young pig. Throughout this enchanting fantasy are woven elements of reality. In describing Charlotte's masterful spelling of words across her web, as no other spider before her had done, White chose to explain in detail the making of a real spider's web. He explained that to the unpracticed eye the completed web would appear to be a single entity of patterned thread, but that a more careful observer could see that the basis for the web was an intricate interrelationship between very distinct components. Each of these components had its separate and indispensable purpose.

For example, several types of thread are possible and Charlotte chooses two: sticky thread for capturing insects and dry, tough thread for writing messages about the pig whose life she is trying to save. Important, too, are the spinnerets and spinning tubes that help play out the threads. The structure of the web requires that there be the circular orb lines as well as the radials that travel straight out from the center. Thus, a number of individual things work independently and together to create the finished web. Each is important in its own right and each is also a component part of a grander design.

We can view the early childhood curriculum in much the same way. When children learn in a way that is most natural to themselves, they unconsciously integrate subject areas into a complex whole based on their current interests. Teachers who consciously adapt this method of learning to the classroom see the curriculum as a fully spun web that incorporates a number of components at one time. However, they also know that it is important to take a careful look at each of these components individually to be sure it is sufficiently represented. Without the radials to connect them, the orb lines in Charlotte's web would surely have collapsed. Without each subject area in the curriculum, the totality would lack strength. Before focusing on the positive ways in which a curriculum web can be woven, let us take a look at how these webs are weakened if the "radials," or subject areas, are deleted from the whole "web."

THE SUBJECT AREAS, OR RADIALS

We will consider each subject area in turn, surmising what might happen if it were to be deleted from the curriculum. As you will see, each area offers its own special strength which, when woven into the whole, provides children with a full and richly rewarding school experience.

1. *Language:* The need to communicate is basic to human beings. Children need many language experiences in school, if they are to learn to communicate with others effectively. Fewer experiences will lead to less effective communication. In addition, children need to understand why we write, read, and talk. Without experiences that give purpose to the learning of letters, words, and sounds, children will fail to understand why they need to learn reading and writing skills. What could be an exciting experience in learning to read and write may become a tedious chore devoid of meaning.

2. *Reading:* This subject might have been included under "Language." Yet, its importance is so critical that it has been given its own listing. Literacy is the foundation of any civilized society. Without success in reading, children are deprived of their rightful membership in the advanced cultures of today. This is not to say that preschool children need to be drilled in reading or even prereading exercises. They do need activities and experiences that show them the importance, excitement, and possibilities offered by the reading they will do one day. In the primary grades, it is amazingly possible to provide the class with reading books, reading groups, and reading assignments and still have little real reading. Real, meaningful, enjoyable reading is what children crave and need.

3. *Mathematics:* Particularly in the earliest years it is tempting to save mathematics for later, for "real" school. This point of view argues for a dull, drill approach to learning mathematics and divorces the subject from real life. Yet, mathematics is all around us, in everyday experiences, waiting to be discovered and explored. Without the introduction of math in the early years, children miss out on learning this important point, and this subject, too, becomes another exercise in tedium.

4. *Science:* Teachers often feel weak in the sciences and so neglect their teaching in the early childhood classroom. To do so perpetuates this weakness in school learning to future generations. This weakness has already been observed across the grades and throughout the entire country. Worse, the deletion of science from the curriculum over recent years is beginning to have a profound effect on an entire society's ability to keep up with the rest of the world in the development of technology. If children have little or no experience with the sciences in the early years, they may never develop an interest in them, or worse yet, they may develop an antipathy or fear toward them.

5. *Social studies:* This is a subject that is often left at the wayside when the day becomes too filled with demands. Yet, learning to participate in their society is one of the most important reasons for children to be educated. Simply passing down the culture from one generation to the next can be done without a study of the social sciences; for children to understand their culture, however, and to learn to make decisions about its future, social studies must be part of the curriculum.

6. *Art:* When the curriculum becomes crowded, this is one of the first subjects to go. Yet when we look back through the history of the ages, the art produced by any society or culture is one of the most salient and telling things about it. The art we and our children produce will be one of the most important legacies we leave for the generations to come. Speaking for the present, art adds richness and beauty to life. It provides children with skills in observation, hand-eye coordination, and methods of communication. Without art the curriculum becomes drier, duller, more tedious.

7. *Movement and drama:* Young children learn, not just with their eyes and ears, but with their entire bodies. To deprive them of movement experiences is to deprive them of a primary method of gaining knowledge. In the primary grades, organized sports are just beginning to be of interest. Throughout all the early years, less organized experiences are crucial to physical, emotional, and intellectual growth. Expressing themselves dramatically is an outgrowth, in part, of children's physical expression. Sometimes when children cannot verbalize what they are thinking and feeling, they can act it out. Without drama, a primary means of communication is eliminated from children's repertoires.

8. *Music:* Like art, music adds richness to children's lives. And like art it frequently disappears from the curriculum. When children are occupied in unsupervised play, they can be observed quite naturally and unconsciously singing, humming, and chanting their way through various activities and experiences. To eliminate music from the curriculum is to eliminate a primary means of children's communication and enjoyment.

It should be apparent that every curricular subject is important to the development of the children we teach. At the same time, as we have seen in our discussion of cognitive development, children do not naturally learn through isolating specific subjects. These have been determined by adult definition. Children's natural learning is more likely to take place across a theme of interest:

building a fort, exploring a sandbox, interacting with the first snow of winter. Teachers can create a good deal of their curriculum by building webs made up of these themes of interest. Done with knowledge and care, a web can be created that incorporates most, or even all, of the required and desired curriculum. In the earliest years, these webs may be built as loosely structured themes. In the primary grades, the requirements and expectations for learning may argue for more structured units. In either case, children's natural inclinations for learning are catered to and exploited in the most positive sense of the word.

DECEMBER AS A CURRICULUM WEB

Probably most teachers create curriculum webs at one time or another, consciously or not. Often, such webs are created during various holiday seasons. As an example, let's see what one teacher might undertake as a curriculum web during the December holiday season.

Making a holiday curriculum web is a tradition of long standing in the preschool and primary grades. This is often true even in classes where the day-by-day curriculum is rigid and divided into self-contained subjects. No matter what their feelings are the rest of the year, teachers seem to accept the idea that in December it is all right to plan learning around a theme. This tradition is so much a part of the culture that what it really is often goes unnoticed: it is a curriculum webbed to meet the interest and excitement of children. A look at some of the more common activities that take place during this time will demonstrate how the December holiday theme covers the entire curriculum.

Language: Learning poems; writing Christmas or Hanukkah cards; learning, writing, and presenting plays and programs.

Mathematics: Learning the sequence of songs and events in a holiday program; measuring ingredients for holiday cooking; making measurements (even primitive ones) when mounting or hanging decorations.

Science: Observing chemical and physical changes during cooking and baking experiences.

Social studies: Working together harmoniously; learning about the music, food, and customs of other lands; learning about the varying December holidays of the cultures represented in the children's own class.

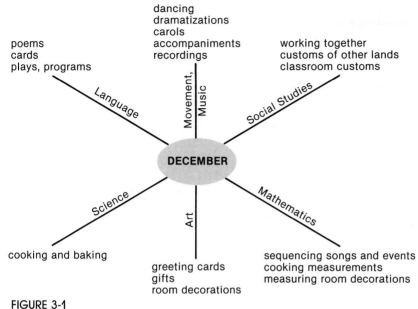

FIGURE 3-1

Art: Making greeting cards; designing and making gifts; planning and making room decorations.

Movement, drama, and music: Dancing to the music learned throughout the month; dramatizing songs and poems; singing carols and other traditional songs; creating accompaniments to holiday music; listening to recordings.

Presented as a straightforward list, the December holiday theme curriculum might contain most or all of the desired components, but let's see what greater possibilities there are by illustrating it as a web (see Figure 3-1).

Here, the same activities are present, but the visual effect is quite different. The web appears less structured, more tentative, and it is these qualities that make it a useful tool for planning. The teacher can choose a theme, create a web, and then add or subtract activities as it becomes apparent that there is too much or too little emphasis in some areas.

WHY CURRICULUM WEBS

We have already hinted at some of the advantages of planning a curriculum through the use of webs. A more in-depth discussion will point up their overall value.

Curriculum Coverage   One concern many teachers have is that if they teach along the line of themes, or webs, some curricular areas will be overemphasized or undertaught. On the contrary, planning with a web provides an overview of the entire curriculum and gives the teacher a basis for decision making of this sort. A look at the December web (Figure 3-1) tells the teacher that science is an underrepresented subject. A decision could then be made between several choices: to work in more science as a part of the theme (perhaps too contrived), to add science that is unrelated to the theme (hard to do in a hectic month such as December), or to wait perhaps until January when the children are interested in learning something entirely new (an opportunity to focus on science by making a science topic the theme of a web).

Natural Learning   As was pointed out in detail in the discussion of cognitive development, children do not naturally learn by focusing first on history, then on science, then on math, and so on. These divisions have been created by adults who may (or may not) learn more efficiently that way themselves. Young children are interested in making sense of the world around them, and they are hungry to learn ever more about what they see, hear, and feel. Breaking their learning down into categories by subject area is less natural, more forced, and therefore less interesting and exciting than is working with thematic webs.

Building on Children's Interests   This advantage to integrating subject matter is an extension of natural learning. Choosing subjects interesting to children means children will be much more involved in the learning process and more enthusiastic about being in school. When learning is simply done by isolated subject matter, it is difficult to heed children's interests as planning is done; through integrated webbing, it is the most natural thing to do.

Skills in Meaningful Context   When learning is done along the line of themes interesting to children, skills need not be neglected. They can have just as much attention paid them as in more subject-oriented learning. They simply need to become part of the planning web. Done within the context of thematic learning, the skills become much more meaningful to children. A spelling word that needs to be right because it is part of an invitation to a holiday party has more meaning than a spelling word that is memorized because it is on this week's list.

Flexibility   Teaching along the line of themes or units takes away the need to be on page 83 by Thanksgiving. It may be more important to read page 155 first and page 72 next month if the current theme calls for that. Further, it is possible to emphasize some curricular areas now and save others for later, as in the case of science in the December curriculum. If the teacher keeps the overall needs of the year in mind, children can cover just as much of the curriculum as is expected (and more), without ever feeling the pressures of getting to page 83 on time.

A Planning Device   Once a teacher has determined that a teaching project or unit will be integrated across the curriculum, the actual making of a web provides a way of organizing that has specific advantages. A web is less structured and more tentative than an outline, while it still provides a focused means of organization. In the case of the December web, the teacher can see quickly that science is underrepresented, that including both other lands and classroom cultures may be too much for a 1-month unit, or that it will probably be better to choose between plays and more general programs in the language section. Further, if the web is regarded as a work in progress, rather than as a finished product, it can be added to or subtracted from at any given time.

Some teachers may find that after creating the web, an outline format is a good finished product. This can be done as a chronology, providing a schedule of activities in their proper sequence. Or it can be done by listing the subject areas. Or, the teacher may find that the web provides enough structure.

The advantages of viewing the school curriculum as a web of learning range from the philosophical (webbed learning as natural learning) to the practical (using webs as a planning device). To see how these six advantages work in practice, let's take a look at one second-grade teacher's experience in planning a unit of learning inspired by the children's interest in a dying flower.

A FLOWER CURRICULUM[1]

It began when Adam brought a cut flower to Ms. Susanna. She let him choose a vase and the best place for its display. Adam chose a pink teacup and a place in the sun "so it won't die." He was both astonished and upset 2 days later when the flower began to wilt and insisted, "But I put it in the sun so it shouldn't be dying!"

---

[1]The teacher in this experience was the author of this text. In 1987–1988 I spent a sabbatical year teaching second grade at the Benjamin Franklin International School in Barcelona, Spain. The children's suggestions provided input for many aspects of this book, including (as demonstrated in "The Flower Curriculum") their insistence on getting my name wrong.

Benny argued that that was exactly the problem. "If you'da put it in the shade it wouldn'ta died." Adam stuck by his original perception, and Ms. Susanna suggested that they could do an experiment with two cut flowers to see if one place was better than the other or not. Soon the whole class was interested in what was happening, and Rachael agreed to bring flowers from her extensive garden.

After a few days it became apparent that both the flower that had been put in the sun and the one that had been placed in a closet were beginning to die. Rachael then entered the argument proposing that it was because she had cut the flowers from their roots that they were dying. William said that if they had been placed in dirt they might have lasted longer, although he thought that perhaps the roots should have been kept on also. Benny said that William might be right but that water was even more important than dirt. The discussion became so heated that Ms. Susanna asked if they might like to do another experiment to help settle the argument.

The children responded enthusiastically and the next day she brought three potted yellow marigolds that resembled each other as closely as three plants possibly could. The class was divided into three teams. One agreed to deprive its plant of water, another of sun, and a third of dirt.

As the children began their controlled experiment to determine a plant's needs for life, Ms. Susanna observed that their interest continued to grow and that they seemed to want more interaction with the plants than the simple experiment offered. She then decided to expand their experiences, not only in the obvious direction of science, but throughout more of the curriculum as well. At first she simply jotted down a few ideas; then, realizing that more organization was needed, she began to construct a web. In its first, tentative stage it looked like Figure 3-2.

On the first day a problem arose. The first team placed its marigold in the sun but didn't water it. The second team gave their marigold water but locked it in a closet, and the third team scooped out their plant's soil, propped it up in its pot and filled the pot with water. The children then posted signs in two languages warning bilingual cleaning staff (and anyone else passing by) not to tamper with the plants.

The following morning Ms. Susanna saw that the plant that was not supposed to be watered had been thoroughly drenched, apparently by a child who lacked understanding of what was to happen. Together she and the children constructed a chart showing what each group should and should not do, and this was added to the planning web under mathematics (see Figure 3-3).

For two reasons, this unit was one that could not be planned in a definitive way. First, it was based on the children's interests, and the teacher made every attempt to accept their guidance as the

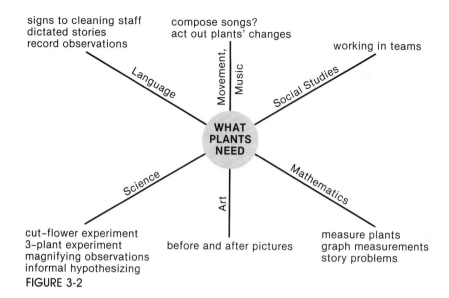

signs to cleaning staff
dictated stories
record observations

compose songs?
act out plants' changes

working in teams

Language

Movement,
Music

Social Studies

WHAT
PLANTS
NEED

Science

Art

Mathematics

cut–flower experiment
3–plant experiment
magnifying observations
informal hypothesizing

before and after pictures

measure plants
graph measurements
story problems

FIGURE 3-2

days and weeks went by. Activities such as in-depth observations with magnifying glasses evolved after the children spent extensive time being "like real scientists." The second reason was that Ms. Susanna had no idea how long the plants would take to change, or which plant might last longer than the others. Thus, it was necessary to create activities as the opportunities occurred. For these two reasons a formal outline was never created.

However, it was possible, on one occasion, to create a completely different type of web. Ms. Susanna had an interest in trying to provide more than academics in this unit. Her class was one which had come from two different schools (and three different classes) the year before and had yet to achieve a feeling of unity. She thought that here might be an opportunity to help the children pull together by working together.

A second nonacademic consideration was that, as time went on, the children became emotionally attached to their plants and ex-

FIGURE 3-3

	Sun Team	Soil Team	Water Team
Sun?	no	yes	yes
Soil?	yes	no	yes
Water?	yes	yes	no

pressed dismay as they shrank smaller and smaller, then began to dry up. It occurred to Ms. Susanna that the academic activities were important in themselves, but that with a bit of extra thought she could incorporate elements to help the children face the emotions they were feeling. After tentatively choosing an activity, she placed it in a different sort of web to be able to determine its usefulness in meeting academic, social, and emotional needs.

The activity was as follows: Each team of children was to look at the pictures they had drawn of their plants the previous weeks. Then, using magnifying glasses they would carefully observe their plants and make drawings of their current state. Below the drawings reports would be written to describe what was different about the plant now. Finally, each team could dance its plant's history and the feelings they had about the changes. The project would take much of one afternoon, so Ms. Susanna felt that it could and should accomplish several things at one time. Figure 3-4 shows the

FIGURE 3-4

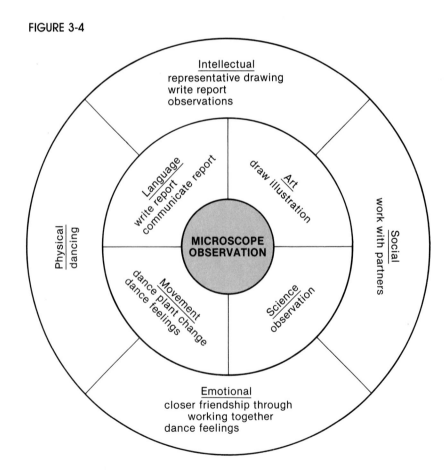

web she drew to see how much of the curriculum was represented and how well the children's intellectual, social, emotional, and physical needs were being met.

The activity was placed in the center of the web. Immediately surrounding the center the curricular areas covered by the activity were placed. The outside of the web showed how intellectual, physical, social, and emotional needs were met.

By creating the web, Ms. Susanna was able to determine if the afternoon activity provided the coverage she hoped it would. In this case, she had already thought through the activity rather extensively and felt that the web simply confirmed what she intended. Another time it might be possible to use the same structure to plan and add on to, just as it would be possible with the curriculum webs pictured in Figures 3-1 and 3-2.

As the weeks progressed, Ms. Susanna added a piece here and there to the original curriculum web until the unit came to its expected conclusion with the final demise of the plants. Looking back at the general curriculum web and at the one-activity web, Ms. Susanna recalled how well movement had met the children's needs when they saw that their plants were dying. It seemed appropriate that as a final activity the children danced both individually and in teams as their friends accompanied them on musical instruments. Their dances told the entire history of each plant and the children's narrations as they danced described their feelings.

Neither this "flower curriculum" nor the "December curriculum" described earlier made use of formal outlines. This does not mean that such outlines have no place. In the case of the December curriculum the web was used to demonstrate the way in which teachers plan across the curriculum—sometimes without an awareness of doing so. And when Ms. Susanna planned the flower curriculum, it was with the intent of following the children's lead. When she felt a need to see if goals and objectives were being met, she used a second form of web. If thorough advance planning had been used to create the flower unit, the second type of web could have been used to combine curricular and other needs. It might have looked like Figure 3-5.

THE DIGGING TO CHINA CURRICULUM[2]

Of course, many (or even most) units of study are planned well in advance (although they, too, need to take into account children's

[2] Many thanks to Jeannine Sadlo for granting permission to use and adapt this unit.

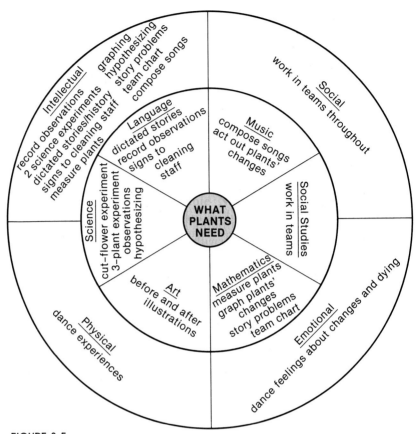

FIGURE 3-5

interests) and it is possible to plan in a more structured way. Let's look now at the way in which one teacher used both types of web as well as the more traditional format for planning a unit. Despite its careful structuring and formality of approach, the subject of the unit was inspired by the teacher's observation of her children's play. Building on a popular recess-time project, she guided them to more extensive learning in a way they enjoyed because of their interest in the topic.

Digging to China is a pastime with a long tradition. Young children seem to find the process engrossing despite their inability to reach the goal. Depending on the age of the children involved, there is the possibility, of course, that there is little or no concept of what or where China is.

One kindergarten teacher observed her children engaged in the time-honored task over a period of several days and finally asked them, "Where's China?"

"Down there," someone said, pointing.

"What's down there when you get to China?" she asked.

"People that look like this." The child put down his shovel long enough to pull his eyes into slanted slits. The others snickered and imitated him.

"Do you know anything else about the people?" The children ignored her, either returning to their digging or pulling their eyes again. The answer was obviously no.

The teacher probed for more. "What is the earth like between here and there? Is it just more dirt?"

"Sure," said some.

"I think there's FIRE!" one added.

"What shape is the earth?" The children just looked at her. "Could it be round like a ball?" Some thought it could and others gave a resounding, "No!"

The teacher left them to their play, realizing that if she so chose, here was an opportunity to create a unit of study and that the first pretest had just been given. Recalling her own childhood experience with the same game, she decided that the learning that could come from such a unit would be both enjoyable and of academic benefit. Perhaps, she thought, the child who believed there was fire down there felt just as she had felt at the same age thinking about it—excited about the possibility, but a bit afraid of success. Before making a final decision, the teacher made a curriculum web to determine whether the unit really could provide the kind of learning she thought her kindergartners should have (see Figure 3-6).

It seemed to the teacher that the unit would be a manageable size, would not interfere with other curricular demands, and

FIGURE 3-6

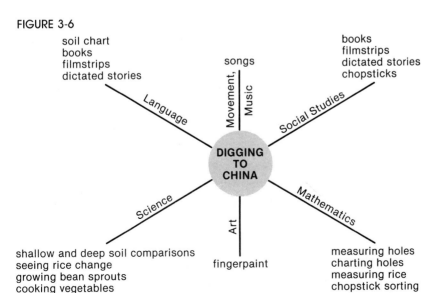

shouldn't take more than a week or two, depending on whether the children continued their interest in digging or not. She then jotted down some notes to determine just what it was she wanted the children to get out of the unit. (A more formal version is given here.)

Anticipated Outcomes

I *Student behavior:* As a result of this unit students will be able to:
  A Hypothesize which holes are deeper
  B Measure with familiar objects
  C Make a three-dimensional graph
  D Classify soil types
  E Compare and contrast Chinese and American school children
  F Participate in a knowledge-based group story about Chinese culture
  G Differentiate between rice and sand through their sense of touch
  H Follow a recipe for cooking rice
  I Manipulate chopsticks as Chinese children do
  J Follow the steps necessary to grow sprouts
  K Cook vegetables using Chinese methods
  L Use music to communicate their experiences
II *Student understanding:* As a result of this unit students will understand:
  A The difference between deep and shallow
  B That they can measure independently anything they need using their own materials
  C That all soil is not the same
  D That children in China are both the same and different, and that they could be friends if they lived close by
  E That rice is a plant and people can eat some plants

To show how this unit covers both academic and other kinds of learning, we can create here the second type of web (see Figure 3-7), the model that was used in the flower curriculum.

Activities Planned

The unit that this teacher created was brief, just eleven activities. She decided, however, that if the children became intensely interested, there was no reason the activities couldn't be expanded. Although the children had a beginning understanding that China was "down there," the teacher chose not to include activities that

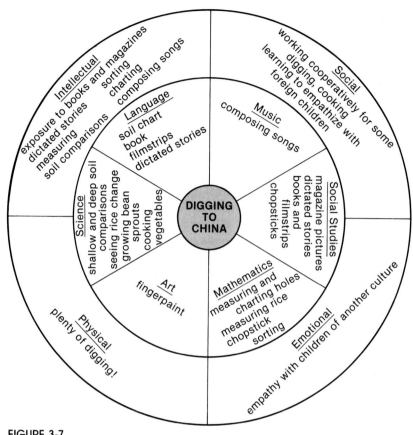

FIGURE 3-7

focused on the shape of the earth. She was well aware that 5-year-olds are rarely truly ready to grasp this concept, as they had demonstrated when she questioned them about the earth's possible roundness. At the same time, she was flexible enough to realize that the question might come up and knew that if it did she could include further activities.

Because the unit was an informal one, based on the children's interests, the teacher decided that she would not make a rigid schedule or time table, but would simply prepare the activities and work them into her county-mandated curriculum. The eleven activities she created are described in their order of introduction, although this, too, was tentative.

I. Measuring Holes

Children observe holes they have dug to determine deepest and most shallow and then use broom or long stick to measure actual depth. Help them record by marking off length on colored tape and cutting it. Use a different color for each tape. Reevaluate initial observation. Ask children how they could make a deeper hole more shallow, or vice versa. Let children experiment, remeasuring to see changes.

II. Charting Hole Measurements

Each child digs a personal hole with his or her own shovel and dowel for measuring. The child digs as desired, then marks depth with colored tape on dowel. The hole remains for a day or two (or several), and each time the child digs, the depth is marked with a different colored tape. The dowel becomes a chart. Informal questioning by teacher should include concepts of deep and shallow.

III. Soil Comparisons

Take children on walk to areas of differing soils. Dig samples and use in classroom for comparisons. Children smell, touch, look, and discuss similarities and differences with each other. Conclusions are dictated to teacher and recorded on chart.

IV. Learning about China

Use books from library, pictures from *National Geographic,* filmstrips, or movies as available. Create a learning center and interact with children informally as they peruse the materials. If artifacts are available for display, include these.

V. China Language Experience

Based on learnings in activity IV, have children dictate stories about what they have learned about China. Collect in a class China Book.

VI. Dig to China Fingerpainting

After children have had experience comparing soils and have learned that rice is a Chinese staple, this activity may be introduced. First, children fingerpaint with usual medium, verbalizing how it feels. Then each child chooses either sand or rice as an addition to the paint, verbalizing feeling again. Teacher notes verbalizations on chart to be hung on low bulletin board. Finished paintings are hung next to chart and children can feel them when desired.

VII. Cooking Rice

Can be done before activity VI if children have little or no experience with rice. Children wash hands and feel their individual small cups of rice. Discuss color, feeling, and smell. Pour all small cups into one big one and note measurements. Pour in cookpot and add a double measure of water. Cook with no salt until soft. Eat and discuss differences in uncooked and cooked rice.

VIII. Growing Bean Sprouts

To be done after children learn that this is an ingredient in Chinese cooking. Place mung bean seeds in bottom of jars with holes poked in lids. Dampen seeds slightly and place in dark area of room or closet. Children may observe seeds whenever they want. Care should be taken that the seeds stay moist. After about 3 days seeds will be sprouted and can be eaten raw or used in activity IX.

IX. Cooking Chinese Vegetables

Use Chinese vegetables as available locally. Display whole vegetables to children, introducing the name of each. Children cut vegetables in pieces (use small groups for proper supervision) while teacher informally repeats new names in conversation. Stir fry, using wok if available.

X. Chopstick Sorting

May be used in conjunction with activity VII or IX or on its own. Children will have learned that Chinese children eat with chopsticks. Use chopsticks to aid in picking up any objects that are to be classified during regular math activities. (Very small objects are harder to pick up.) Children can use two hands or try just one. (Chinese children use one hand to eat, but hold the chopsticks together in their fists rather than in the adult manner.)

XI. Singing While You Work

Use familiar tunes and let children invent songs to sing while they dig or do other unit activities. Example: To tune of "Row, Row, Row Your Boat," children can sing, "Dig, dig, dig your hole...."

How and Why the Unit Worked

That, in its entirety, is one teacher's integrated curriculum unit, using the concept of webbing both as the basic philosophy and as a tool for planning. The format she followed is very similar to the approach used in this book's curriculum chapters. Following her thought processes and planning, the unit evolved sequentially in this way:

• The children displayed an interest in an activity and seemed ripe for further knowledge.
• The teacher made a tentative web of curricular possibilities.

• She then listed the skills and understandings they would attain from these activities.

• To provide a comprehensive overview, both the curriculum and intellectual, social, emotional, and physical learnings were represented on a second web. (Created for this book for demonstration purposes.)

• The activities were listed and described in tentative sequential order.

This curriculum unit also displays some advantages that are related to those that were listed in this chapter's opening discussion:

• Each subject area of the curriculum has been given importance. Although this was potentially a science/social studies unit, the other subjects were also included.

• The activities were largely of the type natural to children. They had already chosen to dig because it interested them. They would continue to dig while learning.

• The unit would be taught because it was a topic of interest to the children. Sometimes interests can be created by the teacher through the introduction of new ideas and topics. Other times the children themselves can inform the teacher, as was the case in this unit.

• Skills were not neglected, but taught in a meaningful context. The teacher did not have to say, "Children, I'm glad you're enjoying yourselves, but now it's time for math." She moved the math class outdoors where the children could see the purpose for learning.

• The unit was a flexible one because the teacher realized that she might not have included all the activities and learnings that would be appropriate for the children. Although the unit had a good, sound structure, it could be readjusted as necessary.

Digging to China was a unit that focused on all areas of the curriculum while teaching them in an integrated format. The curriculum chapters that follow also approach learning from these two directions. Each chapter begins with an in-depth discussion of one curricular area, arguing in each case its singular importance. As it becomes the basis for classroom learning, however, the subject is integrated with others so that the actual learning process becomes more natural. For preschool children, the units are presented in such a way that they truly become an integral part of an informal learning environment. The primary units are more formal, showing how integrated learning can take place within the constraints of the more academic requirements of most schools.

A final word of warning may be in order. Despite the many sound arguments in favor of integrated teaching and learning, of a curriculum that on paper looks like an illustration for a book about spiders, it doesn't always come naturally at first. Make an effort to try the activities suggested at the end of each of the curriculum chapters; they are designed to help you over the first hurdles of planning and teaching.

TO DISCUSS

1 "Yes, but...." See how many problems you can list that might arise when trying to develop a curriculum along the lines of a theme or web rather than according to subject areas. It may be useful to make two lists: one for preschool and one for primary grades. Then discuss ways in which these problems might be solved.

2 Stage a formal debate in which one side argues the case for a linear, subject-based curriculum and the other argues for an integrated curriculum. This will work most effectively if the arguments are confined either to preschool or to the primary grades.

TO DO

1 Observe a class that incorporates integrated learning. Take notes on the following:
   a Academic learning apparently planned by the teacher
   b Academic learning arising spontaneously
   c Social interaction
   d Noise levels
   e Traffic patterns and freedom of movement
2 After observing the class, interview the teacher. Raise questions and concerns that arise from your observation. Learn the degree of formality or informality the teacher uses in planning.

BIBLIOGRAPHY

White, E. B. (1952) *Charlotte's web*. New York: Harper & Row.

Language

Suppose a national polling organization were to pose this question about education: "What is the single most important reason that young children should be educated?" Then suppose we could take this question back through generations and centuries of time. It is highly likely that across the ages a single answer would stand out: "They need to learn to read, of course." Although the reasons for learning to read have been different for different generations, this accomplishment has had such importance in the minds of adults that passion has sometimes outweighed reason in the quest for the perfect reading education. Curiously, other aspects of language development, such as oral expression and listening skills, have often been assumed to develop naturally, while reading is the skill that is assumed to need intensive instruction.

Is there a single best way to teach reading? There have been numerous bandwagons to hop on for those who believe, for a while at least, that they have found it. Should we teach the smallest children the rudiments of reading in an effort to give them a head start? Research may say that the benefits wear off in time, but that doesn't stop people from trying. Should we then wait until children are ready even if they are midway through their elementary years? There are those who think that this, too, has its dangers.

There are no perfect answers to our questions, and there may never be. What we do know is that some very young children learn to read before they get to school and that the way in which they learn is very different from the methods used by most teachers in today's schools. The most exciting research being done on reading today looks at the way children learn informally in the early years and then attempts to transpose those informal methods to the classroom.

Before looking at the current research, and the history of reading and other language instruction that led to it, this chapter describes the experience of a small child who, surrounded by reading and language both at home and at nursery school, broke the reading code on her own. Every young reader's story is his or her own, of course. In Frances's case, it is interesting to note that her preschool had mixed ages so that there were older children to emulate; that the school itself was academically oriented and formal reading instruction of the older children was in evidence if Frances cared to notice; and that at home there was no attempt to teach reading, although the older members of the family read constantly, both to themselves and, quite frequently, to Frances. Further, dinner table conversation was often spirited and even Frances was allowed to enter in. Frequent trips in the car provided opportunities to play games with rhyming words, to learn new songs, and to read simple and familiar signs along the road. Magnetic letters covered the front of the refrigerator and at times Frances would move these around, quietly mouthing a few sounds. In other words, the very stimulating environment Frances experienced was quite mixed. Although the "punchline" of her story will be that she learned to read, all other areas of language experience were present also. Thus, it is difficult to pinpoint the influences that affected her most. This is generally the problem in studying children who read early and the primary reason that research in this area tends to focus on case studies.

Frances was 4, close to 5, when she rather suddenly learned to read. Although it is impossible to interview a child this small to see how the process took place, it is sometimes possible to make close observations and to at least be able to describe the steps that led to a successful reading experience. In Frances's case, her mother was an elementary school teacher who closely observed her transition from nonreader to reader over a period of 2 short weeks. As Frances's story is told, note the very natural, unforced, almost unconscious way in which this preschooler attained the ability to read with great skill.

"I DID!"

Frances attended an academically oriented school in which children between the ages of 3 and 6 were placed in one classroom. One of her favorite ways to spend the morning was to follow along after "the biggest kids" as they engaged in various reading and math activities. Especially fascinating to her were various phonics games in which she could help match pictures to labels, sound out letter combinations, or place labels next to tiny objects. Although she seemed to understand that certain letters referred to names of objects or pictures, Francis did not grasp the idea that writing and reading were for communication purposes. Before long she knew the sound of every letter of the alphabet and many combinations as well, but it did not occur to her that they could be put together into words to mean something. To Frances it was just learning to play a game that the biggest kids had mastered. She enjoyed the status that came with being able to do what they did.

It was after she had achieved the ability to rattle off letter sounds out of context that her mother began to observe a change in behavior. Each afternoon after school, the mother would sit awhile in the living room with a cup of coffee and the evening newspaper. One day Frances decided that she wanted to be there, too, rather than in the yard. She entered the room with a small pile of her favorite books and snuggled down next to her mother. At first she looked at the pictures as she always had, but then her mother became conscious that the pages weren't turning. Frances was staring at the top line of a Dr. Seuss book—staring and staring. Finally she turned the page and again stared a long time at the top line. This behavior continued for about 10 minutes.

The next day the pattern was repeated, but by the third day Frances was looking over the entire page. At first her mother considered discussing the new experience with her but decided that it might be better to let Frances work through the process on her own. By the beginning of the second week, Frances occasionally looked over her mother's shoulder at the newspaper but said nothing. She continued to look silently at the words of her books, seemingly having lost interest in the pictures.

After about 2 weeks, something new appeared in Frances's behavior. Instead of just glancing at the newspaper, she draped herself across her mother's arm and leaned into her lap, although she seemed unconscious that she was doing it. She appeared fascinated with a full-page ad for a major sale in a local department store. Frances's mother wondered if she were able to read the easier words and if Frances could pick up on such things as the fact that *Co.* stood for "company." Just as she was thinking that the time had come to intervene, Frances asked, "Why is the Hecht Co. having a sale?"

Her mother marveled at the natural way the question came out. She had rather expected a drum roll and an excited announcement, "Now I can read!" Instead, this new ability had just quietly and naturally emerged. She did find herself a little puzzled by the fact that Frances could pronounce "Hecht" correctly with its hard "ch" sound but had not intuited that *Co.* stood for "company," since Frances had often visited there and knew the correct name.

Curious as to how well Frances really could read, her mother pointed to a short news story on the opposite page and said, "Can you tell me what this says?" Frances read it with barely a pause!

A few weeks later when a visitor asked Frances who had taught her to read, she answered with a trace of indignation, "I did!" And she had, of course.

WHY LANGUAGE ARTS

In recounting Frances's experience, we focused on the evolution of her ability to read, yet her language experience was wrapped up in more than just reading. She sang in the car, participated in discussions at the dinner table, listened to bedtime stories, and moved letters around the refrigerator door. It may be surmised that the experiences she had with talking and singing orally, listening to stories, and writing on the refrigerator had as much to do with her learning to read as did the actual exposure to older children's reading lessons at school. The whole of language was present in Frances's life experience, with each piece contributing to progress in the others. It is this whole language approach to children's informal learning that is the subject of so much study and teaching efforts today. The history leading to it has been long and varied.

In this country's colonial period, children concentrated first on learning their ABC's, usually using a hornbook. These could be made of wood, various metals, perhaps ivory, and occasionally even gingerbread—an early attempt to encourage interest. The underlying reason for learning to read had primarily to do with attaining the ability to read the Scriptures. Over the succeeding centuries, motivation became more secular and various teaching methods were tried.

After the turn of the twentieth century, interest in reading instruction rather suddenly became the source of much research and newly devised methodologies. In 1909 Edward Thorndike introduced a handwriting scale, and shortly thereafter numerous other tests began to follow, thus instituting this century's scientific movement in the study of education. This period was an intellectually exciting one. To give some idea of the sudden and overwhelming increase in interest: The number of studies about reading done in English before 1901 came to a grand total of 34; from 1910 to 1925 the total rose to 436 in the United States alone. The major change in teaching reading that came from this period was a complete switch from a centuries-long emphasis on oral reading to an equally strong emphasis on silent reading.

In the next decade, from the mid-1920s to the mid-1930s, studies continued to grow in number and increase in depth. The idea of reading readiness became an issue as awareness developed that all children weren't ready in the same way at the same time and that too many were failing to learn to read. There was also the beginning of an argument that exists today: Should children be given carefully planned work in sequential skills? Or should they learn to read as part of what was called an "activity program" in which children chose studies according to their own interests and teachers tried to incorporate these into the larger picture of an integrated curriculum?

In the period from 1935 to 1950 interrelationships between the other language arts and reading began to be part of teaching methodology. In the 1960s a focus on assisting the economically disadvantaged attain higher educational and societal benefits led to government support of new reading programs. New materials were published, basal programs were expanded, help for reading disabilities increased. Not since 1910 had there been such a focus on helping children learn to read.

Yet, for all the excitement, the questions still weren't answered. There was no general agreement then, and there is none now on the best way to teach a child to read. From the mid-1960s to fairly recently the power of the basal reader as the core of reading instruction was undisputed. Other language arts were integrated according to the basal programs' instructions, but the basal was the all-important foundation.

Recently, however, a new movement has been quietly but persistently rising up to challenge the power of the basal programs. This challenger argues that we should make use of our inability to find the one best method and instead attempt to find the methods that work best for each child. It also argues that we should not separate reading from the other language arts but that we should incorporate all of them into a whole, just as children do when they learn language naturally and on their own. Finally, just as learning to read is incorporated into the other language arts, so can language arts be integrated with other areas of the curriculum. Thus, reading is not an isolated skill to be taught in a specified, skill-oriented reading time, but it is part of the everyday life of the classroom.

The name of this new challenger to the status quo is usually given as *whole language instruction*. This method of teaching does not provide the security of a kit or program. It does give the teacher the freedom to make choices based on his or her knowledge of the children and their needs. It will be apparent to anyone with experience teaching the primary grades that this way of teaching runs counter to the prevailing preference for basal-oriented, sequential-skills training.

While most teaching methods and materials have historically been imposed from above, teachers themselves have been a driving force behind the whole language movement. This movement is of sufficient strength to have resulted in at least one new program from a major basal reader company. Teachers also have initiated a nationwide support network with its own newsletter, "Teachers Networking," begun in 1987.

In the first edition of the newsletter, several teachers attempted definition of whole language instruction and what it means for those who teach it. Anything without a program or kit attached becomes open to infinite interpretations, but here is the way one teacher described whole language instruction in this newsletter.

> The focus is always on meaning....Children write across the curriculum for a wide range of authentic purposes....What can visitors to a whole language classroom expect to see? They'll observe students and

teachers collaborating in a content-rich environment, building and creating meaning together through personal narratives, fiction, poetry, journals, letters, research projects, scientific observation, and experiments (Goodman, 1987, p. 9).

This teacher adds that students and teachers can be seen in small groups critiquing each other's work, revising drafts, and discussing literature. While this teacher is describing what goes on in a classroom of children in the elementary grades, the whole language approach applies equally as well to the preschool years. Here, this way of looking at language learning has historically been accepted, if only because most small children aren't able, even with intensive effort, to cope with anything more structured. The proponents of the whole language approach argue that the more natural method of the preschool can be used effectively in the primary grades as well for teaching both beginning and advanced skills.

The theory behind this most recent development in teaching the language arts has been described by Ken Goodman: "Language learning is easy when it's whole, real, and relevant; when it makes sense and is functional; when it's encountered in the context of its use; when the learner chooses to use it" (1986, p. 26). In other words, other, more rigid systems make learning language difficult.

Another aspect of the theory is that there is both a personal and a social side to language learning. The need to communicate comes from inside the child, while the norms of society give shape to the communication. Another important part of the theory for teachers is the idea that "Language is learned as students learn through language and about language, all simultaneously in the context of authentic speech and literacy events." Goodman adds that "Cognitive and linguistic development are totally interdependent" (1986, p. 26).

This moment in the history of language arts teaching is an exciting one. Probably no other area of the early childhood curriculum is so completely on the brink of something new. While some courageous teachers have pioneered the practical application of the whole language approach, they have been given both support and inspiration from the International Reading Association (IRA) and other educational groups. A position statement from the IRA demonstrates just how closely their view and that of these teachers relate. (It should be noted that Ken Goodman, the whole language proponent quoted above, is past president of the IRA.)

Positive school environments for young children, the IRA says, "provide reading and writing opportunities that focus on meaningful experiences and meaningful language rather than merely on abstract skill development, because teaching skills out of context does not ensure use in effective reading and writing..." (1985, p. 1).

This statement, of course, is in consonance with the ideas espoused by those who favor a whole language approach. The IRA's position on young children also points toward this way of teaching; good school environments, they say, do the following:

- Focus learning activities to build upon the functions, uses and strategies of reading and writing that prevail in the children's home background;
- Provide opportunities for children to use written language for a wide variety of purposes, for a wide variety of audiences and in a wide variety of situations;
- View reading and writing as a process that progresses at the child's individual rate. (IRA, 1985, pp. 1–2).

In another position statement, the IRA has gone a step further. Joining with several other groups who have concerns about young children and their learning, they have cooperated in writing a joint statement of recommendations for early literacy development. The other organizations involved in writing this position statement include the Association for Childhood Education International (ACEI), the Association for Supervision and Curriculum Development (ASCD), the National Association for the Education of Young Children (NAEYC), the National Association of Elementary School Principals (NAESP), and the National Council of Teachers of English (NCTE). The concerns of these several groups mirror those of the advocates of whole language teaching. The focus for this statement is on pre-first grade children.

- Many pre-first grade children are subjected to rigid, formal pre-reading programs....
- Little attention is given to individual development or individual learning styles.
- Too much attention is focused upon isolated skill development or abstract parts of the reading process, rather than upon the integration of oral language, writing and listening with reading.
- Too little attention is placed upon reading for pleasure; therefore, children often do not associate reading with enjoyment ("Literacy Development and Pre-First Grade," 1986, p. 110).

This position statement gives fifteen recommendations related to these concerns. In abbreviated form, here are just a few of the most important. Note their agreement with whole language instruction.

- Focus on meaningful experiences and meaningful language rather than merely on isolated skill development.
- Ensure feelings of success for all children, helping them see themselves as people who can enjoy exploring oral and written language.

- Provide reading experiences as an integrated part of the broader communication process, which includes speaking, listening, and writing, as well as other communication systems such as art, math, and music.
- Encourage children to be active participants in the learning process rather than passive recipients of knowledge by using activities that allow for experimentation with talking, listening, writing, and reading ("Literacy Development...," 1986, pp. 110–111).

Conclusion: The current focus on language-teaching research is quite different from that of earlier years. The emphasis is away from isolated skills and sequential drills and toward a more natural, total immersion in every aspect of language with which a young child can and should be surrounded. Those who advocate this new way of viewing language learning argue that the purpose of language is to communicate—orally and in print—and that to help children be successful in speaking, reading, and writing we should integrate these functions in the most meaningful ways we can. Without that element of meaningfulness, children may not grasp the reason for studying the skills to which they're exposed, leaving them confused or bored, or both.

THE TEACHER'S ROLE

The teacher's role in this type of learning is, as might be expected, somewhat different from that found in a classroom where skills are taught in isolation. Who better to explain the teacher's role in whole language instruction than a teacher? In the following excerpts we hear from Dorothy Watson, member of a support group for teachers who espouse the whole language approach. Here are some of her criteria for effective teachers.

- Whole language teachers think learners are terribly interesting and that by watching them intelligently they can find the center of gravity for everything that goes on in their classroom.
- They know that when language is broken into incomprehensible parts that the spell it can weave is also broken, so they present it whole.
- Whole language teachers invite students daily to think and to learn by talking, reading, and writing about important things in science, math, social studies, and life.
- They know that real learning takes place when kids are interested enough to work it out on their own with other learners....there must be time for students to think and talk, sing and dance together.
- Much of their teaching is through invitational modeling. That means that they do what they ask kids to do: they read books, write stories, and they participate in literature study groups (Watson, 1987, pp. 4–5).

Sidney and Iris Tiedt also discussed the teacher's role. Their recommendations closely resemble Watson's, but they also made a few additional points. They say that teachers will:

- Keep a story going at all times in the classroom
- Present language to students in all its diversity (this might include talking about the other languages some of the children or their families speak or listening to the differences in dialects
- Integrate the language arts throughout the curriculum (the language arts can be regarded as a set of tools with which students can learn other curricular areas) (Tiedt and Tiedt, 1987).

One controversial aspect of teaching through the philosophy of whole language is the teacher's attitude toward correcting children's errors. This is true whether corrections need to be made in oral, written, or reading language experiences. The teacher's purpose in all three situations is to be supportive and positive and at the same time encourage young children's progress. The suggestions that follow are designed to help children without being rigidly focused on the correction of errors.

Oral Language   If children speak in short sentences with no connecting words the teacher can repeat what they say, inserting helpful words. If children need a new word, the teacher can use it in the context of natural speech and informally define it within the context of the same conversation. For children who can communicate only in brief sentence segments, the teacher can repeat their ideas in an expanded form. As often as possible, teachers need to provide discussion periods for young children. By listening to others, children begin to emulate the more sophisticated speech patterns. It is important in helping them through all these methods that "children are relaxed, comfortable with their surroundings and free from anxiety" (Wishon et al., 1986, p. 92).

Written Language   Often parents and teachers expect children to make mistakes in oral language and assume that they will grow out of them. They may engage in any or all of the methods just suggested for correction and feel quite comfortable in informally supporting their children. This feeling of ease is often not transferred to their attitude toward written language. Invented oral grammar may be seen as cute, but invented spelling is a cause for alarm. Yet, invented spellings are a child's first attempts at making sense of written communication and progress toward standard spelling in much the same way that oral language progresses naturally to standard forms. The whole language teacher accepts this and helps children as they need it. Some communications with parents coupled with clear classroom criteria should be helpful.

In the preschool years, invented spellings must be allowed to go on and be respected for the progress they represent. When children also invent letters or move from scribbles to beginning writing, this is also cause for praise, not concern.

During the primary grades, as children move toward the beginnings of real writing, it will be helpful to have some activities that do not require any correction of spelling, as well as activities in which children help each other correct themselves. The latter will give children an opportunity to grasp the idea of correct spelling and to learn the words that have meaning and importance to them.

Reading   Judith Newman (1985) interviewed teachers to learn the way in which they themselves dealt with something in their reading they didn't know or understand. Strategies included skipping what they didn't know, using the surrounding context, substituting a word or phrase that had more meaning, rereading the passage, or reading ahead to see if the meaning might be clarified.

She also interviewed children using the same question. She found that the better, more confident readers used very similar techniques. Interestingly, these are not the techniques the teachers generally had taught them. When the same teachers were asked their strategies for helping children, they listed telling them to check out the prefixes and suffixes, having them look for familiar small words within a bigger word, or saying the problem word for the child. Apparently, the better readers ignored their teachers' advice and did what the teachers themselves did.

Then, Newman found, "The children who are having difficulty seem to have a single reply: they 'sound it out.' My suspicion is that unfortunately these less fluent readers have learned, all too well, precisely what we've been teaching them" (p. 64).

In this case, as always, it is important to help children with the meaning of what they are doing. Teaching them the techniques we use ourselves will have longer-lasting benefits. When it is obvious that a child understands the meaning of what has been read, it is more suitable to go back, use the problem word or words and help the child be prepared to read more correctly the next time. The use of favorite stories to be read and reread is an opportunity for this kind of gentle correction.

If any one adjective could be applied to the effective teacher of language skills, it would be "supportive." The role of the teacher in helping children develop oral, writing, and reading skills is one of guidance and encouragement. Learning language is a great adventure for young children and the effective teacher supports the adventurous spirit.

LANGUAGE AND CHILD DEVELOPMENT

Without an understanding of children's language development, effective support may be difficult, however. In this section we look at the way children's competencies in each language area develop. Armed with information about development, the teacher can make knowledgeable decisions in classroom situations.

As in any area of the curriculum, what can be successfully taught to young children largely depends on their level of development. However, in the case of language, particularly reading, parents and school systems often forget this. Fear of reading failure pervades the decisions of adults who often really know better, and children are then left to grapple with difficult concepts that could be learned later with much less struggle. Thus, it is important for teachers to have a knowledge of child development readily available to use and to share with others.

The developmental areas discussed below are divided into oral expression, reading, and writing. In reality, they interact with each other, the development of each providing impetus for the development of the others. Division into three components is simply for the sake of clarity.

Oral Expression

Infants have been observed responding to their own names as early as 6 to 7 days after birth. Oral language has already entered their lives in a major way and will continue to permeate their development in all areas. By the child's tenth or twelfth week it is possible to detect some practice of sounds complete with volume and pitch. During the ensuing months that lead to the first year there is much experimentation, increasing awareness during listening opportunities, and an increased ability to respond to the social world. Greene (1973) points out that during these months "opportunities for increasing the child's linguistic abilities are paramount...an indispensable prerequisite to later, more articulate use of language.... Individual differences in the rate and quality of language development may be evidenced during this period" (p. 9). In other words, language education has already begun with the people in the infant's environment acting as effective or ineffective teachers.

A baby's first word typically appears between 10 and 13 months, and by 15 months a vocabulary of about ten words is normal. About 65 percent of these words are nouns. At 18 to 20 months words are sometimes put together in what has been called telegraphic speech because it leaves out the little connecting words that telegrams also leave out (Dale, 1976).

By the age of 3, most children are moving from telegraphic speech to more complex sentences. By the time they are 4, complex sentences make up between 20 and 25 percent of children's speech (Garrard, 1987). Sometime between age 5 and 7, children attain most of their grammatical understanding. Nevertheless, some children don't master complex structures completely until they are as much as 10 years old (Seefeldt and Barbour, 1986).

Children who have more oral experiences will develop their oral capabilities more fully. In addition, children who attain higher levels of oral functioning will also be better readers and writers, for they have a greater store of verbal knowledge to draw on. As Tway said, "...children write what they hear in the language environment around them....For this reason, it is imperative to maintain a strong oral language program....The classroom where textbooks and workbooks are the sole materials and only written language is stressed is likely to be barren and unproductive" (1983, p. 53).

Reading

Before children can learn to read they need to understand what the purpose of reading actually is. And they need to understand, too, why all those strange little marks are on the page. A knowledge of this is called *print awareness*. One source of confusion for youngsters is the presence of both pictures and print on the same page. While it is obvious to the adult reading a story to a child that pictures are to be looked at and words are to be read, this may not be grasped by the young child. There are some children as old as 5 who believe that pictures can be read just as words are, although there are also children as young as 3 who have not only figured out the difference but have learned to read in the adult sense of the word.

In one study, 3-year-olds were asked questions to test their awareness of print, and they averaged about 45 percent correct answers. The 5-year-olds in the study answered 80 percent or more. A second similar study produced 25 percent correct for the 3-year-olds and 75 percent for the 5-year-olds (Kontos, 1986). The findings of these studies should be a clear warning to educators that there are dangers in insisting that children learn letter names and sounds when they may have no idea what their purpose is.

One way in which children do become aware of the function of print is by reading the more common signs in the environment. Signs that say "McDonald's" or "Stop" are two of the most popular. Although many writers have drawn the conclusion that children's ability to pick up on environmental print will transfer to easier reading, more recent thinking is that this is probably not the case (Kontos, 1986). Further, once these familiar signs are removed from their environmental contexts, prereading children are unable to identify them. Take away the golden arches or the red, hexagonal background and those two popular words lose their easy identity. Nevertheless we may conclude that, "Experiences with environmental print are likely to assist children with their knowledge about reading as opposed to leading them to read independently" (Kontos, 1986, p. 61).

Children's understanding of reading is a field that is still under study. Based on what is now known, Mason (1981) has provided a three-level model to show children's development:

Level 1: Knowledge of the function of print

Level 2: Knowledge of the form of print

Level 3: Knowledge of the conventions of print

Children who are still having trouble with levels 1 and 2 will no doubt have difficulties when they encounter a formalized reading program.

When Vygotsky (1962) looked at the difficulties young Russian children had with learning to read, he concluded that "...it is the abstract quality of written language that is the main stumbling block." Furthermore, a child feels no need for writing and has "only a vague idea of its usefulness." These conclusions, Downing (1969) said, are to be expected if we take Piaget's studies seriously. "At the conventional age for beginning reading, abstract ideas are least appropriate and the child's ego-centric view of his environment is not conducive to a natural understanding of the purpose of the written form of languages—an artificial two-dimensional product of civilization" (p. 219). Given this view, we may well marvel at the ability of some very young children to engage in the abstract reading process, and be more patient with those who are unready.

Writing

In this section we discuss the development of two aspects of writing: the actual physical act of writing and the development of spelling.

Scribbles to Letters   Before children are 1 year old they begin to scribble randomly, enjoying having a crayon in hand but paying no attention to where the marks land. This "uncontrolled scribbling" is later replaced by "controlled scribbling" at about the time children enter nursery school. At this point children seem to have some visible interest in and control over where the scribbles land. A still higher stage of scribbling appears at about 3½ or 4 years: children begin to give their scribbles names. This is generally done after the scribbling is finished, rather than with any intention beforehand (Brittain, 1979).

At about the same time that children develop an interest in making representational drawings, they also become capable of writing (drawing, really) their first letters.

> The parallels between writing and drawing are particularly strong at this age. Just as drawings wander all over the page, so does writing. Even after [a] child understands left-right directionality and top-bottom orientation, if there is no room on the paper, the remainder of the work or message is as likely to go up as it is to go down (Lamme, 1984, p. 68).

Often toward the end of kindergarten children attain another learning related to both art and writing. In their drawings, baselines or grass appear with skies at the top. In writing there is more directionality and visual structure.

Spelling   Adults often express great concern about the inaccurate spellings children produce. However, one writer (Tway, 1983) pointed out that babies just learning to talk don't receive agitated reprimands about their poor pronunciation, but instead are given encouragement and praise. Children should receive the same treatment as they learn to spell. "In the same way, if early writings are given respect and encouragement, the child comes to attach importance to writing" (Tway, 1983, p. 49). Children write what they hear, Tway said, and from this come invented spellings.

Invented spelling appears to have two stages: the first one in which children write down a few letters to indicate complex sounds and a second one in which more letters are added. This second stage is a transitional one that helps children move toward more conventional spelling. Tway observed that many children come to school already knowing how to make many letters and write with invented spelling. "However, they may not know how to make all of the letters yet, and their physical coordination is such that extended writing will usually be difficult, if not impossible (Tway, 1983, p. 50). Thus, again, it is important not to push children too fast and too hard.

THE LANGUAGE CURRICULUM

As this chapter opened, we observed Frances at home and at school, and we saw her apparently combine the two experiences into her first attempt at reading. Most children don't learn with Frances's rapidity, but they do all bring to school their experiences with language. These will include oral language, listening, environmental print, and, often, literature. In determining the early childhood curriculum it is important to keep this fact in mind.

A joint statement by the ACEI, ASCD, IRA, NAESP, NAEYC, and NCTE stresses the importance of recognizing home experiences when planning a child's first curriculum. Here is a brief summary of "what young children know about oral and written language before they come to school":

1. Children have had many experiences from which they are building ideas about functions and uses of language.

2. They have internalized many rules and have conceptualized processes for learning and using language.

3. Many can differentiate between drawing and writing.

4. Many are reading environmental print.

5. Many associate books with reading.

6. Their knowledge about language is influenced by their social and cultural backgrounds.

7. Many expect that reading and writing will be sense-making activities ("Literacy Development and Pre-First Grade," 1986, pp. 110–11).

The statement goes on to say that "Reading and writing experiences at school should permit children to build upon their already existing knowledge of oral and written language" (p. 111). Teachers should not regard even the smallest children as blank slates but as people who have already achieved great strides in acquiring linguistic knowledge.

Regarding point 7, the position paper states, "For optimal learning, teachers should involve children actively in many meaningful, functional language experiences, including speaking, listening, writing and reading." All the language arts must be present in one classroom and be as meaningful to children as they expect them to be. Children are excited about their language learning process and teachers need to develop a curriculum that keeps that excitement alive.

If language learnings are not meaningful to children, it is only a matter of time before their normal curiosity and excitement become dulled by the need to accomplish the teacher's requirements. By then the curriculum belongs to the teacher, not to the children, and what started out as a learning adventure becomes increasingly worklike. It's easy for a teacher to fall into a pattern of dull, lifeless assignments for children. Here are some of the ways this kind of "success" can be ensured.

- Provide each child with a stack of skill sheets each morning to be completed before lunch (or recess or self-chosen centers).
- Assign workbooks that are to be gone through sequentially and then followed by other workbooks.
- Give lots of drills and exercises that break down skills into learning segments.
- Cover every story in every basal in sequential order, following every guideline for skill achievement.
- Demand that every assignment turned in be spelled perfectly and reworked until it is.
- As small children learn their letters, give them lots of drill in learning to stay within the lines.
- Insist that children do their seatwork in silence, not discussing or sharing their work with each other.
- Use written exercises as punishment for bad behavior.
- Make a public example of children who make mistakes in pronunciation and grammar.
- Refuse to let children create or write stories until they are able to spell well and form their letters correctly.

Do many of these sound familiar? Most readers will have experienced at least some of the teaching techniques. Others will have used them in their own classrooms. It might be useful to think back now to the earliest days of schooling. What language experiences gave the most pleasure? Was it the class discussion of a workbook page or listening to the teacher read the next chapter in an exciting book? Was it practicing the formation of letters in kindergarten or role-playing a favorite fairy tale? In previous years, most educators believed that drills were necessary to encourage emergent literacy. Now, a growing body of research has begun to show that reading the exciting book to children and permitting them to dramatize the fairy tale will go further toward promoting reading, writing, and oral language than the drills will. There is no longer reason to squash children's natural interest in and curiosity about language!

Since we now know that it is preferable to avoid the teaching techniques given in the preceding list, it is possible to think of more interesting alternatives. In this chapter we have been talking about a whole language curriculum. Oral, writing, and reading curricula are combined into a total entity, which, in turn, is combined with the entire school curriculum. For example, writing doesn't have to have its assigned time during the day, but can become a necessary tool when there is an exciting new bit of knowledge to write about. Oral language is practiced as children share their ideas, concerns, and questions with each other and with the teacher. Even reading doesn't need to follow the lockstep approach of permanently assigned groups of children plodding their way through the basals. Reading does, however, become necessary when there is something exciting or important to read, and children may be grouped and regrouped as the requirements of learning emerge throughout the days and weeks.

Although, for clarity, each area of the language curriculum has been given its own section in the following discussion, note the interrelationship of each one with the others.

Oral (and Aural) Language Learning

In 1985, *Becoming a Nation of Readers* was published. Sponsored by the National Institute of Education and produced by the National Academy of Education's Commission on Reading, this report took an in-depth look at what research has shown to be the most positive ways for children to learn to read. The conclusion of the commission was that there is no simple answer and that learning to read well is a long and complex journey.

One important piece of this complex puzzle is the development of oral language. "If this foundation is weak," the report states, "progress in reading will be slow and uncertain." The study also found that in kindergarten and first grade learning to listen is important, too. It is, they concluded, "...a moderately good predictor of level of reading comprehension." Further, oral-aural interactions with others must have quality: "When adult questions require children to reflect upon their experiences, mental processes that are needed for proficient reading are stimulated" (National Institute of Education, 1985, p. 30).

Garrard (1987) offers several ways that schools can contribute to speech development of young children. First, teachers need to model complex speech patterns, no matter how young the children are. Modeling coupled with opportunities such as games that require a lot of speech will help children more than drills and corrections. Helpful too are "dramatic play, role playing, puppetry, storytelling, art, building projects, and discussions of direct experiences and special occasions..." (NIE, 1985, p. 20). Other experiences in oral language include telling stories into a tape recorder, show-and-tell, and snack preparation. In each instance the teacher needs to remember to model complex speech patterns.

An important part of the early aural curriculum is reading to children. A review of research by Kontos (1986) showed that reading aloud to children promotes positive attitudes toward reading, high interest in literature, comprehension of reading, a sense of story structure, and greater oral complexity. A number of studies have pointed up the importance of discussing stories as they are read, as this can increase not only comprehension and oral facility but also print awareness. All this from one of the more pleasurable parts of the curriculum!

Learning to Write

Writing can mean either of two processes: simple formation of letters or composing those letters into some meaningful form of communication. According to the report *Becoming a Nation of Readers*, learning to form letters will not help children develop reading skills, but composing will. For some children, learning to read becomes an easy offshoot of their early interest in composing.

It is important that children gain some concept of the purpose of writing, and handwriting practice does not convey this. Further, for many young children, a paper and pencil may be more than their manual dexterity is prepared for. Yet that doesn't mean that writing, in the sense of composition, can't take place.

You may find that children who are newly aware of the purpose of writing will draw pictures with scribbled labels or texts. Ask them to "read" what is said; then print their verbal explanation next to what they scribbled. Additionally, plastic, metal, or felt letters can be used on boards, or cardboard letters can be placed on small rugs; children can then create words and brief stories as they have interest. Dictating stories to the teacher ensures that children's most complex ideas and interests will be transferred to print. Sensitivity to each child's developmental capabilities will guide the teacher to the best approach.

As children develop an interest in composing, a writing center can be established with plenty of tools available: magic markers, crayons, pencils, and paper of varying sizes, colors, and shapes. Older children will probably prefer more "serious" materials. Again, be sensitive to what promotes enthusiasm for writing.

During the primary years, children can use the writing center to compose stories, essays, articles, and books. A new level of activity and challenge·can be introduced. "Publication" of children's writing should be encouraged, which means that some first drafts must be revised until the writing has the best possible presentation, and then they should be bound in some way for others to enjoy. One method for doing this is suggested by Graves and Hansen (1983). It is the "author's chair," a specially designated, and perhaps decorated, chair in which any child may sit to seek assistance and feedback from others. As the author reads what has been written so far, the rest of the class (including the teacher as an equal member) asks questions designed to help the author. The questions may ask the author to clarify, expand, or explain more effectively. Emphasis is on accepting each author's efforts and on providing feedback in a positive way.

Another suggestion for assisting children in their writing is the teacher-child conference. It may take several conferences to make a piece of writing ready for publication and a conference may include:

• Talks with children about how to begin, topic choice, etc.
• Helping children with a story's continuity
• Helping with punctuation, spelling, and grammar but only focusing on one or two per conference
• Becoming the child's first audience for a new creation—a role that other children can begin to take over as they learn to model the teacher's behavior (Turbill, 1985)

Of course, when children get to the point where they can write a draft and then revise it for publication, they have come a long way from their first hesitant steps in placing letters on a paper or from their early attempts at scribbling or invented spellings. Yet, whether they are just beginning to hold a marker or are contemplating placing their book in the school library, children need to be exposed to positive acceptance from their teachers. Invented spelling should be encouraged, not disparaged—corrections will come when it is time for publication. Letter formations can be practiced in the context of what is being written—drills to achieve perfection make writing a burden and stultify creativity. Children should be permitted to write when they have an interest as well as during regularly scheduled times—to be meaningful, projects must be their own, not the teacher's. Writing can and should be a natural and exciting part of children's learning.

Learning to Read

In *Becoming a Nation of Readers* the commission pointed out that the whole language approach to instruction is "used to teach children to read in New Zealand, the most literate country in the world, a country that experiences very low rates of reading failure" (p. 45). The commission also pointed out that in the United States the results of using whole language instruction have been inconsistent, perhaps because we are so wrapped up in our reliance on basal readers. Basal reading programs, it said, "drive" American reading instruction.

A primary problem the study found with basals and basal-inspired instruction was that far too much time and effort is placed on teaching phonics. Phonics instruction, it was found, "drags out over too many years" when it would be better to teach the topic within the context of reading, because the English language contains too many complex phonetic structures. Phonics can, at best, "help the child come up with approximate pronunciations...." An even stronger statement against teaching children to read through a major emphasis on phonics is made by Marie Carbo (1988). After extensively reviewing years of studies that have been used as a justification for emphasis on phonics skills, she concluded not only that the studies were badly flawed but that interpretations of them have been also. Carbo referred to the great success in New Zealand in promoting literacy through whole language training and asked, "If phonics is so effective and so much of it has been taught for the past 20 years, one might reasonably ask why the U.S. ranks 49th (out of 159 UN member countries) in literacy" (1988, p. 226).

Using basal readers and extensive drill in phonics make reading a chore, a difficult challenge to be mastered, certainly with less joy than a whole language approach suggests. Some alternatives:

• Read repetitive books that give children an opportunity to fill in the words as they become familiar with them.
• Read wordless books that permit children to invent their own stories.
• Bring in environmental print. Examples are ads that use familiar names they see on restaurants and stores. They can be posted around the room for reading, or collages might be made from them.
• If several children are reading the same story or different stories on the same topic, have them form a group to discuss and respond to it. Response may include making puppets for dramatization, researching topics of related interest, and so on.
• Use songs, nursery rhymes, poems, and finger plays that can be read over many times, dramatized, and made available for independent reading.
• Have older children read to younger ones to increase children's familiarity with print and to build up their repertoire of stories.
• Sustained silent reading can be done each day for a set time with everyone, including the teacher, joining in.

Of course, it will be difficult for many teachers saddled with a required basal reader regimen to ignore the need to meet programmatic goals. One solution might be that of a first-grade teacher who found four or five basal series stored in a closet. She put several of each on the shelves along with a good assortment of trade books. With this collection she created a whole language approach that included many of the ideas just listed. When criterion tests loomed ahead, she simply coached the children in test-taking procedures, actually role-playing how to use standardized forms and regulation pencils. Further, the stories she read with the children just before the test were from the basal readers that were the basis of the test. She found that teaching to the test for a short period of

time was actually intriguing to the children and made her less nervous as well. The children, of course, performed just fine.

Conclusion: Children learn to read when they have much experience in oral language and a good store of shared literature. Conversely, they learn something about speaking correctly and in complex sentences by extensive contact with the books they read.
Children will write better if they have something to write about,
and reading and talking and writing are important roads to enrich-
ing their knowledge. They will also write better if they have much
experience in seeing how professional authors do it. To summarize:
oral, written, and reading language are totally interrelated, and if
we remember that when planning the curriculum, then language
learning will have much more meaning for children. It is important to remember that these points are true whether children are
very small and reading simply means looking at pictures or are
older and have cracked the code; whether they are small and writing is merely scribbling while telling a story or are older and ready
to make their own books.

INTEGRATING THE LANGUAGE CURRICULUM

One more step remains to be taken in providing meaningful language experiences to young children. Children who talk, write, and
read need something to talk, write, and read about! If we avoid
giving children drills for skills, then something has to take their
place. When language experiences are integrated into the rest of
the curriculum, and vice versa, children will have the richest of experiences. The whole language approach to learning takes this
view and argues strongly for an integrated curriculum.

Many researchers, theoreticians, and educators feel strongly
about the need to integrate language experiences with the whole of
the curriculum. *Becoming a Nation of Readers* states that, "...reading
should be thought of not so much as a separate subject in school
but as integral to learning literature, social studies, and science"
(National Institute of Education, 1985, p. 60). In writing about the
integration of language with science, Judith Newman said, "It is
true that literature is a part of [the] world, but it isn't the whole
world....To exclude the world of science from what we do in the
name of 'language learning' is to miss the wealth of opportunity
science activities offer for helping students develop as language
users" (1985, p. 152). Ken Goodman, speaking of the many advantages of placing language in an integrated curriculum said,
"Speaking, listening, writing, and reading are all happening in
context of the exploration of the world of things, events, ideas, and

experiences. The content curriculum...becomes a broad, rich curriculum that starts where learners are in language and knowledge and builds outward from there" (1986, p. 30).

For preschool children many possibilities for integration exist throughout the day. Virtually every learning material can be labeled with matching labels attached to the proper shelf space. Oral sharing times can be related to any curricular learning. Music activities provide expansion in vocabulary and increased sensitivity to the sound of language. Experience charts help describe science activities and social studies trips. Directions for recipes can be simply written for cooking productions. Oral stories that present mathematical problems can be solved by small groups or the whole class. Literature read during story time can include topics from any area of the curriculum.

Primary children should also have access to language experiences throughout the day. They can solve oral math problems together. Teacher-written math story problems can relate to their own lives and even include open-ended conclusions for the children to complete. Increasingly complex songs expand their oral capacities. Art and reports or stories enhance each other. Written observations of science experiments and thank-you letters to social studies resource people are natural ways to include language in other curricular areas.

Children will spend their lives incorporating language—written, oral, reading—into almost everything they do. By beginning early to integrate with the rest of the curriculum, we are not only making language meaningful to children now but preparing them for the future.

Both the preprimary and primary curriculum in this chapter integrate language with other subject areas. The preprimary unit uses popular children's books to show how their use can be expanded. The primary curriculum is designed to show how language can permeate the classroom in a natural way, providing less reliance on drills and more on meaningful experiences for children of school age.

PREPRIMARY UNIT: A STORYBOOK CURRICULUM

Young children everywhere love to hear stories. And they love to hear the same ones over and over again. The familiarity of favorite characters, the opportunity to join in on remembered words and phrases, pictures to see again and again—all these contribute to repeated enjoyment of a story.

Teachers (and parents) who valiantly act as if they are enjoying the umpteenth retelling of a favorite tale will be glad to know that this repetition goes a long way toward helping young children learn about story structure, the purpose of composition and writing, and reading. We have already discussed in this chapter the language benefits that literature can provide children. Here is one case in which more is better, preferably more of the same thing.

It isn't necessary, however, to treat a story repetition in the same way each time it is brought back into the classroom. Yes, children love to hear the same story again and again, but they also enjoy acting it out, singing about it, role-playing the characters in the dress-up corner, and seeing it appear during activities that—to adult eyes—might not seem at first to be related. In short, it is possible to really live a story for a while.

The stories chosen for this unit are familiar and easily available often in more than one version. All of them are fantasy stories that include characters, such as talking animals, who could not truly exist. Use of fantasy literature with very young children has historically been the source of some controversy. We know that children in the preoperational years have difficulty sorting reality from fantasy. We do not know, however, if it is better to provide children only with stories that are reality-based to help them differentiate between reality and unreality, or whether it is preferable to let them enjoy the fantasy years, realizing that any psychologically healthy child will outgrow the period without difficulty.

Since there are currently unanswered questions and arguments on both sides of the issue, it may be well when using these favorites to give children some assistance in understanding. Taking time before or after a story to talk about which elements could be real, and which could not, can assist them in making the differentiation.

Consider these stories and activities just a beginning. Browse through the school library and see what other possibilities are available. Look for books that have clear, colorful illustrations that use language in a way that is clear to children and gives them opportunities to repeat words and phrases, and that lend themselves to additional activities such as those suggested in the unit. Finally, choose stories for extended activities that the children have already heard once and for which they have shown enthusiasm.

Activities

I. The Little Red Hen (LRH)

A *Summary of story:* In the barnyard live a number of animals, all of them lazy with the exception of the Little Red Hen. When she decides to make bread (or a cake), none of the animals will

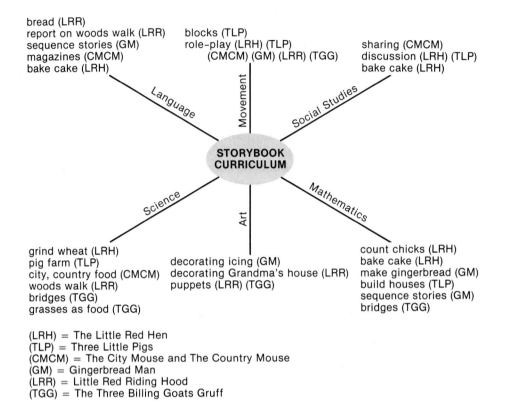

bread (LRR)
report on woods walk (LRR)
sequence stories (GM)
magazines (CMCM)
bake cake (LRH)

blocks (TLP)
role-play (LRH) (TLP)
(CMCM) (GM) (LRR) (TGG)

sharing (CMCM)
discussion (LRH) (TLP)
bake cake (LRH)

Language   Movement   Social Studies

STORYBOOK
CURRICULUM

Science   Art   Mathematics

grind wheat (LRH)
pig farm (TLP)
city, country food (CMCM)
woods walk (LRR)
bridges (TGG)
grasses as food (TGG)

decorating icing (GM)
decorating Grandma's house (LRR)
puppets (LRR) (TGG)

count chicks (LRH)
bake cake (LRH)
make gingerbread (GM)
build houses (TLP)
sequence stories (GM)
bridges (TGG)

(LRH) = The Little Red Hen
(TLP) = Three Little Pigs
(CMCM) = The City Mouse and The Country Mouse
(GM) = Gingerbread Man
(LRR) = Little Red Riding Hood
(TGG) = The Three Billing Goats Gruff

Note that some activities are listed twice because they are integrated into more than one area of the curriculum.

FIGURE 4-1

help her in the processes that are necessary: planting the seeds, cutting the wheat, threshing it, carrying it to the mill for grinding into flour, baking the bread or cake. So she does it all herself. When the animals volunteer to help with the final stage—eating—the hen responds that they didn't help make it so they can't help eat it. She and her chicks eat it all.

B *Activities:*

1 Bake a small, simple loaf cake with children, using picture instructions for the recipe. The teacher plays the part of the hen, the children are her chicks. When the cake is finished, the children help count themselves and their "mother hen" before she cuts the cake in the correct number of pieces. Stuffed animals can represent the animals who don't get to eat. While the "chicks" eat their cake, they can discuss whether the other animals should get any or not.

2 Grinding wheat is a process that most children (or adults) don't have the opportunity to see or partake in anymore. Hand grinders can be found in antique stores (expensive) or by contacting parents and others for help in finding one to borrow. Children can help with the rather arduous process and observe the change from grain to flour.

3 This story is fun to role-play, but a large burden is placed on the character of the hen. For very young children, the dramatization may work best if the teacher takes the role of the hen. If there is a child who can do the job, the teacher may wish to play the part of a chick, making comments or asking questions to help move the story along.

4 Children toward the end of the preschool years are beginning to think about what is and is not fair. After reading the story two or three times, hold a brief discussion about this issue as it appears in the story. Some suggested questions are: Should any of the animals have cake even if they didn't help? If so, who? And how much? Is it fair that the chicks got cake but didn't help? Why? Would it have been fair if the hen had eaten it all? Why do you think she didn't?

II. The Three Little Pigs (TLP)

A *Summary of story:* Three young, male pigs leave home to seek their fortune. Each builds himself a house: one of straw, one of wood, and one of brick. When the big, bad wolf comes to eat them up, he huffs and puffs but can only blow down the first two houses. Each of the pigs in turn, runs to the brick house for safety. When the wolf then tries to climb down the chimney of the brick house, the pigs are ready to catch him with a kettle of boiling water.

B *Activities:*

1 In the block corner or outside, have children replicate the pigs' homes. This can be part of a role-play effort, or the building can be done for its own sake. Informal discussion as the project progresses will help point up the obvious superiority of brick as a building material. Red construction paper can be wrapped around blocks for bricks, while other blocks can serve as wood. Pine branches can be substituted for the straw.

2 Role-play this story using tables that can be crawled under as houses. All three pigs may remain male with a mother pig added to say goodbye and with a female wolf, one or two pigs may be female. For younger children, the teacher should play the part of one of the pigs to help the story movement. Sometimes an entire class will refuse to play the part of the (scary) wolf. This then becomes the teacher's part.

3 Find out what real pigs look, feel, sound, and smell like. Visit a pig farm or other farm and concentrate just on the pigs. Discuss the difference between real pigs and fantasy pigs.

III. The City Mouse and the Country Mouse (CMCM)

A *Summary of story:* The city mouse comes to stay with his country cousin and is somewhat condescending about the inelegant surroundings and food. He extends a return invitation to come to his more sophisticated city home, and the two of them set off. At first the country mouse is impressed with city living but is soon happy to return to the more simple country life when their safety is threatened by snarling attack dogs.

B *Activities:*

1 From magazines cut a large collection of city and country pictures. After discussing the differences, mix them in one pile and let children classify them. Label each pile, or label two shallow boxes.

2 For snack one day eat small samples of "city" food as shown in the version the children are reading. "Country" food will follow the next day. If the class has been studying nutrition, city food can be represented by refined, nonnutritious products and country food by simple, healthy items.

3 Most versions of this story stress the idea that the country mouse was a host who acted from a motive of sharing. Discuss with children the unmannered behavior of the city mouse. Role-play more appropriate behavior. As a follow-up, children can bring a toy from home one day to share with others. Try one-on-one sharing (trading) of each item, having the children act out their parts as if they were well-mannered mice.

IV. The Gingerbread Man (GM)

A *Summary of story:* While a little old man is out working in the fields, his little old wife bakes a gingerbread man who surprises her by jumping out of the oven and running away. The man and woman give chase, as do other people and animals, but no one can catch the gingerbread man. At the end he is outsmarted by a fox who offers a ride across a river on his head. The fox lures the unsuspecting gingerbread man close enough to his mouth to do what is supposed to be done to gingerbread men: The fox eats him.

B *Activities:*

1 Use packaged gingerbread mix to make dough, providing a picture chart for directions. As a math experience, have children count out specific numbers of raisins or candies for prebaking decorations. When the cookies are done, a plain icing can be mixed and colored for creative decorating.

2 Photocopy the pictures in the story and mount them on tagboard. On the backs write the numbers that place them in

sequential order. Make a tagboard strip with sections marked off for placing the pictures. Each of these should be numbered. Children place the pictures in order, checking the backs for accuracy. They can then tell the story to each other, to themselves, or to the teacher.

3 This is a good story to role-play because so many children can have a turn. The teacher may need to play the gingerbread man in a class of very young children. Lay out the "escape route" and chasing rules very clearly before beginning.

V. Little Red Riding Hood (LRR)

A *Summary of story:* Little Red Riding Hood's mother sends her through the woods to visit her sick grandmother. On the way she is waylaid by the wolf, who has evil intentions. Unsuspecting, she tells the wolf where she is going and he then sneaks to the grandmother's house and eats her up. When Red Riding Hood arrives, she encounters the wolf tucked into bed and thinks it is her grandmother. After discussing "grandmother's" strange appearance, the wolf attacks Red Riding Hood, intending to eat her. She is saved by a woodsman passing by, who then saves the grandmother as well. (Some books reduce the traditional gore of this tale by having Grandma hide in a closet.)

B *Activities:* (adapted from Milner, 1982)

1 The plot of this story is direct and simple enough that it is appropriate for the dress-up corner or for independent role-playing. Use a cot for Grandma's bed and give it plenty of blankets and pillows. Make two or three red capes by cutting rectangles of red cloth and fastening with a big safety pin. (The neck end of the cape can be gathered for better fit.) Any type basket will do, and blocks can be used for the "goodies" that go in it. Use shower caps and old plastic glasses for Grandma's costume. Have extras of these also. An old, fur hat is ideal for the wolf, but any brown knit hat can be used. Let children role-play informally, providing direction only if they are very hesitant.

2 Take a walk through the woods (it need only be a small area with trees). Find flowers, acorns, pine cones, etc., for decorating Grandma's house. Write an experience chart about the trip.

3 Make stick puppets using paper plates, pipe cleaners, fur, and construction paper. Let each child make favorite characters for more role-play, either directed or free.

4 Make bread or cupcakes to take to Grandma. Use a package mix and provide children with simple directions using pictures. Once these are made, children can all pretend to be

Red Riding Hood taking them to Grandma. The teacher can be Grandma, who then shares the gift with all the Red Riding Hoods.

VI. The Three Billy Goats Gruff (TGG)

A *Summary of story:* The three goats have eaten all the grass in their usual territory and decide to head for the very green grass in the meadow on the other side of the bridge. However, under the bridge lives a fearsome troll who may eat them up. They then follow a unique plan for arriving safely. First, the smallest goat crosses the bridge and answers the troll's challenge with the suggestion that he wait for a larger goat to eat. The middle-sized goat does the same. After each has arrived safely in the meadow, the largest goat responds to the troll's challenge with one of his own. The two fight, and the goat succeeds in knocking the troll off the bridge and permanently downstream.

B *Activities:*

1 The simple sequence of events makes this a good story to role-play. Choose a sturdy, low table to use as a bridge. Use a strong chair at each end as a step.

2 In the block corner, design bridges of varying styles and sizes. Use available dolls to determine which styles and sizes of bridge are the most useful and appropriate.

3 Using a homemade bridge, enact the play with stick puppets. The children can make these by pasting pictures of the characters on popsicle sticks. If the completed materials are left out as a center, children can enact the story as often as they like and with as many goats and trolls as they need at the moment.

4 People don't ordinarily eat whole leaves of grass as goats do, but they do eat parts of edible grasses and some greens that resemble grasses. Further, they do not chew them with the teeth that are meant for meat consumption, but with their grinding teeth—teeth similar to those of the goats gruff. Point out these teeth to the children and then have them consciously use these teeth to eat such things as bean sprouts and finely shredded lettuce.

The Teacher's Role

To make this, or any other unit, work successfully you will need to play several roles, sometimes more than one at one time. Some of the activities lend themselves to facilitative teaching, others to more direct instruction. Using the categories of teacher's roles discussed in Chapter Two, here are suggestions that should help you use this unit successfully.

Facilitating   Activities that need some teacher guidance but give children inventive freedom include: role-play (LRH) (TLP) (GM) (LRR) (TGG), blocks (TLP) (TGG), magazines (CMCM), city and country food (CMCM), sequence stories (GM), woods walk (LRR), stick puppets (LRR) (TGG), and bridges (TGG).

Instructing   Some of the more challenging activities, particularly those related to cooking, require more direction from the teacher. You will find yourself being more directive in these activities: bake a cake (LRH), grinding wheat (LRH), discussion (LRH) (TLP), pig farm (TLP), sharing (CMCM), make gingerbread (GM), and grasses as food (TGG).

Providing Play   Each of the stories should be role-played in a free way once the children are familiar with the stories. Props should be left available in a center for this purpose. After the children know more than one story, it is sometimes advantageous to put props from two or more stories in one center. Expect to see much creativity emerging.

Managing   The role-play centers should be easily managed. There will be few arguments about who plays which role because young children readily invent new roles or let several people be one character. When initiating the dramatic activities, be sure that every child who wants an opportunity to play a role gets to. Be equally sure that children are not forced into acting if they are timid. The cooking experiences will require more vigilance. These work best when you interact with only a few children at a time. Choose a free-play period, perhaps when everyone is involved in their own activities over an extended period of time. Call children to you as needed.

Observing   Use the free role-play times to observe children's social interactions, particularly leader and follower patterns. Encourage unsure children in their participation by temporarily taking part in the role-play with them, perhaps suggesting dialogue or asking, "What happens next?" As soon as possible, step back and observe what progress has been made.

Evaluating   As you observe, evaluate the activities and the children's interactions with the materials. Reread the stories when ever the children seem interested. As you read, leave out words and phrases for the children to fill in.

Reflecting and Planning   After observing and evaluating, take some time to think about what did or didn't go well and why. If the children don't take well to one story, try another before giving up on the unit. If they are enthusiastic about what is happening, consider adding other stories and extending the unit. You could either add extra activities to the most popular stories already under way or add new stories with new activities.

PRIMARY UNIT: LANGUAGE ACTIVITIES

For this chapter we depart from the primary unit format used in the other subject areas in Chapters Five through Nine. Throughout our discussion of the language arts there has been an emphasis on learning to read, write, and speak in a natural way, through activities that have meaning to children. The trend in schools for more than 25 years has been to focus ever more narrowly on specific skills, breaking them down into carefully learned but meaningless exercises. Yet research has shown that when words have meaning to them, children learn more readily and become more enthusiastic about reading and writing.

The most important thing is to provide an environment rich in language experiences. Thus, all areas of the curriculum need to have language embedded in them in some way most of the time. The ideas that follow provide suggestions for doing just that and can be adapted to whatever topics are being studied in the various curricular areas.

Ordinarily, we use a curriculum web to aid us in planning. Here the web is used as a table of contents (see Figure 4-2).

Mathematics

I. Number Stories (adapted from Tiedt and Tiedt, 1987)

Let children get to "know" their numbers better by writing stories about them. Each child chooses a favorite and gives it personal characteristics, an age, perhaps a family, and finally a plot to follow.

II. Math Letters (adapted from Tiedt and Tiedt, 1987)

As children gain new math concepts, they can write letters about them to their friends in the class, or their parents, or even to the

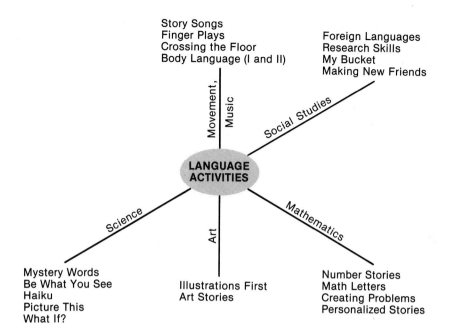

Story Songs
Finger Plays
Crossing the Floor
Body Language (I and II)

Foreign Languages
Research Skills
My Bucket
Making New Friends

Movement, Music

Social Studies

LANGUAGE ACTIVITIES

Science

Art

Mathematics

Mystery Words
Be What You See
Haiku
Picture This
What If?

Illustrations First
Art Stories

Number Stories
Math Letters
Creating Problems
Personalized Stories

Note that some activities are listed twice because they are integrated into more than one area of the curriculum.

FIGURE 4-2

class pet. The definition of a geometric shape or the steps in a division problem could be subjects for a letter.

III. Creating Problems

As children are learning new mathematical processes, they can make up story problems to demonstrate the processes. Encourage creativity and the use of each other's names.

IV. Personalized Stories

Create story problems using children's names. This can be done orally, particularly with younger children. Written adventures can be created for those who can read. Use vocabulary that can be read easily by children who are the most reluctant readers. One idea to try: Leave the final problem with an open question in the story's plot. Let children finish the story as they also finish the problems.

Science

I. Mystery Words

Every new science unit is bound to have a list of unfamiliar words. Rather than simply teaching them as drill vocabulary, use them as an enticement into the unit. List the words on the board, challenge the children to intuit what they have in common, and then look up those that remain mysteries. An abbreviated dictionary or glossary can be made for later reference.

II. Be What You See

When studying insects in the schoolyard, pets in their homes, or wild animals in the area, the children have an opportunity to engage in creative writing. Ask children to take the point of view of one animal and to write a story about life from that animal's point of view.

III. Haiku

This ancient Japanese poetry form focuses traditionally on subjects of nature. Second- and third-grade children enjoy combining their appreciation of nature's beauty with the simple syllabic framework of the haiku. To help them get started, it may be useful to clap the rhythm of the syllables. The haiku structure is:

5 syllables

7 syllables

8 syllables

IV. Picture This (adapted from Tiedt and Tiedt, 1987)

Either individually or on a group mural, children make a picture of the animal or other science topic they have just studied. In outline form around the picture, write words to describe what they know about the animal or topic. A picture of a cardinal might be outlined in such words as "red," "migrates," "insects," "crested," and so on.

V. What If?

It is best to wait until second grade to do this activity, when children are able to separate reality from fantasy. As a group on an experience chart or, for some advanced students, individually, children imagine what would happen if certain scientific principles were not true. Some suggestions:

What would happen if waterfalls flowed up instead of down?

What if magnets repelled instead of attracted?

What if Earth and Pluto changed places? Earth and Mercury?

What if ships could go as fast as airplanes?

Social Studies

I. Making New Friends

At the beginning of the day, hand each child a partial card with half the name of a geographical place, historical person, or other social studies piece of information. The children search out their matching cards and thus attain their special friend of the day. Depending on the day's projects, they can work together as either they or the teacher find appropriate.

II. My Bucket

If the day has been going well, a child's bucket is "full"; if not so well, it may be "empty." It is the class's task to help fill each other's buckets. After lunch children gather together and share individually and voluntarily their feelings about the day's progress. They can discuss personal matters, academics, or whole class interactions. The ensuing discussion will focus on ways to fill an empty bucket or provide an opportunity to express happiness about a full one.

III. Research Skills (adapted from Hanna, Potter, & Hagaman, 1955)

Frequently, first attempts at research are made in social studies. It is possible to begin toward the end of first grade with just one or two basic steps included. By third grade the entire class should be ready for research at some level. Whatever the topic, here are some suggestions to help beginning researchers on their way to success:

• Have the reading materials already in the classroom rather than requiring children to find them in the library. Provide a wide range of reading levels.
• Slip a piece of paper into the books to show where the needed information can be found.
• Occasionally recall and reread with each child the original question that provided the impetus for research; keep the direction of the study clear.
• Let children choose or help guide them into a choice of working alone, in pairs, or in committees.
• Keep alert for whatever problems some children may be having with the research process. If several children seem stuck on one aspect, call them together as a group for additional assistance.
• Allow enough time, but don't let it drag on. Young children will probably complete a research project more quickly than older children.

IV. Foreign Languages

When learning about other countries, try to learn some of their language as well. Just learning that other people communicate differently is new to some children and exciting knowledge to gain for all of them. If several languages are to be tried, it is good to learn the same expressions in each for the sake of comparison.

Art

I. Illustrations First

Reverse the usual order, in which a story is written and then art work is used to illustrate it. Often children who complain of writer's block can overcome it by drawing a picture first, and then creating the story to go with it.

II. Art Stories

From museums or the library obtain posters and prints of high-quality artists. Choose a balance between abstract and realistic. Allow children to choose between at least two paintings and have them imagine who they are in the painting. They can then write a story about what is happening or has already happened. Or they can describe the scene, embellishing on what they see.

Movement and Music

I. Body Language I

Have children pair up or work in teams to create letters or phonetic sounds. The whole class can work at once on one sound and observe each other's solutions. Or they can secretly decide what they will create and let the rest of the class guess the result.

II. Body Language II

As the children learn parts of speech, have them act out ideas for each. Some suggestions;

Nouns: airplanes, clowns, rain

Verbs: creep, slide, stretch

Adjectives: happy, frightened, cold

Adverbs: joyfully, sadly, carefully

III. Crossing the Floor

Challenge children to think of as many ways to cross the floor as they can, writing them on the board and then reading them aloud.

IV. Story Songs

Short songs or song segments are often sung on records that tell favorite children's stories. Other times these can be found in anthologies of music. When reading or telling old favorite stories, make use of these song segments. Giving the children an opportunity to "interrupt" the story at intervals to insert their song segment keeps interest and attention up. If samples are not readily available, children can compose their own. Another possible source is the school music teacher.

V. Finger Plays

In the preprimary years children have usually learned a number of finger plays with preset movements. Now, as they learn new poems and songs, challenge them to create their own finger plays. This may work best in small groups or pairs.

The Teacher's Role

The activities in this section will, no doubt be spread out over time rather than used as a single unit. They may be introduced and adapted to fit into different topics you are studying. As a teacher you will approach different activities in different ways.

Facilitating   Illustrations first, art stories, number stories, math letters, creating problems, personalized stories, finger plays, be what you see, what if?, making new friends, and research skills are all activities that require some teacher assistance in getting started. They are principally designed, however, for children to be able to work freely on their own, making their own decisions.

Instructing   Story, songs, body language I and II, crossing the floor, mystery words, Haiku, picture this, my bucket, and foreign languages will, for the most part, require some direction from you. However, if you see that children are doing well without your help, be sure to give them the freedom to work on their own.

Providing Play   Illustrations first, art stories, number stories, math letters, be what you see, and making new friends are all activities that may well go from needing your facilitation to a play mode. To do this, keep the necessary materials available for the children to choose from as they wish. If children have enjoyed doing the activities as a class, they will choose to repeat them on their own and, importantly, expand and invent as they want.

Managing   The activities that require your facilitation are almost all appropriate for work in centers. Consider limiting the number of children that can work at one time by simply placing, over the center, a card with the maximum number allowed written on it. This will give children an opportunity to interact with others without being overwhelmed by too much activity.

Observing   As children work on their own, take time to read their work in progress, offering assistance and suggestions. Be available in case you are needed, but don't intrude if they prefer privacy during creative times. Have them read their creations to each other while you observe informally.

Evaluating   Evaluation should be done by the children as well as by you. Create an "author's chair," where a child can read a work in progress to others for critiquing. Be sure to create a ground rule that critiquing must be done supportively.

Reflecting and Planning   Since these activities are meant to be introduced into the curriculum at varying times, reflection and planing should be ongoing. Determine which kinds of activities are most successful, based on children's participation and on the appropriate level of challenge. Introduce similar experiences across the curriculum during the school year.

TO DISCUSS

1   No matter what type of reading instruction is used in a primary classroom, some children will be more advanced than others. Discuss first the feelings that children of all levels will have about these unavoidable inequities. Then discuss which approach—whole language instruction or traditional reading groups—deals best with the problems of feelings, self-concept, and social interaction. Try to suggest some specific methods or activities that will make the class atmosphere more positive.

TO DO

1   As a group, determine a specific skill that could be taught in each of the available classes of young children. In some classes teach the skill as its own entity; in others embed the skill within a larger language experience. Compare experiences.

BIBLIOGRAPHY

Brittain, W. (1979) *Creativity, art, and the young child.* New York: Macmillan.

Carbo, M. (1987) Reading styles research: "What works" isn't always phonics. *Phi Delta Kappan, 68(6):*431–435.

Carbo, M. (1988) Debunking the great phonics myth. *Phi Delta Kappan, 70(3):*226–240.

Corcoran, G. (1976) *Language experience for nursery and kindergarten years.* Itasca, IL: F.E. Peacock.

Dale, P. (1976) *Language development.* New York: Holt, Rinehart & Winston.

Downing, J. (1969) How children think about reading. *The Reading Teacher, 23(3):*217–230.

Erickson, F. (1984) School literacy, reasoning, and civility: An anthropologist's perspective. *Review of Educational Research, 54(4):*525–546.

Garrard, K. (1987) Helping young children develop mature speech patterns. *Young Children, 42(3):*16–21.

Goodman, G. (1987) TAWL topics. *Teachers Networking, 1(1):*4–11.

Goodman, K. (1986) *What's whole in whole language?* Portsmouth, NH: Heinemann.

Graves, D., and Hansen, J. (1983) The author's chair. *Language Art, 60:*176–183.

Greene, G. (1973) *The development of the language arts.* Lincoln, NE: Professional Educators Publications.

Hanna, L., Potter, G., & Hagaman, N. (1955) *Unit teaching in the elementary school.* New York: Rinehart.

International Reading Association Board position statement on reading and writing in early childhood. (1985) Newark, DE: International Reading Association.

Kontos, S. (1986) Research in review: What preschool children know about reading and how they learn it. *Young Children, 42(1):*58–66.

Lamme, L. (1984) *Growing up writing.* Washington, D.C.: Acropolis Books.

Literacy development and pre-first grade: A joint statement. (1986) *Childhood Education, 63(2):*110–111.

Mason, J. (1980) When do children begin to read: An exploration of four-year-old children's letter and word reading competencies. *Reading Research Quarterly, 15(2):*203–226.

Mason, J. (1981) Prereading: A developmental perspective (Tech. Rep. No. 198). Urbana: University of Illinois, Center for the Study of Reading. (Quoted in Kontos, 1986.)

Milner, S. (1982) *Effects of curriculum intervention program using fairy tales on preschool children's empathy level, reading readiness, oral language development and concept of a story.* University of Florida: Unpublished doctoral dissertation.

National Institute of Education (1985) *Becoming a nation of readers: The report of the Commission on Reading.* Washington, D.C.: National Institute of Education.

Nessel, D. (1987) Reading comprehension: Asking the right questions. *Phi Delta Kappan, 68(6):*442–444.

Newman, J. (Ed.) (1985) *Whole language theory in use.* Portsmouth, NH: Heinemann.

Raines, S. (1986) Teacher educator learns from 1st- and 2nd-grade readers and writers. *Childhood Education, 62(4):*260–264.

Saracho, O. (1985) The impact of young children's print awareness in learning to read. *Early Child Development and Care, 21(1):*1–10.

Seefeldt, C., & Barbour, N. (1986) *Early childhood education: An introduction.* Columbus, OH: Merrill.

Tiedt, S., & Tiedt, I. (1987) *Language arts activities for the classroom.* Boston: Allyn & Bacon.

Tschudi, S., & Tschudi, S. (1983) *Teaching writing in the content areas.* Washington, D.C.: National Education Association.

Turbill, J. (1985) *No better way to teach writing!* Rozelle, N.S.W., Australia: Primary English Teaching Association.

Tway, E. (1983) The development of writing in a language arts context. In B. Busching & J. Schwartz (Eds.), *Integrating the language arts in the elementary school.* Urbana, IL: National Council of Teachers of English.

Vygotsky, L. (1962) *Thought and language.* Cambridge: Massachusetts Institute of Technology.

Watson, D. (1987) What is whole language? *Teachers Networking, 1(1):*4.

Wishon, P., Brazee, P., & Ellen, B. (1986) Facilitating oral language competence: The natural ingredients. *Childhood Education, 63(2):*91–94.

_____ chapter five

Mathematics

The world of the written word is an obvious one. Billboards, road signs, newspapers, TV ads, magazines, and books surround us. Mathematical messages are more subtle, although equally a part of our everyday life. Looking out across a cityscape we see buildings that could not have been constructed without extensive use of mathematical principles. In the grocery store we buy a vast variety of food, knowing that every item we pay for has been measured, weighed, or packed according to volume. To get to the store we climb into a car that has been built using mathematical calculations, fill it with carefully measured gasoline, and drive mathematically derived distances. Once our food is home we can put it into a refrigerator cooled to a mathematically calculated temperature or into an oven heated with similar calculations. Even the simple act of making a bed is a mathematical one as we toss fresh (rectangular) sheets into the air, let them land in a symmetrical position, and, at least casually, calculate the measurements of bed and sheets to ensure a reasonable ordered finished product.

Somehow, as adults we often neglect to communicate to children the mathematical nature of the world around them. We are much more conscious of providing exposure to the written word. Perhaps it is because the messages of mathematics are so subtle that both adults and children absorb them without awareness of them. Yet our days are full of mathematical problem solving, and it would be well if we made ourselves more conscious of these incidents and communicated them to children. Then when it is time to introduce children to mathematical systems they will be able to see the long-term payoff because they will have had sufficient real-life experiences. Learning mathematics and learning to read can both be exciting and fun, but they can also be work. Children need to know that in both cases there is a real-life reward waiting for them.

A primary focus of this chapter is the real-life purpose of mathematics. We begin with a very ordinary sort of day in a preschool in which children use mathematical principles in a comfortable, nonthreatening social atmosphere. The discussion that follows includes a look at two views of mathematics learning: the concept of math as a drill subject versus real-life problem solving. Both the preprimary and the primary units focus on the need to increase children's mathematical awareness in their everyday lives.

AN ORDINARY EVENT

An aware teacher can make use of everyday experiences to teach a wide array of skills and concepts. Many of these are mathematical in nature, as can be seen in the following observation of a private nursery school. This observation was made near the beginning of the school year and thus presents an interesting description of a teacher helping children adjust to a new environment. Mrs. Hawthorne's class was a mixture of 3- and 4-year-olds, and the 4-year-olds were largely returnees from the year before. For the past 2 weeks, Mrs. Hawthorne had encouraged the 4-year-olds to show courtesy and kindness to the new children and had given them daily opportunities to practice both. A second, and equally important, theme had been to help the older children review and reinforce last year's academic learning by having them teach the new children some of their acquired skills. One of these skills was the application of one-to-one correspondence, and this is the lesson that was taking place when the following observation was made. The description, written in the present tense, is a "fleshed-out" version of the original terse notes made by a visiting observer.

Today's snack is vanilla pudding and orange juice, requiring for each child a cup, a small bowl, a spoon, and a napkin. The food is served family style, but the dishes and silver are placed on the tables beforehand by the day's helping team. Today this team consists of three 4-year-olds and three 3-year-olds, working in older-younger pairs.

Mrs. Hawthorne asks the children to count the number of chairs at each of the several tables and notes that the three younger children have no difficulty in this task. She then provides each older-younger pair with a small basket of spoons and instructs them to put one spoon on the table in front of each chair. The 4-year-olds handle the job with the confidence that comes from remembered familiarity. But two of the younger children seem confused. Although their older partners show them exactly what to do, they randomly place the spoons around the table. The third 3-year-old tackles the job with intense seriousness and concentration. When he is finished, a pleased smile crosses his face and he sighs with what seems to be contentment. Mrs. Hawthorne makes no comment, however, on his success or on the other children's failures. The spoons are correctly placed in any event due to the 4-year-old facilitators.

Next the bowls are placed around the tables and a second new child begins to understand the logic underlying what she is doing. The remaining 3-year-old continues to place dishes randomly and his partner, Timmy, begins to be impatient.

"No, no, like this!" he exclaims, then responds to Mrs. Hawthorne's quiet reminder to "help, not boss" by standing alone, for a minute, looking tense. Then, in a moment of inspiration, he puts a bowl in the younger child's hand, holds his own hand over the other's, and gently helps him place the bowl next to a spoon. "Like this," he says in an elaborately gentle voice. He looks at Mrs. Hawthorne to see if she has noticed his victory over himself. She smiles and he smiles back.

At just this time the other 4-year-olds discover that their baskets contain more spoons than are needed. Immediately they come to Mrs. Hawthorne, great concern written on their faces, "Hey," says one, "we got too much spoons."

Mrs. Hawthorne surveys the baskets carefully and seriously. "Hmm," she says, "too many spoons. How about you, Timmy? Do you have too many spoons?"

"Oh, yeah. I got two too much—too many."

"And how many extras do you have, Rachel?" Rachel counts four.

"Jackson, how about you?" There is just one.

"Well, then. Jackson has one, Rachel you have four, and Timmy you have two. Shall we just put them all together and keep them in the drawer here?" The children agree, but Mrs. Hawthorne asks that they stop for just a minute to see what their collective remainder is.

"Let's put the extra spoons right here on the table and see how many extra we have altogether." As the spoons are placed in a row, teacher and 4-year-olds count in unison.

During the entire problem in practical addition, the younger children hang quietly in the background. They watch with modest interest but seem to have no desire to join in the activity.

WHY MATHEMATICS

In this very ordinary, natural sort of experience we can see that it takes only a little extra effort to turn everyday events into mathematical learning. For a preschool teacher, the challenge is to keep constantly aware of potential lessons. For the teacher in the primary grades, the challenge is to avoid being bogged down by curricular demands to the exclusion of real-life problem solving.

In this section we discuss the basic goals of mathematics education now and through history. Sometimes these goals have shown an awareness of the importance of real-life problem solving and occasionally it has been at least somewhat disregarded. We will leave the reader to determine what happened when.

"Problem solving must be the focus of school mathematics." This position statement by the National Council of Teachers of Mathematics (NCTM, 1980, p. 4) may sound too obvious to be worth mentioning. If we observe classrooms, however, we find that this straightforward, common-sense declaration is frequently forgotten or ignored. There is often such pressure, particularly in the primary grades, to achieve ever higher skill levels that we feel there is no time to allow "work on problems that may take hours, days and even weeks to solve" (NCTM, 1980, p. 4). Some of this work might include posing questions, analyzing the questions, and communicating results through illustrations, charts, and diagrams. Even very young children are capable of such activities. Looking back at our observation of Mrs. Hawthorne's class, we see that some of them were represented in the informal experience of the preschool children.

For example, although no illustrations or diagrams were made on paper, the children did have to analyze the set-up of the table: how many people there would be and how many utensils were required to make the one-to-one correspondences. They translated the results of their thinking to the act of setting the table, and, since this was a relatively new skill, they used trial and error to attain satisfactory results. No one was upset by the ambiguity of the situation when there were varying remainders in the spoon supply, and tentative conclusions about the numbers they needed were finally replaced by a satisfactory resolution. In everyday settings, in other words, even very young children can and do engage in complex mathematical analysis. As an early childhood educator, Mrs. Hawthorne saw that a major task in teaching mathematics was to enhance what the children were already doing in their own natural world.

Her point of view is an important one to consider. The ultimate reason for mathematics is, after all, not just to solve problems as presented in a text or worksheet but to solve problems that present themselves in many phases of life. The complexity of life today is many times greater than that in earlier centuries, and we are discovering that young children are capable of mathematical thinking that is much deeper and broader than we had ever before realized.

From the vantage point of the late twentieth century some ideas seem very simple: reading a number, using it as a symbol for a known quantity, doing basic addition and subtraction. Such simplicity has not always been so apparent. The first time someone tried to represent a number symbolically it probably came out as a series of hash marks. The earliest record we have of this attempt is on a wolf bone from the Paleolithic times and the hash marks were divided into groups of five. So perhaps our ancestors of 30,000 years ago were already using their fingers as counting aids and as bases for numbering systems.

The symbol for zero was invented by the Babylonians, probably about 700 B.C., later by the Mayans around A.D. 400, and again by the Hindus in A.D. 800. If the invention of the zero doesn't seem earthshaking, think how much trouble the last sentence would have been to write without it.

By the Middle Ages finger reckoning was still the order of the European school day, and children were considered sufficiently educated if they could count. Today we assume that even the youngest children can use their fingers to count to 5 and that a zero means something is all gone. Older children are expected to go much further. In the first part of the eighteenth century, algebra, geometry, and trigonometry were introduced into colleges in the United States. A century later these subjects were moved down to the high school level. By the end of the nineteenth century, there were recommendations that children from the sixth grade onward should be exposed to concrete forms of geometry and introductory algebra. After centuries of grappling with these mathematical concepts, people were finding them so easily understood that they were working their way from the colleges to the elementary schools. Today we routinely expect children in kindergarten to have a rudimentary understanding of numbers and geometry.

In addition to expecting more of today's children, we have also spent this century pondering the method by which mathematics should be taught. When nothing more was expected of children than that they could count, rote learning and memorization reigned supreme as the logical methodology. In fact, this is still the preferred approach for some of today's educational researchers.

Stimulus-response methods based on behavioristic techniques have been the primary way of updating the centuries-old tradition of rote learning. It will be recalled from the discussion of cognitive learning in Chapter One that arithmetic is regarded by B. F. Skinner as one of "the drill subjects." This point of view argues for the use of such modern inventions as teaching machines and computers, math games that test skills, and a progressive introduction of increasingly complex skills.

An early childhood application of this methodological viewpoint grew from one of the original Head Start programs of the 1960s. Sigfried Engelmann, from the original Head Start research team of Bereiter and Engelmann, reteamed with Doug Carnine to develop the DISTAR arithmetic program. Their approach was to choose a limited set of objectives and then to program the learning of them into small, incremental steps. Behavior modification techniques would reinforce the child each step of the way.

Despite the efficiency of such an approach for small children, it has been criticized, in part because it is, perhaps, too efficient (Osborne & Nibbelink, 1975). One critical factor in achieving real mathematical understanding is the opportunity to play around with concepts, and this system allows almost none of this.

The controversy over the definition of arithmetic as a drill or nondrill subject was already taking place by the 1930s. At that time William Brownell argued that "children must understand the basic concepts that underlie what they are learning if learning is to be permanent" (Kennedy, 1986, p. 6). Brownell and others attacked the drill theory of arithmetic for a number of reasons: Children don't understand or enjoy arithmetic, they can't apply their skills to new situations, they forget quickly, focus is on the subject rather than on the needs of the learner, and, finally, this type of learning has almost no relationship or tie to the real world. Theorists and researchers of that time began to consider a newly controversial question: Should children learn mathematics incidentally as a part of their natural environment, or should it be taught as a systematic subject?

By the end of World War II, the general consensus, and the position of the National Council of Teachers of Mathematics, was that "Mathematics, including arithmetic, has an inherent organization. This organization must be respected in learning. Teaching, to be effective, must be orderly and systematic; hence, arithmetic cannot be taught informally or incidentally" (Trafton, 1975, p. 21).

This did not mean, however, that systematic instruction had to be formal. The needs, interests, and developmental level of the child were all to be taken into consideration. Informal experiences were sanctioned for the early years, "involving the child actively, and providing many opportunities for using arithmetic in socially significant situations" (Trafton, 1975, p. 21). Thus, a compromise position between learning by drill and incidental, real-life learning was effected.

The mid-1950s brought yet another major reform movement, which was often referred to under the umbrella term of *new math*. The concern of educators moved from methodology to content. The ability of the Russians to send the satellite Sputnik into orbit led to a questioning by Americans of mathematical training in schools. After looking at math instruction across the country, it seemed that there was a need for greater substance and higher expectations.

As mathematics programs were reconstructed, the early years were viewed as an appropriate time to learn geometry and graphing, sets, open sentences, and properties. The use of computational skills was newly emphasized, although there was controversy over the importance of memorizing facts or of discovering them through work with meaningful problems. This issue was never settled during the approximately 20 years in which new math evolved. Other unsettled issues concerned the training of teachers, who learned more substance but less about how to impart it to children, and the problem of focusing on materials that could best be understood by top students but might leave others behind.

Although the era of new math has been labeled by some as a mistake or failure, there was much progress that we can apply today to early education: Revitalization in curriculum and pedagogy accompanied the searching for answers; new content such as geometry and graphing was introduced into the early years; planned but informal programs became accepted for young children; mathematics became more exciting to teach and to learn; more research was done on the content and processes of children's thinking (Trafton, 1975). In other words, this period of ferment was a time for much thinking and growth.

Today, a main emphasis in mathematics for young children is on achieving balance. Earlier centuries leaned heavily in the direction of rote learning; the 1930s overcorrected in their emphasis on meaningfulness; the 1980s focused too highly on content. Now, the attempts of researchers have been toward balancing informal, real-life learning with the attainment of necessary skills. Using developmental theory it has been possible to realize that some mathematical learnings, such as geometry, graphing, and fractions, can be introduced earlier in very concrete ways. It is equally useful to know that too much computation at an early age serves merely to bore and confuse children. Let us consider now how today's teacher can approach this new emphasis on balancing the historical approaches to learning.

THE TEACHER'S ROLE

The world of the young child is full of possibilities for mathematics learning. Often, although we are aware of the possibilities for language learning in everyday life, we fail to see, or simply ignore, the less obvious math possibilities. Most of our communications during the day are, after all, concerned with words, not numbers. Yet, with not too much effort, it is possible to expand everyday learning to include mathematics as well.

When exploring a new plant with 3-year-olds, we can calculate the number of leaves and petals or identify the various shapes of its parts. In class we can turn naturally occurring events into mathematics learnings as Mrs. Hawthorne did when it was time to set the table. In other words, just as it is important to keep aware of potential language experiences for fostering children's growth, it is also important to be alert to everyday possibilities for mathematics learning.

Sometimes teachers themselves never learned mathematics in a natural way but only as a drill-and-competency subject having no relationship to the real world. Teachers with this unfortunate background may thus be part of a vast number of people with math phobias, fearful not only of mathematics for themselves but concerned about their ability to teach the subject to even very young children. It is encouraging to note that many beginning teachers find that when they help young children understand the world in mathematical terms, they begin to understand mathematical concepts and processes better themselves! Whatever the teacher's background, it is important that he or she help children feel comfortable and natural about the use of mathematics.

As important as natural, comfortable learning may be, it is also important, of course, to consider structure. As we discussed in the last section, the current focus of educational researchers is on achieving a balance between the two extremes. As teachers work toward a successful balance, there are three important areas to consider: concepts, skills, and applications (Trafton, 1975). *Concepts* are important to focus on because, for small children, they are generally hazy and tentative if guidance is not provided. *Skills* are critical, too, because they provide the tools necessary for future growth in mathematical understanding and because they give children a feeling of dominion over new experiences. Finally, *applications* are important because when children apply learning from one situation to another, they demonstrate that they really understand the concept and have achieved the skill necessary to use it.

Some children are able more quickly than others to attain concepts and skills and to make applications. Others have difficulty with one or more of these three areas of learning. Thus, it is necessary to consider some individualizing of instruction. In a structured classroom this will mean that some children are introduced to methods and materials sooner than others. In more open settings, learning will be individualized as children are allowed to choose to learn the things that interest and challenge them most. If we follow the lead of the two mathematics councils, we can adopt both these approaches to individualization and apply them at the appropriate times.

Trafton suggests that individualization must include "acceptance of each child as an individual worthy of adult respect," and that to this should be added "an acceptance of the child's ideas, a provision of opportunities for pupil input in developing and selecting learning experiences, a concern for the quality of the child's intellectual development, and a willingness to take time to know the child as an individual" (1975, p. 39). If we agree with the current search for achieving the proper balance between natural and structured learnings, then Trafton's view is important to think about. As teachers we need to provide both balance and individual attention so that children can learn with both joy and competence. To be able to do this however, we must know more about our children than their test scores and mathematical likes and dislikes.

MATHEMATICS AND CHILD DEVELOPMENT

Between the preprimary and primary years a great change takes place in children's mathematical development. The preprimary child has limited abilities in conservation, classification, seriation, and ordering of numbers. The primary child has gained, or is gaining, competence in all of these. Thus, for children in kindergarten and first grade, it is important to provide experiences that will help them make the transition between the two stages of thought. It is essential to strike a balance between giving children sufficient challenge and taking care not to try to push them into a stage they can't yet achieve. Studies have shown that when children are trained to learn mathematics above their reasoning level, there may be positive results at first but they are "rarely retained unless the child is already in transition from one level to another" (Suydam & Weaver, 1975, p. 47).

Although affective development may not be as obvious in mathematics learning as it is in other subjects, it is still important to consider. Children in the primary grades may have concerns about their performance. According to Erikson's theory (1964) these children are at the beginning of the stage of industry vs. inferiority, a time when it is important for them to feel positive about their own ability to perform mathematically in order to avoid long-term negative feelings about themselves and the subject.

Affective development related to mathematics can also make use of Piagetian (1932) theory. Children in the preprimary years are egocentric in their play and work, often preferring to have their own materials while working next to someone else. Children in the primary grades, however, have begun to be intrigued by games played in teams, by the rules that accompany them, and by the negotiations that must take place for a game to progress smoothly. The implications for teaching are that older children may learn best in small groups or teams and that mathematical problems can be provided for these social interactions.

The ways in which children learn mathematics change considerably between the two groups, as we have seen. What children can learn is also subject to change. In the following sections we discuss the development of conservation, classification, seriation, and ordering. Research in these areas in the past few years has aroused some controversy and, where applicable, that will also be discussed.

Conservation

Conservation refers to the child's ability to realize that two equal quantities or groups remain equal in amount or number, no matter how they may be transformed in shape or position. Conservation comprehension can be applied to number, liquid, mass, or length. The following experience demonstrates both the theory about conservation of number as well as the controversy surrounding it.

A Head Start teacher had been studying Piagetian tasks and decided to prove, or disprove, their correctness with his own children. He began with the conservation of number and, knowing that pennies were important and interesting to children, chose them as his testing materials.

The teacher began with Lola, a 4-year-old. Placing the pennies in parallel rows of eight each, he asked Lola to count the number in each row. She did so with no difficulty, declaring that she saw "the same much" in each row. Then the teacher spread out one row of eight so that it produced a longer line. This time Lola stated, with great assurance, that the spread-out row had more pennies.

Here, the teacher tried to help Lola relate the experience to real life. "Suppose you wanted to buy some candy," he said. "Which row would be best to take?" Lola chose the spread-out row because "it has mucher."

After attaining the same results with several other children, the teacher interviewed Samantha, also 4 years old. At first she also believed that the spread-out row contained more pennies. But when the teacher asked her which she would choose if planning to buy candy she looked thoughtful for a moment and then said, "What does it matter? They're both the same!"

The teacher, wanting to see how far Samantha's reasoning could go, restocked the rows so that one had nine pennies, the other seven. He then squeezed the nine pennies close together and spread out the seven to make a longer row. "Now," he asked, "which row do you want to spend?"

"You're trying to trick me, aren't you?" she asked. "I want the row that has nine."

This experience, a variation of a classic Piaget test of conservation ability, demonstrates in two ways the controversial aspect of tests of this ability. Piaget's observations indicated that children obtain conservation between the ages of 6 and 8, and yet Samantha clearly was acquiring understanding at age 4. This surprising finding is related to a second one in which researchers have found that children can conserve earlier if the objects are more interesting to them or related to their lives in some way.

One explanation for this apparent departure from Piaget's findings has been provided by Kamii (Castle, 1986). In her work with the Piaget research institute in Geneva, Switzerland, she has learned that children are achieving conservation at earlier ages than they did a generation ago. The important issue is, she has argued, that children do attain conservation developmentally and that they cannot truly understand number and numeration without an understanding of conservation.

A number of studies (Suydam & Weaver, 1975) have shown that, indeed, children who conserve early can also perform more easily in beginning arithmetic and at an earlier age. Several researchers have concluded that tests of number conservation could be used to determine arithmetic readiness because this ability does seem so necessary to success.

Other types of conservation were mentioned earlier in this section and they, too, are related to early mathematics learning. The ability to conserve length and area will influence the type of geometry learnings children can attain. An example of a test for conservation of length includes laying four sticks of equal length in a straight line. Four more sticks of the same length are then laid below them in a zigzag pattern. Children must have attained conservation of length in order to understand that the two rows are equal.

To test for conservation of area, four square pieces of paper can be laid out in a row with their sides touching. Below this are placed four equally large sheets of paper, placed so that the four squares create a larger square. Again, it is necessary to have achieved conservation in order to see that the areas of both configurations are the same.

Classification

When a child draws a picture of assorted animals and then circles all the birds, then all the dogs, and so on, she is placing them in classes. An infant just learning to talk may learn to say "dog" and then apply that label to all furry animals. This, too, is classification, although primitive, and it soon gives way to more accurate labeling. In both cases just described, the classification is a simple and singular one: birds are understood as different from dogs, but the concept of them as part of a larger group called animals is as yet too complex. Young children can classify on just one level at a time.

This can cause limitations in a couple of ways. If preschool children are presented with the traditional wood or plastic geometric shapes of different colors, they are likely to group them according to color. Older children will be interested in classifying by size also, and in the primary grades they should be able to coordinate the two. For example, they might place small green circles in one pile and large green circles in another.

Another limitation in early attempts at classification is that of class inclusion. If a child is given six miniature dogs and two cats and asked if there are more dogs or more animals, the answer will vary depending on age. A preschooler will answer that there are more dogs, whereas the child in the primary grades can generally see that one class (dogs) is included in another (animals).

Piaget's colleagues observed that the understanding of class inclusion was developmental. Kamii (1985) has concluded that what appear to adults as wrong conclusions, are actually developmental steps, and at each progressive stage these conclusions will be better coordinated and closer to the adult perception of correct (Kamii & De Clark, 1985). This finding is important to consider when offering children activities that include classification. The experiences are necessary to achieve more adequate understanding, and patience needs to be expressed as children work their way through a hierarchy of wrong-to-right answers.

Seriation and Ordering

Alex was new to nursery school and his mother was explaining to the teacher that he already knew a lot about math. For example, she said, this 3-year-old could count to 20. When asked to perform, Alex at first refused and then shyly counted quickly and accurately to 20.

The teacher praised him and then asked Alex to count a row of 10 popsicle sticks. Alex began accurately enough until he got to the fourth stick. This one became "4, 5." He then skipped over the next stick and described the following one as "6, 7." By the time Alex finished there were 12 sticks as far as he was concerned.

His mother looked embarrassed. The teacher assured her, however, that Alex's behavior was quite normal and that in nursery school there would be a focus on understanding, rather than simply repeating, numbers. It would be awhile, in fact, before Alex even needed to work with numbers directly.

Understanding the ordering of numbers and placement of objects in a series is yet another skill that needs to emerge before number can be understood and used as a tool for mathematics learning. At times children can point to objects and name the numbers that go with them, but they don't always think of the numbers in the same way adults do. If the teacher had asked Alex to show her the number-10 stick, Alex might well have thought its name was actually Ten, just as if it had been Sam or George.

A further difficulty emerges when children are asked to place objects in a row in order of size. Preschoolers tend to have difficulty doing more than finding the smallest and the largest. Even through the first or second grade, children often need to find the proper order through trial and error. It is only in second or third grade that most children can logically lay out a series correctly or place a second series of objects below the first one so that they are matched one to one.

Conservation, classification, and seriation are important attainments in their own right. Additionally, as children learn these concepts they prepare for a later understanding of number. For example, when they play with their toys and place together a group of dolls on one side of the room and a pile of books on the other, they are classifying their belongings into mathematical sets. Although, when they are very young, they won't consciously count the dolls and the books, the children will perceive that there are more objects than one. Arranging the dolls in a row with the biggest at one end and the smallest at the other teaches seriation and pre-counting. And while the pile of books and the row of dolls may be too many objects to count, there are other objects in the children's lives that can be understood in the plural. The concept of *two* comes naturally when it is noticed that there are two shoes to wear or two cookies to eat.

These early learning experiences are intuitive and natural ones. For true mathematical understanding, real thinking is eventually needed. During the years that children comprehend prenumber and number concepts, they are not yet conscious of their thinking. In the primary years, first steps in making children conscious of their thinking should be taken, although they have not yet grown completely out of intuitive thinking. To make their learning experiences most beneficial it is important to let children construct their own learning and understanding. If they are drilled and pushed, they will probably perform fairly well, but they will simply be mimicking adult behaviors. Long-term learning will be achieved more readily if children are permitted to invent their own ways of dealing with their new concepts.

THE MATHEMATICS CURRICULUM

The NCTM Standards

In the past few years, the Commission on Standards for School Mathematics of the NCTM has spent much time reviewing the curriculum for kindergarten through high school. In 1988 they published their first overview of the work they had been doing toward reforming school math, including a set of thirteen standards for kindergarten and the primary grades (Commission on Standards, 1988). We will use these new standards as the basis of our curriculum discussion, adding implications for the earlier years as well.

Standard 1: Mathematics as Problem Solving   Children need to use "problem-solving approaches to investigate and understand mathematical content; formulate problems from everyday and mathematical situations; develop and apply strategies to solve a wide variety of problems..." (p. 6). Since children in the early years do not yet think logically, they will undertake this work in their own trial-and-error mode. As they do this, they will be preparing themselves for the emergence of logic. If children are permitted to wrestle with problems on their own rather than forced to work from prefabricated adult systems, their understanding will be much deeper.

One way to encourage the problem-solving approach is to give first- and second-graders addition and subtraction problems informally before teaching them any systems (Driscoll, undated). One researcher (Colvin, 1987) discovered in her work with first-graders that children who learned word problems first and number facts later were clearly superior in their use of the mathematical processes and in understanding the meanings of mathematical problems. In addition, their memorization of addition and subtraction facts was equivalent to that of children who had focused on the facts first and on problem solving second.

Standard 2: Mathematics as Communication   Children need to have many opportunities to communicate their math learnings so that they "relate physical materials, pictures and diagrams to mathematical ideas; reflect upon and clarify their thinking about mathematical ideas and situations;...realize that representing, discussing, listening, writing, and reading mathematics are a vital part of learning and using mathematics" (p. 6).

This is an argument against letting mathematics exist in a vacuum. Communication puts mathematical thinking into the context of real life and enhances its importance to children by letting them share and discuss their problem solving with others. Making graphs from real objects, such as types of shoes children are wearing or the kind of bread they choose for a snack, gives the youngest children three-dimensional concrete objects to work with. Picture graphs for older children provide the next step in understanding (Barrata-Lorton, 1976).

Standard 3: Mathematics as Reasoning   Reasoning should be emphasized so that children can "draw logical conclusions about mathematics;...justify their answers and solution processes; ...believe that mathematics makes sense" (p. 6). The development of language makes reasoning possible in one sense because teacher and child can reflect together on the experience the child is having. On the other hand, logical thinking takes many years to develop, at least until the completion of elementary school. So, reasoning for your children can be thought of as a preparation for logic. Teachers who ask questions that point to "what next" and "why" encourage growth in the right direction.

Standard 4: Mathematical Connections   Children should have opportunities to make connections so that they can "recognize relationships among different topics in mathematics; use mathematics in other curriculum areas; use mathematics in their daily lives" (p. 6). This standard is the one of the thirteen that speaks most directly to the principle focus of this textbook. Mathematics should not be taught in isolation but in relation to everyday happenings (such as the vignette that opened this chapter) and to other parts of the curriculum. The meaningfulness of mathematics becomes more apparent to children when they have opportunities to make connections.

Standard 5: Estimation   Children should have experiences in estimation so that they can "recognize when an estimation is appropriate; use estimation to determine reasonableness of results; apply estimation in working with quantities, measurement, computation, and problem solving" (p. 6). Very young children estimate wildly, having as yet no concept of number. Until they begin to understand number, there is no point in considering activities that include estimation. Although groups differ, a teacher might expect to try a few activities toward the end of first grade. In one school there was a contest to guess the number of jelly beans in a quart jar. The child who guessed most correctly would win the jar to take back to his or her class. To prepare her children for the contest, one first-grade teacher spent several days doing estimation activities with her class. When the day came to submit their estimates, every child in the class suggested a number that was at least as reasonable as those suggested by children in the upper elementary grades. In fact, one of the first-graders actually took second prize.

Standard 6: Number Sense and Numeration   The "mathematics curriculum should include whole number concepts and skills so that students can: construct number meanings through real-world experiences and the use of physical materials; understand our numeration system by relating counting, grouping, and place-value concepts; develop number sense" (pp. 6–7). The development of number sense is based on the development of other basic skills as we discussed in the preceding section, "Mathematics and Child Development." Thus, it is important to give young children many experiences with concrete objects, adding written numbers only as they are ready to understand them. This will be true all the way through the primary years, although, of course, numbers as symbols will be much more clearly understood as children mature.

Standard 7: Concepts of Whole Number Operations   Children should have in their curriculum addition, subtraction, multiplication, and division of whole numbers so that they can "...relate the mathematical language and symbolism of operations to problem situations and information language;...develop operation sense" (p. 7). As children work with sets of objects they will begin to discover the concept of addition and, eventually, subtraction. With teacher direction they can see that both combining two sets to make one larger one and breaking up a set into smaller ones are addition processes. Understanding that subtraction is related to addition is difficult at first, particularly if based on real-life experiences, such as the actual taking away and disappearance of objects. But if objects are removed and kept in sight, the understanding will be simpler.

Multiplication begins to come naturally as children learn to count in twos, threes, and so on. Teachers can encourage this behavior in natural ways when counting objects in the environment: shoes, eyes, mittens, dolls, wheels on trucks, and so on. Traditionally, division is thought of as the most difficult of the processes to understand. Yet children use two types of division from a very early age: sharing such things as candy with friends or trying to find out how many objects they can purchase with the money they have (Williams & Shuard, 1970).

Standard 8: Whole Number Computation   The curriculum should include whole number computation so that children can "model, explain, and develop reasonable proficiency with basic facts and algorithms;...select and use computation techniques appropriate to specific problem situations and determine whether the result is reasonable" (p. 7). The process of selecting and using the right techniques and operations is done intuitively by children in the pre-number years. When children enter school, this intuitive understanding is often taken away as teachers begin to focus on drill and textbook learning. Real-life experiences and applications can make it easier for children to make logical choices of computation techniques.

Standard 9: Geometry and Spatial Sense   Children should have experience with two- and three-dimensional geometry so that they can "describe, model, draw and classify shapes; develop spatial sense; recognize and appreciate geometry in their world" (p. 7). Williams and Shuard (1970) give some good real-life reasons for young children to learn geometry. First, children need "a picture of the spatial structure in which we live...the shape of our earth and the properties of its surface...." Second, "It is equally important for children to know that both living and non-living bodies have characteristic shapes and structures...." A spider's web, a snow crystal, man-made structures and mechanisms are all of interest to small children. Third, children will learn to appreciate patterns and forms that people use and create for their enjoyment. Fourth, mathematical activities such as "sorting, combining, partitioning, matching, ordering..." (p. 93) are all included in the manipulations of geometric space.

Standard 10: Measurement   Measurement should be included in the curriculum so that children can "understand the attributes of length, capacity, weight, area, volume, time, temperature, and angle;...make and use measurements in problems and everyday situations" (p. 7). Even preschool children can begin to engage in measurement activities. This does not mean they need to use numbered rulers; indeed, they would no doubt fail in the attempt. However, everyday objects can be used so that a block might be three pencils long and two wide. Pieces of yarn can be used to measure objects with curves and corners. As children develop an understanding of number, real rulers, scales, thermometers, and so on can be used.

Standard 11: Statistics and Probability   Children should have experiences with data analysis and probability so that they can "collect, organize, and describe data; construct, read, and interpret displays of data..." (p. 7). For children in the early years, the concept of probability is out of reach, but collecting, organizing, and describing data are possible activities from preschool onward. Activities involving displays of data are possible when children begin to understand number as well as number symbols and written words. When preschoolers collect fall leaves, classify them into heaps based on their red or yellow colors, and then tell what they have, they are engaged in an experience that will prepare them for later activities involving symbols. Primary children might take empty milk cartons back to the classroom after lunch and construct a three-dimensional graph showing how many children drank chocolate milk and how many preferred white. More abstract systems can come later.

Standard 12: Fractions and Decimals   The curriculum should include fractions and decimals so that children can "develop concepts of fractions, mixed numbers and decimals; develop number sense for fractions and decimals;...apply fractions and decimals in problem situations" (p. 8). Certainly, children who do not yet understand whole numbers are not yet ready for fractions. By second grade, many children are ready to work with concrete examples and to begin to write their symbols. Using the traditional rectangle, triangle, or circle "is a valuable method because the equality of the parts which make the whole and the equivalence of different forms of the same fractions are so easily seen" (Williams & Shuard, 1970, p. 175).

Standard 13: Patterns and Relationships   Patterns and relationships should be included so that children can "recognize, extend, describe, and create a wide variety of patterns; represent and describe mathematical relationships..." (p. 8). Patterns are especially appropriate for young children, right from the earliest ages. In the pre-number years, patterns should be two- and three-dimensional objects with plenty of opportunities to create repeated patterns. In the primary grades, patterns of numbers can be recognized and should thus be built into some of the work that children do. For example, a teacher-made worksheet might include a row of problems in which all the answers are the same or each answer is one more than the previous one.

Summary

As a way to summarize what we have discussed about history, development, and curriculum, let's go back to the beginning of this chapter and the observation of Mrs. Hawthorne's preschool class. In this experience, older children were given an opportunity to help the younger, newer children with the practical mathematics of setting tables. This everyday sort of experience demonstrates a number of things that have been discussed during this chapter.

History of Mathematics Education   Speaking in very broad terms, the evolution of mathematics teaching to young children has gone from centuries of rote learning to high emphasis on meaningfulness to strong focus on content and, finally, to our current attempt at balance between all the elements of teaching. In Mrs. Hawthorne's class there was an experience in which the learning was informal and meaningful, drawn from everyday experience. However, at the same time she balanced this informality at the end of the experience with a more challenging and slightly structured lesson for the older children.

Developmental Implications As the children in Mrs. Hawthorne's room dealt with each group of tableware, they had an opportunity to practice classification. As they placed objects in order around the table, seriation was necessary for success. As we saw, the 3-year-olds had trouble with this new activity while the 4-year-olds knew what to do based on previous experience. We also saw, however, that the younger children began to understand what was going on during the informal part of the activity and so, even for them, this experience was appropriate. They were not, however, ready to begin the follow-up lesson with the older children that introduced the idea of number.

Curriculum Problem solving is the first of the standards discussed by the NCTM, and for every one of the children, this was a problem-solving experience. In addition, the children were able to apply mathematics to everyday situations, think about the reasonableness of the results, and intuit appropriate computational skills, all found within the descriptions of the standards. The likelihood of multiple learnings, such as in this experience, is increased when we approach mathematics through integrating the curriculum.

Integration In Mrs. Hawthorne's class, mathematics learnings were integrated into the fabric of everyday preschool life. In addition, there were social studies learnings: care of the younger children by the older, family-style serving of food, cooperation required to get the job done. Within this natural experience, individualization was provided; 3-year-olds participated to the best of their own abilities; 4-year-olds were presented with a lesson about remainders, while the younger children tuned out.

Integrating mathematics naturally into a preschool's daily events helps children feel comfortable about a subject area that will have applications throughout their lives. A commentator on early mathematics learning in Britain has summarized this view of the long-term need for math:

> Without mathematics, children would not come to terms with their environment. Mathematical education should awaken in children the significance of mathematics to their lives—an appreciation of its aesthetic qualities; its role in the maintenance, protection, and development of society; its use in their ordinary lives; and the need for it in their careers. Mathematics, therefore, possesses values which are essential for

human beings who wish to live a full and active life (Choat, 1978, p. 125).

PREPRIMARY ACTIVITIES FOR INTEGRATING MATHEMATICS

Throughout the day we can introduce mathematical learning. At the preschool level this is best done in informal ways with an alertness to situations as they present themselves. The integrated mathematics activities for the preschool years included in this section reflect this orientation. Later in the primary grades, informal learning is still valued, but planning is more formal.

Our discussion of the importance of incorporating mathematics into everyday school life has been extensive. The following activities show a number of ways this can be done, frequently with very little preparation and few, if any, materials.

Some of the activities blend into the regular life of the classroom so thoroughly that children will probably have no awareness that mathematics is being learned. Some examples of this type of learning are Silver Sorting, Block Play, and Playing Store. Other activities are more clearly definable as mathematics but still fit into the school day. Examples include Schoolyard Walk and Bouncing Ball.

As can be seen by the curriculum web (Figure 5-1), several subject areas other than mathematics can be learned at the same time. The first four activities fit simply into the everyday routine.

Activities

I. Silver Sorting

Use plastic tableware drawer inserts that have the shapes of the different pieces indented in them. Place tableware in unsorted piles. Direct very young children to first feel the outlines of the indentations. Leave children free to sort the tableware. This may be done as a process activity that is always out and as a practical activity in actual classroom life. A picture of each utensil may be placed in the bottom of each section.

II. Everything in Its Place

For use in storage shelves within reach of children, make cut-out patterns from laminated construction paper that are the same shape as the material to be stored. Children use these as guides to replace materials when they are finished using them.

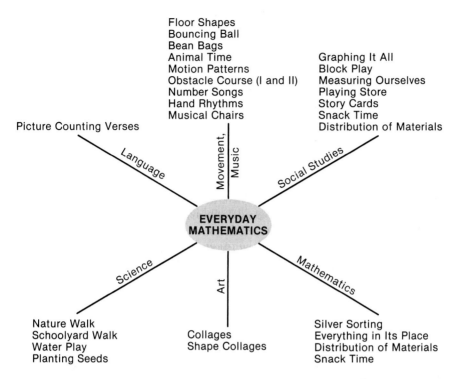

Note that some activities are listed twice because they are integrated into more than one area of the curriculum.

FIGURE 5-1

III. Distribution of Materials (Kamii, 1982)

Ask children to bring "just enough cups (or other material) for everybody at your table." Keep the number small enough to be manageable.

IV. Snack Time (Kamii, 1982)

Ask children in pairs or individually to divide the total amount of snack food among children at their table. They should figure out themselves the fair distribution, and, if everyone is satisfied, perfect equality is not essential.

V. Picture Counting (Brown, 1982)

When you read to children and show them pictures, help them find and count various items

VI. Story Cards

These can be purchased commercially or cut from coloring books. Have children place picture cards (usually no more than three)

in correct order from left to right and then tell a story. Children should be permitted to define "correct" order.

VII. Verses

Use counting verses throughout the day: at line-up time, on the playground, on the way back from a field trip. Here are two traditional choices to start with.

A. Ten little monkeys jumping on the bed
   One fell off and bumped his head.
   Called the doctor and the doctor said,
   "That's what you get for jumping on the bed."

(This is a good whole-body exercise. Choose the most active children to be the final monkeys out.)

B. One little brown bird, up and up she flew
   Along came another one, and that made two.
   Two little brown birds, sitting in a tree
   Along came another one, and that made three.
   Three little brown birds, here comes one more

   What's all the noise about? That made four.
   Four little brown birds and one makes five
   Singing in the sun, glad to be alive.

VIII. Playing Store (Broman, 1982)

If a store has been set up for classroom play, tape a penny on each item to be sold. One child is storekeeper; the others buy items for one penny each. As soon as this is understood, put different amounts of pennies on the items, which will then need to be matched by the customers.

IX. Measuring Ourselves

Have each child lie down while two others (or one child and the teacher) roll out an adding machine tape from head to foot and then cut it, to show the child's height. Write each child's name on the strip. Lay a strip of masking tape in a straight line on the floor as a base and then lay the children's tapes in correct order from smallest to largest. (It is easiest to begin with the smallest on one end and the largest on the other as the first two.)

X. Block Play

Take walks to bridges, buildings, and roads. Feel them, observe any apparent bricks, blocks, and so on. Ask children to recreate the structures with unit blocks.

XI. Graphing It All

Make bar graphs of eye colors, hair colors, number of people in family, favorite foods, and so on.

XII. Musical Chairs

Have enough chairs for everyone the first time through. As a chair is removed, announce that *one* chair is being taken away. After the music is played, announce that *one more* child has no chair. At this age it is important that children continue to play and that there be no winners or losers. Therefore, as the music begins again each time, continue to keep all the children walking. Each time the music stops, count the children now seated on the floor instead of on chairs.

XIII. Hand Rhythms

The teacher claps a very simple pattern with the hands. The children repeat it.

XIV. Number Songs

Choose songs to memorize that use counting: "Six Little Ducks," "Ten Little Indians," "The Ants Came Marching." The youngest children will be learning sounds by rote; as they become a little older they can hold up their fingers or clap their hands on their knees as they count.

XV. Nature Walk

After a nature walk have children classify objects using free choice. After much experience with this self-initiated learning, they can be encouraged to try classifying by color, type of tree, large or small object, and so on.

XVI. Schoolyard Walk

Take children outside to count objects of their choice. Tell them to make hash marks on paper as they see each object. Large objects such as trees can be counted in a large area. Small objects such as rocks or marigolds should be confined to a small territory. The name of the object may be dictated to the teacher before the counting begins.

XVII. Water Play

Using tubs of water and containers of various sizes and shapes, have children experiment freely to discover the capacities of the containers. Follow-up questions by the teacher may include: How many little bottles of water do you need to fill this large can? Which one of these holds more? and so on.

XVIII. Planting Seeds (Brown, 1982)

Plant four seeds in a flower pot or jar, counting them out and placing a card with the numeral on the side of the pot. As seeds germinate, count them to see if they equal four. If not, have children calculate how many did not come up and how many did. (This can be done with other numbers, of course, but keep the total number of seeds to a few.)

XIX. Obstacle Course I

Place furniture around the classroom as an obstacle course. Direct children as they move single file to walk *around* the chair, *under* the table, *over* the big block, and so on. As children follow the directions, they may repeat them.

XX. Obstacle Course II

Place furniture around the classroom as above. Put number cards on each piece in the order children should engage them. Choose from these or other means of achieving the course:

A. Challenge individual children to pass through the course: Hop over no. 1, crawl through no. 2, slide over no. 3.

B. Let children pass through any way they prefer, but announce their positions: I'm crawling through no. 1, now I'm hopping over no. 2.

XXI. Motion Patterns

Have children repeat and continue patterns such as two jumps, one clap, twirl about; one step in, one jump, one clap.

XXII. Animal Time

Use cards with large dots. Give each child one card with any number of dots from one to five. Whisper the name of an animal in each child's ear. Have the child count the number of dots and make the appropriate animal noise that many times. Ask others to guess the animal.

XXIII. Bean Bags

Make a rectangular cloth with felt geometric shapes glued on. Have each child throw a beanbag at the cloth, announcing in advance what shape he or she is aiming for. Play as a game without winners, simply giving children an equal number of turns.

XXIV. Bouncing Ball

Using a playground ball, have children sit in a circle with the teacher in the middle. Roll the ball to a child and say a number.

The child bounces the ball that number of times, counting out loud, and then rolls it back to the teacher.

XXV. Floor Shapes

Make large geometric shapes from butcher paper and tape them to the floor. Have children lie, stand, or sit on the shapes either individually or in pairs in order to "make" the shapes. Encourage them to say the shape names.

XXVI. Collages (Kamii, 1976)

Use beans of varying colors, yarn, and other collage materials. Give each child the same number of some of their collage objects. Collages should be made as desired. Then children can count their beans, yarn, and so on and observe the equal amounts.

XXVII. Shape Collages

Cut out geometric shapes from scrap paper. Expand on the usual square, rectangle, circle, and triangle repertoire to include pentagons, parallelograms, trapezoids, and so on. Collages may be made in a variety of combinations:

   A. Provide all one shape in different sizes and colors.

   B. Provide two familiar shapes and one new one. Mention the new name several times in informal conversation.

   C. Provide all one color and size, but several shapes.

The Teacher's Role

Children need as many opportunities as possible to invent their own mathematical understandings. As has been pointed out in this chapter, however, some intervention by the teacher is frequently necessary to tune children in to math in the environment and to get them started on their way. In this chapter's math activities, even those that are primarily play must usually have some teacher introduction.

Facilitating Distribution of Materials, Snack time, Measuring Ourselves, Hand Rhythms, Nature Walk, Obstacle Course II, and Collages work best as facilitated activities.

Instructing More teacher direction is needed for Picture Counting, Story Cards, Verses, Graphing It All, Musical Chairs, Schoolyard Walk, Planting Seeds, Obstacle Course I, Motion Patterns, Bouncing Ball, and Floor Shapes.

Providing Play Silver Sorting, Playing Store, Block Play, Water Play, Bean Bags, and Shape Collages are all activities that children can do freely without intervention.

Managing   These activities provide much variety. Some are designed for large or small groups and others for individual work or play. Additionally, some are definitely more noisy than others. Determine beforehand what category any activity belongs in, and then decide if new rules are required, if prior discussion is needed, or if the materials can simply be put out without comment.

Observing   This is a good time to make notations of children's understanding of mathematical principles. Try carrying a clipboard (recommended in other chapters also) on which you jot children's names and any special problems they have or any activities that they've obviously outgrown.

Evaluating   As you make notes on the clipboard, you'll be able to see if some activities are too easy for most children or too difficult. Keep materials out and available for children who haven't yet understood the activities, and, at the same time, provide new things for those who have advanced.

Reflecting and Planning   Think about the amount of mathematical experiences in your classroom in relationship to other subject-area experiences. Be sure that children have continual opportunities to work with mathematical ideas and plan for new ones as they outgrow the old.

PRIMARY UNIT: IT'S ABOUT TIME

It's a matter of survival for young children to learn to tell time, read a calendar, and learn the sequences of events. Yet despite the demands for these skills in everyday life, the concepts underlying them are not fully understood by children until their thinking is well into the concrete operational stage. For a number of Piagetian tasks involving an understanding of time, children are about 9 years old before they can move from trial and error to a logical approach for problem solving. Clock time can be confusing; even through the primary grades many children believe that when they do an action quickly, the clock also moves quickly. Sequences of events are not always understood; some children believe that a child who is actually younger may be older simply because she is larger.

For most of the primary years, then, children's concepts of time are gleaned on an intuitive or trial-and-error basis. By the third grade, many children will be attaining a logical ability when working with concepts of time. The activities suggested for this unit are appropriate for children at either the trial-and-error or the beginning logic stages.

Anticipated Outcomes

I *Student behavior:* As a result of this unit students will be able to:
   A Place days of the calendar in sequence
   B Differentiate days, months, and seasons
   C Identify hours and minutes that indicate regular daily events
   D Use sand timers and stopwatches as timing devices
   E Construct simple graphs dealing with time
II *Student understanding:* As a result of this unit students will understand that:
   A Months are longer than days and days than hours, etc.
   B Historical events can be placed in sequential order
   C It is not the same time everywhere
   D Time can seem to move slower or faster than it really does

The activities in this unit do not need to be done in the order in which they are listed. They can be introduced as a part of study in other subject areas or as children express a need or curiosity to learn. The curriculum web for this unit is shown in Figure 5-2.

Activities

I. Calendar Time Line
Fold a long strip of butcher paper in half, lengthwise. Break up a wall calendar into individual months and glue each in sequence on the strip. Place this time line on the wall at child height and X off each day as it occurs. Leave a space under each month so children can write or dictate highlights of each month as they occur.

II. Matching and Reading
Laminate a 1-month calendar. Cut a second, identical calendar into pieces and laminate each numeral and the name of the month. Children work with this activity in sequence:
   A. Build the cut-up calendar on top of the whole one.
   B. Build the cut-up calendar to the side of the whole one.
   C. Build the cut-up calendar on its own and use the whole one as a check when finished.

III. Personal Calendar
Provide each child with a photocopy of a calendar for personal use. At the beginning or ending of each day, have children mark off

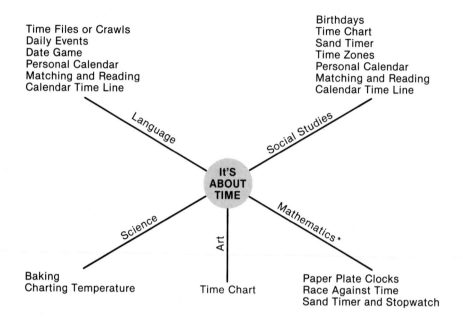

Time Files or Crawls
Daily Events
Date Game
Personal Calendar
Matching and Reading
Calendar Time Line

Birthdays
Time Chart
Sand Timer
Time Zones
Personal Calendar
Matching and Reading
Calendar Time Line

Language

Social Studies

IT'S ABOUT TIME

Science

Art

Mathematics *

Baking
Charting Temperature

Time Chart

Paper Plate Clocks
Race Against Time
Sand Timer and Stopwatch

*All activities are mathematics–based. These are not integrated with other subjects. Note that some activities are listed twice because they are integrated into more than one area of the curriculum.

FIGURE 5-2

the day and note the number of days completed or yet to be completed in the week or month. As an additional aid, the teacher can verbally stress terminology such as, "Today is Monday, the second of October."

IV. Date Game (Day, 1983)

On sturdy tri-wall or other board, mount three pockets made with envelopes. Label them: Day, Month, Season. Make several appropriate word cards for each. Have children shuffle and sort them. Self-correcting identification can be placed on the back of each card.

V. Paper Plate Clocks

Make a collection of clocks from paper plates by placing numbers in appropriate places using marking pens or glued-on stencils. Cut clock hands from tagboard and fasten with a paper fastener. Have children explore the clocks informally, comparing times to the classroom clock or "setting" them for future events, such as music class or lunch.

VI. Time Zones

On a large map of the United States, draw time zone lines, or emphasize them with a marker if they are already there. Using paper plate clocks, set one at a "correct" time and ask the children to set the others at their appropriate times to match.

VII. Daily Events

Below the classroom clock, place a paper plate clock for each of the day's events. Set the clock at the appropriate time and label below with the activity. Children read both the label and the classroom clock for an accurate comparison.

VIII. Baking

During any cooking project that requires timed cooking or baking, set a paper plate clock to the time when the food will be ready. Place it under the classroom clock for accurate reading and comparison.

IX. Race Against Time

When it is clean-up time, challenge students to do a fast job by setting a paper plate clock to the desired finish time.

X. Sand Timer

Children can be challenged, or can challenge each other, to see how many times they can run the width of the playground, bounce a ball, hop, and so on before the sand runs out. To encourage cooperation, divide children in pairs for clean-up or arithmetic drills, and so on.

XI. Sand Timer and Stopwatch

Have children use a simple stopwatch to see how many items can be done in a minute; an example is how many simple addition problems. In a quieter mood, children can observe the sand timer and use the stopwatch to see how long it takes to fill the bottom. Repeated experiences will give an understanding of consistency.

XII. Time Flies or Crawls

Ask children to sit in silence. After a minute, stop, but don't tell them how long they sat in silence. Then ask them to talk to the children around them and time that for a minute. Discuss which activity they thought lasted longer and then explain that they were equal. Discuss the way our feelings can trick us into thinking that time moves faster or slower.

XIII. Time Chart

When studying any historical sequence, post a long sheet of butcher paper on the wall. On separate sheets, draw (or cut out) pictures of historical figures and/or events. Discuss their chronological order, place them in correct order, and glue them to the chart. (Children will probably not be able to make the accurate divisions of a real time line.)

XIV. Charting Temperature

On chart paper, write the days of the month across the top. Down the left side of the paper, list degrees in 5-degree increments using temperatures most likely to be experienced at the time of year. Place a dot in the correct square on the grid and, as the days progress, connect the dots with a marking pen.

XV. Birthdays

On chart paper, write the names of the months across the top. Have children paste on colored-paper squares (starting at the bottom) to show how many were born in each month, thus creating a bar graph.

The Teacher's Role

Over many centuries, various methods have been invented to keep track of time. It is only since the industrial revolution, however, that people have become so thoroughly governed by it. For primary-grade children, the whole concept is one of novelty and interest, but it can also be difficult to grasp. Be sure to keep the activities positive and don't feel obligated to force time concepts on children that they're not ready for yet.

Facilitating   Calendar Time Line, Personal Calendar, Baking, Sand Timer and Stopwatch, and Birthdays will need some facilitation, although children can direct their own learning to a great extent.

Instructing   Time Zones, Daily Events, Time Flies or Crawls, Time Chart, and Charting Temperatures work best as directed learning.

Providing Play   Matching and Reading, Date Game, Paper Plate Clocks, Race Against Time, and Sand Timer lend themselves well to a play setting.

Managing   Most of these activities don't work as well when done by individuals as they do when children are in pairs or small groups. Find ways to group the children heterogeneously so that there will always be someone available who can assist the others.

Observing   These activities offer a good opportunity to observe informally using a clipboard. (See "Observing" in the preprimary math unit.)

Evaluating   Use some of the activities themselves as evaluation tools. For example, Personal Calendars offers an opportunity for you to see what each child understands of other activities related to calendar time. As children play with Paper Plate Clocks you will be able to see if other clock-time activities have been understood.

Reflecting and Planning   If your school is typical, your children will be expected to achieve rather specific goals in relation to understanding time, particularly clock time. As you observe their interactions with the materials and with each other, determine how far they have to go before they attain the required concepts. Then provide sufficient opportunities for them to play around with the materials, adding other materials as it seems helpful. The idea of "playing around" is advisable here. The topic of time is often quite difficult for children to understand. A lot of drills just frustrate them, but repeated playful interaction with time-related materials can help them toward success.

TO DISCUSS

1   Divide into groups according to the ages or grades of children with whom you are working. Describe your classroom situations and learning styles to one another. Brainstorm the greatest number of ways possible in which mathematics learnings might be incorporated naturally into the day.

TO DO

1   Refer to the experiment done by the Head Start teacher on page 146. Replicate this experiment with young children in your classrooms or your neighborhood. Compare your experiences.

2   Try to implement some of the ideas from the discussion above. Then discuss your successes and problems.

BIBLIOGRAPHY

Barrata-Lorton, M. (1976) *Mathematics their way.* Menlo Park, CA: Addison-Wesley.

Bell, F. (1980) *Teaching elementary school mathematics.* Dubuque, IA: Wm. C. Brown.

Broman, B. (1982) *The early years in childhood education.* Boston: Houghton Mifflin.

Brown, S. (1982) *One, two buckle my shoe.* Mt. Rainier, MD: Gryphon House.

Castellano, J., & Scaffa, M. (1974) *Unimath.* Silver Spring, MD: Lehman-Scaffa Art and Photography.

Castle, K. (1986) Conference update: 1985 NAECTE keynote address. *National Association of Early Childhood Teacher Educators Bulletin, 7(1):*1–2.

Choat, E. (1978) *Children's acquisition of mathematics.* Windsor, England: NFER Publishing.

Clements, D. (1985) *Computers in early and primary education.* Englewood Cliffs, NJ: Prentice Hall.

Colvin, S. (1987) *Introducing addition and subtraction symbols to first graders.* University of Florida: unpublished doctoral dissertation.

Commission on Standards for School Mathematics of NCTM (1988) *Overview of the curriculum and evaluation standards for school mathematics.* Reston, VA: National Council of Teachers of Mathematics.

Copeland, R. (1984) *How children learn mathematics.* New York: Macmillan.

Day, B. (1983) *Early childhood education.* New York: Macmillan.

Driscoll, M. (undated) *Research within reach.* Reston, VA: The National Council of Teachers of Mathematics.

Erikson, E. (1964) *Childhood and society.* New York: Norton.

Gelman, R. (1969) Conservation acquisition: A problem of learning to attend to relevant attributes. *Journal of Experimental Child Psychology, 7:*167–187.

Isenberger, K. (Ed.) (1950) *A half century of science and mathematics teaching.* Oak Park. IL: Central Association of Science and Mathematics Teachers.

Kamii, C., & DeVries, R. (1976) *Piaget, children and number.* Washington, D.C.: National Association for the Education of Young Children.

Kamii, C. (1982) *Number in preschool and kindergarten.* Washington, D.C.: National Association for the Education of Young Children.

Kamii, C., & DeClark, G. (1985) *Young children reinvent arithmetic.* New York: Teachers College Press.

Kennedy, L. (1986) A rationale. *Arithmetic Teacher, 33(6):*6–7.

Maffei, A., & Buckley, P. (1980) *Teaching preschool math.* New York: Human Sciences Press.

McLeod, G. (1971) An experiment in the teaching of selected concepts of probability to elementary school children. *Dissertation Abstracts International, 32A:*1359.

Osborne, A., & Nibbelink, W. (1975) Directions of curricular change. In J. Payne (Ed.), *Mathematics learning in early childhood.* Reston, VA: The National Council of Teachers of Mathematics.

Papert, S. (1980) *Mindstorms: Children, computers, and powerful ideas.* New York: Basic Books.

Piaget, J. (1966, 1932) *The moral judgment of the child.* New York: Free Press.

Piaget, J., & Inhelder, B. (1975) *The origin of the idea of chance in children.* New York: W. W. Norton.

Resnikoff, H., & Wells, Jr., R. (1973) *Mathematics in civilization.* New York: Holt, Rinehart & Winston.

Suydam, M., & Weaver, F. (1975) pp. 43–68. Research on learning mathematics. In J. Payme (Ed.) *Mathematics learning in early childhood.* Reston, VA: The National Council of Teachers of Mathematics.

Trafton, P. (1975) pp. 16–41. The curriculum. *Mathematics learning in early childhood.* Reston, VA: The National Council of Teachers of Mathematics.

Williams, E., & Shuard, H. (1970) *Elementary mathematics today.* Menlo Park, CA: Addison-Wesley.

chapter six

Science

The back-to-basics movement of recent years with its accompanying emphasis on skills attainment has often meant the disappearance of science from the curriculum. This has been true not only in the primary grades but often in nursery school and kindergarten as well. Yet science learning in the early years deals with what is most interesting, exciting, and appropriate for children to learn about: the real, tangible world around them. As children gain knowledge and appreciation of their environment, they become enthusiastic and even excited about the study of science.

In this chapter we discuss the "crisis" in science learning that now exists in the United States due to long-term neglect of the subject. On the more positive side, and in more depth, we explore the possibilities for science experiences with young children based on their developmental capabilities.

ONE DAY IN THE WOODS

It sometimes happens that teachers who have come through an educational system that has deemphasized science study are often unaware of the potential science offers for exciting learning. Yet science learning is such a natural part of everyday life that it occasionally appears, unbidden, as an unexpected and serendipitous experience. Such was the case in the experience described below. Here was a situation in which the teacher had the best of intentions for her children's progress, but it took a rabbit and a few messy construction workers to show her what broader possibilities existed.

It was in the early 1980s that Jan began her first teaching job in a small, southern town. Her county had recently become devoted to achieving higher scores on standardized tests, and so her induction as a new first-grade teacher included encouragement in using a back-to-basics approach in her classroom. Although Jan's teacher training had focused on a broader-based, child-oriented philosophy, Jan was too excited and nervous about doing well in her first job to be very concerned about any discrepancies in point of view.

Early on it was made clear to Jan by the other teachers that there was little or no time for such frills as social studies, science, art, or music until the year was well under way and the first round of testing had taken place. So Jan fell into the routine of the school, handing out dittoed seatwork and trying hard to keep the children up to schedule in the required texts and workbooks. One day, in a hall closet, she noticed a collection of science curriculums stacked in boxes against the wall. Jan wondered, a bit wistfully, if the children would ever have the opportunity to use the materials or if they were simply a reminder of a no-longer-valid approach to learning.

One break in the routine was often provided when Jan took the children to a small wooded area at the edge of the school property for their lunch. There they could listen to the wind in the trees and the water flowing in a nearby stream. An occasional rabbit or less frequent snake provided added interest. It did not occur to Jan that here were curricular opportunities until a change in the idyllic surroundings suddenly took place.

Across the street work began on a new, small shopping center. During their breaks the construction workers found refuge from the hot sun in the little forest. The children began to notice discarded aluminum cans and cigarette stubs. Then, more alarming changes took place as the creek began to fill with silt and discarded building materials. The rabbits were nowhere to be seen. One day it occurred to a few of the girls that the construction workers were directly to blame, not only for the refuse in the forest but for the disappearance of the rabbits as well. Jan, who had been fairly disturbed by the changing environment, suddenly became angry herself.

"Is there anything we could do about this?" she asked the class. "Would you like to talk to the construction workers and see if they could change some of the things they do?"

At the suggestion of a direct confrontation, the children immediately lost courage. However, the question prompted an involved discussion that finally concluded in a unanimous decision to write a letter—to be hand delivered by Jan. As Jan crossed the road to seek out the project's foreman, it suddenly and clearly occurred to her that by developing and acting on their concern for the environment the children had actually been engaging in both science and social studies learnings. And all during the lunch hour!

Fortunately, the foreman had a sense of humor and a genuine liking for children. Not only did the workers change their behavior at this request, but he even wrote a letter back to the children. Further, at Jan's request he came to school to talk to the children about the construction project and to explain the measures that were taken to clean up the environment as they worked. He told them that after the project was over the creek would be clear again and the rabbits would no doubt return.

A new idea occurred to Jan. The children could keep careful watch over the changes in the creek, keeping a journal as the weeks went by. They could also watch the changes in the seasons both in the plant life and the animals. Everything would be documented in writing. Additionally, anything that could be counted—ant hills, rabbits (or no rabbits), snakes, and so on—would be graphed over the weeks and months. As she began planning, the curriculum didn't look quite so dreary anymore.

WHY SCIENCE

In 1982, the National Science Teachers Association (NSTA) published a position paper that stated bluntly, "There is a crisis in science education." Although in 1985 the paper was updated and amended, this statement remained. Some of the problems the Association observed: Public appreciation of science education has declined although our personal and national welfare require that we appreciate more; many of the problems related to our quality of life are related to science-generated technology; public support for science education is decreasing just as the impact of science and technology is increasing; the United States is falling behind many other countries in the production of scientific and technological goods and services; and in science and technological careers there is an underrepresentation of women, minorities, and handicapped people. The NSTA has deplored the apparent fact that much of the U.S. population might be described as "scientifically illiterate." The goal for science education today should be, "to develop scientifically literate individuals who understand how science, technology, and society influence one another and who are able to use this knowledge in their everyday decision making."

If we think for a minute about the need to balance science and society, we can also see the need to integrate science and social studies in school learning. In the 1980s we finally began to understand the social and moral implications of the scientific decisions we make, and the NSTA believes that science should begin grappling with these issues at the earliest educational levels. The scientifically literate person, they argue, is one who has had a long educational experience in science and therefore "has a substantial knowledge base of facts, concepts, conceptual networks, and process skills that enable the individual to continue to learn and think logically."

For young children, the NSTA suggests that science "should be used to integrate, reinforce, and enhance the other basic curricular areas so as to make learning more meaningful for children." Daily opportunities for learning are recommended in which children will learn the scientific processes and inquiry skills while being given time to nurture their natural curiosity about the world. Appreciation for the world around them as well as an understanding of it will aid in the creation of adult citizens who are not only scientifically aware but societally responsible.

Historically, science education has had a moral dimension to it from earliest times, but for quite different reasons. For example, in the last half of the eighteenth century nature books were brought from England to the United States with the intention that children would glean from them a greater appreciation of God's handiwork. As one book review of the time stated:

> In infant and elementary schools generally these volumes will be found of great service, in awakening the mind to an early interest in the study of Life, that peculiar manifestation of creative Wisdom (Underhill, 1941, p. 26).

The study of science was generally a hands-on affair, with little time devoted to hypothesizing or studying theory. Partly because both Locke and Rousseau had been arguing for concrete learning and partly because it was felt that children would appreciate God's handiwork most if given the objects themselves to admire, the science curriculum for young children was, in today's terminology, developmentally appropriate.

It is important to remember that during the late 1700s education was primarily for those who could afford to pay for it. By the beginning of the nineteenth century, universal schooling had evolved and schools were becoming more and more crowded. Although the desire to teach science through the use of objects remained, the need to provide an education for many children at one time meant that discussion and pictures began to be more the norm.

Toward the end of the century an attempt was made to return to the use of objects, but the teaching methods promoted rote learning of isolated bits of information. With the advent of a new explosion in technological expertise and invention it became clear that something more was needed. An "elementary science movement" grew out of educators' concerns, and soon a structured, knowledge-based approach was recommended for children's learning.

A counterforce was at work, however, prompted by influential religious interests and by the fact that the economy was still largely agrarian. The "nature study movement" promoted nature study that would be unstructured and built on children's interests, emotional development, and imagination. For some, such an approach provided children with appreciation for their Creator and for the fruits of the earth, thus making them more content with rural life. For many early childhood educators, a further benefit seemed to be that the nature study approach was more in the spirit of Froebelian tradition and, thus theoretically acceptable.

In hindsight it isn't difficult to see that in the battle between these two opposing approaches to science education it was inevitable that the more structured, knowledge-based approach would win out in an increasingly technological society. The issue was not dead, but dormant, and it has erupted once again in recent years.

In the meantime, the elementary science movement provided the materials and methodology until the mid-1950s. Kindergartens were the site of experiential hands-on exploration while elementary children studied science topics from graded readers developed largely in the 1920s. Then in 1957 an alarming thing happened: The Soviet Union launched the world's first satellite and the entire United States asked how Soviet technology had become more advanced than ours. Part of the answer seemed to be the out-of-date school science programs and, shaken from its complacency, the science community responded. For the next 20 years, with funds provided by the federal government, projects were instituted ranging from course development to graduate degrees for science teachers. Of most importance to the early childhood field was the development of a variety of curriculums that school systems could purchase, all of which focused on and provided materials for carefully programmed hands-on exploration.

Throughout the second decade of federally supported programs, concerns for and problems arising from the civil rights movement replaced worries about Russian technological superiority. Science education took a back seat to study about human rights and, in 1976, when the National Science Foundation studied the status of science education in the United States, it was found that study of science in the elementary schools had virtually disappeared. By 1982, when the National Science Teachers Association wrote its first position paper stating that "there is a crisis in science education," the civil rights issue had been replaced by the back-to-basics movement. Science was not considered basic.

Noting that the devaluing of science education has produced a situation in which American schools no longer produce graduates sufficiently knowledgeable to take on scientific and technological jobs and that the populace as a whole has become, yet again, scientifically illiterate, the National Science Foundation (NSF) announced in early 1989 a $50 million development project for elementary education. The NSF, a federal agency, thus began a 4-year project to upgrade and expand elementary science study through the development of books, learning materials, software, and teacher training. One major intent of the project is to move away from text-oriented, read-and-recite learning; another is to integrate science with other curricular areas. The project is, in effect, an update of the federally funded programs of the 1950s and 1960s and is designed for children in kindergarten and above.

The current outlook for children in kindergarten and the primary grades is bright. Whether we teach these children or younger children in nursery school, it is important to have some basic philosophical views about curriculum and teaching. For young children through the primary years the National Science Teachers Association provides the following positions. Each is important to think about in planning for the teaching of science.

- *On the environment:* "NSTA supports activities that promote increased awareness and responsible educational use of terrestrial, aquatic, atmospheric, and human-designed components of the environment." Further, "firsthand interaction...is considered both relevant and necessary...to develop the kind of reasoned thinking that will result in responsible decision making regarding human/eco-system interaction."
- *On sexuality and human reproduction:* "We hold that education in this field is feasible at every curricular stage and can, therefore, begin at the earliest grade or level."
- *On the metric system:* "Because the metric system is used in all industrial nations except the United States...we urge that use of the metric system be integrated into all curriculum subjects and at every grade level."
- *On energy education:* "Energy education is a program that uses an interdisciplinary approach to help students use knowledge from the humanities, natural sciences, and social sciences to enhance their understanding of themselves and to benefit the quality of life and living for human beings....Decision making based on knowledge and facts with concern for questions of ethics, values, morals, and aesthetics is a major activity....The curriculum should utilize the community as a reservoir of issues for study as well as a source of enlightenment."
- *On responsibility for classroom animals:* "A teacher must have a clear understanding of and a strong commitment to the responsible care of living animals before making any decision to use live animals for educational study." Important considerations include being sure that the animals are healthy, that their quarters are spacious, that handling is gentle, food is adequate, and drinking water is clean. Unwanted breedings should be controlled.
- *On curriculum integration:* "Science should be an integral part of the elementary school program. It should be used to integrate, reinforce, and enhance the other basic curricular areas so as to make learning more meaningful for children."

• *On the overall focus of science learning:* "The focus of the elementary science program should be on fostering in children an understanding of, an interest in, and an appreciation of the world in which they live."

These positions taken by the NSTA refer in part to science curriculum and programs and in part to teachers. In the next section we focus on teachers and the ways in which these positions affect teaching.

THE TEACHER'S ROLE

Of the seven NSTA positions that have just been discussed, five (environment, sexuality and reproduction, energy, animals, and focus on appreciation) have elements that make them societally controversial in some way. Nevertheless, the NSTA argues that, "As professionals, teachers must be free to examine controversial issues openly in the classroom." At any level of schooling, the community at large and parents in particular may be reticent to grant such a degree of freedom to teachers. At the early childhood and primary levels, the issue may often be a conflict between the need for children to remain children and the need for them to have a better understanding of the world around them.

Good parent communication is an important place to begin dealing with the problem of controversy. Letters home explaining new units of study should be accompanied by invitations to come to school to discuss what is happening, to help with the program, or to simply observe. A second way to diffuse controversy is through curriculum integration. As an issue becomes part of a larger picture, it may lose its intensity.

The NSTA's support of "firsthand interaction" and inquiry learning fall within the theoretical framework of this textbook and provide the most meaningful way to learn about the potentially controversial issues. Teachers can take their children out into the community to learn about environmental issues such as keeping parks clean and cared for, rivers and lakes unpolluted, and neighborhoods fit for living in. Community resource people can provide the knowledge and incentive children need to become responsible, perhaps taking on class projects in the environment. (We saw this idea in action in our opening account of Jan's classroom.)

Curricular integration comes when the focus on citizenship that comes from these projects makes them a fit topic for the social studies. Art projects can draw attention to the children's concern as can short essays and stories, either dictated or written on their own. Even environmentally oriented folk songs—an American tradition—can be composed. When opportunities are taken to graph or chart changes and observations, math is also brought in as a curricular area.

When children learn to appreciate their environment through inquiry and firsthand experiences, they are participating in what might be called, historically, a combination of both the nature study movement and the elementary science movement. This is perhaps fitting for a postindustrial society when we are no longer enthralled by every technological advance, but rather receptive and wary, realizing that there are benefits to be had by technological advances but that we must be careful to appreciate the planet on which we live.

SCIENCE AND CHILD DEVELOPMENT

The developmental attributes children acquire that are related to science learning are, in some respects, similar or identical to those in other areas of learning. For example, the understanding of conservation, classification, and seriation and ordering are necessary to children's understanding of number; thus, we have discussed these attributes extensively in the mathematics chapter. As children develop their understanding of time and space they can participate more fully in science learning, but these developmental attributes are also related to the social studies and are discussed at length in that chapter. We shall not, then, give more than a brief review of each as it applies to science in particular.

Conservation, it will be recalled, is the ability to understand that two equal quantities or groups remain equal in amount or number even when they are transformed in space or position. In doing science experiments this understanding may be crucial if liquids are poured into containers of different sizes and shapes or when mud, sand, or playdough are used to understand the stability of weight and mass.

The discussion on classification in the mathematics chapter described the difficulties of preprimary science in focusing on more than one class at a time. Classes of animals were used as one example and these, of course, will relate to numerous science experiences, as will classification of plants. In other words, the nursery school child may see that there are red flowers and white flowers but have difficulty understanding that they are both roses or that one is a carnation but that both are in the flower family. The child in the primary grades should be more capable of grasping class inclusion and can participate in more complex science experiences.

Seriation and ordering of numbers or objects are as important to science as they are to mathematics. Very young children cannot place things in any kind of order, but by the nursery school years they can do so through trial and error. Logical thinking begins to appear anywhere from kindergarten through the second grade. Thinking in logical order is necessary to many kinds of science experiences, such as determining the processes that contribute to the successful growth of plants or understanding the importance of keeping the steps of an experiment in order.

Children's concepts about time were discussed in the social studies chapter in relation to the study of history and as the integrated unit for primary children in the mathematics chapter. The confusion that young children feel about the passage of history will be felt also in their attempts to understand prehistoric animals, extinction, and other aspects of science history. On a more immediate level, it will be difficult for preprimary children to do experiments that require many days' duration or observation over time.

The concept of space is related, in the social studies chapter, to the study of geography. There the discussion focuses on the need for young children to see geographical use of space as immediate, related to self, and three-dimensional. Children who have achieved concrete operations can begin to use two-dimensional materials such as maps and will have some idea of scale. As related to science learning, this growth in the concept of space means that primary-age children will enjoy making realistic drawings of their experiments and will be able to visually comprehend the changes and measurements that are made in them. Younger children will probably be more comfortable spending the same time with the objects themselves.

Other aspects of development are related most specifically to science learnings. A discussion of them will demonstrate why true scientific experimentation is impossible with very young children and that it must be carefully introduced in the most basic way in the primary grades. How children look at concrete objects is an important place to begin.

Concrete Information

At the preoperational stage, children understand objects by physically handling them, turning them over to see all sides, and feeling the differences in surface. Objects that present optical illusions or those that look different from different perspectives cause confusion. However, concrete operational children can take varying viewpoints in stride because they aren't so bound by their perceptions.

Yet concrete operational children have their own limitations. Although they can see varying viewpoints and physical relationships, they have a hard time theorizing about possibilities. If given an experiment in which they must find possible solutions to a problem, they will probably assume that the first solution they find is the only one. For an example of this phenomenon, note the behavior of Timmy in the next section.

Isolating, Controlling, and Testing Variables

In doing science experiments, the manipulation of variables is often a necessary capability. A graduate student in child development once used his three children, ages 5, 8, and 13, to test this capability and his description of the results provides a good illustration of the way children develop.

Five identical clear, plastic bottles were placed in a row with each one filled with its own clear liquid (sulfuric acid, water, hydrogen peroxide, sodium thiosulfate, and potassium iodide). Two small open dishes each held a clear liquid also (water in one, a combination of the sulfuric acid and hydrogen peroxide in the other). As each child was called into the kitchen, the father added just a little potassium iodide to the open dishes and they both watched while one of the liquids turned greenish yellow. The child was then told to try to duplicate the color by mixing as he or she desired. Each child took a different approach illustrative of his or her developmental levels:

Janie (age 5): After staring silently for a few moments at the open dishes she murmured, "It's gotta be magic." Her father assured her that it wasn't, and Janie began a random selection of containers, from which she poured and mixed, with increasing frustration. Finally, she pushed the experimental container away from herself, announced, "I'm too little for this," and departed in disgust.

Timmy (age 8½): After observing his father, Timmy began by combining water and sodium thiosulfate. His father asked how he chose them and he answered incongruously, "If I knew what they were I'd probably figure it out." For a time he tried various combinations, realizing aloud that he might have already done some of them. Finally, he combined the sulfuric acid and hydrogen peroxide and got a faint yellow. His father suggested that a third liquid might be in order and suddenly Timmy remembered seeing him add the potassium iodide. He watched in great satisfaction as the proper color appeared and excitedly declared, "I did a sinetific expermint!"

Audra (age 13): Audra began by adding the potassium iodide to each of the liquids in order. When nothing happened she exclaimed, "Wait, maybe it could take three mixtures or all five." She then mixed all five together and expressed disappointment that it didn't "at least turn a light *shade* of yellow." Audra then wished she had a piece of paper to organize her efforts, but turned down her father's offer of one. She then tried to remember which combinations she had made as one by one she attempted to replicate the correct color. At last the correct combination was stumbled upon.

Looking back at the efforts of the three children we see that Janie's attempts were primitively random, that Timmy was vaguely aware that some kind of system was possible but acted as randomly as Janie, and that Audra had yet to reach a truly formal operational stage in which she could methodically isolate, control, and test the variable. It should be obvious from this illustration that science experiences that require systematic manipulation of this sort are beyond the capabilities of younger children.

Rules, Procedures, and Models

In order to accomplish scientific experiments in the fullest sense, it is necessary to set up procedures, develop theoretical models, and create rules for handling objects or situations.

One Saturday, Richard (age 15) discovered some large, half-dead batteries in the trashbin behind a nursing home. Always one for scavenging and experimenting, he took them home and carefully, methodically, and with some creativity analyzed the properties and uses of the batteries, and then experimented with some new ways to use them. It wasn't long before one of the neighbor boys, Buddy (age 13), came by and joined in the experimentation. Buddy worked systematically and methodically following Richard's lead, with no apparent interest in doing the original research. When Buddy's little brother Wilson (age 8) came looking for him, he, too, got caught up in the spirit of invention. His participation, however, was limited to observation and occasional gofer jobs as new materials were needed. The next day, quite on his own, Wilson repeated the processes of the day before as well as his memory would serve him.

Here it can be seen that a child of primary-grade age can take part in scientific processes if there are strong models for him or her to follow. Wilson was quite content in this case to follow the lead of others but would not have known, much as Timmy (in our last section) did not know, how to create the processes on his own. If we were to add a preschool child to this account, he or she would more than likely have no interest in the processes at all. The preschool child, if drawn by a desire to be with the other children, might, however, enjoy doing some of the mundane, decisionless work involved.

Causality

To carry out science experiences with real understanding it is necessary for children to grasp logical cause and effect beyond the early childhood dependence on animism, artificialism, or magic as explanations of various phenomena. Piaget explains *animism* as being the belief that things, such as objects in nature, act the way they do because they want to. (The sun might set because it's tired.) *Artificialism*, Piaget says, is the belief that God or man has made the entire world and its contents in human fashion. (God might be seen as both creator of wind and inventor of sailboat building so that the wind might be enjoyed.) The concept of *magic* is used by children to link cause and effect. (When Susan was 6 she saw her first shooting stars and assumed that they must have sent the tooth fairy who, shortly afterward, flew in her window and left 25 cents under her pillow.)

In the primary years, some children will still occasionally lapse into such explanations when there seem to be no others available. For the most part, however, they are beginning to understand scientific causality if concrete materials are present.

Transformation

Perhaps one reason that small children have a tendency to believe that changes may be caused by magic is that they are unable to see transformations taking place. They can focus on the beginning and on the end, but the change process eludes them until they are in the primary grades. The story is told (Forman & Kuschner, 1983) of a teacher who showed a 4-year-old boy a caterpillar and an anesthetized butterfly. The butterfly, she told him, used to be a caterpillar. The child was completely confused and no doubt wondered how the apparently dead butterfly could ever have been a caterpillar—perhaps even that caterpillar—when the caterpillar was still alive and in its caterpillar state. Children this young do not have the capability to imagine what transformations might have taken place unless given the opportunity to witness them firsthand and at a speed that helps them make sense of the world.

Throughout our discussion of children's development in science-related concepts, young children can be seen trying to make sense of their world. Logical thought is beyond possibility for the very young and so they rely on their ability to invent answers that seem quite sensible to them at the time. With experience and maturation of thought, it becomes possible in the primary years to drop most of the reliance on fanciful explanations. With guidance and concrete experiences some logical thought is possible in science learnings. In choosing activities for the science curriculum, it thus becomes essential to help children sort out fantasy from reality, to observe how phenomena change, and to present all activities in the most concrete way possible.

In the hectic rush to attain higher scores on standardized tests, it is often science that gets left by the wayside, particularly in the primary grades where learning to read is a major curricular focus. Based on observation and work with children, however, it has been shown that the confusions about causality, natural phenomena, animism, and so on may not be dropped through simple maturation (Howe, 1975). What is needed is experience coupled with maturation, or children may not progress in their scientific thinking as they could. It is important to consider the long-term implications for children who are not provided with this aspect of their education.

THE SCIENCE CURRICULUM

If a school's science curriculum were to be evaluated, what criteria might be used? The National Science Teachers Association (Mechling & Oliver, 1983a) suggests four criteria, each of which relates to the early years in important ways.

1. The first criterion is "a balanced emphasis among the life sciences, earth sciences, and physical sciences" (p. 6). Appropriate experiences are possible for young children in all these areas just as they are for older students. Life sciences, for example, include biological studies, and for young children the opportunity to learn more about the lives of the plants and animals that inhabit the world around them is always exciting. Ecology is a natural follow-up as children learn about the interactions between plants and animals and the earth itself. Further explorations in geology teach children to understand the differences in various earth forms and to observe formations firsthand. Even physics and chemistry are not beyond the capabilities of small students. For example, in everyday classroom life children learn about speed, balance, gravity, and simple machines. Chemical properties begin to be understood as children observe changes made during cooking experiences. All the varied sciences have application to the lives of young children and, when presented to them in an appropriately concrete way, provide children with an interesting, even exciting way to learn.

2. The second criterion for a good science program is that curriculum materials "include a study of problems which are relative to us now and in the future..." (p. 6). Among the topics suggested by the NSTA are some that are appropriate for use with young children: air and water pollution, energy production, perhaps even world hunger. The classroom experience that opened this chapter demonstrates the ability of children to understand in a concrete way the implications of mistreating the environment. The primary unit for this chapter is directly concerned with helping children understand the need to face the problems we must deal with in the environment; the preprimary unit indirectly does the same.

3. A third criterion for a good science curriculum according to the NSTA is that materials "encourage children to explore, discover, and find answers for themselves rather than telling them how things turn out..." (p. 7). In this book we have frequently discussed the need for children to discover the world through concrete experiences. Numerous studies have shown that children learn more when given the opportunity to learn in this way. Mechling and Oliver (1983) extensively reviewed the literature on this topic. In their review of twenty studies that focused on general academic achievement, it was found that classes who had activity-oriented science learning produced percentile scores far higher than classes that were textbook-oriented. Another thirteen studies looked at children's progress in science process skills, and the results showed that children who had been taught in hands-on programs scored 18 to 36 points higher than did the children who had textbook-based curriculums. Even writing and math skills can benefit from an activity-based program. Their review of thirty-one studies showed that children who participated in activity-based science programs scored up to 8 percentile points higher than did the children in textbook-oriented classes. Last, but certainly not least of these issues, is the attitude children bring to the study of science. Another review of twenty studies showed that children had more positive attitudes toward science in general and even toward themselves when they were in activity-based programs. Scores were up to 20 percentile points higher.

Obviously, the advantages of learning science by discovering, by inquiring, and through firsthand experiences are great, both academically and psychologically. Almost three decades ago Jerome Bruner (Carin & Sund, 1970) summarized the advantages of this kind of learning with four basic points, all of which can be justified by the research just reviewed. First, he argued that this kind of learning produces an increase in intellectual potency; we have seen that in the many studies cited above. Second, Bruner said, that with discovering and inquiring there is a shift from extrinsic to intrinsic rewards; the last group of studies argues for this conclusion. He pointed out that children will learn the heuristics of discovery; the research reviewed above shows that hands-on study is more effective than text-oriented study in helping children learn how to discover new ideas in science. Fourth, Bruner argued that discovery learning provides an aid to memory processing; the academically oriented tests described above required children to do at least some memorizing, giving validity to his argument.

The impulse to tell children how things turn out is sometimes strong, particularly when teachers feel pressured to keep up with a text or the need to demonstrate an experiment in order to do it "right." The evidence is, as we have seen, that the other way around has more positive results.

4. The fourth and final NSTA criterion for a good science curriculum is that children be provided with experience in the scientific processes: "observing, measuring, predicting, inferring, classifying, recording and analyzing data, formulating and testing hypotheses, and designing and conducting experiments..." (p. 7). At the youngest ages not all these processes may be appropriate, but they may be picked up as children mature. Neuman (1978), for example, suggested that preprimary children should focus on four: observing (through using the five senses), classifying (through sorting objects), quantifying (through comparing, counting, and measuring), and communicating (through verbally shared findings).

Some helpful suggestions for introducing young children to the scientific processes come from Richards and Holford (1983):

1. Help students to raise questions and to put questions into a form which can be answered by a fair test

2. Encourage children to predict and say what they expect will happen

3. Prompt closer and more careful observations

4. Help students to see ways in which their tests are not fair and ways in which these can be made fairer

5. Encourage students to measure whenever it is useful

6. Help students to find the most helpful way of recording their evidence so that they can see the patterns in their observations

7. Encourage children to think about their experiences, to talk together, and to describe them to others

8. Help children to see the uses they can make of their findings (Adapted from p. 57)

Most important, Richards and Holford argue, is that children in the primary grades talk and work together so that they can plan, investigate, and develop their shared ideas as a group. This, of course, is counter to the textbook approach to learning science, but totally appropriate to the tendency of children in the primary grades to want to work with others.

One result of letting children explore the world firsthand and with less direction from their teachers is that through the natural learning process more than science is included. We have already seen in a group of studies reviewed above that the implications for reading and math scores are positive. As we shall see in the next section, integrating science with the other areas of the curriculum provides a natural and effective way for young children to learn.

Science and the Integrated Curriculum

At the beginning of this chapter we met Jan, a first-year teacher who despaired of breaking out of her school's back-to-basics routine until she realized that it was already beginning to happen. When her first-graders took an interest in maintaining the integrity of the environment, they combined social studies and science. As they observed the habits of animals they engaged in a scientific process. Their letter to the construction workers was, of course, a language experience and, as a bit of social activism, social studies. To all this Jan planned to add record keeping over the ensuing weeks (language) and graphing (math). Only the arts were missing from Jan's plans and, with some extra effort, she could have included them, too. A simple song might have been written, for example, or perhaps a very short play. Leaves and rocks could be used for artistic rubbings; berries, bark, and leaves could be the basis of homemade dyes. Although Jan didn't do these things, she definitely took a large step in the direction of integrating the class curriculum through an everyday sort of experience.

It is the position of the National Science Teachers Association that such integration is an important way for science to be learned effectively and that, working in reverse, science can easily be incorporated into other subject areas (Mechling & Oliver, 1983b). Here are some suggestions the NSTA makes for integration.

1. "Science and math can and should be integrated because they are interdependent" (p. 22). For example, when plants are grown, there are opportunities for measurement. Temperatures are read and then graphed over time. Objects collected from nature walks are counted and classified. Objects are weighed, and rainfall is calculated and graphed. An NSTA curriculum committee has been quoted as saying, "Mathematics is the language by which one describes the order in nature and which in turn leads to a clearer understanding of that order" (p. 24).

2. Art can be derived from science as well. The NSTA suggests beginning with the obvious, but often overlooked, schoolyard. Here trees, leaves, patches of lawn, bushes, and pavement offer children opportunities to observe, interact, draw, paint, sculpt, and so on.

3. Making musical instruments in the classroom provides children with an opportunity to learn scientific principles while having a musical experience. Further, they can compose songs about countless science experiences.

4. When science and reading are integrated, the former may go a long way toward improving the second. The NSTA argues that unless children have real-life experiences they will have no knowledge base about which to read. Children must have the opportunity to hear and use language through direct exploration: "Definitions of words are invented after children have had experience with the objects or concepts that the words represent" (p. 33). As mentioned earlier, research has shown that experiences in activity-based science actually raise reading scores. Additionally, science can provide motivation for children who are having difficulties in reading and other language arts. In the primary years there will be times when science materials need to be read, and if used wisely, this activity can provide a bridge between experiences or motivate a visually-oriented child to want to learn more.

5. Science, as we have seen in Jan's story, goes hand-in-hand with social studies also. In previous centuries society's influence on the physical earth was less noticeable because society was, simply, smaller. Now however, "Science and technology influence every aspect of our lives. They are central to our welfare as individuals and to the welfare of our society.... The natural sciences and social sciences cannot be divorced from one another. The study of human activities, coupled with climate, vegetation, soils, and landforms, makes social studies a truly integrated topic" (p. 39).

Truly, science is appropriate for integration into the curriculum as well as having an importance of its own. Our welfare as a civilized culture depends heavily on the advances of science. At the same time, we have learned that science can be (and has been) used to negative effect. As world population grows and science discoveries increase, it will become increasingly necessary to combine our science knowledge with high ethical standards. This combination can and should begin at the earliest ages. The science units that follow focus on this kind of integration.

PREPRIMARY ACTIVITIES FOR INTEGRATING SCIENCE

Most very young children are fascinated by nature. They take delight in the colors and shapes of flowers, the changing scenery of the sky, and the antics of animals. It takes little encouragement to make them aware of the beauty around them. Without that encouragement, many children eventually become oblivious to much of nature as they are increasingly lured away by friends, television, neighborhood games, and long hours at school. The purpose of the activities that follow is to heighten children's awareness of the natural beauty around them. The appreciation of nature they develop at this age can be continued and augmented by the environmental awareness and activism espoused by the primary unit that follows next.

Although other scientific processes are used in these activities, observation is used most prominently. The activities can be taught as a curriculum unit or as individual activities integrated throughout the year into the broader curriculum. The curriculum web for this unit is shown in Figure 6-1.

Activities

I. One Beautiful Thing

Use the entire schoolyard or mark off a permissible search area. Ask children to find one beautiful thing and bring it to you. When the collection is complete, return the objects to their owners and have the children sit in a circle. One by one have each child explain why the found object is beautiful and then share it with another child as a gift. (Only one gift for each child of course!)

FIGURE 6-1

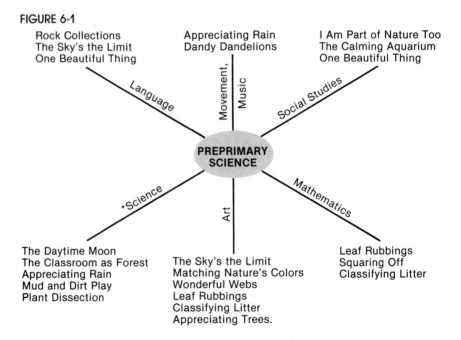

Rock Collections
The Sky's the Limit
One Beautiful Thing

Appreciating Rain
Dandy Dandelions

I Am Part of Nature Too
The Calming Aquarium
One Beautiful Thing

Language — Movement, Music — Social Studies

PREPRIMARY SCIENCE

*Science — Art — Mathematics

The Daytime Moon
The Classroom as Forest
Appreciating Rain
Mud and Dirt Play
Plant Dissection

The Sky's the Limit
Matching Nature's Colors
Wonderful Webs
Leaf Rubbings
Classifying Litter
Appreciating Trees.

Leaf Rubbings
Squaring Off
Classifying Litter

*All the activities are science-based. These are not integrated with other subjects. Note that some activities are listed twice because they are integrated into more than one area of the curriculum.

II. The Sky's the Limit

On a day when there are fast-moving cumulus clouds, have every-one lie down looking skyward. (This may well be the children's first opportunity to play the age-old game of finding shapes in the clouds.) Focus the discussion on the beauty of the shapes and sky colors also. After returning to the classroom, have children use crayons to draw white clouds on light blue paper or shape cotton and glue it on the paper.

III. Matching Nature's Colors

Take a tray containing paints in the primary colors (as well as white, black, and brown) outside to the garden or woods. In empty pots let children attempt to mix colors that match those they ob-serve in individual plants. Follow up with paintbrushes and art pa-per attached to clipboards. While still in the environment, have children paint as directed.

IV. The Calming Aquarium

Psychologists have long recommended aquariums for their calming effect. Permit children to simply sit and gaze at the fish and other aquarium life whenever they need to take a break from interacting with others. Rules for caring for the fish should be given to the children as the aquarium is introduced into the classroom. As a group they can decide the rules for observation.

V. Wonderful Webs

Before school each morning check the grounds for spiderwebs wo-ven the night before. Teach children to keep a respectful distance but gather around close enough to observe. If the group is small, children may want to watch the spider and its web for some time. Although most young children cannot achieve much in the way of representational art, a web with a single spider (and possibly a vic-tim) may emerge in drawing.

VI. Leaf Rubbings

This well-known art project becomes a science and math learn-ing when children are asked to find two leaves whose shapes and/or sizes are different from each other. Most children will be able to tape the leaves to a piece of paper on their own, tape a second sheet of paper over the top, and choose any color crayon to make a rubbing by using the side of the crayon. Cut the tape and discard the sheet with the leaves, unless the children want to keep that, too.

VII. Squaring Off

Have children choose any measuring stick they prefer, whether it is something from the classroom or a stick dropped by a tree. Assist them in using their measuring stick to lay out a straight line and then, with another small stick, to draw the line in the dirt. Repeat on three other sides to make a square. Ask each child to observe his or her own plot for a few minutes and then share with others interesting observations about insect life or plants.

VIII. The Daytime Moon

Keep track of the moon's orbit and, when it is in the sky during the daytime, take the children outside to observe it. This may assist them in growing out of such misconceptions as the idea that the sun goes to bed and the moon wakes up at night.

IX. Classifying Litter

Take a walk through the nearest park or wooded area that is visited frequently by people. Give each child a bag in which to put litter dropped by plants or by people. Returning to the classroom, classify the entire collection into two piles. Discuss the implications for the beauty of the area when people leave litter behind. Collages can be made with the natural litter. Some older children may be interested in adding one piece of litter made by people to the collage and then dictating a story about its ugliness.

X. Dandy Dandelions (adapted from Nicklesburg, 1976)

If your schoolyard is beset with dandelions, make full use of them. Pull growing plants apart to see how the flowers are constructed. When the pappus (seed parachute apparatus) has appeared, have the children blow the seeds away and observe where they land. Uproot a plant and admire its strong root, a major factor in promoting its success as a plant. Make whistles from the stems by holding them in front of the mouth and blowing across the top. Have children dance as if they were dandelions swaying in the wind or as if they were the pappus blowing away.

XI. Rock Collections and What to Do with Them

Children often begin collecting rocks because they admire their beauty. When this happens, start a classroom rock collection in the science or nature corner. Hammer one of each type of rock to see which are soft and will break up. (They may wish to reclassify as the results are observed.) Have older children search in rock reference books for pictures of similar examples. Search for fossils in the rocks. Use a magnifying glass to observe differences in each group. Have children dictate a story about what they have observed. Place the written story on the wall above the rock collection.

XII. The Classroom as Forest

From the ceiling hang assorted plants as there is room. Be sure to hang them low enough that the children are aware of them, even if it means that adults must carefully wend their way through the forest. Bring them down as necessary for the children to water. Have a class discussion about the way having the plants in the room makes the atmosphere different.

XIII. Appreciating Rain

When a rainstorm is coming, small children (like animals!) often respond to the change in atmosphere and their behavior changes. Make use of this time. Have them sit still and sense the change in the temperature and the feeling of the air, listen to the wind, smell the earth as the first drops hit, dance as if the wind is pushing them, and simply sit and stare out the window at the rain. If the storm is not electrical, the weather is warm, and children have raincoats, take a walk in the rain. Splash in puddles, feel the rain on the face, listen to the differences in sound as it hits varying surfaces. Observe the effect it has on different plants.

XIV. I Am Part of Nature Too

When having a picnic outdoors, practice leaving the environment as clean or cleaner than when it was entered. When walking anywhere where footprints are left, observe their sizes and shapes. Emphasize that footprints are the only things people should leave behind when they hike.

XV. Appreciating Trees

Sit very quietly under a group of trees, or choose one special tree. Notice the birds and squirrels that regard the tree(s) as their habitat. Feel the bark of the tree(s) and discuss the texture. Follow up by making rubbings on sturdy paper. Join hands around individual tree trunks and count how many children it takes to circle each one: discuss which is larger, which is smaller. Collect, compare, and make rubbings from the leaves as in activity VI.

XVI. Mud and Dirt Play

Section off a small area outdoors that is just for exploring dirt and mud. Equip it with small sprinkling cans, small cans of water, and assorted spoons. Have on hand old rubber boots to wear or (in warm weather, of course) go barefooted. Let children experiment with different textures, asking them occasional questions about their observations.

XVII. Plant Dissection

Provide a center in which children can pull plants apart to see how they are constructed. Have one of each type as a model that is off-limits to experimentation. Be sure that the plants you choose are nontoxic!

The Teacher's Role

In this collection of activities, more than in some other science units, there is quite a bit of teacher direction. When introducing children to nature it is important for safety reasons to keep close watch on what is happening. Nevertheless, two activities are devoted strictly to play.

Facilitating   Some teacher direction is needed, but children should be left free to experiment as soon as they can in The Sky's the Limit, Matching Nature's Colors, The Calming Aquarium, Leaf Rubbings, Squaring Off, Classifying Litter, Dandy Dandelions, Appreciating Rain, and Appreciating Trees.

Instructing   You will probably need to remain with the children, directing most of their learning in One Beautiful Thing, Wonderful Webs, The Daytime Moon, Rock Collections, and The Classroom as Forest.

Providing Play   Mud and Dirt Play and Plant Dissection are designed as free-play activities. Matching Nature's Colors and The Calming Aquarium should turn into play experiences as children are left on their own.

Managing   For the play experiences, be sure to stay in the background, available if children need you or if you see that things are not going as they ought to. Try not to hover, however, so that children feel as though they are really on their own.

When you are about to go on a nature walk or related activities, role-play in advance the proper procedures and behaviors. It's actually fun to imagine discovering flowers (admiring but not touching them) or spiderwebs (observing them silently). During the actual activities, children can be reminded, with special signals such as a finger to the lips, about the correct behaviors.

Observing   Some small children have a tendency to act violently toward nature. Sometimes this is pathological, but usually they don't understand what they are doing because they are not clear about what is real and alive and what is a human-made toy. During science experiences, be sure to observe their behaviors well so that you can deal with children who need your help. Role-playing with individual offenders will usually terminate any problems. If not, a conference with parents may be in order.

Evaluating   Your observations will tell you whether children are developing a good relationship with nature or not. During storytime, choose some books that have nature elements in them and encourage open (but brief) discussion about the topics.

Reflecting and Planning   As you observe children in their interactions with nature and each other and as you listen to their responses to nature elements in stories, determine what gaps remain in their experience that are appropriate to fill during the current school year. See how this might be done in the context of thematic units you are planning, or make a nature experience part of the more stable parts of the children's daily schedules.

PRIMARY UNIT: OUR ENVIRONMENT IS CHANGING— ARE WE HELPING OR HURTING?

Even without our help the environment is always changing: Volcanos erupt, earthquakes realign whole communities, hills erode, and coastlines expand and contract. In more primitive times, human beings interacted with nature and its changes with a certain respect for the power of natural phenomena. But as societies have grown in size and knowledge, the human tendency has been to try to interfere and to grasp some of nature's power. In early Egypt building dams and other irrigation projects was a budding science; today, we build huge, sequential dams on ever larger rivers. In earlier centuries we walked or rode horses on trails that animals had created; today we have built extensive road systems over those same trails or have created roads in whatever directions provide convenience for us. To shelter our families and businesses we blast out hillsides, drain swamps, and create landfills. The list goes on. The growth of the technology that has made it possible to create so many changes has been so rapid that it is only in recent years that we have begun to be aware of what we are doing to the environment. Some changes are reversible, some are not. Some changes are benign, most are harmful.

  In recent years, various organizations and study groups have tried to warn us of the consequences of our actions. In order to slow the tide of irreversible harmful changes, it is important for children to learn at the earliest possible time that what they do to the environment affects more than themselves. During the primary years, children are developmentally ready to begin to look at the consequences of their actions. They are beginning to understand the concepts of conservation and reversibility. As they reach out in a social way to their community, they are also able to reach out in an environmentally responsible way.

This unit is designed to help children in the primary years understand that natural changes are taking place constantly, that some changes are positive for humans and some are negative, that some can be reversed and some cannot. Most important, a major purpose of this unit is to help children understand that they can have some effect on the condition of the environment and have a right and a responsibility to help others in the community understand also.

Anticipated Outcomes

I   *Student behavior:* As a result of this unit students will be able to:
   A Use conservation principles in caring for their environment
   B Identify irreversible changes
   C Take steps to increase others' awareness of change
II *Student understanding:* As a result of this unit students will understand that:
   A Some changes cannot be reversed
   B Human beings can make environmental changes for good or bad
   C The environment is continually changing
   D Even children can influence the conditions of the environment
   E Animals have special needs for survival
   F Plants have special needs for survival

The activities for this unit are divided into two sections: an awareness/informational section and an activist section. Activism should follow knowledge, but within each section activities may be done in any order or adapted to individual needs.

Activities to Increase Awareness of Change

I. Identifying Irreversible Changes (adapted from Peterson, Bowyer, Butts, & Bybee, 1984)

Make a class mural that demonstrates changes in nature that cannot be reversed. Use photos, drawings, or pictures from magazines to illustrate. Examples might be small animals that have grown

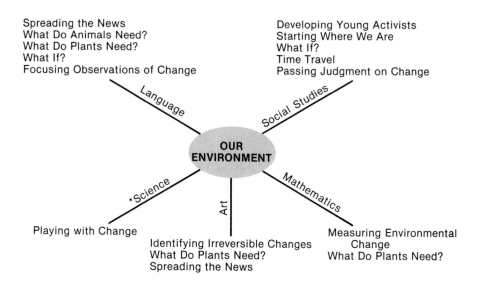

Spreading the News
What Do Animals Need?
What Do Plants Need?
What If?
Focusing Observations of Change

Developing Young Activists
Starting Where We Are
What If?
Time Travel
Passing Judgment on Change

Language
Social Studies

OUR ENVIRONMENT

Science
Art
Mathematics

Playing with Change

Identifying Irreversible Changes
What Do Plants Need?
Spreading the News

Measuring Environmental
Change
What Do Plants Need?

*All activities are science–based. This one is not integrated with other subjects. Note that some activities are listed twice because they are integrated into more than one area of the curriculum.

FIGURE 6-2

large, baby humans that have become adults, raw vegetables that have been cooked, milk that has come from the cow. Small objects can also be taped or tacked on the mural; worn-down pencils from the classroom and leaves that have turned brown are examples.

II. Measuring Environmental Change

Be alert to measurement opportunities. Use whatever measuring tools and system (English or metric) you are using in your math curriculum. Keep records of changes in temperature, size of melting ice cubes, length of worn-down pencils, height of a pile of writing paper or books, size of growing plants, and so on. These changes can be charted. One suggestion is to divide the chart into human-made changes and nature-made changes; this will increase awareness of societal responsibilities.

III. Passing Judgment on Change (adapted from Bybee, 1984)

Divide a chart into three columns labeled good, bad, and neutral. Each day children observe changes in weather, the natural environment, and the human-made environment both at home and at school. These are discussed as a class and entered in the appropriate column based on the class decision.

IV. Focusing Observations of Change (adapted from Bybee, 1984)

As part of any activity concerning change, divide children into small groups or pairs. Assign each team to observe and list changes according to a single word such as "color," "population," "environment," "habitat," "organisms," or "structure." This activity is best done outside if a natural environment for observation is available.

V. Time Travel

Choose a modern invention that children take for granted as part of everyday life. Research what was used to serve the same purpose in previous cultures. Determine which invention, resource, or change altered the environment more and in what ways. If irreversible changes were made, these should be noted. Changes can be charted according to centuries or by dividing between good, bad, or neutral changes or between reversible and irreversible changes. (It may well be discovered by the children that earlier societies also used the environment unwisely. Discussion may focus on our greater awareness today and the resulting increase in our need for responsibility.)

VI. What If?

Ask children to look at the long-range consequences of environmental change by writing about them. Individualized essays can be written, but more ideas may emerge from small group brainstorming. Present each child or group with a question at the top of a page. Some examples: "What would happen if all the water on earth got polluted?" "What would happen if all the dogs became extinct?" "What would happen if all the garbage dumps got filled up?"

VII. What Do Plants Need?

Purchase three small, flowered potted plants. Deprive one of light by placing it in a dark closet (but give it necessary water). Deprive a second one of water by placing it in sufficient sunlight and giving it no care. Deprive a third one of soil by pulling the plant from its dirt and placing it in a pot of water. Divide the class into three teams to draw before, during, and after pictures; to graph sizes of plants over time; and to write a diary of observations. Have a final discussion in which there is a focus on people's responsibility toward plants that come under their care.

VIII. What Do Animals Need?

Obtain several animals of different classes so that children can compare the needs of mammals to those of fish, reptiles, or birds. Introduce the animals one at a time, giving careful instructions for the care of each. After they are all in the classroom, divide the children into study teams to research the food and habitat needs of each animal and then determine if their needs could be better met.

Make changes as appropriate. Through discussion between groups, compare the needs of one class with the others. "What If?" essays may be written focusing on the consequences of each animal not having its needs met (see activity VI).

IX. Playing with Change

Create a center in which children can experiment to learn what changes are reversible and which are permanent. Some suggestions: making mud from dirt; mixing water that has had different shades of food coloring added; collecting magazine pages to cut up; trying to get toothpaste back into the tube; hammering soft rocks into dust. As you pass by, informally question the children about the implications of what they are finding.

Activities to Promote Active Environmentalism

X. Starting Where We Are

Have children help identify consumables used in the classroom. Discuss ways in which conservation efforts would be beneficial and then follow through. Some examples: Use both sides of paper when possible; use washable cotton towels in place of paper ones; if the thermostat is controlled in individual rooms, encourage children to wear sweaters and to keep the temperature turned down; never leave the drinking fountain on longer than necessary.

XI. Spreading the News

As children become aware and interested in conserving, they can make posters to be placed schoolwide. Short articles can be written for the school newspaper describing their conservation efforts. It may even be possible for the class to start a schoolwide conservation program.

XII. Developing Young Activists

Make students aware of human-made and natural environmental changes as described in newspapers and on television. Discuss whether the changes are good, bad, or neutral. If they are good, it may be appropriate to write a brief class letter of thanks. If they are bad, another kind of letter may be in order. If changes are local, there may be more the children can do. Second- and third-graders, for example, can be enthusiastic members of neighborhood clean-up campaigns. The important consideration is to be certain that the chosen tasks are suitable for young children.

The Teacher's Role

Children in the primary years are just beginning to be aware of harmful human-made changes within the environment. They are often idealistic and excited about what they can do to help (and sometimes judgmental about practices they see at home). Be sure to permit them to think of activities on their own that will keep their enthusiasm going.

Facilitating   In the following activities, children can largely manage on their own after some assistance from you: Identifying Irreversible Changes, Focusing Observations of Change, What If?, What Do Plants Need?, What Do Animals Need?, and Spreading the News.

Instructing   Measuring Environmental Change, Passing Judgment on Change, Time Travel, Starting Where We Are, and Developing Young Activists will work best when you direct the learning.

Providing Play   There is just one activity that is truly play in this unit, but keeping the Playing with Change center up during the entire unit will provide continual play possibilities. Be sure to change the materials frequently.

Managing   The enthusiasm young children generally develop for this kind of unit leads to work in small groups for many of the activities. They may enjoy working in teams, each one choosing to focus on its own specific interests. For greatest success, be sure that grouping of children is done heterogeneously across ability levels. Before beginning group projects as a whole, it is a good idea to let the entire class suggest two or three rules for smooth functioning and behavior. A brief discussion before new activities begin will help them remember what the rules are.

Observing   When children are working in groups it gives you an opportunity to observe their interactions with each other, noting who the leaders and followers are. Academic help can be given when groups need it.

Evaluating   The final three (activist) activities may be considered evaluative ones. If children are gaining interest in environmental activity, then they are learning to understand the needs of earth and society.

Reflecting and Planning   Invite children to reflect with you on the progress of what they are doing. Are there other things they would like to learn about? Are there new ways they would like to become more active? Would they like to call in outside experts to give them more ideas? Plan extensions together.

TO DISCUSS

1 Collect a number of books for very young children. Survey them to discover how many portray a fantasy view of natural events (sun rising, wind blowing, flowers growing, animals talking, and so on). Are there more that portray fantasy or more that portray reality? Discuss the implications for young children's understanding and cognitive growth. Will they become more confused than they already are about natural events? Should books such as these be saved for a time when fantasy and reality are sorted out in children's minds, or is it better to simply accept the idea of fantasy books for very young children?

2 Discuss ways in which science can become part of the general early childhood classroom day. Divide this discussion into two parts: preprimary and primary. Discuss what regular events and classroom (or outdoor) materials lend themselves to incorporation of science without actually taking time for formal science activities.

TO DO

1 Use this chapter or any science activities book. Find an activity that could be presented to children either as discovery learning or as a teacher demonstration. Experiment in one of the following ways:

   a Pair up with another student. Each choose one method of presentation and compare results in terms of student learning, enjoyment, and receptivity.

   b If you have access to two classes of similar age, try both yourself. Compare as in part a.

BIBLIOGRAPHY

Bybee, R. (1984) *Teaching about science and society.* Columbus, OH: Merrill.

Carin, A., & Sund, B. (1970) *Teaching modern science.* Columbus, OH: Merrill.

Craig, R. (1981) The child's construction of space and time, *Science and Children* November:36–37.

Forman, G., & Kuschner, D. (1983) *The child's construction of knowledge.* Washington, D.C.: National Association for the Education of Young Children.

Gardner, P. (1975) *The structure of science education.* Hawthorn, Australia: Longman.

Howe, A. (1975) A rationale for science in early childhood education. *Science Education, 59(1):*95–101.

Mechling, K., & Oliver, D. (1983a) *Characteristics of a good elementary science program.* Washington, D.C.: National Science Teachers Association.

Mechling, K., & Oliver, D. (1983b) *Science teaches basic skills.* Washington, D.C.: National Science Teachers Association.

Mechling, K., & Oliver, D. (1983c) *What research says about elementary school science.* Washington, D.C.: National Science Teachers Association.

Neuman, D. (1978) *Experiences in science for young children.* Albany, NY: Delmar.

Nicklesburg, J. (1976) *Nature activities for early childhood.* Menlo Park: Addison-Wesley.

NSTA Positions on Issues in Science Education. (1985, 1982). Washington, D.C.: National Science Teachers Association.

Peterson, R., Bowyer, J., Butts, D., & Bybee, R. (1984) *Science and society.* Columbus, OH: Merrill.

Richards, C., & Holford, D. (1983) *The teaching of primary science.* New York: Falmer Press.

Smith, R. (1981) Early childhood science education: A Piagetian perspective. *Young Children,* January:3–10.

Underhill, O. (1941) *The origins and development of elementary-school science.* Chicago: Scott Foresman.

_____ chapter seven

Social Studies

It is sometimes said that education for effective citizenship is, or should be, the school's primary function. Although any area of the curriculum can be adapted to this purpose, the social studies (being by definition about human beings in their societies) provide the most logical and easily developed source of citizenship curriculum. This chapter focuses on the use of the social studies as a means to citizenship education in the early years. Because young children learn best when they are actively involved, a major purpose of this chapter is to demonstrate that even the very youngest students can participate in their society, taking on some of the responsibilities of citizenship in a democracy.

The chapter opens with an example of children learning about another culture as a way to know themselves better. This is followed by a discussion of just what is needed in the schools for learning about citizenship: the teacher's role in promoting it, the qualities that need to be fostered in children, and the historical and philosophical support for letting children learn about citizenship actively. An in-depth discussion of child development related to the social studies is followed by a discussion of appropriate curriculum. Because active learning about democratic citizenship is the important underlying theme of this entire chapter, there is a final section devoted to practical suggestions for implementing democracy in the preprimary or primary classroom. The two teaching units that complete the chapter are both focused on citizenship as well.

OF COWBOYS AND INDIANS

Sometimes when we lack knowledge of our heritage and culture, a well-timed, interestingly presented course or class brings us both knowledge and appreciation. Other times, we can learn much about ourselves by comparing and contrasting our own culture with another. Either approach to learning—studying ourselves or making comparisons with others—can be effective at any age, from the early years through adulthood. The following story is an illustration of both methods being used simultaneously in one kindergarten class. As you read this story, note the very natural, perhaps unconscious, use the Native Americans made of an integrated curriculum. Their purpose was to teach an overview of their culture, not to break it down into lessons in art, literature, dance, and so on.

Trudi taught kindergarten in Oregon. One year, two of her students were Native American boys from two different Plains tribes. They had been adopted by Anglo-Saxon families who each hoped that its boy would develop an appreciation of his heritage. During that year a local coalition of Native Americans received a government grant to develop an awareness program for use in the elementary schools. Although the program was targeted for third grade and up, Trudi decided that interaction with the Native Americans would help provide self-esteem for the two boys and expanded cultural awareness for all the children. She invited the Native American group to work with her class and enthusiastically they agreed to bring their 8-week program to the kindergarten.

On the first day, four Native Americans, all adults, arrived and gathered the class around them to explain a little of their background. It was the first time that the subject of Native Americans had been brought up in the classroom, and the children were unaware that two boys, Gabe and Aaron, were themselves Native Americans. The two didn't even know it about each other.

As a first activity, one of the men gave a simple pretest. "Tell me what you know about Indians," he said. The general consensus seemed to be that "Indians are bad guys who shoot cowboys." Without looking the least surprised, he responded, "Well, we're Indians and we're here to show you that Indians are a lot more than that. Let me tell you a story...."

For more than an hour the class sat transfixed as he told one Native American legend after another. Although Trudi worried that the children would become restless, no one moved. Clearly the occasion was an important one. Over the following weeks more stories were added and old ones were revisited. Women taught beadwork, bringing in a collection of the tiniest beads in a multitude of colors. Again, Trudi worried about the appropriateness of the materials for 5-year-olds. After all, she had just recently shown the children how to string complex patterns in wooden beads many times larger than those of the Native Americans. But one of their children, herself 5 years old, came with her mother bringing her own intricate beadwork and demonstrated that even a very young child could manipulate small materials if the motivation was there. The other children were impressed and tackled the challenge with enthusiasm, never losing patience despite the many frustrations.

Games, songs, and dances were introduced with ever-increasing complexity, and most of the children caught on. They began to look at books about Native Americans and to ask for stories during the daily story hour. Native American themes began to appear in the children's fantasy plan. Clearly, the curriculum had become integrated and related to a single theme with the children themselves responsible for much of the trend.

As the weeks went by, many of the children began to talk informally about the differences they observed between Native American culture and their own. Trudi observed that the two Native American boys, Gabe and Aaron, never joined in these conversations. She wondered what they were thinking but hesitated to force the issue. Then, late one morning the two boys, quite suddenly and on their own, awoke to their heritage together. It was just after an extended free-play period. The entire class had finished cleaning up and was headed for the story corner. By coincidence, Gabe and Aaron were the last two to finish cleaning. They came from opposite sides of the room, nearly ran into each other, and then, in unison, stopped and stared. Gabe put a hand on Aaron's dark, straight hair. "Are you Indian?" he asked.

"Yeah," Aaron answered shyly.

"So am I." Gabe put his arm around Aaron's shoulder and Aaron did the same to Gabe. Together they walked to the story corner to join the others.

With that experience, Trudi felt she had achieved her goal: All the children had had the experience of comparing and contrasting two cultures, and two Native American boys had achieved an appreciative awareness of their native culture. Further, they all learned something about themselves—that they were capable of participating successfully in another culture's traditions, even if the skills required (e.g., bead stringing and complex dancing) were difficult to acquire. Thus, in increasing their self-esteem and their appreciation of another culture, the children had taken an important step toward the ultimate goal of attaining the skills necessary for living in a democratic and pluralistic society.

Once they reached the upper elementary years, it would be appropriate for these children to study about their cultural heritage. They would be able to read U.S. history to learn about conflicts with and displacement of Native Americans—and would get a clearer picture of Native Americans who shot cowboys. They would be able to study more fully about Native American culture and anthropology as well as to learn the economics of conflicts between Native Americans and the U.S. government. Such formal studies are appropriate for older children, whereas in the preprimary and primary years, concrete involvements, such as those experienced in Trudi's kindergarten class, provide more meaningful learning. This learning may not always work smoothly toward a predetermined goal as it did in the case of Aaron's and Gabe's recognition of their common heritage. But one purpose of such early concrete learning is to plant the motivational and cognitive seeds from which later social studies learnings can emerge.

These concrete social studies experiences may take various directions: for example, the unit on Native American culture might be followed by community experiences and this, in turn, might be followed by attention to environmental care, and so on. Ultimately, however, all of these experiences have a single goal: the beginning of consciously responsible citizenship.

WHY SOCIAL STUDIES

Stated quite simply, social studies education has one goal: to produce effective citizens. In a time when many argue that our schools should go back to the basics, it would be well to remember that, ultimately, the most basic goal of all is to create citizens who will know how to participate in and help maintain their democratic form of government. This training for citizenship need not and should not be confined to the upper grades; it ought to be a core part of the early childhood curriculum as well. The important social interactions that are so much a part of the early childhood classroom provide both a natural opportunity and a definite necessity for learning citizenship.

Citizenship refers to the rights and responsibilities of the people living in a society. Of course, privileges are more attractive than duties, so that children (and probably most adults) will be more easily drawn to the former. It is much more pleasant, for example, to take your turn telling the class about your weekend than to listen quietly to others. And it is certainly more enjoyable to be involved in a limited-access learning center than to wait impatiently for a turn. But learning the kind of fairness required for living in a cooperative society with limited resources is an essential step in learning to be a successful citizen. While home and church contribute much to children's development as citizens, the school offers the best opportunity for learning to relate well to people of varying races, abilities, and opinions. Thus, it becomes both the right and the responsibility of teachers to assist young children as they grow toward effective citizenship.

Early education for citizenship is a concept that first took root in the United States in the last half of the nineteenth century. At that time there was a dramatic increase in the number of nursery schools, most notably those provided for children of recent immigrants. Previously, nursery education had been the privilege of those who could afford to pay for it. Now, with an ever-growing wave of new arrivals, a need for citizenship education was perceived. Patriotic philanthropists funded nursery schools whose purpose was to socialize children to their new country and to plant the seeds of responsible citizenship. Parent involvement was an integral part of this new kind of nursery education. Mothers, particularly, were encouraged to participate. The ultimate goal for both parent and child was the same: socialization to a new culture and responsible citizenship.

Over the decades early childhood settings have evolved continuously until few, if any, of today's schools resemble those of the last century. Yet the question of preparation for citizenship remains. The National Council for the Social Studies (NCSS) has addressed this issue with its "Social Studies Curriculum Guidelines" that are recommended for kindergarten through grade twelve (Osborn, 1979). The NCSS's global definition of citizenship demonstrates the evolution of school philosophy during this century: "The basic goal of social studies education is to prepare young people to be humane, rational, participating citizens in a world that is becoming increasingly interdependent" (p. 262).

Children can be encouraged toward "humane, rational, and participating" citizenship from the earliest years. The NCSS equates humaneness with a provision for human dignity: "Each person should have the opportunity to know, to choose, and to act" (p. 262). Rationality, they say, "denotes a critical and questioning approach to knowledge but also implies a need for discovering, proposing, and creating: the rational person doubts but also believes" (p. 262). And concerning participation they say, "...without action, neither knowledge nor rational processes are of much consequence....Commitment to human dignity must put the power of knowledge to use in the service of humanity" (p. 262).

A quick look around a class of young children might make one wonder if the NCSS statement is appropriate at the earliest school levels. Should such young students have classroom opportunities to "know, to choose, and to act?" Are they ready for a critical and questioning approach to knowledge and "discovering, proposing, and creating?" How can young children participate in "the service to humanity?" The Early Childhood Committee of NCSS answers these questions indirectly when it declares, "...it is increasingly clear that early childhood is a formative period for the rapid development of the concept of the political self, a sense of self marked by growing attitudes about how the system works. The ingathering of experiences and the shaping of attitudes through interactions in the environment are part of the process of children becoming citizens, setting foundations for adult citizen actions" (Pagano, 1978, p. 41).

It is necessary to realize that the everyday experiences of young children can involve "discovering, proposing, creating and choosing." They are natural manifestations of the constructivist view of early childhood education. For example, letting children participate in choosing their academic activities provides not only an effective cognitive learning experience but also the kind of decision-making skills necessary for life in a democracy. Discovering is also an integral part of constructivist views of learning, as are proposing and creating. One school-based example of how they might be combined involves the problem of playground litter. First, children could be guided into discovering the litter and perceiving it as a problem: then they could propose and create solutions for a clean-up campaign. In just one activity, children would have discovered, proposed, created, and participated in "the service of humanity."

THE TEACHER'S ROLE

Permitting young children to discover, propose, and create takes some courage on the part of the teacher. The results may be unexpected, untidy, and a little noisy at times! At the same time, the teacher needs to respect children's ability to observe the world around them, to see wrongs and want to put them right, and to be able to follow through on a course of action.

Obviously, to allow young children this much freedom requires that the teacher be willing to promote independence of thought and action. This is sometimes difficult because it is during these same early years that children most express their warmth and desire for closeness to the teacher. It is a rare teacher who is not touched by this outpouring of genuine affection. Carried too far, however, it can create too much dependency and stifle decision-making skills and creativity. Fostering dependence, then, means doing a disservice to the children. It is better to rejoice with children when they say, "I did it myself!"

Promoting independence means allowing children to make occasional mistakes as they choose some of their own academic activities. They should even be permitted to choose between working and playing alone or within groups. Most of all, the teacher needs to provide a secure atmosphere in which children are unafraid to make choices that are provided them. They should be helped to see more of the world around them and to make improvements where they are needed. This does not mean that children should be pushed into growing up sooner than they are ready, but that they are offered the opportunity to be full participants in their school experience. In this way they will be taking the beginning steps toward full citizenship.

Both Piaget and Montessori believed that children should be helped toward independence by their teachers. They argued for independence as the most humane and efficient road to cognitive learning as well as the best way to create effective citizens, children who would be prepared to live in a democracy. In arguing for a democratic structure in the preschool, Montessori (1969) referred to a "society in embryo." Both of them were also acutely aware of the developmental limitations of young children and did not have unrealistic expectations about their ability to participate in a real democracy. Thus, in working toward citizenship, as in other curricular areas, it is important for teachers to be keenly aware of child development. Before discussing the social studies curriculum, then, it is important to look at the developmental implications of what is taught in the social studies.

SOCIAL STUDIES AND CHILD DEVELOPMENT

In Chapter One we saw how young children's cognitive growth progresses through the preoperational into the concrete operational stage. During this period their growing intellectual abilities make children excited by learning but they are still ego-bound. At either stage, children's intellects are best served by concrete experiences focused on the here and now.

In the affective domain, children are also working through stages characterized by ego-centered concepts. Preschoolers see discipline and moral issues as matters related to authority rather than fairness, whereas primary-grade children are beginning to develop a sense of autonomy in their moral decisions and are more able to see the viewpoints of others. In Erikson's developmental structure, preschool children are most likely experiencing "initiative vs. guilt" and primary children, "industry vs. inferiority" (see Chapter One). In the earlier stage children develop a sense of initiative based on their new-found language abilities and their increased mobility. In the latter stage, tasks, responsibilities, and expanded role identities are predominant.

To illustrate how development affects social studies education, we focus now on the emergence of spatial concepts, temporal concepts, and racial awareness. Concepts such as these are at the heart of the social studies curriculum and, consequently, teachers must be sensitive to how these and similar concepts develop.

Spatial Concepts

When young children create a primitive map of their school or trace from a map the route they take to get home each day, they are gaining a sense of belonging to their own community. As they get older and use maps to locate their community within state and country or study the migration patterns of their ancestors, they become aware that their immediate community is connected to a much larger world. This physical awareness is an important step in understanding the interconnectedness of the entire world community.

To a great extent, the reason children's early maps are primitive and the later ones are more complex and global is that children only gradually develop their spatial awareness. It is sometimes difficult for adults to see space from the child's point of view, as the following story illustrates.

A group of elementary education students was studying mapping skills. They had been presented with large pieces of butcher paper and instructions to map various parts of the building as they thought kindergarten children would do it. In four of the five groups the students returned from their assignment with what seemed to them childlike drawings. The fifth group, however, came back looking amused and a bit chagrined. One member of this group had brought her 4-year-old son to class and, of course, he had been invited to help with the group's map.

The result was a dramatically different map. Around the edges were the childlike drawings done by the education students, but spread across one entire half of the paper was a door with an outside doorknob that had obviously been drawn by the real child. His mother told the class that on the way to their assigned map-making area, her little boy had held the door open for everyone. While he had been delighted at this grown-up privilege, he had also been overwhelmed by the enormity of the door and it had become the focal point of his map drawing. His interpretation of space was thus much more personal and less objective than his adult companions'.

It is only from the adult viewpoint that visual space is logically and mathematically represented. Young children have much more subjective perceptions of space that need to be taken into account when introducing geography into the curriculum. Both Piaget and Jerome Bruner (Jantz and Klawitter, 1985) believed that children could not successfully use and understand mapping techniques until the logical thought attained in the formal operations stage had been reached. The skills they referred to include not only map reading but analyzing, abstracting, and inferring information.

Another researcher (Stoltman, 1979) observed that children's abilities to work with maps progress from the concrete to the abstract based on a stage-like development. Map-reading skills progress from a simple ability to see symbols on a map to understanding the symbols, recognizing patterns, working with a numerical scale, and, finally, making inferences based on the reading.

Similarly, map drawing starts at a primitive level with little relation to reality, proceeds to maps that are representative of the actual environment, and finally to an ability to infer information from the mapped objects.

Stoltman's observations support the use of caution in introducing maps to young children. It is important to remember that any map is an abstraction and that the beginning stages of map study should be concrete and personally related to the children. One study done with both preschool children and student teachers (Liben, Moore, and Golbeck, 1982) demonstrates how concrete it is possible to be and the way in which young children understand best that which is most personal and concrete. Each of the groups in this study, the preschool children and the student teachers, was asked to reconstruct the children's classroom, first by using a model of the room and second by actually using the room itself after the furniture had been removed. The results showed that the student teachers could perform either task, but that the children performed far better when working with the actual classroom furnishings. Working with the scaled model required a degree of spatial abstraction that the children found difficult.

Temporal Concepts

Probably more important than geography to the development of good citizenship is the study of history. Learning about one's ancestors and the heritage they created gives a sense of continuity to citizenship. Understanding and avoiding the mistakes of the past while attempting to build on the positive is synonymous with good citizenship.

To even begin to understand history, however, requires a basic understanding of the passage of time. Very young children have little grasp of time and have difficulty sorting out yesterday from tomorrow, last night from this afternoon. Attempts to teach children about historical events can have amusing results as the following incident illustrates.

The first-grade teacher was trying to help her children understand just how long ago it was that the Pilgrims had landed on Plymouth Rock. "Before your parents were born, before their parents were born, and before their grandparents even, that's when the Pilgrims came and the native American Indians helped them survive." Follow-up questions and discussion revealed that, no, there had been no cars, televisions, air conditioning, or even refrigerators. The children seemed to have a good feel for the historical distance between themselves and the early settlers. But just as the class was about to move to the next activity one child raised his hand and asked the teacher, "Were you alive then?"

This child's confusion about the passage of time, while amusing, also points up the need to understand children's temporal concepts before introducing the study of history. As with the problem of spatial concepts, more research must yet be done before we can speak knowledgeably about each step of cognitive development. Piaget (1969) studied children's developing concepts of time and concluded that these moved from the simple and confused to the abstract.

Interestingly, one conceptual step children must take is to be able to separate time from space, and this is accomplished during the preoperational years. During the preoperational years, children learn the basics of sequencing but have difficulty differentiating between short and long segments of time. During the concrete operational years, children gradually develop the ability to understand long and short time spans as well as the complexity of simultaneous events. At about age 5 children begin to develop the adult sense of time. The concept of a day seems to be understood first, then longer chunks of time such as a week, month, and year. The short time periods such as minutes and hours are understood next. At about age 8 children can look at the future outside their everyday lives (Bauer, 1979).

Not until the upper elementary years, however, can children acquire a historical perspective of time. Thus, the confusion of the first-grader about the Pilgrims and his teacher is understandable. This is not to say that the story of the Pilgrims isn't valuable for young children, only that we shouldn't expect them to have our understanding of the historical time span.

Racial Awareness

Children's understanding of racial characteristics as well as their attitudes toward their own and others' races has implications for several areas of the social studies: history, sociology, anthropology, international education, current events, values development, and, perhaps most important, citizenship education. Racial awareness develops along two distinct but overlapping tracks: simple awareness and the appearance of attitudes. Simple awareness begins first, in the very early years, as the following story illustrates.

Over the kitchen sink was a window looking out at a rather dismal workingclass neighborhood. On either side of the window were two framed Japanese woodblock prints of nineteenth-century geishas. As soon as Peter was big enough to sit in the high chair he ignored the scene through the window in favor of the portraits. When he grew big enough to ask what they were his mother answered simply, "Japanese ladies." For a while, whenever Peter was put into his highchair, he pointed to the pictures and stated with solemnity, "Japamese ladies."

It was when Peter was 3 that his mother decided to take him for his first visit to the local library. Although the sight of shelves crammed with books was interesting to him, Peter was most attracted to a glass display case in the center of the room. It stood just high enough to be at Peter's eye level if he stood on tiptoe. Inside was an intricate model of an Indonesian village and countryside. Peter's attention was soon focused on the small wooden figures of people and their decidedly non-Western faces and clothing. After staring quietly for a time, Peter suddenly pointed with excitement at a couple of women walking on the country road. "Japamese, Mommy, Japamese!" he exclaimed.

This kind of early awareness of differences has been studied in young children. The ability to identify, or to be aware that there are differing racial groups, normally appears in children by age 4 or 5. (Peter's precocity can probably be explained by his 2 years' experience with the Japanese prints.) This early awareness is a simple, physical one that lacks understanding of precise racial discriminations (as in Peter's identification of Indonesians as Japanese) and a sense of racial continuity over time. By the primary grades, children are generally able to understand their own race in relation to others, can classify races, and have a sense of their historical continuity (Semaj, 1980).

While the development of cognitive awareness of differences is important in teachers' choice of teaching methods and materials, it is of even more importance to be aware of the development of racial attitudes. The eight formative steps listed below appear to be discrete but, in actuality, will sometimes overlap each other (Katz, 1976). They demonstrate the interaction of cognitive and affective development.

1. Observation of racial cues (e.g., Peter's first awareness of "Japanese" ladies)

2. Formation of rudimentary concepts (child is aware that people may label other races positively or negatively)

3. Conceptual differentiation (feedback of a positive or negative nature influences the child's perceptions more fully)

4. Recognition of the irrevocability of cues (child learns that racial identification never changes)

5. Consolidation of group concepts (child can identify, label, and recognize members of a group; appears about kindergarten age)

6. Perceptual elaboration (differences between groups are empha-

sized over differences within groups; appears at preschool through elementary ages)

7. Cognitive elaboration (complex racial attitudes begin to develop; what teachers and peers say is important in changing or maintaining attitudes)

8. Attitude crystallization (may appear at end of elementary years)

The fact that attitude crystallization may appear by the end of elementary school, and that differences between groups are emphasized as early as the preschool years, indicates the importance of helping children work through their understanding of race relationships. Even in the early years it may be difficult to erase stereotypical viewpoints and negative connotations given some racial labels. To see just how difficult it can be, we'll return to the opening story in which we left Aaron and Gabe entranced with each other's Native American identification. Unfortunately, the story does not have a happy ending.

It was the last day of the program and once again the story teller drew the children around him, this time for a posttest.

"We've been seeing you children for a long time now," he began, "and we've enjoyed it. Have you?"

"Yes!" was the unanimously enthusiastic response.

"Well, tell me what you know about Indians now."

Two boys immediately raised their hands, and although he called on one, both responded in unison, "They're bad guys and they kill cowboys."

It was then that Trudi realized how difficult it is to erase racial stereotypes, even in the early years. She remained enthusiastic about the overall experience, however. She said later, "That scene between Gabe and Aaron will last me for a lifetime. And I don't really think that last stereotyped comment is all the children were thinking either. I believe they learned a lot more and that they won't forget it...at least not everything. Now that I see how difficult it is to change our preconceived ideas about people, I think we need more of this kind of thing in school, not less."

THE SOCIAL STUDIES CURRICULUM

The preceding discussion regarding the developmental limitations of preschool and primary social studies education contains one underlying theme: children's cognitive development and social development begin at a very concrete level and progress through the elementary years to the beginnings of abstract understandings. At each step of the way, positive and negative attitudes toward self and others are increasingly internalized and it is these attitudes that mold and shape children into adult citizens. As we have seen in Trudi's kindergarten, it is never too early to be concerned about this judgmental facet of development.

Given children's limited understanding of such things as time and space, coupled with the early development of attitude crystallization, there is a definite need to shape the social studies curriculum around citizenship development. As we have seen, the National Council for the Social Studies has stated that the primary goal of the social studies is citizenship education. A subgroup of the NCSS, the Early Childhood Committee (1978) has developed a set of guidelines for implementing this goal in the early childhood curriculum. These guidelines form the basis of our discussion about an appropriate curriculum for the early years.

The NCSS Guidelines

The Early Childhood Committee has provided a detailed description of guiding principles for the curriculum, citizen competencies, and "enabling processes" or teaching methods. Some of the most important of these are summarized below.

Guiding Principles These principles set the stage for the curriculum. Note the two themes that run through the principles: the importance of active learning about democracy and the need to provide a wide diversity in the curriculum.

• Citizenship education is specific and therefore it "involves children in active learning to help them develop democratic behaviors and gain knowledge and understanding of basic concepts and principles of American democracy."
• Citizenship education is explicitly interrelated and therefore it "infuses democratic themes, values, and processes into the full range of the curriculum."
• Citizenship education is person oriented and therefore it "considers the developmental capabilities and unique learning styles of individual students" and "emphasizes the interdependence of people."
• Citizenship education is dynamically interactive and therefore it "promotes instructional programs that are content- and process-oriented, that respond to individual and group needs, and that emphasize personal growth and social responsibility" (Pagano, 1978, pp. 51–54).

Citizen Competencies Children are capable of a large number of citizen competencies. The following list for early and middle childhood is just a sampling of the committee's much lengthier version. In this section, note that every one of the competencies can be applied across the curriculum. They are not confined to the social studies.

Early Childhood
- Actively listens to what another thinks, feels, intends
- Learns to take turns talking, listening, sharing, helping
- Develops a personal sense of cooperation, participation, interdependence
- Recognizes that different people have different thoughts, feelings, experiences, information, interests, needs
- Recognizes that there are also commonalities among people
- Becomes aware of rules as a way of establishing boundaries and protecting group life and knows the democratic process for changing them
- Grows in personal freedom and self-discipline by learning to make choices and to determine personal values
- Understands roles and responsibilities of leaders and demonstrates competencies in leadership among peers

Middle Childhood
- Shows increasing awareness of the rights, needs, and feelings of self and others
- Can alter behavior for more effective interpersonal relationships
- Has "knowledge of the general purpose of functions of government"
- Understands the principles of America's two-party system
- Can compare the principles of our Constitution with the political orientation of other countries
- Can use negotiation, compromise, and due process in conflict situations
- Can see beyond desire for immediate solutions in view of long-range consequences

Enabling Processes   The point of view of the Early Childhood Committee, as of this book, is that young children construct their own learning by interacting with their environment. It follows that teaching methods should be less directive and more facilitative of children's independent learning. Consequently, the committee has preferred to call teaching "enabling processes." Four examples the committee gives of this kind of teaching are group discussions and meetings, role taking and role-play, field trips, and game sessions.

The social studies curriculum should be taught using an interdisciplinary approach according to the committee. That is, subject matter such as economics, history, and geography should not be separated out but integrated as a means to citizenship education. At the same time, the committee has also adopted a suggestion from Arthur K. Ellis's *Teaching and Learning Elementary Social Studies* (1977) that each of the social sciences can be defined in terms of the young child's ego-based interests. Examples of what very young children can study:

History—my past

Geography—the environment in which I live

Psychology—my needs and desires

Sociology—how I fit into the society in which I live

Anthropology—how my culture has shaped my life

Political science—the influence I exert on others and the influence they exert on me

Economics—how I am supported financially

Each of these examples is focused on the child's concept of space and time: the here and now. As children mature through the elementary grades it is both possible and desirable to move from ego-centered social studies to a focus on the rest of society.

The concept of beginning with the here and now, then building on it, has its historical base in the work of Lucy Sprague Mitchell (1934). While Mitchell's ideas originated a half century ago they are current and viable today. Her "here and now" curriculum was based on the philosophy of John Dewey and was meant to counteract the traditional practice of teaching children directly and through rote memorization. Mitchell's idea was to make social studies learning for young children an outgrowth of their own experience, something that had more meaning to them than repetition of facts. It is significant that she titled one book *Young Geographers*. With Dewey she believed that children should be social scientists (in this case geographers) not simply consumers of information (students of geography).

Summary Theory, research, and practice all indicate that social studies for young children are most effective if based on, but not confined to, their immediate lives. If a curriculum begins with the here and now, then branches outward, it can cover any area of the social sciences. The teaching methodology or enabling processes would allow children to be not simply recipients of preordained facts but social investigators themselves—geographers, historians, economists, and anthropologists. Taken together and applied to the early years, these social sciences should be adapted in such a way that the long-range goal will be to help create effective citizens. In our culture, this means creating citizens who will feel at home in the very demanding society called a democracy.

Classroom Democracy

Although democracy can be the object of formal study, it can also be learned incidentally as part of the very fabric of classroom life. The teacher's role is to transmit the idea of democracy, by example and modeling, to children. The children's role is to be actively involved in here-and-now learning. Democracy and learning firsthand how to make it work is critical to citizenship education. This section gives both a philosophical perspective and specific ideas for teachers.

If teachers want young children to begin learning the lessons of citizenship, and if they believe that children learn best by being active social scientists rather than passive recipients of information, then children must be given some firsthand experiences in democracy. For the teacher this takes some courage. On the surface, it is far easier to be an authoritarian teacher in a quiet, well-disciplined classroom than to give children the opportunity to help run the classroom. Teachers must then step down from their pedestals of authoritarianism and open up the possibilities of unexpected problems in the social structure. While too little freedom can breed both dependency and rebellion, too much of it can be the cause of chaos. Is the risk worth it? A strong affirmation has come over the years from various psychologists and educators who have tried classroom democracy. Here is what a few of them have to say.

John Dewey

A society is a number of people held together because they are working along common lines, in a common spirit, and with reference to common aims. The common needs and aims demand a growing interchange of thought and growing unity of sympathetic feeling. The radical reason that the present school cannot organize itself as a natural social unit is because just this element of common and productive activity is absent...the tragic weakness of the present school is that it endeavors to prepare future members of the social order in a medium in which the conditions of the social spirit are eminently wanting (1964, p. 300).

Maria Montessori

The only social life that children get in the ordinary schools is during play-time or on excursions. Ours live in an active community....It is interesting to see how, little by little, these (children) become aware of forming a community which behaves as such. They come to feel part of a group to which their activity contributes. And not only do they begin to take an interest in this, but they work on it profoundly. ...Once they have reached this level, the children no longer act thoughtlessly, but put the group first and try to succeed for its benefit (1969, pp. 224, 232).

Jean Piaget

...the problem is to know what will best prepare the child for its future task of citizenship....For ourselves, we regard as of the utmost importance the experiments that have been made to introduce democratic methods into schools....If one thinks of the systematic resistance offered by pupils to the authoritarian methods, and the admirable ingenuity employed by children the world over to evade disciplinarian constraint, one cannot help regarding as defective a system which allows so much effort to be wasted instead of using it in cooperation....it is even immoral to wish to impose upon the child a fully worked-out system of discipline....(1932, pp. 363, 404).

John Dewey's philosophy was that children need to experience a thing to learn it, and that included democracy. Piaget concurred, developing much of his pro-democratic stance as a young peace advocate during World War I. Montessori's words are particularly meaningful for she personally felt the sting of Mussolini's fascism when all her schools in Italy were suddenly closed and she was forced to leave the country until the end of World War II. Taken as a group, all three of them believed strongly that lecturing to children about democracy was meaningless and that the experiencing of it could and should be begun at the earliest possible age.

But how to do it? While preparing children to be effective citizens in a democratic society is the ultimate goal of the social studies, at the early childhood level the formal study of social and political systems is difficult and probably an impossibility. There, something less formal than study and certainly more active than lecturing is needed. The ideas that follow in the next section give examples of how this can be done. Many of them are adapted from the techniques that Montessori used in her own classrooms.

One important distinction should be made between the pre-school years and the primary grades. To use Montessori's words, a preschool class can only aspire to the status of "embryonic society" (1969). A true democracy will only begin to emerge in the primary years. However, many of the following techniques and attitudes are equally valid at both levels of education.

1. Teacher attitude is the beginning point, for with the proper teacher attitude all other suggestions will fail. It may also be the most difficult to accomplish. So often people choose to teach younger children because of their warmth, friendliness, acceptance, and...their dependency. Yet it is this very dependency that teachers must discourage. While they can still be affectionate and outgoing to children, teachers must also be sure that they are not themselves dependent on the warmth these children so naturally share. The attitude of teachers in a democratically oriented classroom should encourage the following:

- *Teaching style that is facilitative rather than directive:* If teachers simply tell children what to do, they will never learn to make decisions, and decision making is what democracy is all about.
- *Teacher modeling of appropriate behavior:* If they treat others (children, teachers, parents, principal) in a democratic fashion, the children will usually imitate their behavior.
- *Teacher trust:* Teachers must trust children to help care for the environment, to direct at least some of their own learning, to make most of their own rules, and to accept the consequences.
- *Teacher acceptance of the children's mistakes:* Democracy, even at the adult level, is always an experiment, a society in transition. Mistakes must be allowed.
- *Treating children with dignity:* This means practicing the golden rule: Unless teachers want to be treated condescendingly, talked down to, spanked or otherwise disciplined imperiously, they should not do the same to their children.

2. Children should be allowed to teach each other. This aids in understanding the responsibility required of participating citizens. Academically, it provides the child who does the teaching with reinforced learning and the other child with some one-on-one attention. A spirit of helping each other in the classroom naturally helps build a cooperative society. It is important that the teacher help all children find something they are good at and can help teach to others.

3. In the preschool, especially, children should be able to choose when to be social and when to work or play alone. Young children are only beginning to understand what group participation means; if teachers force the issue, they encourage the authority-follower relationship rather than independence.

4. Teachers need to continually seek ways to achieve group management without resorting to punishments and other authoritarian modes. Two Montessori techniques are particularly interesting. The first is for use when a single child is misbehaving and involves the teacher asking, "Is my teaching approach wrong? Are the materials interesting to the child? Can I direct this child to something that will engage him or her more successfully?" Two things should be obvious from this approach: the focus of "blame," if there is any, is placed on the teacher, not the child, and the child is not corrected for misbehavior but redirected through the use of the curriculum.

The second Montessori technique is useful when the whole class seems to be falling apart. Rather than focusing first on the most badly misbehaving children, the teacher searches out those least affected by the chaos and quietly redirects them to their work. The teacher then repeats this process with the next best group and so on. This provides a gradually calming effect. Both these techniques rely less on the teacher's authority than on the teacher's guidance and the children's increasing sense of internal self-control, a personal quality needed for living in a democracy.

5. Real tools should be provided for real work. This is usually done in the primary grades but rarely in kindergarten and preschool, where miniature plastic replicas are usually provided. Children need the real thing in order to take responsibility for their environment. All that is necessary is to find the smallest size available for each tool, then adapt as necessary—perhaps by shortening a handle or providing nontoxic substitutes for cleaning solvents.

6. Teachers must insist that children earn the right to freedom, democracy, and independence. If these are offered as gifts at the beginning of the school year, anarchy rather than democracy is likely to develop. There is nothing wrong with starting out in a somewhat authoritarian mode and gradually increasing the children's freedom. This should, however, be done as rapidly as feasible.

Democracy can be incorporated into any area of the curriculum by selecting or adapting these ideas. Thus, in a very natural way the social studies, through active experience with classroom democracy, are made part of an integrated curriculum. The Early Childhood Committee of the NCSS (Pagano, 1978) takes the point of view that the social studies can even be used as the basis for integrating the entire curriculum, while still separating out individual subject areas when appropriate. They argue that, "Citizenship education...could be viewed as the goal of all education" (p. 84). With this in mind, it is possible to place all subject areas under the single umbrella of citizenship/social studies:

Taken in this broad sense, such a goal includes mathematics and the ability to compute time, distance, and personal finances. It includes reading and writing because these skills are essential to effective functioning in today's society. Following this line of thought, all learning could be considered social studies and all teaching in early childhood could be called social education (p. 84).

PREPRIMARY ACTIVITIES FOR ENCOURAGING DEMOCRACY

This unit for preschool children is not a formally structured one but a series of classroom activities that help very young children build an "embryonic society" (see Figure 7-1). They should be introduced as appropriate throughout the year.

Care of the Environment

A concerned citizen is one who is aware of the environment and works to keep it healthy. Very young children can develop environmental awareness in their own classroom.

I. Room-Care Corner

Have materials available for cleaning and polishing every surface possible. Nontoxic materials include hand lotion for wood polish, a tiny bit of vinegar in a large amount of water for glass spray, Lava soap chopped in small pieces and melted over low flame with

FIGURE 7-1

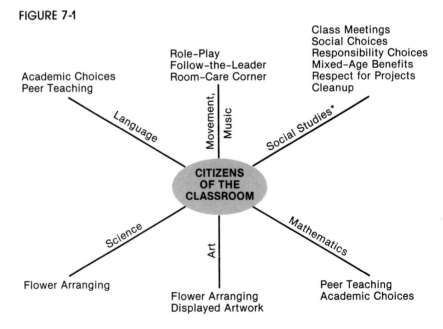

*All activities are social studies-based. These are not integrated with other subjects. Note that some activities are listed twice because they are integrated into more than one area of the curriculum.

a bit of water and then molded into a small dish for metal polish. Have a bag handy for dirty rags. A laundry tub can be used for washing the rags. Each of these cleanup activities can have its own box or basket with a descriptive label on the container and a matching one at its place on the shelf.

II. Flower Arranging

Have available assorted garden flowers and greens and junior baby food jars to use as vases. Have children arrange, add water, and place where desired to enhance the room's beauty.

III. Cleanup

When introducing any new material, demonstrate specifically where it should be put. Stress the idea that putting materials away is simply the closing step of any activity, whether done alone or in a group.

IV. Follow-the-Leader

Using recorded music, lead the class on tip-toe or walk through the room—in and out of the furniture and around whatever materials are out. There is one rule: Don't touch anything. Conclude by pointing out the need to move carefully through the classroom at all times to avoid damaging property or disrupting activities. This game should be played the very first week of school.

V. Displayed Artwork

If (and only if) children want to leave their work at school, let them choose where they would like to hang it. Their choices may not be the same as an adult's, but the children will enjoy the beauty they have created themselves.

Care of Each Other

A responsible citizen is one who cares about others and helps them when they are in need, or can determine when to help them help themselves. Awareness of others is a major step out of egocentrism and toward responsible citizenship.

VI. Respect for Projects

After playing Follow-the-Leader (activity IV), communicate daily the need to walk around, not over, each other's project, blocks, or toys. Say out loud, "I'm walking around your castle, Sandy, so I won't hurt it."

VII. Peer Teaching

Make a personal chart of at least one thing each child has superior ability in. (Everybody has something!) Make sure all children have an opportunity to teach something to someone else. When children come for help in almost anything, try to find a child who can help instead. Encourage children to ask each other for help.

VIII. Mixed-Age Benefits

If there is more than one age in the class, take advantage of it. Give children increasing responsibility for each other as they get older and lead younger children to expect and ask for help from the more mature.

IX. Role-Play

When conflicts arise, try letting children play each other's roles. At this age they can develop a beginning sense of what it is like to step into another's shoes.

Making Choices and Decisions

While any society imposes some restrictions, a democracy has the least. Competent citizens know how to make knowledgeable and thoughtful choices, but this takes practice and it is never too early to start. Begin by offering the very youngest just two choices. Over time expand so that finally you can say, "What would you like to do this morning?" and the child will not feel overwhelmed.

X. Academic Choices

If there is material the children need to cover, give them limited choices. "Would you like to do this math game first and then go out and play, or would you like to play a short time before doing the math?" Another option is, "Would you like to play this math game or the one on the shelf?"

XI. Responsibility Choices

If there is work to be done and it is not clearly one person's responsibility, give choices such as, "Would you like to help put blocks away or clean up the housekeeping corner?"

XII. Social Choices

Young children need to be given the choice of working and playing alone or with other children. They should also be allowed to choose between finishing what they are doing and joining the larger group for another activity. Try giving the occasional hold-out the opportunity to work alone provided she or he doesn't disturb the rest of the class. If the whole-group activity is attractive enough, the child will either soon join everyone else or will continue working on the preferred project while watching (or singing or reciting) what the class is doing.

XIII. Class Meetings

"Town meetings" in all their varieties are more successful when the participants have had practice in the appropriate skills. In preschool these meetings should be short, purposeful and usually teacher directed. The following guidelines are appropriate.

A. With children participating, set up at the very beginning only two or three rules pertaining to taking turns, listening courteously, and so on.

B. If all the meetings have the same general purpose, follow a set pattern or sequence of events.

C. When children behave in a way that is against the rules, try simply repeating the rule or, better, ask the child to repeat the rule out loud.

D. If steps A through C are followed in a somewhat ritualistic manner, children will soon begin to mimic the teacher's role. Children of kindergarten age may then be able to run their meeting without adult help. Rehearse the rituals with them first, and in the beginning choose the most mature to run the meetings. Try "working" a short distance away in case the need for help arises.

The Teacher's Role

Since your function in this social studies unit is to encourage democracy, you will, of course, want to provide guidance only as necessary and opportunities for children to govern themselves whenever possible. Most of the activities require some facilitation from you, but they can, to a great extent, become more child directed as children gain experience and confidence.

Facilitating   Cleanup, Displayed Artwork, Respect for Projects, Peer Teaching, Role-Play, Academic Choices, Responsibility Choices, Social Choices, and Class Meetings will need your help at first, but children should be given as much freedom as possible.

Instructing   Follow-the-Leader is one activity that will probably always work best with your leadership, unless some children understand its purpose well enough to take over from you.

Providing Play   The Room-Care Corner and Flower Arranging can be left open for children's free use. (Room care to a very young child really can be classified as play.)

Managing   Teaching children to assume responsibility requires a special type of management. First, you need to be very explicit as to what the expectations are. Demonstrate proper use of equipment and let children role-play. Stay positive rather than being punitive. In other words, emphasize the need to be careful so that materials will stay in good condition and the room will be beautiful. This is very different from telling children they must be careful or they will be punished. Let the children help you make a rule or two that will help ensure a smoothly running day. If you take these precautions in the beginning, you will be able to turn over much of the running of the classroom to the children, even if they are very young.

If you note that there are infractions of the rules and the demonstrated procedures, try repeating demonstrations and role-play or ask a child to recite the pertinent rule to you. If problems persist, remove materials and activities for a while as necessary.

Observing   You will need to continually observe children's progress in their independent decision making and cooperative behavior. If you are disappointed in their progress, consider having an outsider observe for a while. Sometimes another teacher (preferably one who is sympathetic to your ideas) can see interactions between children or between you and children that are too close for you to notice. As you observe that the children are gaining in self-confidence, give them new responsibilities.

Evaluating   Evaluation for these activities will be most successfully done through your careful observations. Democratic behavior is not something that can be graded on any kind of scale but must be suited to each class's own temperament.

Reflecting and Planning   To repeat, as the children grow in competence and self-confidence, give them more opportunities to make their own decisions and direct their own classroom.

PRIMARY UNIT: HELPING THE COMMUNITY HELPERS

Traditionally, children have studied their community during the primary years, usually in the first and second grades. Developmentally, this is an appropriate step out from the self-focus of the earlier years, and there are so many facets to learning about the community that it is a natural choice for applying the concepts of an integrated curriculum.

It is important for children to learn who in the community is there to help them. In the unit presented here, one addition to the traditional unit has been made. Because education for citizenship means encouraging children toward independence and self-confidence, it seems a bit shortsighted to study only the helpfulness of the helpers. Rather, it is important to find ways, even minor ways, that children can help the helpers.

In this unit the community starts within the school and home and works outward. It can be taught in its entirety, or a few helpers may be chosen from the larger list (see Figure 7-2). Since the list given here is designed to be representative, not exhaustive, others can certainly be added. Many of the activities are integrated with the rest of the curriculum.

Anticipated Outcomes

I *Student behavior:* As a result of this unit students will be able to:

  A Identify service careers in the community

  B Describe the helping functions of selected community services

FIGURE 7-2

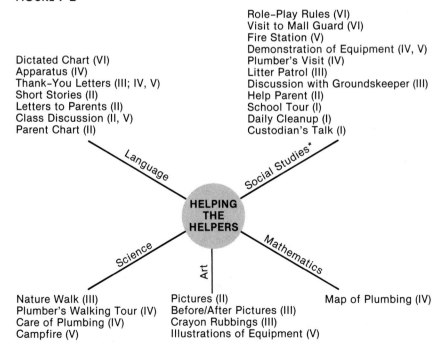

Role-Play Rules (VI)
Visit to Mall Guard (VI)
Fire Station (V)
Demonstration of Equipment (IV, V)
Plumber's Visit (IV)
Litter Patrol (III)
Discussion with Groundskeeper (III)
Help Parent (II)
School Tour (I)
Daily Cleanup (I)
Custodian's Talk (I)

Dictated Chart (VI)
Apparatus (IV)
Thank-You Letters (III; IV, V)
Short Stories (II)
Letters to Parents (II)
Class Discussion (II, V)
Parent Chart (II)

Nature Walk (III)
Plumber's Walking Tour (IV)
Care of Plumbing (IV)
Campfire (V)

Pictures (II)
Before/After Pictures (III)
Crayon Rubbings (III)
Illustrations of Equipment (V)

Map of Plumbing (IV)

*All activities are social studies-based. These are not integrated with other subjects.

C Contact community helpers for assistance in an emergency

D Follow the basic rules, regulations, and laws pertaining to the appropriate agencies

E Use democratic processes more effectively in the classroom

F Suggest and act on ideas for contributing to the welfare of the community

II *Student understanding:* As a result of this unit students will understand that:

A Service agencies are created with the purpose of helping every community resident

B People can help each other through working in commercial enterprises

C Rules, regulations, and laws are created to keep the community functioning effectively

D Children can contribute effective service to the community

E Everyone in the community deserves to have met their basic needs of food, shelter, and safety

F All people in the community need to work together to make the best community possible

Helpers and Related Activities

I School custodian

A Questions to be answered

1 How does the custodian help our classroom? The school?

2 How can we assist the custodian to make his or her work easier?

3 What tools does the custodian use? Which are adaptable to us?

B Activities

1 *Custodian's Talk:* Invite the custodian to class to demonstrate tools, describe his or her responsibilities, suggest ways children can help.

2 *Daily Cleanup:* Incorporate custodian's suggestions into daily cleanup routine.

3 *School Tour:* Tour school to identify results of custodian's work and places class could volunteer to help.

II Parent responsible for primary housekeeping responsibilities (usually a mother, but an available "househusband" would be an educational alternative)

A Questions to be answered

1 What jobs must be done to keep the home functioning smoothly?

2 Which jobs are essential on a regular basis and which are done only occasionally?

3 What happens if the jobs are not done?

4 Which jobs affect us (the children) most directly?

5 What jobs can we safely help with?

B Activities

  1 *Parent Chart:* Have a visit from a parent. List on a chart the jobs that need doing in the home. Discuss ways these are best done and ways we as children could help.

  2 *Help Parent:* Visit same parent's home and help with jobs determined by school visit.

    a Parent shows where tools are kept, demonstrates their use, shows the dirt to be cleaned, and so forth.

    b Children help in small groups.

  3 *Class Discussion:* Back at school, discuss the relevance of the trip to our own lives.

    a What new ways can we help in our own homes?

    b What will happen if the jobs we've helped with aren't done?

  4 *Letters to Parents:* Write letters to children's own parents volunteering specific help with something we haven't done before at home and/or asking for suggestions for ways we can help.

  5 *Pictures:* Illustrate our experiences at the house.

  6 *Short Stories:* Write short stories to accompany the pictures.

  7 *Class Discussion:* In a class discussion, compare upkeep requirements of school to home. Consider new cleanup and care assignments.

III Groundskeeper at public park

  A Questions to be answered

    1 How does caring for the outdoors differ from caring for the school?

    2 How does the groundskeeper help maintain the natural environment? The playground area? The more formal gardens?

    3 How can children best help keep the park clean and useful?

  B Activities

    1 *Nature Walk:* Go on a nature walk that includes identification of natural elements and human-made intrusions.

    2 *Discussion with Groundskeeper:* Discuss with groundskeeper his or her responsibilities and ways children can help.

    3 *Litter Patrol:* Hold a litter patrol as a class project.

    4 *Before/After Pictures:* Draw before and after pictures of litter patrol.

    5 *Crayon Rubbings:* Make crayon rubbings of leaves and of paper-type litter.

      6 *Thank-You Letters:* Write a thank-you letter to the grounds-keeper that includes ways the class intends to help.

IV Plumber

  A Questions to be answered

    1 For which repairs is a plumber responsible?

    2 What are the basic workings of a plumbing system?

    3 What are the necessary tools and how are they used?

    4 What are some ways we can help the plumber?

  B Activities

    1 *Plumber's Visit:* Invite a plumber to visit either the school or a home of one of the children.

      a *Plumber's Walking Tour:* Take a walking tour and have plumber point out pipes and outlet.

      b *Demonstration of Equipment:* Demonstrate the tools and give children an opportunity to try some out.

      c *Care of Plumbing:* Ask plumber to discuss proper care of plumbing apparatus including problems caused by introduction of foreign objects.

    2 *Apparatus:* Using a resource book such as *What Makes It Go, Work and Fly?*, make models of plumbing apparatus from materials on hand.

    3 *Map of Plumbing:* Create a map of the school (or student's house) and draw in the plumbing operation.

    4 *Thank-You Letters:* Write a thank-you letter to plumber that includes awareness of ways in which children can help.

V Fire fighter

  A Questions to be answered

    1 What different functions does the fire department carry out?

    2 What are the tools and equipment necessary for each function?

    3 In what ways can we help the fire department?

  B Activities

    1 *Campfire:* In an outdoor, sandy area of the building, demonstrate the way fire spreads easily from paper to leaves to sticks. Discuss: What would happen if sand didn't surround this? If we were to blow on it or a strong wind came up? Why must we be extremely careful around fires? And not start them ourselves? How do we call for help if we see a fire?

    2 *Fire Station:* Make a visit to a fire station.

      a *Demonstration of Equipment:* Thoroughly inspect each type of vehicle to see how its equipment works.

      b *Class Discussion:* Discuss with the fire chief or representative ways we can help prevent fires. Review the procedures for calling for help.

      3 *Thank-You Letters:* Write a thank-you letter that includes a list of ways we can help.

      4 *Illustrations of Equipment:* Make illustrations of equipment and written descriptions of their function.

VI Mall guard

   A Questions to be answered

      1 How does the guard help us if we are lost or frightened?

      2 How do we locate a guard? Who else can help us in an emergency?

      3 What can we do to make the guard's job easier?

   B Activities

      1 *Visit to Mall Guard:* Visit a guard in the office at a mall. Actually walk through the steps to take if you are lost.

      2 *Role-Play Rules:* Role-play safety rules to follow at a mall, such as staying with parents or others in charge.

      3 *Dictated Chart:* Have the class dictate the suggestions for nos. 1 and 2 and write them on a chart.

To add other occupations, make note of what community helpers are represented by the parents of children in your class, survey the community itself, or discuss possibilities with the children to build their own interests.

The Teacher's Role

This unit is designed to provide children with an opportunity to mature in their actions and concepts of themselves as participating members of the community. Although much of what they undertake can be done with independence and interstudent cooperation, most activities will require at least some teacher facilitation.

Facilitating   Help children get started and then give them independence as much as possible for the following: Clean-Up Routine, Tour of the School, Visit to a Parent's House and the follow-up Illustration, Discussion with the Groundskeeper, Litter Patrol, Thank-You Letters, Models of Plumbing Apparatus, Plumbing Map of School, and Visit to the Fire Station.

Instructing   These activities will require more direction from you: Visits from the Custodian, from a Parent, with the Plumber and with the Mall Guard; Letters to Parents; Clean-Up Discussion; Nature Walk; Campfire; Role-Play of Safety Rules.

Providing Play   Crayon Rubbings.

Managing   As children go out into the community it is a good idea to discuss, as a whole group, society's expectations for their behavior. From each discussion glean two or three key phrases to describe the way they should behave. Write these on the board or on a chart far enough in advance that the children will see them several times before departure or before a guest's arrival. They will then remember them when you make brief mention of one or more during a trip or interview. If you are in public and a child, or children, misbehave, you can keep the situation private simply by keeping them near you. Children at this age will be interested in identifying with their school and you can also remind them that outsiders will see them as representatives of the school. Whatever else you may do, do not take a trip away from a child because of advance misbehavior unless it directly pertains to the trip itself and it is necessary for the success of the trip. Intentionally spilling milk in the lunchroom, for example, does not have any relationship to a field trip.

Observing   The children's enthusiasm will be important to observe. This will give you an idea of the directions in which you should go with the activities. Observe also the extent to which children cooperate with each other, interact with the community's representatives, and keep on task during projects.

Evaluating   To determine if children are attaining the understandings listed at the beginning of this unit, try having a class discussion in which they think of other ways they might assist the community. Let children invent their own extension activities, with you as their supportive facilitator.

Reflecting and Planning   If your observations tell you that children are very interested in one or two representatives from the community, consider studying them more in depth rather than using the entire unit. If the children show interest in extending the variety of experiences during the classroom discussion just suggested, let them help in the planning.

TO DISCUSS

1   Introducing democracy into the classroom will be slightly different for different ages of children. Make a group chart that reserves a space for each age group and/or grade. Then discuss age-appropriate ways that children can take on more responsibilities of democratic citizenship.

TO DO

1 If you are employed as a teacher, or if you are student teaching, look at your lesson plans for the current week. List as many places as you can find that would benefit from the addition of a social studies learning. Try to follow through on at least two of them.

2 (This might follow from the suggested discussion above.) Observe your own class or one you work with. List ways in which a more democratic atmosphere could be created. Try one or two of them on a temporary basis. If the children are old enough, poll them for their responses to the change. Take notes that include successes and difficulties. Discuss these with the class.

BIBLIOGRAPHY

Bauer, D. (1979) As children see it. In K. Yamamoto (Ed.), *Children in time and space*. New York: Teachers College Press.

Dewey, J. (1964) The school and society. In R. Archambault (Ed.), *John Dewey on education*. New York: Random House.

Ellis, A. K. (1977) *Teaching and learning elementary social studies*. Boston: Allyn & Bacon.

Jantz, R., & Klawitter, K. (1985) Early childhood/elementary social studies: A review of recent research. In *Review of research in social studies education (1976–1983)*. Boulder, CO: ERIC Clearinghouse for Social Studies/Social Science Education.

Katz, P. (1976) The acquisition of racial attitudes in children. In *Towards the elimination of racism*. New York: Pergamon.

Kaufman, J. (1971) *What makes it go, work and fly?* New York: Western.

Liben, L., Moore, M., & Golbeck, S. (1982) Preschoolers' knowledge of their classroom environment: Evidence from small-scale and life-size spatial tasks. *Child Development, 53(5):*1275–1284.

Mitchell, L. S. (1934) *Young geographers*. New York: Bank Street College of Education.

Montessori, M. (1969). *The absorbent mind*. Kal, India: Kalakshetra Publications. [First published in 1949.]

Osborn, R. (Chairperson) (1979) National Council for the Social Studies position statement: Revision of the NCSS social studies curriculum guidelines. *Social Education, 43:*261–274.

Pagano, A. (Ed.) (1978) *Social studies in early childhood: An interactionist point of view*. NCSS Bulletin 58. Washington, D.C.: National Council for the Social Studies.

Piaget, J., & Inhelder, B. (1967) *The child's conception of space*. New York: Norton.

Piaget, J. (1965, 1932) *The moral judgment of the child*. London: K. Paul, Trench, Trubner.

Piaget, J. (1969) *The child's conception of time*. London: Routledge & Paul.

Semaj, L. (1980) The development of racial evaluation and preference: A cognitive approach. *Journal of Black Psychology, 6:*59–79.

Stanley, W. (Ed.) (1985) *Review of research in social studies education: 1976–1983*. Boulder, CO: ERIC Clearinghouse and Washington, D.C.: National Council for the Social Studies.

Stoltman, J. (1979) Geographic skills in early elementary years. *Indiana Social Studies Quarterly, 32:*37–42.

Art

One warm but misty day a 4-year-old boy sat on a large rock next to his father, quietly watching the surf of the ocean pound the shore. Suddenly he sucked in his breath and exclaimed, "Oh, look at the beauty!" Half an hour later the child sat at the little table in his bedroom, swirling gray and blue crayons around on a piece of paper, all the while saying, "Pssh, pssh," in an apparent imitation of the sea. Not long after that, the paper lay awkwardly bent on the floor between a few toys that were now of more interest.

This brief experience demonstrates several attributes of children's approaches to art. An adult might have been inspired by the beauty to create a picture, too. But the child entered into the endeavor with his voice and body, becoming the ocean himself. What was produced on paper was secondary to the process of creation. Once he had relived the experience, the little boy had no more need of the paper and it lay on the floor, crumpled and forgotten. Perhaps most important, the child's experience was a very natural one, moving from his seaside exclamation to the role-play on paper in one unself-conscious flow.

It is this very naturalness that makes art with young children such a rewarding experience. Children are appreciative and accepting of beauty and love being a part of its expression. When their home and school experiences support this attitude, children can take a very positive first step in a lifelong love of the visual beauty that is called art.

The importance of art to life itself is the first topic discussed in this chapter. We will focus, in fact, on the need for art in the kind of society we live in. It is often the artwork of a culture that is most remembered centuries later, so it is important to consider what our culture's art is saying to the coming generations.

ART AND THE FIELD TRIP

Before beginning our discussion of art and the young child, we'll observe an art lesson in action. The class is a third grade, and art is used here as a follow-up activity to an experience that was part of the science curriculum.

The children had just returned from a morning at the zoo, where they had been observing characteristics of mammals. Now they were taking grapefruit-size chunks of clay from a large box and working with them individually at their desks.

As they settled down, their teacher, Steve Janes, said, "Close your eyes and imagine the mammal you've chosen to sculpt. Can you see it?" Some of the children could and some couldn't, so they all closed their eyes again. Steve went on, "Think about your animal in the position you want it to be. Close your eyes and let it move slowly so that it's sitting or lying or standing—just as it will be when you make it. Don't open your eyes until you can remember everything you need. When you know you can see your animal, start sculpting it. Whenever you can't see it right, just close your eyes again until you can."

At first the room was almost silent as the children began manipulating the clay. Soon, however, the sound of pounding, rolling, and intermittent animated chatter filled the room. Occasionally a child sat in total silence, eyes closed, concentrating. This was followed almost immediately by more pounding, rolling, and chatter.

Steve walked throughout the room, talking informally with the children, reviewing their knowledge of mammalian characteristics. "Now, be sure you don't forget to give these animals feathers."

"Feathers?!" Several children answered, laughing.

"Mr. Janes," one girl said, "You're always kidding us. You mean fur."

"Oh, yes," he answered as if just remembering, "it's fur." The children continued as before until one boy declared, "But I can't figure out how to make the fur!" Immediately, another boy who had been working steadily and quietly answered, "Look, you can do this." He displayed a partly completed grizzly bear with scratched-in lines along its back. "See? I did it with this broken pencil." Several children looked on with interest and soon a number of pencils had taken on a new use.

As Steve moved throughout the room, observing and offering help, he noted that some children had broken the clay into small pieces and were putting it together bit by bit. Others had retained the original chunk and were pulling, squeezing, and molding. He knew that the animals made by the first group of children could never be fired successfully but made a decision not to correct their method. They were involved, happy, and working in creative ways and that, he decided, was more important this time.

Then Steve introduced a science-related idea again. "Wings!" he said suddenly. "You've all forgotten the wings."

"Wings!" the entire class shouted, several children adding, "Mammals don't fly."

"Are you absolutely positive?"

"Positive," a couple answered. Others looked uncertain.

"Well, what about the bat that was in my garage last night?" Suddenly the children recalled what they had learned, and one girl ventured, "Well, most of them can't fly."

"You're right," Steve agreed and smiled. The child smiled back, knowing that in this class it was okay to be wrong sometimes.

WHY ART

When Steve's class took their trip to the zoo they were getting better acquainted not only with the mammals they went to study but also with a community resource. The entirety of their experience—the trip to the zoo, the clay work later—would long be remembered by most of them. As third-graders they were old enough to see the zoo as a useful and interesting part of the community, and this learning could be solidified and expanded through the art experience.

Preparing for Democracy   Art, in fact, can be used in many ways to help children understand their society better. June McFee (1970) has written eloquently on the place that art has in the preservation of our society, its democratic basis, and the environment in which we live. She argues that teachers need to do better in teaching children that part of their responsibility as citizens is to help maintain the visual attractiveness of the environment. Among other things, children need to "be able to see what is going on in the visual environment...to understand that appearance is related to use...and...to understand how changes affect the quality of the environment they all share" (p. 340).

Increasing Respect   McFee also argues the importance of art in a multicultural society such as ours. She points out that within the United States such subcultures as the various Native American tribes have been able to maintain their sense of identity through their art. It follows that children "can learn to respect their own and other subcultures through their art forms." To do this, we must help them understand the symbolic meanings in their own environments as well as those in other subcultures.

If we look at our democratic society as a whole and each individual's place in it, we can see ways in which art education has something of value to offer even the youngest children. In Table 8-1, note on the left the assumptions about people in a democracy and on the right the kind of art experiences that might encourage the cultivation of each assumption.

Traditionally, art in the early childhood program has not been thought of as a way to teach about democracy. Yet, as can be seen

TABLE 8-1   Art Education in a Democracy

Assumptions About People in a Democracy	Related Art Experiences
People have infinite value.	Give children an opportunity to develop their unique potential through creativity.
People need and have capacity for freedom of choice.	Give children independent decision making through art activities.
People have equal rights with others to develop their potential.	Flexibility of results in art activities helps provide equality of opportunity.
People have the capacity for self-government.	Children learn to evaluate their own work as well as others'.
People have the capacity to work with others as equals.	Group-planned art projects help children understand an interdependent society.
People are able to use reason.	Art processes necessitate anticipation of new outcomes.

Source: Adapted from McFee, 1970, pp. 345–346.

from Table 8-1, the integration of art and learning about one's society comes quite naturally to the art program.

Increasing Cognitive Perception   More basically, art can be regarded as an important influence on the cognitive development of young children. Until about the age of 10, there is a strong relationship between art ability and intellectual ability (Burkhart, 1962). Taken at face value, this statement relates simply to development, not to curriculum. However, Lambert Brittain (1979) has suggested that art activities both reflect and help form the "inner" child, and encourage concept development.

Brittain says that when young children draw, even in the early scribbling stages, they are symbolizing an event. The drawing becomes a concrete, visible reminder of the event as well as a way to clarify and organize it cognitively. This is especially important for very little children when their verbal abilities are limited; their expression through art provides a kind of shorthand to describe feelings, visual memories, and actions. This use of art as a concrete cognitive experience could certainly be observed in the seaside experience of the 4-year-old boy. It also helps unite various areas of the early childhood curriculum. And art can help make any subject area more concrete as seen, for example, in the science-related activities in Steve's class.

Providing Creativity   Related both to learning about democracy and to cognitive growth is the issue of creativity. The importance of art as a contributor to creativity in the classroom cannot be underestimated. Creativity, as defined in Table 8-1, is an avenue toward developing each child's unique potential. It is the essential ingredient needed by people in a democracy where they must rely on their own resources, both for survival and for "the pursuit of happiness." Creativity is a critical element in the creation of new goods and services that form the basis of a capitalist economy. When education focuses primarily on the basics at the expense of creative experiences, a lifelong pattern of noncreativity may begin, which will deter children from eventually participating in their society to the fullest. While any area of the curriculum can be taught in such a way as to foster creativity, art is inherently appropriate for the task.

Giving Aesthetic Enjoyment   For young children, art has strong benefits. It helps organize their cognitive perceptions of their world and their place in it. It provides creative experiences and ways of thinking. Art can provide preparatory experiences for living in a democratic society. As children learn to understand and respect themselves and others through art experiences, there are psychological benefits. To be able to appreciate and enjoy an aesthetic creative experience, or the result of another's, adds richness to life. Through recognition of the contribution that art can make to the curriculum, the aware teacher can do much to enhance children's classroom experiences.

THE TEACHER'S ROLE

Using classroom art as a means of providing creativity, increasing cognitive perceptions, preparing children for democracy, increasing their respect of self and others, and giving them aesthetic enjoyment is asking a lot. Yet success is possible if the teacher's attitude and teaching approach and the developmental levels of the children are all carefully considered.

For a definition of the teacher's role, we can begin with advice from The National Art Education Association (NAEA). From the viewpoint of the NAEA, there is no single best way of teaching art, and the association prefers that teachers remain open-minded and flexible about the way they teach:

> No single approach to art teaching can fill all...the roles by which art can make itself recognized as a force instead of a frill in the schools. To meet these many needs, a wide variety of approaches, concepts, and philosophies are necessary....Art education by its very nature escapes

categories and rigid structures; and it must remain flexible and open (Greenburg, undated, p. 33).

More important is for the teacher to feel and respond to the qualities of the world and "to know with sympathy and joy, with tenderness and understanding" (Greenburg, undated, p. 33).

Although the NAEA states the case for creativity of teaching approach, the organization is also in favor of integrating art into the curriculum as a whole. Once long ago, it says, art was integrated into everyday life, but then, "The industrial revolution disrupted the harmonious development of art forms and of social life; never has it been clearer that a new harmony of these must be achieved" (Greenburg, undated, p. 85). This can and must be done in the school by making art a part of the child's whole existence, "helping him as he explores nature, builds bridges, relives history, performs and enjoys music and drama..." (Greenburg, undated, p. 85).

For the young child, art is learned simply by observing and discovering the world all around: its shapes, sizes, colors, and movement. The pictures children draw or paint provide a way to express and communicate ideas and feelings about their world. The primary role of the teacher is to offer young children a wealth of experience and to remember always that they are sensory learners.

More specifically, some teaching suggestions given by the NAEA include the following.

• Professional artwork should be displayed; those that use much color and imagination are usually most enjoyed. Examples of artists that may be used include Matisse, Klee, and Chagall.
• "Cute" drawings by adults should be avoided for display as children may try copying them instead of developing their own ideas.
• Materials should be kept in perfect condition and in organized storage places.
• Cleanup duty gives children a sense of responsibility and a respect for tools.
• Tools should be of high quality. They will be less frustrating to children, last longer, and cause fewer accidents (Adapted from Lord, 1981, pp. 59–73).

These suggestions offer a good start for the teacher, and Ritson and Smith add several other positive things that teachers can do for children.

• Teachers should realize that ability to express oneself is developmental and that each stage is temporary.
• Teachers should make materials easily accessible.

- Materials should provide stimulating sensory experiences, promote experimentation, and be adaptable to varying abilities and ideas.
- Teachers need to provide art experiences that are open-ended, providing children with real problems to be solved.
- Teachers should not expect realism in children's products.
- Teachers should continuously help children develop their creative ability.
- Teachers need to help children develop their perceptions, making them aware of what they see, feel, and hear.
- Teachers need to help children become more sensitive to the feelings of others as well as to phenomena in the environment.
- Teachers should help children build a sense of design, arranging materials so they are functionally located as well as pleasing to the eye.
- Teachers should develop their own sensitivity to beauty to model and pass on to children.
- Children need to acquire and practice skills, and teachers need to arrange situations to permit this. Even copying is sometimes necessary to perfect a technique or acquire a new one.
- Thinking and creative behavior need to be encouraged, accepted, and rewarded. The teacher must recognize that sometimes the best teaching is no teaching at all (Adapted from Ritson & Smith, 1975, pp. 159–162).

Within these two lists of teaching suggestions can be found ideas that contribute to the achievement of the goals set forth in this section: increasing children's cognitive perceptions, providing them with creativity, preparing them for living in a democracy, helping them respect themselves and others, and contributing to their aesthetic enjoyment. Unfortunately, it is remarkably easy for teachers to undermine the achievement of these goals. After observing many teachers at work, Brittain concluded that he could make a list of advice, too—one that would tell teachers how to approach art creativity in all the *wrong* ways. He based his list on his own observations.

- Teachers should place materials in a safe place, just out of children's reach.
- Children should draw or paint only within the prescribed time set by the teacher.
- Every lesson should be demonstrated before children start so there is no opportunity for spontaneity.
- Every activity should have a definite end product determined by the teacher in advance.
- Children should display their finished products in unison as they progress.

- Daily, or at least weekly, teachers should run off dittos for coloring or practice in staying between lines.
- Rewards should be given for neatness and orderliness.
- Only those products that meet the teacher's standards should be praised.
- Children who can't stay in the lines or cut well should have extra exercises to reinforce their failures.
- Every holiday should have stereotyped dittos with patterned art (Adapted from Brittain, 1979, pp. 154–158).

Experienced teachers may read this list with an occasional twinge of guilt or defensiveness. If so, it may be well to consider again the teaching goals set out earlier for cognitive growth, creativity, democratic experience, respect for self and others, and aesthetic experiences. It is unlikely that a case for any of these can be made with any of the items on Brittain's list of ineffective teaching methods.

Other readers may feel that the many expectations provided in these lists are beyond the reach of the teacher with average or little artistic talent or creativity. Frequently, however, classes taught by someone with above-average artistic talent or creativity are actually at a disadvantage. These teachers may do so much work in enhancing the aesthetics of the classroom that there is little left for the children to do. What is needed, instead, are an attitude and an approach to the children that will encourage them to discover their own talents.

Whether teachers are artistic or not, they can encourage children by modeling appreciation of art, both professional and school-produced. Artistic or not, they need to experiment with some of the materials the children use. In this way they can determine their quality and condition and feel what it is like to work with them. Artistic or not, teachers should not hang their own creations as models to inspire children; their eager students will try faithfully to copy them in every way.

What teachers should desire is to communicate to children their own love of art (even if they have to develop it first!) and to provide them with the tools and skills to be able to learn in their own way. Brittain has said that this way is, "Playfulness, freedom to structure one's own activities, openness to experience, curiosity..." (1979, p. 161). The successful teacher of early childhood art (1) provides children with both direction and freedom and (2) values creativity over perfection.

Finally, the teacher must realize that children pass through developmental stages in their art abilities. It is important to have some awareness of these in order to avoid expecting too much or too little from children, and to understand better the processes and products of their art experiences.

ART AND CHILD DEVELOPMENT

Although children advance through stages in their ability to draw, paint, and sculpt, it is often difficult to pinpoint their exact place in development. There are other environmental elements that enter into the expected regularity of stagelike progression, as we shall discuss later. For now, we can describe each of the stages, realizing that the assigned ages are broadly defined. As given here, the stages come from the work of Lowenfeld and Brittain (1975) and Brittain (1979).

Stages in Drawing (with related commentary on painting)

Stage I: Random Scribbling (ages 1–2½)   For these young children, motor development and observation of lines on the paper are most important. Their grip on the drawing tool is tight and the wrist moves very little. They may watch the lines appearing on the paper, but it is out of curiosity rather than for visual control of movement.

Stage II: Controlled Scribblings (ages 2½–3½)   To the adult, the drawings don't look much more advanced than those in stage I. Yet, by observing children, we can see that their wrists are now more flexible, they look at their paper more often, and they appear to have visual control over their marks.

Stage III: Naming of Scribblings (ages 3½–4)   Children usually don't announce in advance the topic of their artwork. Rather, they generally begin a session of controlled scribbling, realize that the set of marks reminds them of something, and give it a name.

In all the scribbling stages, the representations may not be visual at all, but simply there to evoke a mood or a sensory memory. A wild, circular scribble, for example, may be a child's representation of the family dog chasing its tail.

The scribbling stages last longer for painting than for drawing because control of the materials is more difficult. Simply filling the paper with paint may be enough to interest a child who, if given a marking pen, would be inventing names for the resulting scribbles.

Stage IV: Representation Attempts (ages 4–5)   When children's drawings begin to take on the characteristics of something recognizable, we need to realize that they are not necessarily trying to capture a photographic likeness. Although there is certainly a visual element of representation, we can still see traces of the previous period when feelings and emotions were as important as visual memories. A child who has just been spanked may draw a picture of his mother with outsized hands; a loved pet may be larger than the person standing next to it. Early attempts at representation should be considered symbols for objects and people rather than poor attempts at likenesses.

At this stage, the objects represented in a picture will be facing forward and floating in space. There seems to be no concept of what may be in the background, that people might be looking at each other instead of at the viewer, or that they need to stand on something.

Stage V: Preschematic Drawing (ages 5–7)   There is much experimentation during this stage at working out a concept of form, or a scheme. A baseline for figures to stand on appears, and at the top of the paper children put a line for the sky. Human beings move from having only head and legs to appearing with all the essential body parts. Clothing is added eventually, and legs may be drawn as double lines to indicate volume. Pictures of the family show people in approximately correct relationship regarding size.

Painting now moves out of the scribble or mechanical use of the brush stage. Representational pictures appear, although they are still not as advanced as those that are drawn.

Stage VI: Schematic Stage (ages 7–9)   The baseline grows thicker; the characters portrayed as well as the other objects march straight across the page. The same technique for drawing a human is repeated again and again without the experimentation of the earlier stage.

Stages in Claywork

The progress that children make in their work with clay parallels that of drawing and painting. At the same time they are scribbling, children also pound clay aimlessly. The period of controlled scribbling is represented in clay by the formation of balls, which may be rolled into snakes, joined together to make other shapes, or punched down with assorted holes. When shapes get this complex it is about the time that children begin to name their scribbles, and names may also be given to the shapes of clay. At about age 5, children can announce in advance what they are making and the figures take on increasing complexity. They are, however, generally laid flat on the table with three-dimensional pieces added on top. Free-standing figures may not appear with regularity until age 7 or so.

Development of Cognition and Art

The Piagetian stages of cognitive growth can quite usefully be compared to the Lowenfeld and Brittain art stages. By considering the two side by side, it is easier to plan appropriate art projects and to integrate art into the academic curriculum.

Piaget's preoperational stage is represented by controlled scribbling, naming of scribbling, early representation attempts, and preschematic drawing. During these art stages, children are much more concerned with processes and materials than with finished products. Therefore, adult-inspired activities that require systematic steps for completion are, quite bluntly, a total waste of the child's time. Teachers who provide hole punchers for putting together little books, for example, may well find children sitting happily at the art table punching random holes through paper after paper. First experiences with scissors may result in a heap of random shapes spread across a table rather than the cut-out picture the teacher had planned.

In the primary grades, children enter Piaget's concrete operations stage while they also become capable of schematic drawing. Now, product becomes important to them and there is a greater interest in conquering techniques in order to achieve a goal. At this point, planning ahead for class art projects, decorating individual books, and so on begin to make sense. (Some patience with side excursions with the hole puncher and scissors is in order, however.)

The difference between the preoperational and concrete operational stages, as they relate to art, can be seen at the end of the school day. If there are paintings lying out in the hallway to dry and the children cannot identify their own or even remember how many of them are theirs, they are certainly preoperational. Even the primary years are too early to expect children to wait while clay is fired and they, too, may forget which product is theirs.

One important qualification must be made about developmental stages in art. As with any other stages, the ages are approximate and will vary according to genetics, environment, and experiences. Within one kindergarten classroom, a teacher may have everyone from a scribbler to a child drawing complex profile portraits. McFee has listed a number of variables that might enter into any child's response to art experiences.

- Influence of child's culture on his attention

- Child's cognitive style
- The ways the child relates self to three-dimensional space
- Amount of encouragement from home and school environment to develop creative traits and a playful attitude
- Perceptual-conceptual skills of the adults who teach child
- Richness or dullness of the visual environment
- The child's adaptations to the school environment
- The child's attitudes toward art activities (Adapted from McFee, 1970, pp. 231–232)

These intervening variables must be considered along with developmental stages as the curriculum is planned. Of course, it is just about impossible to take them all into account while being cognizant of each child's stage in drawing, painting, or sculpting. This argues for a curriculum that is flexible, providing opportunities for choice and creativity.

THE ART CURRICULUM

NAEA's Six Essential Goals

The National Art Education Association (NAEA) has listed six "Essentials of a Quality School Art Program" (Greenberg, undated). We will use these six essentials as the basis of our discussion on the art curriculum for young children. They are clearly supportive of the goals we set forth earlier for art teaching: cognitive development, creativity, experience with democracy, respect for self and others, and appreciation of aesthetics.

1. A quality art program should provide children with an ability to "have intense involvement in and response to personal visual experiences" (p. 6).

These experiences may be either the enjoyment of the art created by others or the creation of one's own work. In either case, for very young children an intense involvement is a supremely natural state; thus, a primary target of the curriculum is an atmosphere that fosters it.

Involvement with Others' Art: Look carefully at classrooms for young children. How many of them have artwork posted at heights of 5, 6, or even 8 feet above the floor? Try squatting down to the children's level. How does the artwork look to them? Will they even pay attention to it? Before posting anything on walls, it is a good idea to try seeing it through the eyes of children. Above their eye level, broad expanses of color and design are appropriate, but not detailed work that asks for two-way communication.

If mobiles or other pieces of art are hung from the ceilings, it makes good sense to have them low enough that children can see them well. This poses something of a hazard for the teacher moving about the room, but it is a small price to pay for the children's involvement.

It is good to note how long artworks have been placed in their current positions. Long enough to fray at the edges, fade, or even rip? If a picture is a sentimental favorite and no replacement is available, there is an excuse to leave it up. Otherwise, the beauty of perfection is certainly to be preferred! At the same time, artwork should be left up long enough that children grow familiar with it, and this is particularly true with the youngest children, who enjoy the stability of the familiar.

Involvement with One's Own Art: For small children, involvement can mean experiments in modes of touching, in the sounds made by some media as they are used, or in their smells. An occasional child is offended by the smell of tempera, disgusted with the feel of finger paint, or intimidated by the muscular effort required of clay or play dough. It is important to be sensitive to children's responses and not to assume that every one of them will react positively to everything we introduce.

Some intervention may be appropriate for those who have negative feelings. For children who object to an odor, a different form of paint could be the answer. Adding soapflakes to tempera negates some of the strong smell; using watercolors is another alternative. One technique that has worked is to give children who dislike finger paint a very small amount of paint and have them use just the very tips of the fingers until they get used to the idea. If even that is too much, small, wooden spatulas or other tools may be the answer for a while. When children have problems with clay, the teacher can manipulate it for a while, warming it up and making it easier for the child to handle. Children with small hands need smaller amounts of clay to work with; breaking it into smaller pieces before children begin work is helpful.

2. A quality art program gives children opportunities to "perceive and understand visual relationships in the environment," that is, to help children become "visually literate" and even "make informed visual judgments" (p. 6).

The young child as art critic? Why, yes! Children can learn to look at classic art prints with a knowledgeable eye, and they can be taught to critique their peers' work as well as their own. It can all be done in a positive way with the teacher modeling the appropriate behavior.

For some reason, teachers who don't hesitate to critique children's work in every other area of the curriculum somehow feel that doing so in art will stifle and hurt children. Done negatively that is, of course, true—just as negative criticism in any curricular area will stifle and hurt children. What must be done is to make criticism a natural mode of looking at art. As children look at professional art prints they can discuss the use of color, the comparative sizes of objects, and so on. Older children can learn such things as the concept of making objects smaller to give them distance.

If this kind of criticism is taken for granted, then children will be willing to criticize and be critiqued when classroom art is produced. Children in the preschool years who are primarily interested in process will not be able to relate to this kind of activity. But children as young as those in kindergarten can begin to look at what they've done more closely. Teachers can find at least one good thing to say about each work of art; a graceful line, an interesting use of color, and unusual subject matter are all candidates for praise. Frequently children can see for themselves where a technique didn't work and it bothers them. A critiquing time offers an opportunity to help each other with ideas for improvement. Critiquing sessions need not be done as a whole class, although that's possible. Small groups can offer a comfortable atmosphere of supportiveness.

3. A quality art program lets children "think, feel, and act creatively with visual art materials" giving them the same opportunity a professional artist has to transform materials "into a whole work of art" (p. 6).

When children are viewed as small, but very real, artists, a new emphasis on quality materials and programs must follow. Respect for children as real artists suggests that materials be of high quality, unstructured enough to inspire creativity, and basic and simple enough to give children confidence as they work. A list of materials for the early years might include:

tempera paints

brushes of high quality and varying sizes

crayons of varying sizes

watercolors

finger paint

chalk

collage materials of varying textures

assorted scraps and wood glue for sculpture

newsprint, manila, and white drawing paper

4. A quality art program provides opportunity for each child to "increase manipulative and organizational skills in art performance appropriate to his abilities. The development of skills is an important outcome for every student" (p. 7).

The position of the NAEA is that skills are attained only through much practice. "Through using materials one does increase manipulative and organizational skills; it is the chance to work with art materials and to think that allows one to begin to THINK, FEEL, ACT CREATIVELY WITH VISUAL MATERIALS" (p. 7). (The emphatic capital letters are theirs.) It would seem that the once-a-week art specialist, no matter how talented, will not provide children with the practice they need to become skillful. While we often provide preschool children with plenty of art materials, we more frequently neglect them in the primary years. Just having them available for children to use at odd moments during the day not only will provide practice in skills but also can go far toward making the most of the time that is available. Children should be permitted to use art materials between work assignments, after tasks are completed, and so on. More important, art should be integrated into other areas of the curriculum on a regular basis.

Children also need some instruction in method, especially when being introduced to a new medium or when learning to make new applications with a familiar material. It is during these times that a sensitive teacher can pick up reluctance on the part of some children to deal with some media. (Return to point 1 for suggestions in dealing with this problem.)

5. A quality art program should help children "acquire a knowledge of man's visual art heritage.... Youngsters can begin to see connections between what has happened in the arts, ways in which different people have lived, and what they are trying to make and do in their own lives" (p. 7).

It is never too early to start! One teacher of 3- and 4-year-olds hung inexpensive museum prints of works by the French impressionists throughout her classroom. The 4-year-olds seemed interested in learning what techniques the artists used to achieve different results, and the teacher found herself giving them suggestions. Soon two or three of the older children were actually trying to imitate the pointillists. They could be heard in one corner of the room gently beating the points of their magic markers against the paper as they chanted, "Dot, dot, dot...."

One morning a mother walked in with her 3-year-old and began looking carefully at each print. Finally she said to the teacher, "I was sure I'd see it here somewhere, but I don't." She explained that she had taken her child to the art museum for his first visit and that he had been transfixed by a particular painting. No matter what else she showed him, he kept returning to it, asking to be picked up to see it better. The mother described the painting, and the teacher thought for a minute and then laughed. "Do you remember my concern that Jamie was spending so much time in the bathroom? Well, that's where the picture is!"

Although these children were too young for a class field trip, they were already responding to museum art in a very positive way. In the primary grades a field trip may be beneficial, but only if the museum is small or if the class concentrates on one school of painting or on one artist. The trip should be supplemented with art prints in the class that become old friends. Other resources can include films, slides, and books of art prints.

6. The quality art program should assist the child in using "art knowledge and skills in his personal and community life. As students grow they must begin to assume responsibility for their own actions, personally and publicly" (p. 7).

The key phrase to children's responsibility is, of course, "as they grow." Nevertheless, even preschool children are not too young to transfer their school learning to a sense of aesthetics in the home and community. There is a story that Maria Montessori liked to tell about the children in her slum school who took their newly acquired aesthetic sense home with them. She had encouraged the children to beautify the classroom in various ways, including the use of little pots of flowers throughout. Before long she observed that the apartments surrounding the school were displaying pots of flowers in their windows and learned that parents had put them there at the encouragement of their children.

Most children are at least minimally aware of the natural beauty around them and, with the teacher's encouragement, can become more conscious not only of beauty but of everyone's responsibility in its upkeep and longevity.

Summary

This chapter began with a description of Steve's art experience, a lesson he used to reinforce the children's science experience at the zoo. His informal and lighthearted discussion with them as they worked provided a review of biological details, which were then expressed in the sculpted products. Of course, he could have tested the children on their knowledge of mammals more formally. However, not only would the atmosphere have been more tense, but the learning would not have been as concrete, as visual, or as enthusiastic—and probably not as permanent.

There are many opportunities throughout the day and the curriculum for incorporating art. As in Steve's experience, art can be used for reinforcement of any academic learning or for informal testing. In writing experiences, art can be used to illustrate, once something is dictated or written; when used first, art can also be used to provide inspiration for a story. Art can decorate any paper of which a child is proud. Art in any form can be used to calm an upset child.

Returning to Steve's classroom, we can also see that one experience can demonstrate how the criteria for a quality art program can be met. Here the criteria are summarized with a description of the way this happened.

1. A quality art program should provide children with an ability to "have intense involvement in and response to personal visual experiences" (p. 6). In Steve's class, each child was intensely involved in one way or another. This was natural as the art experience grew from another involving experience: the field trip to the zoo. The quietness as each child began sculpting and the subsequent excited sharing were manifestations of the class's involvement.

2. A quality art program gives children opportunities to "perceive and understand visual relationships in the environment," that is, to help children become "visually literate" and even to "make informed visual judgments" (p. 6). In Steve's third grade class, one boy offered guidance for the others as he shared his solution to the problem of representing grizzly bear fur. It is important that the children with problems were quite open about their inability to create what they needed and that the solution was taken in stride without any need for external reinforcement, reward, or critical acclaim.

3. A quality art program lets children "think, feel, and act creatively with visual art materials" giving them the same opportunity a professional artist has to transform materials "into a whole work of art" (p. 6). The material in Steve's class was clay that could be fired, a professional medium. At the same time, he was accepting of children whose methodology was such that firing would be impossible. He made this decision based on his observation of the children's involvement. At a later date he would probably give a demonstration of technique before the children became so intensely interested in other aspects of the project.

4. A quality art program provides opportunity for each child to "increase manipulative and organizational skills in art performance appropriate to his abilities. The development of skills is an important outcome for every student" (p. 7). This statement is, of course, related to point 3 above. In addition, we can see that Steve expressed the NAEA's intent that children learn skills through practice. No doubt he uses art in other curricular activities as well.

We can see that in just one art activity, four of the six criteria for a quality art program have been met. Further, art can be used to enhance and build on the learning from another curricular area. The preprimary and primary art activities that follow are designed to meet all six of the criteria (although, of course, not all of them at the same time). While both preprimary and primary activities integrate curricular learning, they do it in rather different ways.

PREPRIMARY ACTIVITIES FOR INTEGRATING ART

Art is one curricular area that children may well integrate with their other learnings even without teacher direction. If a variety of art materials is available and within reach, children will usually experiment and learn on their own. For example, upon return from a trip to the zoo, a child who is at the stage of representational attempts may use crayons to draw the family of chimpanzees she observed. Another, at the scribbling stage, may represent the chimpanzees by enthusiastically brushing brown all over a large paper on the easel.

Informality of this sort can lead to much creativity of expression. It is also possible, however, to keep a maximum of creativity while introducing some structure into the curriculum. The ideas for preprimary children have been chosen for this purpose (see Figure 8-1). They are grouped by separate artistic skill areas.

Because children in the early years may be at such widely varying stages of development, it is a good idea to provide activities that lend themselves to everything from scribbling to representation. The ideas included here are flexible enough that they can be

FIGURE 8-1

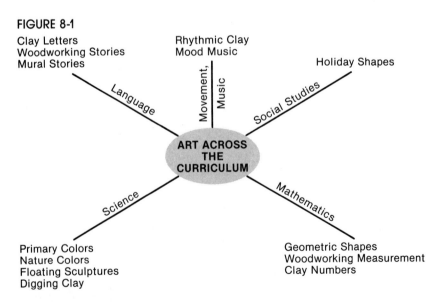

Clay Letters
Woodworking Stories
Mural Stories

Rhythmic Clay
Mood Music

Holiday Shapes

Language

Movement, Music

Social Studies

ART ACROSS THE CURRICULUM

Science

Mathematics

Primary Colors
Nature Colors
Floating Sculptures
Digging Clay

Geometric Shapes
Woodworking Measurement
Clay Numbers

All activities are art–based.

adapted by the children at any of the stages likely to be found in the preprimary years.

Painting Activities

Easels may be a convenience, but they aren't a necessity. Table-tops, outdoor floors, or any other washable surface may be used. Adding soapflakes to tempera paint will make it easier to clean up. One idea for making the painting "center" portable is to put cans of paint in soft drink carrying packs.

If children are to use only one brush in several cans of paint, be sure to carefully demonstrate how to clean the brush each time. For younger children, it is usually less messy to put one brush in each can of paint.

Language   Young children love to work side by side, although they cannot be expected to cooperate on a mural based on a specific theme. On a large sheet of butcher paper, let children work alone or in small groups to make a mural by adding whatever they find beautiful. Use the mural as a background for dictated Mural Stories, announcements of upcoming events, and other visual displays.

Mathematics   Again, cut the painting papers, this time into Geometric Shapes. Informally discuss the name of the shape as children paint or as you help remove the paper when they are done. Don't confine shapes to the square-circle-triangle triad. Children are equally capable of saying and seeing rhombus, trapezoid, and parallelogram.

Science   Supply only the three Primary Colors. Challenge children to invent as many colors and shades as possible. Discuss with them the varying ways different children achieved their results.

Match paint colors to your nature observations. Watch for the arrival of different kinds of birds and discuss the Nature Colors that can be seen in them. Note the varying colors of leaves on the trees. Supply paint and let children mix it to get the right shades. This in itself is one activity for preschoolers. Have children pair a swatch of paint on one side of the paper with an artifact of nature on the other.

Social Studies   As a break from the usual rectangular sheets of paper, supply the paint center with precut thematic Holiday Shapes: hearts for Valentine's Day, shamrocks for St. Patrick's Day, and so on will provide recognition of the holiday without resorting to stereotyped patterned "art." If specific colors are associated with the holiday, they can be provided in the paint jars while others are temporarily removed.

Music   Painting to Mood Music is usually interesting and pleasant for children. Use the opportunity to introduce the sound of new instruments and compositions. In one sitting you might want to choose just one mood or, perhaps, contrasting moods. If the latter, be sure that the differences are starkly obvious. Provide a variety of colors, but don't expect children to choose the same colors for the same moods that an adult would. Black may very well make a child happy!

Woodworking Activities

Check local lumberyards and factories for scraps. Just one or two cooperative sources should keep you in lumber for the year. Choose soft, lightweight types for easier manipulation. Leave no source unchecked; one teacher relied for years on a mousetrap factory!

Even the youngest children enjoy hammering, but, of course, some supervision is required. Using very lightweight wood, it is possible to create assorted sculptures and other objects with wood glue. Joining two or three pieces of wood together may be all the sculpting the smallest children need. Kindergarten children will enjoy hammers, nails, and saws, particularly when a workbench and vise are provided.

Language   When interesting things are happening in the woodworking corner, the experience can be enhanced by Woodworking Stories dictated to the teacher. Have children describe what they have made and attach these descriptions to the object. Or have children describe the steps they took and follow up with a story focusing on sequential events.

Mathematics   This subject is virtually unavoidable in woodworking. For any project children undertake, some form of Woodworking Measurement is necessary, whether formal or primitive. Even the experimental gluing and banging of the youngest children will produce an expanded knowledge of spatial relationships. Older children can learn to choose one piece of wood as a measuring rod and compare it against other pieces of wood. Or something else in the classroom, such as a pencil, can be used as a unit of measure when choosing pieces of wood of the "right" size.

Science   Observing which objects float and which don't is a popular activity in preschool. In the woodbox, provide pieces of varying density and size. In a nearby tub of water have children experiment and hypothesize about what will float and why. They might also nail two or three pieces of wood together in varying configurations to see what will float. Some children will see these Floating Sculptures as "boats," a good springboard for discussion as to what real shipbuilders must look for in their designs.

Clay Activities

Homemade or commercial play dough and hand-dug or purchased clay all provide children with a unique sensory experience. Some children really get into it—literally and figuratively—thumping, rolling, squashing, and manipulating. Others are more reticent and want to work only with their fingertips. This latter group can be encouraged to participate more fully by suggesting to them that this time, just for a minute, they try pushing down with the side of the hand. Next time introduce something else that can manipulate the clay: the elbow, palm, or knuckle, for example.

Language and Mathematics   A number of 4-year-olds and an occasional 3-year-old will be interested in the formation of numbers and letters although their dexterity isn't yet developed enough to write with pencil and paper. Clay offers a large-motor outlet for their budding interest. Begin with the Clay Letters of their names or the Clay Numbers that are their ages or some other symbol of real interest to them. Usually children will make any of these by rolling out snake shapes and then manipulating them into the proper shapes.

Science   Having children dig their own clay (Digging Clay) gives them a heightened understanding of what a source of supply really is. (In our modern culture that's not always easy.) Comparing the texture and malleability of clay with other substances such as sand and dirt gives practice in classification as well as an increased understanding of the positive elements of clay as an art medium.

Music   On a rainy day when energy needs an outlet, or at the end of an intense week, pounding clay to the rhythm of favorite records is a satisfying learning experience. Try using those that have strong rhythms. Singing very rhythmic songs is also fun to do but is more of a conscious effort and may detract from involvement with the art experience.

The Teacher's Role

Art activities that require much teacher intervention are most frequently those that are uncreative, uninspired, and based on adult-made patterns. Thus, you will find that the activities in this unit fall primarily in the categories of facilitating and providing play.

Facilitating   The activities that require some teacher facilitation can all eventually be modified as free-play experiences. The principle need is to get children started, making sure they understand what they are doing. These activities are Primary Colors, Nature

Colors, Mood Music, Floating Sculptures, Woodworking Measurement, Woodworking Stories, and Digging Clay.

Instructing Making Clay Letters and Clay Numbers is the one activity that will, at least at first, require teacher assistance. If children enjoy the activity, they may in time do it on their own.

Providing Play Holiday Shapes, Geometric Shapes, Mural Stories, and Rhythmic Clay are all activities that are immediately playful.

Managing Good preparation—preparation of materials and of children—will be your most important management tool. Be sure that everything children need is easily reached, accident-resistant, and in good supply. Prepare children by demonstrating proper use of materials, particularly in regard to cleanup. Consider role-playing as a class the ways in which paints are mixed, papers are put away, and so on.

Observing Give children as much freedom to work on their own as possible. Observe their interactions with the materials from a little distance, giving them plenty of opportunity to experiment on their own. If a child seems frustrated, wait in the background for a bit to see if he or she can work out the problem before you intervene.

Evaluating Through observation and conversational interaction you should be able to determine whether children are comfortable or intimidated by materials and activities.

Reflecting and Planning As you think about how things went, consider the levels of challenge that were provided the children. In the case of art, repetition for the purpose of further experimentation is preferable to continual new experiences. For this reason, it is a good idea to plan to have similar materials available at all times but with slight modifications to provide new challenges.

PRIMARY UNIT: THE BEAUTY AROUND US

In the primary years it is disturbingly easy to forget the importance of developing children's aesthetic sense as we go about the business of teaching them to read, write, and compute. One argument that is sometimes posited for ignoring visual aesthetics is that children still have many hours at home for this kind of thing. This may or may not be the case. Latchkey children must usually stay locked inside, without any kind of encouragement. Those in afterschool programs can find little escape from the busy noise all about them. Others, by choice or from lack of imagination, will spend hours in front of a television set. Clearly, the school has the resources and an obligation to fill the gap.

One method for introducing art into a busy academic program is to incorporate it into other curricular areas. (We saw Steve do this with his science unit.) This type of experience takes as much or as little time in the curriculum as we are willing to give.

A second solution is to wrap other curricular areas around art, and this unit does just that. While we may not often have the luxury of time to make art the core of the curriculum, it is usually more possible at the beginning of the school year. This is the time when we set the tone for the entire year. Providing children with an opportunity to appreciate the beauty around them at the beginning will also provide a reason to enjoy school in the months to come.

In this unit children are encouraged to be aware of the aesthetics of their classroom and school and to help create the visual attractiveness of that environment. While these activities can be done at any time during the school year, they may be most effective if introduced at the beginning as a means of setting the stage. The activities may be introduced in any order (see Figure 8-2).

Anticipated Outcomes

I   *Student behavior:* As a result of this unit students will be able to:
    A Manipulate several art media with confidence
    B Make aesthetic judgments about their own and their peers' art products
    C Make aesthetic judgments about the visual attractiveness of their school environment
    D Suggest alternative solutions to visual problem areas
II   *Student understanding:* As a result of this unit students will understand that:
    A Everyone is responsible for the visual attractiveness of the environment around them
    B It is possible to improve the visual attractiveness of the environment
    C Critical analysis of visual attractiveness can be non-threatening and can result in greater competence

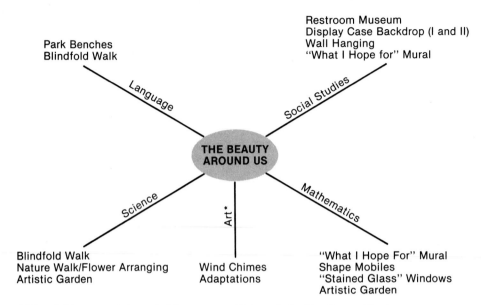

*All activities are art-based. These are not integrated with other subjects.
Note that some activities are listed twice because they are integrated into
more than one area of the curriculum.
FIGURE 8-2

Activities to Beautify the Classroom

I. Blindfold Walk (Bringing the Outdoors In)

Use strips of fabric or make blindfolds from construction paper.
Have children line up outside, each one blindfolded, with one
hand on the shoulder of the person in front and the other hand
holding a supply of crayons. Lead children slowly through the
schoolyard and tell them to listen to the sounds around them. Stop
in a comfortable place, remove the blindfolds, and describe and
discuss the sounds. On manila art paper have children draw the
visual representation of favorite sounds. Use the final products to
decorate a wall or a bulletin board.

II. Nature Walk/Flower Arranging

Take children on a walk around the schoolgrounds and adjacent
property as available. Snip small branches and flowers (multiples
of each for later use) and identify the ones you know. Using reference books, identify the remaining flowers and branches. Place
them in water in like groups and make labels. Then ask children to
place them throughout the room in any way that they perceive as
beautifying.

III. "What I Hope For" Mural

Have children measure a large bulletin board or wall space and then cut butcher paper to match. (This may require more than one attempt.) With a selection of tempera paints, have small groups of children fill this background paper with designs. Introduce just two rules for making the designs: they should be nonrepresentational and they should be unlike those any other child is making. (The first rule provides a better background, the second encourages creativity.) When the designs are finished, discuss their likenesses and differences and the ease or difficulty the children had in being original.

On this background, have children tack pictures of themselves drawn with markers or crayons, doing what they hope will be possible during the coming school year. Beneath each picture write an explanatory label that describes the child's hope.

IV. Shape Mobiles

Provide children with cardboard patterns of varying geometric shapes in several sizes. Include some that are new to them. Have children choose shapes, sizes, and colors of construction paper to outline and cut out. Use a hole punch at the desired position and with heavy black thread attach the shapes to wire hangers. Let children experiment on their own to achieve the right balance; let them hang their hangers on doorknobs or hooks while they work to test the balance. Hang the finished products low enough so that children will be aware of their presence without straining to look up.

V. "Stained Glass" Windows

For the "lead," use 8- by 11-inch black lightweight paper. Cut off one end so that the paper becomes a square, 8 by 8 inches. Have children fold the paper in half, in half again crosswise, and then into a triangle. With scissors, have them cut desired designs in each of the three sides. When paper is opened it will have several large holes. Have children experiment with varying colors of cellophane, putting two or three together to create new colors. Several combinations will be possible in one windowpane. Tape the finished products to classroom windows. Discuss the types of cuts made to achieve each shape and the colors used to create new shades.

Activities to Beautify the Schoolgrounds

VI. Wind Chimes

Use cured clay to make small, flat designs. With the point of a compass or an ice pick, poke one hole near the edge of each. Choose one object and give it two holes; this will be the top chime. Fire the clay objects. Tie the top one to a fairly thick and sturdy string; hang others from thinner strings. Make sure they touch just slightly in order to make a noise when the wind blows.

Hang the chimes from low branches or available crossbeams near the schoolbuilding. On the first windy day, take the class outside to lie in the grass, eyes closed, to listen to the sounds. See if they can hum to match the sounds.

VII. Artistic Garden

Buy packets of flower seeds that will bloom in the fall. On large charts have children work in groups to design arrangements of the available varieties. They will need to discuss the final height of each full-grown plant as well as color composition and the location of the garden. Using their charts, have children plant the seeds, fertilize according to directions, and keep the correct watering schedule in each group. Permit each group to assign responsibilities for planting and upkeep. Keep a written record (wall chart) of these duties. Also keep a chart or diary of the emergence and growth of the plants. Discuss the success or failure in carrying out the original plans. Suggest alternative ideas for future attempts.

VIII. Park Benches

You will need donated old chairs and benches. One good source is often the school district warehouse where discarded furniture is kept. Have children sand down the old paint and varnish the furniture. This takes time and patience and is best done in small groups. Use water-based outdoor paint to repaint the furniture. Place it in the school courtyard or other shady place. Extend written invitations to all classes and office staff to enjoy the finished products.

Activities to Beautify the School

IX. Adaptations

Any of the projects already suggested can be adapted for use in the school hallways, principal's or secretaries' offices, cafeteria, and so on. The essential ingredient is a planning discussion with the children in which they determine which areas of the school could benefit most from beautification and then decide on the appropriate art activities.

X. Wall Hanging

Cut a large rectangle of burlap, narrow enough so that children can sit on each side of it and reach the middle easily. On square pieces of white cloth (an old sheet will do), have children use magic markers to draw self-portraits. These are then sewn onto the burlap after a design is decided on and, if appropriate, after measurements are made. Sew labels with children's names beneath each portrait or use them as an integral part of the picture. Make a tunnel at the top of the hanging by folding over the burlap and sewing it; then place a dowel through it and attach a sturdy string hanger at each end. At the top of the hanging, sew a sign from the class welcoming visitors to the school. Then place the hanging in a conspicuous hallway.

XI. Display Case Backdrop I (Adapted from Linderman & Linderman, 1977, p. 437)

Many elementary schools have display cases in the hall areas. This activity and the one following provide an opportunity for the class to contribute to the school's appearance by enhancing the cases that all the grades will use. Use butcher paper or a piece of plain cotton fabric large enough to fill the back of the display case. Cover a rolling pin with paper and tape the ends together for a snug fit. Glue yarn or string onto the paper to make any type of pattern. Place a large sponge in a shallow dish and soak the top of the sponge in tempera paint. Roll the pin on the sponge and then on the paper or cloth. Have children work in teams or as individuals, depending on the size of the backdrop. Designs can overlap each other slightly, if desired.

XII. Display Case Backdrop II (Adapted from Linderman & Linderman, 1977, p. 425)

Use potatoes and any other vegetables that can be sliced to reveal a flat surface. Cut the potato in half, and then use a paring knife, melon ball cutter, pencils, nails, scissors, and sticks to carve simple designs. Dip the cut potato into thick tempera and print on cloth or paper.

XIII. Restroom Museum

Children can make simple frames for professional (and inexpensive) art prints or for their own best artwork. After choosing large pieces of construction paper, have the children cut holes large enough to frame each print. Abstract designs made with markers or crayons or just one or two neutral colors are the least distracting as frame decorations.

More complex frames can be made with scrap lumber if framing-size strips are available. Second- and third-graders can learn to measure corners with a miter box and then use a saw to attain the correct size. Frames can then be painted with tempera or water-based wall paint. An activity that helps children see color more accurately is to pick a shade from the art print to use in the frame and then try through experimentation to mix it correctly.

Hang finished products in restrooms throughout the school. Occasional shifting of the artworks will keep interest up.

The Teacher's Role

In this unit, the teacher is a facilitator. There are no activities that require total direction, thus providing children with much opportunity for experimentation and decision making. At the same time, none of the activities are designed just for play. It is important to keep this in mind and to provide children with experiences such as those in the preprimary unit. As a part of the regular classroom curriculum there should be art resources available, such as paints, magic markers, crayons, and so on.

Managing   In a unit that provides children with opportunities for self-direction, it is important that the teacher have a clear understanding of appropriate behaviors. This understanding must then be successfully communicated to the children, and they must enter into a spirit of cooperation and self-reliance. Each class will be different, so achieving this may be different from year to year. In general, it is helpful to discuss the situation openly with children in advance. Explain that the activities will require them to act and make decisions on their own. Describe the possible pitfalls: other classes disturbed by too much noise, possible messes, interpersonal disagreements, and so on. Then ask children to help design at least one rule to deal with each of the possible pitfalls. If you have established a good rapport with children, an occasional reminder of the rules may be all the help you'll ever need. If your class hasn't yet achieved this stage, don't let any activity even begin to get out of control. As soon as you sense that things are about to go badly, call the group together and briefly discuss the rules that are being broken or the new ones that need to be made. Then send children back to try again.

Observing   Since this unit is designed to let children make many of their own decisions and to learn to cooperate, you should have a number of opportunities to observe. Look for their interest in the artwork, but also note the children's interactions.

Evaluating   The social pride and activism that are the basis of this unit indicate a need to evaluate such attributes as cooperation and planning skills as well as artistic products. Informal self-evaluations as the children progress will be useful for them, and these may either arise spontaneously as they work in groups or be encouraged by the teacher.

Reflecting and Planning   The activities as presented here can be adapted and expanded, depending on children's interests. Look to the children for more ideas as they learn how rewarding it is to beautify their environment. Perhaps they will be most interested in contributing more beautification projects to the school or in organizing them for all the grades. Or they may wish to make their own room more beautiful. Listen to their suggestions and be supportive, perhaps contributing ideas for dealing with various obstacles such as bureaucracies and limited materials.

TO DISCUSS

1   Return to Brittain's list of teaching techniques for destroying artistic creativity on pages 241–242. Discuss the reasons that teachers might be drawn to these behaviors. Suggest satisfactory alternatives for each one.

TO DO

1   Observe at least two art activities in early childhood classrooms. Match them with the NAEA's criteria for quality art programs. Design ways in which more criteria might be met, or analyze the reasons the maximum has probably been reached.

REFERENCES

Brittain, L. (1979) *Creativity, art and the young child.* New York: Macmillan.

Burkhart, R. (1962) *Spontaneous and deliberate ways of learning.* Scranton, PA: International Textbook.

Greenberg, P. (undated) *Art education: Elementary.* Reston, VA: The National Art Education Association.

Linderman, E., & Linderman, M. (1977) *Crafts for the classroom.* New York: Macmillan.

Lord, L. (1981) The role of the teacher. In *Art for the preprimary child.* Reston, VA: The National Art Education Association. pp. 59–73.

Lowenfeld, V., & Brittain, L. (1975) *Creative and mental growth.* New York: Macmillan.

McFee, J. (1970) *Preparation for art.* Belmont, CA: Wadsworth.

Ritson, J., & Smith, J. (1975) *Creative teaching of art in the elementary school.* Boston: Allyn & Bacon.

Music and Movement

Much of the music for and by young children very naturally incorporates physical movement. For example, the long-term popularity of "The Eensy Weensy Spider" would surely have been less without the accompanying movements. Small children singing to themselves almost always do it while they are also engaged in some sort of physical movement; conversely, young children engaged in physical activity frequently accompany their activity with music. Chants and songs for jumping rope and bouncing balls are common, and children invent songs and chants to communicate with each other during their active play. In the real life of young children, many curricular subjects are naturally integrated, as we have pointed out throughout this text. Music and movement are so frequently inseparable that they have been integrated into this single chapter.

Some segments of "Music and Movement" separate the two subjects: child development and history, for example. By and large, however, this chapter combines the two much as children do in their own lives. It is not only children who do this, of course. Many cultures have a rich tradition of songs and chants "composed" by people engaged in physical labor.

This humanly natural expression of music and movement is the topic of the examples provided in the following section. When children feel comfortable and uninhibited during their free-play periods, music and movement emerge in a natural rhythm. That is to say, spontaneity means that there will be spurts of time when virtually everyone seems to be engaged in a physically musical activity of some sort. Other times the atmosphere will be much quieter with, perhaps, an occasional child or two humming under his breath or briefly moving her body to a remembered dance fragment.

NATURAL MOVEMENT AND MUSIC

The examples of music and movement given below were observed over a period of time during a number of free-play periods. The notes were kept by Eleanor, a student teacher in a class of 3-, 4-, and 5-year-olds, and were pulled from a larger set that included other curricular areas as well.

Eleanor had not really thought about integrating music and movement. It just happened. She did not even realize what had taken place until she looked back at her notes. Then she saw repeated examples of children engaging in the two simultaneously. In these selections from Eleanor's notes, the experiences took place during free-play time unless otherwise indicated.

• Robert, Paul, and Ricardo are at the listening center playing records. They know they have to avoid disturbing others by wearing headsets. That doesn't keep them from singing and dancing to the music—with their headset cords seeming to trail in every direction.

• It's a beautiful day out, but the kids in the housekeeping corner are chanting, "It's raining, it's pouring..." as they play. The words don't seem to relate to the plot of their play. The song is just background noise.

• Mercedes and Charles are using two saws to slice through a couple of boards. They've somehow gotten in rhythm with each other and are inventing a nonsense song as they go along. It sounds something like "Squeechy, squeechy little saw-w-w."

• Every day the 4- and 5-year-olds try for perfect balance on the balance beam. It's always been quiet concentration, but today it finally seems to be easy for them, and they started singing to each child who was walking the beam. (The one on the beam doesn't seem to have the nerve to join in.) Any song they know seems acceptable.

• Ramon has never had a music lesson and there's no piano at home, but he's able to pick out the melody of almost any song on the class piano. He just spent 10 minutes working through the new one they learned yesterday, and five or six others gathered around to watch. Two of the girls started twirling around and giggling, but nobody tried singing. The song is probably still too new.

• There are little pieces of masking tape on some of the piano keys. They are the ones used by the teacher when she plays a special melody to call the children to group time. Some of the older children have learned the melodic pattern and can pick it out with the aid of the tape. Today when it was time to clean up, Rusty played the tune and then decided to repeat himself. He got carried away with the idea and played it over and over. I was going crazy, but the kids didn't mind because as soon as they'd finish their cleaning they'd come over and sing, "Nyah, nyah,..." to the tune and dance around more or less in rhythm.

• On the playground, three of the little ones were sitting in the sandbox, mostly just shoveling sand in their buckets and talking to themselves. But Sarah started shoveling in rhythm and each time some sand would go in the bucket she'd chant, "Pup!" Then the "pup" became more singsong, and for a short time she almost had a little song and dance going.

These selections from Eleanor's notes do not include observations of music and movement activities that were chosen by the teacher as part of the curriculum. Instead, they are representative examples of the natural relationship between music and movement during informal times in the children's school day. Anyone who observes small children at play will see that these events usually emerge unannounced and that they can easily be overlooked or interrupted when other things appear to have more importance. But music and movement are both natural and important parts of children's lives and deserve our attention.

WHY MUSIC, WHY MOVEMENT

"The value of movement experience in teaching music stems from the pleasure the child has in moving and the intimate relationship that exists between movement and sound" (Andress, et al., 1973, p. 2). This statement, the point of view of a music educator, demonstrates the integrated importance that music and movement have in the lives of young children. For the purposes of this discussion, however, we will separate the two.

Why Music

Music, like art, gives a specific culture its trademark. Whether we are observed today by others or many years from now by our descendants, it is the fine arts that are tangible indicators of what we have been about. Today we live in a culture that places children in schools from an early age, thus giving schools much of the responsibility for teaching whatever fine arts will be passed along. The Music Educators National Conference (MENC) has stated that, "Virtually every individual or group that has made a major contribution to Western educational thought since Plato has included the arts among the basics..." (MENC, 1986, p. 12). "Music is basic. Every young American should receive a solid program of instruction in music in school" (p. 12).

The MENC argues a ten-point rationale for including music in the curriculum, most of which apply to preschool and all of which are important in the primary grades.

1. Music is worth knowing—for every member of society.

2. A glorious part of our cultural heritage is passed on through music.

3. All children should be given the opportunity to test the limits of their potential in many fields, including music.

4. Music provides an outlet for creativity and self-expression.

5. Music is an important way to learn about other cultures.

6. Music provides success for some children who may not find it in other curricular areas.

7. By increasing musical concepts and skills, children also derive more enjoyment from making and listening to music.

8. Music is a powerful symbol system, important to learn along with verbal and mathematical symbols.

9. Because it is more subjective than quantifiable, music is more like real life than are most other curricular disciplines.

10. A major societal role music plays is to transform the human experience and to exalt the human spirit (Adapted from MENC, 1986, p. 13).

Having decided upon this ten-point rationale for music, the MENC then takes the position "that the fundamental purpose of teaching music in the schools is to develop in each student, as fully as possible, the ability to perform, to create, and to understand music" (p. 14). This threefold purpose, intended for even young children, is of relatively recent invention. Looking back to our country's earliest years, we can see that the ability to perform has traditionally been considered the prime reason to teach music, understanding is a possible second, and creation is a distant third that is reserved for those with a well-defined talent.

The Pilgrims and the Puritans brought with them an enjoyment for music, primarily devoted to religious purposes. A hundred years after their arrival, however, the Puritan Cotton Mather gave some clue that music had been secularized when he found it necessary to deliver a speech that decried teaching children "trifles" at dancing school (Keene, 1982). At the same time, singing schools were begun in order to teach young and old how to sing psalms more effectively. Throughout the eighteenth century these schools retained their popularity, providing a major source of music training for everyone.

As towns and cities flourished, music education continued to grow in importance. For example, in eighteenth-century Philadelphia there were fashionable boarding schools that educated "young ladies" in dancing, singing, and the playing of instruments. By the next century, some attempts were made to introduce music into the public schools, but there were critics and the going was rocky.

Nevertheless, throughout the nineteenth century, schools did begin to incorporate music and a philosophical argument began that sounds much like the arguments that accompany the philosophies of reading. Should children learn many songs just for enjoyment and then, much later, learn the mechanics of reading the notes and other symbols? Or should they first learn the tools and how to use them before learning to sing? The arguments on both sides continue today. By 1864 the first series of singing books for younger schoolchildren had been published and several others followed soon after.

The turn of this century brought first the mechanical player piano and then the phonograph into the schools, thus making music appreciation possible as a course of study. Younger children were given little instruction in what they were listening to and were simply left to be entertained. In 1920, however, the book *Music Appreciation for Little Children* was published by Victor Co. to give teachers direction in helping small children learn to experience and to love music. The book's philosophy clearly was on the side of those who present music first for enjoyment and later for skills learning: "Children should hear music long before they are asked to master the symbols of the printed form, the rules of grammar of its language, or the techniques of its performance" (Keene, 1982, p. 257).

This argument was echoed by Carl Orff in Germany in the middle years of this century. He felt that too many young children learned to play instruments without ever having experienced music. The system of music education he developed was imported to this country and, at least in part, continues to influence the music education of young children.

Rhythm was Orff's starting point and it grew out of children's speech patterns: "For the child, as for primitive man, speaking and singing, music and movement cannot be isolated" (Keene, 1982, p. 343). Percussion instruments were to be used along with body movements. Children worked in groups and were introduced to basic instruments such as drums, cymbals, and water-filled musical glasses. Orff himself composed melodies largely to traditional nursery rhymes and songs. Creativity was an important part of music education, and children were expected to integrate their music making with poetry, movement, playing, and dancing—all part of children's natural activities.

From Hungary came another imported method for teaching music to young children. Zoltan Kodaly (*Kō*-dye) held many beliefs that were similar to Orff's, but he was influenced more strongly by his country's highly academic, structured educational system. Rather than beginning children's training with Orff's playful music experiences, Kodaly preferred to start their education with national folk songs. He was inspired to do this after hearing student teachers in a university preparing songs to teach to their elementary children. He considered their selections insipid and shallow and determined that instead children should be exposed to their rich national heritage. When his method was introduced in the United States, he suggested that the 40,000 folk songs available in the Library of Congress would be a generous source.

Hungarian children begin their music training in nursery school, and Kodaly believed that their best curriculum would be movement and singing games. As soon as children were ready, reading and writing of musical notation should be introduced. The method, although structured, is simplified in its presentation and uses role play, pictures, and body movements.

Although both Kodaly and Orff sought to make use of the natural development and interests of small children, they approached training in opposite directions. Orff argued for much experience with music before symbols were introduced; Kodaly felt that even very young children could learn notation if taught properly. In theory and in practice, both methods have much to recommend them, and the two are sufficiently compatible that ideas from both could be used in one classroom. Books devoted to the two systems are usually available from music curriculum offices and can be adapted for use by regular classroom teachers.

A third approach to young children's music emerged at the turn of the century, was ignored for a while, and has regained popularity. It was begun in Switzerland by Émile Jaques-Dalcroze and demonstrates, perhaps best of all the approaches, the efficacy of integrating movement and music. He was in agreement with his countryman from the century before, Heinrich Pestalozzi, that music's power to evoke feelings made it a desirable course of study for young children. And he agreed with Pestalozzi that the "purpose of education was to foster the harmonious development of moral, physical, and mental capability" (Brown, 1987, p. 89). Jaques-Dalcroze, in applying this philosophy to music for the young, stressed the importance of integrating music with rhythm and body movement, thus focusing on educating the whole person.

The Dalcroze eurythmics (Greek for "good rhythm") begins in nursery school with relaxed listening, the playing of singing games, and acting out the musical accompaniments of stories. As children get older, they coordinate body movement, ear training, and improvisation at the piano. The Dalcroze philosophy is that there is a "coordination of brain, nerves, and muscles when the child responds with physical actions to musical stimuli. This then creates a greater depth of feeling and sensitivity to music" (Bayless & Ramsey, 1978, p. 171).

The philosophies of Orff, Kodaly, and Dalcroze all point to movement as an integral part of creating and learning music. Now, let's focus on movement itself.

Why Movement

In 1981 the American Alliance for Health, Physical Education, Recreation and Dance (AAHPERD) published a series of pamphlets and books in an effort to bring together current theory, philosophy, and practical ideas for the use of teachers of young children. AAHPERD argued that children between the ages of 2½ and 8 need movement education because:

- They want to feel good (health concerns).
- They want to look good (bodily appearance).
- They want to do better (locomotor movements).
- They want to get along (psychosocial concerns).
- They want to "turn on" (aesthetics).
- They want to survive (body alignment and injury prevention) (Adapted from Riggs, Dodds, & Zuccalo, 1981).

Such a broad-based view of the benefits of movement education is both new and very old. Bits and pieces of it have been present in educational philosophy for many centuries, but not usually in unified form as they are in AAHPERD's philosophy. The early Greeks and Romans incorporated play into their education for young children, and before them the Egyptians trained young boys in tumbling, dancing, tug-of-war, ball games, juggling, wrestling, swimming, and more.

Later, in the Middle Ages, physical education was decried as being too focused on the satanic physical and this potential evil was removed from the curriculum in cathedral schools. Boys in the royal court schools, however, learned to swim and dive, use various bows, joust, wrestle, and fence—all activities that would be useful when they were later admitted to knighthood.

The Renaissance brought a return of the attitudes of the Greeks and Romans, and physical education again had wide acceptance. Nevertheless, this acceptance was primarily practiced in the upper classes, and the poorer children suffered ill health, crowded conditions, and little time for physical play. Thus, as the American continent was first colonized, "a combination of hard physical labor and puritanical fervor left little inclination for play among early settlers" (Shephard, 1982, p. 15).

By 1852, however, some schools in the Boston area began incorporating gymnastics, and St. Louis and Cincinnati soon followed suit. By 1866 California was requiring physical education in all its schools. The first public playground appeared in Boston in 1885 and 4 years later the same city required Swedish gymnastics in the schools. The primary purpose was to provide children with a break from study and did not address other needs such as those listed by AAHPERD. In fact, the gymnastics could be done right in the classroom between heavy study sessions. At the turn of the century, John Dewey introduced games and dancing as part of young children's physical education into the University of Chicago laboratory school, but, for the most part, schools didn't change from formalized gymnastics programs until after World War I.

Physical education finally came into its own as an important subject for schoolchildren after World War II, a period notable for the emergence of "movement education" as an appropriate approach for younger children. Begun in Germany with the work of Rudolf Laban, expanded in England, and then imported by the United States, movement education takes a different approach to what is expected of children when they are educated physically. The traditional teaching of progressive skills, the same skills to all children in a group whether they are ready or not, is rejected. In its place, children's physical and emotional development are enhanced by using games, gymnastics, and dance in a less competitive and more creative way. Four categories of movement provide a framework for the curriculum:

- What the body can do (body awareness)
- Where the body can move (space awareness)
- How the body can move (qualities of movement)
- Relationship to other performers and to apparatus (Kirchner, 1978, p. 10)

The several goals of this type of program are quite different from those traditionally associated with physical education, particularly in the primary grades. Even though preschools have traditionally focused less performance and competition and more on creativity and games, the goals of today's movement education are broader still:

- Children will become physically fit and skillful in a variety of situations.
- Children will understand the principles of movement and become aware of what their bodies can do.
- Self-discipline and self-reliance are encouraged.
- There are opportunities for self-expression and creativity.
- Children develop confidence in meeting physical challenges.
- Cooperation and sensitivity to others are encouraged (Kirchner, 1978, p. 4).

If only some of these goals are achieved, children will attain much more than has historically been expected by any kind of physical education. The fact that games, gymnastics, and dance are the primary vehicles for achieving these goals means that there is an excellent opportunity to incorporate music, and this is frequently done. While music and movement have historically been separated more often than not, teachers today can take advantage of the many opportunities to unite them.

THE TEACHER'S ROLE

The varying philosophies of music for young children and of movement education have a number of points in common that relate to what teachers should consider doing and being. Several of these points suggest that teachers be models for child behavior and/or become like children themselves. Teachers who feel they have no talent for music or for physical movement need to remember that young children are so delighted when their teachers enter into their activities that talent is not a consideration. Teachers who still feel hesitant because some other adult might see, can simply close the door and enjoy! Try these suggestions for successful classroom experiences.

1. *Choose child-centered over teacher-centered learning.*The creative aspects of both music and movement will be greatly enhanced by this decision. If teachers lecture or demonstrate and try to get children to follow, they may increase technical performance for some children, but it will be the teacher's dance or music, not the children's. As children grow in their understanding of music, such demonstrations are at times appropriate, but they should not be the exclusive methodology.

Child-centered learning also means learning by discovery. This may take a little longer than simply telling children a musical or movement solution, but the final result is a more profound understanding. The mode of teaching should be: Here's a problem; can you and your partner(s) figure out how to do it?

2. *Individualize learning.*This suggestion is related to child-centered learning. It does not necessarily mean that every child will have a personal tutoring session every time teaching takes place. It does argue, however, that teachers should start where the children are, rather than expecting them in advance to meet some perhaps unrealistic set of criteria. Rigid music curriculums and old-fashioned physical education skills require this behavior of children. The teacher who individualizes learning observes children to determine what their interests, strengths, and needs are and then acts on those observations.

The teacher who individualizes learning takes care to help children in a positive way. Reinforcement should be positive, thus bringing joy and creativity to children's participation.

3. *Be a frequent observer*. Child-centered learning, with its time for exploration, provides teachers with observation time, which can be used to carefully calculate where children are in their progress. The teacher can move about the room or playground as children test out their ideas, perhaps making an occasional suggestion but mostly simply making notations for future use.

4. *Use teachable moments*. Music and movement do not always need to be rigidly scheduled. They can be incorporated into the entire school day in such a way that use can be made of spontaneity. Do two or three children interrupt their work to begin chanting or pounding in rhythm while others watch and wonder if it's "all right" to join in? The teacher can join in, too, letting them know that it is indeed all right. New rhythms can then be added, with the quietest saved for last, thus bringing the class back to its original on-task behavior.

5. *Be a playmate to the children at times.*The example of a teachable moment fits here also. Music and movement are times of physical and emotional release, and children are at times hesitant or else they overreact to the situation. Becoming one of them sets the tone for behavior. If children tend to feel inhibited, it helps them feel more natural about the activities.

6. *Be a composer and an improviser*. The teacher should observe the children's own inventions in movement and music and then help extend them. If a child is rambling through a spontaneous song, the teacher can first join in and then expand on it, inviting the child to do likewise. The same can be done with tentative dance steps and configurations.

7. *Be a learner as well as a teacher*. Be a teacher who can create music and movement. As teachers, we expect young children to be uninhibited and open to new attempts, and we need to expect the same of ourselves. If we want children to be positive in their attempts, then we must be sure we feel positive ourselves. If a teacher has never had lessons in music or movement, this just might be a time when it would be fun to try!

8. *Be aware of approximate developmental levels*. Teachers need not analyze the exact stage of every child during each music or movement encounter. But some general knowledge of what abilities are within the norm will assist them in making curricular decisions.

MUSIC AND MOVEMENT AND CHILD DEVELOPMENT

In Chapter One, motor development and physical growth were discussed at length and it may be useful to make a cursory review of it before beginning this section. While Chapter One dealt with general stages of development, we focus in this chapter on what you might expect to see children doing at different ages. We will again combine music and movement because they are so naturally combined in development, particularly in regard to dance and rhythm skills.

The sources for this section come from the literature in both physical education and music and include Nelson (1955), Andress (1980), Andress, Heimann, Rinehart, & Talbert (1973), Bayless & Ramsey (1978), Beaty (1986), Burton (1980), Haines & Gerber (1984), Humphrey (1980), McDonald (1979), Peery & Peery (1987), and Skinner (1979). The descriptions of what you might expect to observe at each age are followed by implications for you to consider in future planning of the curriculum.

Infants through Age 2

In very young infants, the close observer will notice abilities that seem to be far beyond their age. In Chapter One we mentioned the reflex motions of walking and swimming, both of which disappear later. To these we can also add the ability to imitate tones on-key. This musical capability also disappears with time and, like the other two, can be observed between 3 and 6 months of age. At this time, infants are trying out many movements and sounds. When either one is reinforced by some result, such as a crib mobile wiggling or an adult imitating the infant's vocalizations, the baby will repeat the movement or sound over and over. This kind of repeated response to environmental stimuli was called *circular* by Piaget.

At about 6 months, babies begin using somewhat rhythmic whole-body movements in response to music. In the ensuing months they will learn to clap, point, move backward, crawl, slither, roll, push, and pull—all important movements for responding to music.

Learning to walk, usually sometime after the first birthday, offers vast freedom to infants. By 18 months they will bounce to music or to their own inner sense of rhythm. They enjoy being rocked and sung to, bounced in rhythm on an adult knee, or swung in the air to music and rhymes. Some children are able to sing parts of songs. When creating their own movement, they enjoy making plenty of racket using their enthusiastic physical energy.

The developing capabilities and enjoyment of infants come in response to the environment, a fact with important implications. If the environment is rich, so will be the infant's responses. A number of studies have shown what deprivation can do—for example, in orphanages with few care givers available. Children as old as 2 may not be able to sit up; 4-year-olds may not be able to walk.

Blind babies (in any setting) may not become interested in crawling because they have no visual stimuli.

Those who care for infants can enhance the atmosphere with plenty of talking, singing, and rhythmic activities appropriate to their ages. Mobiles in the crib, wind chimes in the window, playing musical instruments for the child to listen to—all provide possibilities for growth.

The 2-Year-Old

The abilities of walking and talking as well as better overall body control make new activities possible and old activities more skillfully done. For example, we can still expect children to prefer banging pots and pans to create wonderful (to them!) noises. Now, however, they may pick and choose which pots they prefer. Still, there are limitations in that they may choose two pot lids as cymbals because they are the same size, not because they are auditorily preferable. At this age, their visual discrimination is ahead of their ability to make choices in sound.

Two-year-olds run, gallop, walk on tiptoe, and jump rhythmically. They can walk up and down stairs, at first with both feet on a step, then later just one. They enjoy rolling balls and can throw overhand as well as kick from a standing position. Arms are used for balance and to keep rhythm, and hand-clapping is rhythmic. The rhythm of older 2-year-olds is more competent and they become more interested in imitating the rhythms of others. Musical commercials on TV or radio now catch their attention and they will sing snatches of a song. A few children can sing whole songs, sometimes while rocking a doll. There are spontaneous songs, too, usually growing out of motor activities. These often use the minor third (as in "Rain, Rain Go Away").

Because children at this age are more self-sufficient, lack of adult attention may not be as devastating as it is for younger infants. Nevertheless, if a child is to learn to throw a ball, then someone must be around to demonstrate and help. If children are to respond to music in rhythmic and tuneful ways, then there must be music present. Of course, 2-year-olds still prefer solitary and sometimes parallel play, so they should not be forced into group situations for movement and music activities. Two-year-olds also crave independence, so they are happiest when adult direction leads to independent capabilities. Since their attention shifts quickly from one thing to another, it is a good idea to alternate active with more sedentary activities. Most of all, 2-year-olds need happy reinforcement of their attempts at improving their skills: running faster, walking up and down stairs, climbing around and over things, and dancing to music and rhythmic beats.

The 3-Year-Old

Now children walk in a way that looks much more adult. They swing their arms, rather than using them for balance, and the rhythm is right. Their speech is quite fluent, making it more possible for them to sing lyrics and recite short poems.

Now that their coordination and rhythm are improved, simple, imaginative dramatic play becomes attractive. They are likely to introduce some variety into their body movements and to experiment with their use of space. A lot of energy goes into movement, and children may occasionally lose control and fall (but at least it's not too far to the ground!). The ability to ride tricycles gives much more mobility, and no preschool can possess too many of life's first vehicles.

General movement capabilities increase for the 3-year-olds. They can walk forward and backward on a straight line, walk up and down stairs with more ease, jump off the bottom step or two, run with a more even stride, balance for a moment on one foot, and maybe even hop a bit. They can now kick a ball while running, and some children can bounce it fairly well. Galloping, jumping, running, and walking are now done with such ease that 3-year-olds can keep fairly good time to music. Most can even stamp their feet while clapping their hands at the same time.

For some children there can be a temporary relapse before they turn 4. There may be days when everything goes well and others when they seek the reassurance of an adult hand going up or down stairs or when they can't get the beloved trike to do what it ought to. This appears to happen during growth spurts, when the body seems to need to adjust to new changes.

Generally speaking, however, 3-year-olds are making great strides in coordination. This is a good time to introduce rhythm and melody instruments as well as singing games. They may fall a little behind with the words when they sing, but they enjoy trying. Because 3-year-olds are cooperative, loving, and friendly and want adult approval, it is important to encourage them in their attempts. They are just beginning to be able to share and take turns, thus suggesting encouragement and reinforcement but not high demands.

The 4-Year-Old

Four-year-olds are agile, energetic, and more active than ever before. They run up and down stairs, can throw a ball overhand, and are learning to skip. Jumping is great fun as they learn to do it from a running position. Four's will climb as high as they can on playground equipment or trees, and then they sometimes can't get back down again. Stunts and tricks are popular activities. They can march in time, and some can hop on one foot. They are beginning to like to do things in groups, such as singing, but most times they like to do things their own way without too many interfering directions.

Children of this age are able to classify and to order sounds, and they can organize them to express a story. Because they are beginning to remember sequences, they can make use of them in songs, memorizing or inventing their own. Nonsense words and silly plots or phrasing are as entertaining to 4-year-olds in songs as they are in stories.

The implications for working with 4-year-olds include being sure that there is plenty of space and time for energetic movement experiences. There should be climbing equipment and supervisors to be sure all goes well. This is a good time for dramatic play; acting out stories in free interpretation, possibly with song, is excellent also.

The 5-Year-Old

Five-year-olds offer a respite from the energetic year before. Refining and consolidating already acquired abilities is more the keynote than is exploration and expansion. A good sense of balance is pretty well established by now, and fine motor development is improved. For most children, but not all, handedness is established. Children can walk the balance beam, execute simple dance steps, and, in general, control bodily activity more smoothly. Hopping and skipping are now no problem, and skipping rope is an attainable challenge for many. Some children can hit a swinging ball, play two-handed catch, and bounce the ball repeatedly, but none of these skills is at a mature level. Body rhythm is confident and natural, and both body awareness and body image are increasing.

Five-year-olds still have a vivid imagination and as yet cannot always differentiate fantasy from reality. Dramatic play and pretending are enjoyable still. Cognitively, 5-year-olds can combine simple ideas into more complex ones and apply them to new situations, thus making them capable of more complex musical experiences. Because they are now more capable of cooperative play, they can also cooperate to create or reproduce musical events.

Musically, children can respond more accurately to rhythm. They can repeat musical and rhythmic patterns. They can begin to sort out the multiple musical sounds of a band or an orchestra. Many can sing back a musical pattern, on-key and in rhythm.

Although 4-year-olds can begin to participate in drama and group songs, it is the 5-year-olds who can really produce. Providing them with opportunities to explore movement and song is important. They can differentiate between types of instruments and their functions, including making decisions about what instruments might best accompany recorded musical pieces. Five-year-olds no longer have the all-out constant physical exuberance of 4-year-olds, so a balance between active and more passive activities is a good idea once again.

The 6-Year-Old, 7-Year-Old, and 8-Year-Old

By the time children enter first grade, they are also entering an important new stage in their development. Although there is change and progress between the ages of 6 and 8, the course is more steady and unvaried than it was in previous years. Thus, we can cluster several ages together in one group.

After the "breather" that the 5-year-olds provide, the 6-year-olds demonstrate again what energy and activity young children are capable of. By now, if all has gone well, children have, at the least, a simple mastery of the fundamental motor skills. You will recall from Chapter One that these are the skills necessary for future use in sports and recreational activities. They include those we have discussed: running, jumping, hopping, skipping, galloping, balancing, climbing, and throwing, bouncing, catching, kicking, and hitting a ball. These fundamental skills are important enough to children that teachers need to observe them knowledgeably and support children's progress in refining them. By elementary school, physical education teachers become a part of children's lives, but unless you are in the rare school district that provides a class every day, you will find yourself supervising much of the children's outdoor activity. At such times it would be a good idea to observe these skills and provide help—or seek it from physical education professionals—when it is needed. Children who become competent in the fundamental skills will feel much more competent as they begin new sports. And that is true all the way through life. Following are some ideas of what to observe:

• *Running:* First-graders can run in much the same fashion as adults; all the coordination elements are present. They aren't, of course, as fast, for speed comes over the next 3 years with growth and practice. First and second grade are generally a time of great increase in speed, both for fast dashes and for longer runs. Boys tend to be just slightly faster than girls.

• *Hopping, galloping, and skipping:* In this instance it is girls who outperform boys, usually acquiring all three skills a little earlier. It is in first grade that skipping is usually mastered, although girls may be more graceful and boys more heavy and flat-footed.

• *Jumping:* Before children enter first grade their jumping interests have focused more on jumping down rather than up, over, or far. Now, however, children begin to learn about long jumps and high jumps in their physical education classes, and a different interest grows. As they enter school, girls have a slight edge over boys in distances, but boys then improve more rapidly and by the end of third grade have become more adept at jumping than girls.

• *Throwing:* Between the ages of 7 and 11, children increase their throwing distances by 100 percent. However, boys outdistance girls markedly at all ages.

• *Kicking:* Again, boys perform better at all ages, both in velocity and distance. For both sexes there is great improvement between the first and third grades.

• *Balance:* There are four interrelated types of balance: postural balance (walking and sitting upright), static balance (keeping a position without moving), dynamic balance (controlling posture while moving through space), and gymnastic balance (needed for stunts and complex movement combinations). Studies of children working on balance beams (dynamic balance) showed great improvement between first and third grades, with boys and girls almost identical in their abilities. Various apparatuses have been used to measure static balance and, curiously, children improved through age 7, tapered off at age 8, then increased performance again at age 9. Coming into first grade, boys were less capable than girls but were then able to catch up.

The acquisition of the fundamental skills by first grade signified the future need not only for refinement but also for the introduction of new uses for these skills. Changing social interests, including more focus on the importance of peers, means that children are developing an interest in activities that require teams and groups. The significance for musical experiences is that more complex interactions and projects are now enjoyed. Planning performances together is more important than individual effort or impositions from above.

Acquisition of fundamental skills also indicates that children are now capable of rhythmic movement and coordinated dance steps while working in groups. Marching, simple square dances, or a Virginia reel are possibilities.

Concerning children's abilities to produce musical pitch, carry a melody, and perform metrical tasks, the most important influence appears to be experience and contact. Some first-graders can do all these things well and others take a number of years, although researchers don't yet know why. But one thing seems certain: The children who have more contact with musical experiences become more capable sooner.

As primary-grade children attain the Piagetian concrete operational stage, they become capable of new and more complex musical experiences. For example, children who can perform concrete operational tasks involving number can also combine musical sounds in their memories. By third grade, children are competent in reading and notating music, but they often prefer to fall back on the rote learning they have done in all their previous years. Third-graders are also able to sing simple two-part songs and in rounds if they have had sufficient training.

Children make great strides in their movement and music capabilities. Between infancy and the third grade many changes take place, and these differences will influence what is included in an effective curriculum. Although rather specific ages were given in this section for the development of skills and capabilities, it still must be remembered that individual children develop on different schedules. Further, each individual's development will usually show some unevenness. For example, one child may be far ahead physically but behind musically, while another child may demonstrate the reverse. Use the age divisions as guidelines only.

THE MOVEMENT AND MUSIC CURRICULUM

In this section we begin first with a discussion of appropriate movement curriculum. Then, after a discussion of the music curriculum, we combine the two to show the ways in which their integration is a natural and appropriate curricular design.

The Movement Curriculum

Since the youngest children are concerned with developing fundamental skills, the curriculum should be designed to identify and enhance those skills. By the second and third grade, children are beginning to enter the period of refinement of skills and have a growing interest in team sports and games, and the curriculum needs to reflect this change.

For example, *body awareness* entails not just an internal understanding of body parts and their relationships, but also an understanding of what one can and cannot do with the body. *Spatial awareness* refers to an understanding of the body's relationship to objects in space as well as to a good perception of the relationships between objects themselves. Children also need to have an awareness of the two sides of the body and to directions such as up/down or front/back/sideways, which is referred to as *directional awareness*. *Manipulative skills* include such things as throwing, bouncing, kicking, rolling, catching, or trapping a ball. The difference between locomotor and nonlocomotor skills is the degree of movement. *Nonlocomotor activities* include such things as leaning, twisting, bending, and so on that permit the child to stay in one place. Movement from one place to another is involved in *locomotor skills*.

These are essential elements that should provide a foundation for movement education; other goals don't all relate directly to movement itself but to the grander picture of children's physical lives:

1. To develop respect for the rights and ideas of others

2. To help children become happy, helpful people

3. To develop a positive, stable self-concept

4. To form a realistic view of personal strengths and weaknesses

5. To enhance children's creativity

6. To encourage children to solve simple problems

7. To awaken children to intellectual challenges (Adapted from Gallahue, 1982, p. 375)

These goals show how much further the movement curriculum can go. In recent years public concern has grown about lifelong *fitness* and a focus on attitudes that produce wellness. Even young children can learn what movement-related activities promote well-being and can learn to enjoy them. Activities that promote endurance, flexibility, and muscular strength are all important in achieving a healthful outlook and being. The interpersonal skills suggested by numbers 1 and 2 are important for success in team sports. Although we have not listed them as physically fundamental skills, they are certainly fundamental to good teamwork. Thus, it is important for the youngest children to grow in their social abilities so that in the primary years they will have the foundation necessary to progress to the interactive social stages that relate to teamwork.

All seven elements should be included in the preprimary and primary curriculum, and you will see them represented in the units at the end of this chapter. It is important to realize that helping children to understand their bodies' capabilities, to move them through space, and to have an understanding of healthy bodily practices and good interpersonal skills is not just preparing children for success in sports. Throughout our lives we need these skills, and making young children comfortable with their bodies and with what they can do creates a curriculum with broad and long-term benefits.

Of course, basing our curricular choices on the related developmental levels of the children we teach is of major importance. Gallahue has listed a number of these for both preschool and elementary children.

Preschool Curriculum Choices Based on Development

1. Plenty of undirected and directed gross motor play

2. Lots of movement exploration and problem-solving activities

3. Positive reinforcement to enhance self-image

4. Progression from simple to complex in locomotor, manipulative, and stability (nonlocomotor) activities

5. No separation of boys and girls

6. Plenty of activities designed specifically to enhance perceptual-motor activity

7. Activities that include drama and imagery to enhance children's imaginations

8. Activities that require object handling and eye-hand coordination

9. Introduction of bilateral activities: skipping, galloping, and hopping

10. Children permitted to progress at their own rates

Primary-Grade Curriculum Choices Based on Development

1. Opportunities to refine fundamental movements until they are fluid

2. Activities to help children make the transition from the fundamental movement phase to the sports-related phase

3. Continued encouragement and positive reinforcement

4. Opportunities to experiment with movement to enhance perceptual-motor efficiency

5. Progressively greater amounts of responsibility introduced to promote self-reliance

6. Gradual introduction to group and team activities

7. Use of story plays and imaginary and mimetic activities

8. Use of music and rhythmics to enhance fundamental movement and creativity

9. Integration of movement into the academic curriculum to enhance learning

10. Climbing and hanging activities to develop the upper torso

11. Discussions about sportsmanship: taking turns, fair play, cheating, and so on (Adapted from Gallahue, 1982, p. 129 ff.)

So that you have a more specific idea of activities that are based on developmental levels, here are some suggestions for different age groups.

Preschool Activities

- Active games that require simple counting
- Dramatic play
- Climbing and jumping off medium-size boxes
- Simple rhythms and marching
- Time for individual play
- Low, inclined planks; jungle gyms; and building blocks for climbing
- Practice in starting, stopping, dodging, and changing direction
- Throwing and catching with slow-moving objects (beachballs, balloons)
- Walking the balance beam
- Challenges to run faster and faster
- Practice riding tricycles up inclined planes and around objects
- Practice dribbling ball with feet
- Use of music, words, stories, and sound to stimulate creative movements
- Simple singing games
- Games lacking in competition

Kindergarten and First-Grade Activities

- Activities requiring speed, starting and stopping on signal, and changing directions
- Jumping over barriers with gradually increased heights
- Hopscotch and related grids or patterns for hopping
- Skipping to a distinct rhythmic beat
- Versatile play structures for climbing
- Individualized challenges when learning ball skills
- Use of music in the background and for rhythmic activities
- Animal stunts
- Creative rhythms and movement sequences with themes from songs and stories
- Games with individual roles and few team games and relays
- Simple stunts and tumbling

Second- and Third-Grade Activities

- Use of team concept in activities and relays

• Challenging movement problems: critical demands in stunts, tumbling, and apparatus work
  • Teaching of safety and good judgment
  • Dodgeball and other active games
  • Organized practice in skills: throwing, catching, moving, and so on
  • Rules and playing fair during games; stress on social customs and courtesy during movement activities
  • Creative rhythms and action songs
  • Folk dances
  • Introduction of simple sports skills
  • Avoidance of highly organized ball games that demand quickness and accuracy
  • Ball bouncing and dribbling skills to rhythm (Adapted from Burton, 1980, pp. 52–62; Pangrazi & Dauer, 1981, pp. 13–16)

To make the curriculum work for you, there are a few general principles that will be helpful to remember. Try thinking about yourself when you have learned a new adult sport. At the beginning you probably thrived on encouragement and positive reinforcement. In the initial stages you were no doubt much more tense than you were when you felt at ease and the movements began to flow more effortlessly. Until you built up strength and skill, short and frequent sessions were preferable to long, extended, and intense ones. Your skills progressed from the simple to the complex and (if applicable) from the muscularly gross to the refined. Practice was necessary, but it did not necessarily make perfect; your own abilities were not always the same as others. As you progressed in your skills, it was helpful to get feedback from instructors or friends on your progress. This feedback needed to be more specific (and perhaps more honest!) than the initial positive reinforcements.

If you can mentally transfer your own evolution in a new sport to the experience of young children across all their movement learning, you should have a good feel for what is necessary, helpful, and possible. During the preschool and early primary years, positive reinforcement is important. During second and third grade it is important, too, but feedback on skills is usually highly sought by children newly aware of what it takes to achieve sports-related success.

A last word should be said about safety. Preschool children are at risk during physical activity because they have yet to get their bodies under dependable control. Primary children also are at risk because of their enthusiasm for new physical challenges. Before planning a program of activities, check the facilities and determine their safety. And before beginning any activity, make sure children understand what safety measures are their responsibility. Then be sure there is adequate supervision during every experience and that you know the proper procedures for any emergency.

The Music Curriculum

Just as there were essential elements in the movement curriculum so there are for music. The same elements pertain to both preschool and the primary grades although, of course, the focus is different as children develop.

1. Listening and describing

2. Singing

3. Playing instruments (melodic and rhythmic)

4. Performing rhythms (movement and dance)

5. Reading

6. Valuing

Listening is the foundation for all music experiences. It can stand alone as an activity, or it can underlie the others. *Describing* signifies the demonstration of the attention that was paid during the listening process. Children can describe what they have heard through words, song, rhythmic movement, or their own interpretation on melodic or rhythm instruments. *Singing* is both fundamental and sophisticated. The smallest infants, experimenting with their voices make sounds that are as much like singing as they are like talking. Singing attains its greater complexity through training and acculturation. *Instruments* for the youngest children are typically rhythmic, providing basic sounds and beats to explore. As they get older, children can coordinate the double requirement of melody and rhythm using instruments that provide the possibility of both. *Rhythms* can be of the whole body as well, and for the youngest children melodic experiences are unquestionably accompanied by a bodily response. *Reading* music is often saved for later rather than introduced sooner, yet often the youngest preschooler can learn to tell the difference between musical notation and the printed word.

Next to listening, *valuing* may be the most important element as applied to lifelong learning. A love of music can begin early and continue throughout life. Valuing includes a critical element as well, and even young children have their preferences. As children listen closely, describe carefully, and participate by playing instruments and moving to rhythms, they learn to critique their own and others' work and to develop preferences.

Our expectations for what children can do at each age will, as usual, depend on the developmental levels we have discussed previously. Here are some curriculum guidelines based on developmental considerations as provided by the Music Educators National Conference. The MENC has chosen to describe curriculum expectations in terms of what children should be able to do as a result of teacher's efforts.

Preschool Expectations

Children should be able to:

- Improvise singing as they play instruments
- Play and explore sounds of rhythm instruments
- Walk, run, jump, gallop, clap, and freeze to the sound of percussion instruments
- Label printed music as music
- Listen attentively to music
- Move spontaneously to many types of music
- Recognize the difference between singing and speaking
- Show by their movements that they recognize beat, tempo, and pitch
- Enjoy singing and being sung to
- Enjoy listening to music and other sounds
- Enjoy making sounds with body, instruments, and other objects in the environment

Kindergarten Expectations

Children should be able to:

- Sing in tune most of the time while in their own range
- Through movement and instruments, show awareness of beat, tempo, dynamics (loud/soft), pitch, and phrasing
- "Read" music using pictures, geometric shapes, and other symbols
- Improvise songs spontaneously
- Express ideas and moods using instruments and body or environmental sounds
- Listen attentively to a larger repertoire of music
- Describe similarities and differences in musical elements using movement or language
- Classify instruments (classroom or traditional) according to shape, size, pitch, and tone quality
- Have a beginning vocabulary of musical terms
- Enjoy singing nonsense songs, folk songs, and song games
- Be aware of music as a part of everyday life
- Enjoy moving to music and playing instruments
- Respect music and musicians

First- through Third-Grade Expectations

By the completion of third grade, children should be able to:

- Sing in tune alone or with a group
- Have a repertoire of folk and composed songs
- Sing with appropriate musical expression
- Clap, walk, run, or skip in beat to the music
- Play simple pitch patterns on simple melodic instruments
- Play simple rhythmic patterns on simple percussion instruments to accompany songs
- Sing rounds
- Respond rhythmically to notational rhythm patterns
- Use correct notational symbols for pitch and expression
- Use a system for reading notation (syllables, numbers, and letters)
- Sing or play a classroom instrument in answer to an unfinished melodic phrase
- Create short, melodic patterns on instruments or by singing
- Improvise songs and instrumental accompaniments to movement
- Create short pieces using sounds from the environment
- Create new stanzas to familiar melodies
- Dramatize songs and stories
- Recognize contrasting sound patterns such as slow/fast, major/minor, and repeated/contrasting phrases
- Recognize the sound of classes of instruments such as wind, string, and percussion
- Feel respect for music and its performance and creation
- Show joy when participating in music
- Use music as a means of personal expression (Adapted from MENC, 1986, pp. 18–22)

Some ideas for activities based on children's characteristics at different ages could include the following.

Preschool Activities

- A noisy corner where a collection of different items that can make sound is kept (small blocks, bells, spoons, pot lids, and so on)
- Informal singing all day long
- Songs with plenty of action
- Rhythm instruments (with something for each child)
- Recorded music for listening with strong rhythms and variations in mood
- Repeated experiences in listening, playing, and singing the same music
- Free movement accompanied by a limited selection of music

Kindergarten and First-Grade Activities

• A simple record player for children to use on their own (headsets can take care of noise problems)
• A few rhythm instruments near the record player for free choice
• Recorded music played in the background during appropriate quiet work periods
• Discussions of recorded music after several listening experiences (focus on mood, pitch, rhythms, and so on)
• Visitors who can play and describe instruments; follow-up listening experiences to identify instruments in music
• Use of own bodies to make many and varied sounds, including use of rhythm
• Development of a repertoire of favorite songs to use during field trips, during cleanup, and so on

Second- and Third-Grade Activities

• An expanded collection of songs
• Making up new words to old favorites
• Singing simple rounds
• Dramatizing songs or writing plays that incorporate favorite songs
• Continuing of listening to recorded music and learning about new instruments
• Folk dances of this and other countries
• Experimenting with possible sounds on classroom instruments and environmental objects (Adapted from MENC, 1986, pp. 18–22)

Children in the preschool years, including kindergarten, enjoy having music throughout their day, and to some extent many or most schools have traditionally followed this format. Unfortunately, teachers in the primary years often neglect music completely, feeling that it doesn't represent "real" work. Yet music is there to enjoy during our entire lifetimes, and a once-a-week visit to the music teacher is hardly sufficient to provide children with all they might learn and enjoy. Music need not take extra time in the regular classroom. Recorded music can be played in the background during worktimes. Songs can be sung during cleanup or while getting into line. An exploratory center can be set up along with other centers to be chosen as part of the day's work.

Music and Movement Together

Whether it is in preschool or in the primary grades, one of the most enjoyable parts of a child's day is often when music and movement are combined. Here we will talk about teaching music through movement and movement through music. In the minds of young children the two are often one and the same thing, and it is frequently to their benefit if teachers acquire the same attitude.

Creativity and freedom of exploration is particularly important in the preschool years as children are still forming their own body awareness. For the youngest children formal dance training with prescribed steps is unnecessary and premature (Stinson, 1988). Far better to have opportunities in exploring bodily movement, developing a sensitivity to rhythm and melody, and feeling increasingly comfortable in the environment. If offered these opportunities, children in the primary grades will feel at home in continuing to explore the relationships between movement, rhythm, and music. At the same time they are ready to learn simple folk dances that can be done in groups or individually. Their facility in movement is such that they can coordinate the music and rhythm they hear with the movements they wish to make with their bodies. Finally, their cognitive development makes it possible for them to take on the complexities of varied and repeated movement patterns and memorize them. Here are some activities you might try.

Movement and Music for Preschool and Kindergarten

• Mirror images: To recorded music, move rhythmically while children imitate; children can be leaders as they gain confidence.
• March from one type of activity to another with appropriate musical background.
• Play the drum(s) in varying rhythms and have children move as they feel inspired.
• Using piano or recorded music, instruct children to hop, skip, gallop, jump, and walk.
• After hearing a story about particular animals, ask children to move to music as the animals might.

Movement and Music for the Primary Grades

• Continue interpretive movement to a musical background, making ideas more challenging.
• Challenge children to invent new movements and dance steps for old songs (can be done in small groups).
• Do some folk dances, including some simple square dancing.
• On field trips, have children sing and change types of movement as they walk, march, hop, skip, and so on.

A Note About Creativity   You will find many books on movement and music that suggest "creative" activities with singing games and action songs. Often, however, specific movements are given for each phrase or idea in a song, and this can hardly be called creative. It might be cute and it might be fun, but the authors have already done the creating for you and for the children. You might, for example, have the children gathered around singing "The Eensy Weensy Spider." They are trying very hard to get their thumbs and index fingers to climb up the spout correctly when, actually, several children just might see themselves as great, big, hairy, monstrous, gray spiders. If they do, and if you really wish to promote creativity, then they should be permitted to throw their whole bodies into being big and hairy. Sometimes you will want the children to learn specific, sequential movements and at other times to be creative. Be sure you keep your goals matched to your activities.

A Note on Management   Children moving around the room with the sound and beat of music need not get out of hand. If you are a beginning teacher you might want to try working with just a few children at a time. As you feel comfortable and work with more, keep a few principles in mind.

• Be sure children understand the basic idea of what they are doing before beginning.
• Allow plenty of room for movement; push extraneous furniture out of the way.
• Children who frequently have trouble controlling their behavior should be placed close to you.
• Vary raucous rhythms with placid quiet movement.
• Make necessary management instructions part of the activity.
• Always, always terminate an activity with quiet, calm movement.

To demonstrate how these suggestions might work in practice, here is one activity, appropriate for preschoolers through, perhaps, first grade. It is described from the point of view of the teacher. Mentally follow this teacher's instructions, and you will see how she includes management within a noisy, creative session. For this activity, the teacher has chosen to let each child explore one large piece of paper from the morning newspaper. As she begins, the children are seated around her in a large circle, one folded piece of paper in front of each child.

> Pat your paper gently. Pat it all over.
> Blow gently on your paper. Did it move just a little?
> Now blow harder. Did it move farther this time?
> Stand up; then reach over and pick up your paper with just one thumb and two other fingers.
> Listen to the music as it begins and move with your paper. Pretend it is sailing in the wind.

Now take your paper down to the floor again.

Open it up.

Can you smash it into a little ball?

Now throw your ball in the air. Does it come down fast? Is it slow?

Listen to the music and dance with your paper ball.

The music stopped, so you stop too.

Stand very still and crunch your paper ball next to your ear. Can you hear it?

Hold your paper ball in front of you and hop up and down.

Do you see the big wastebasket I just placed in the center of the room? Watch me throw my ball in.

Dance with your ball a little more; then throw it in the basket.

That's right. One at a time.

When your ball is in the basket, dance on tiptoes back to your place and quietly sit down.

The children are now quietly back in a circle and ready for their next activity.

MUSIC AND MOVEMENT IN THE INTEGRATED CURRICULUM

We have mentioned briefly the idea of music and movement throughout the day. Our final discussion of the two will focus on their place in the integrated curriculum. If music and movement are used throughout the preschool day, in both formal and informal ways, it's difficult to avoid integrating them into the entire curriculum. In the primary grades, a more conscious effort to integrate may be necessary.

Songs and singing games that include math concepts are common in the preschool years. From "Ten Little Indians" to "Six Little Ducks" there are plenty of opportunities for young children to learn counting skills. But math includes spatial and temporal concepts, too, and movement activities help internalize an understanding of space while repetitions and song verses promote an understanding of time. For primary children, songs can be invented to help learn math skills. I once observed a third-grade girl who could only regroup or carry in an addition problem if she sang the little jingle her teacher had taught her many weeks earlier.

Language is integrated with music the instant that words are added. Learning verses to songs adds richness to a child's language growth. Movement connects with language when children use their bodies to make letters, perhaps moving them through space as they do.

Art integrates with movement as young children learn to control the tools of their creativity—brushes, scissors, and so on. Large murals call for large movements, needlework for small ones. Painting to music helps to create moods and new artistic ideas.

Social studies can be enhanced by learning songs appropriate to the theme of current interest. Acting out the roles of people that are being studied gives a more personal meaning to the study.

Preschool children love to portray animals and, in doing so, can come to see and feel how the animals really move. Suitable background music can be introduced as they experiment. Older children can role-play the science principles they are learning.

The alert teacher seeks ways throughout the day to enjoy movement and music on the childrens' own terms and to integrate them into the curriculum being studied. By so doing, the school experience becomes both memorable and joyous. In this chapter's preprimary unit, suggestions are made for including music and movement experiences in some typical preschool curriculum topics. The primary unit demonstrates the use of movement and music in a student-created theatrical activity. The experience includes much of the school curriculum during its creation.

PREPRIMARY ACTIVITIES FOR INTEGRATING MOVEMENT AND MUSIC

Many opportunities present themselves for incorporating music and movement into the regular school day. Our focus here will be on activities that can be considered part of cognitive and affective learning experiences. They are sample suggestions of what might be included across the curriculum (see Figure 9-1). Some of them, such as What I did This Weekend, would fit into the regular day. Others, such as Songs for Stories might be part of a theme.

Language Activities

I. What I Did This Weekend
Have children share what they did over the weekend while you record mentally or on paper. Then, call out each activity and have the entire class "do" or act out what various children reported.

II. Describing Words (Adjectives)
Make a list of words that describe objects or people. Ask children to act them out individually or in groups. Some suggestions are slippery, sticky, hungry, stuffed, frightened, lonely, and happy.

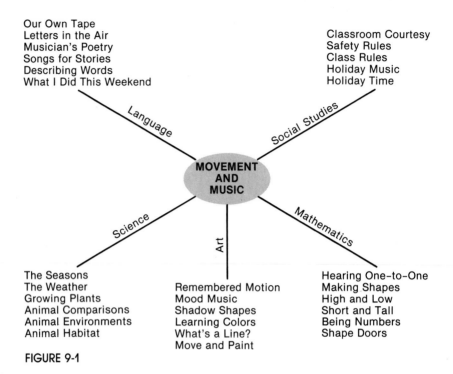

FIGURE 9-1

III. Songs for Stories

Have individual children create snippets of songs that illustrate a repeated set of words from a familiar story. Have the whole class use these during the reading or telling of the story. From "The Gingerbread Man," for instance, a song can be made to accompany just the last part of his chant: "...and I can run away from you, I can, I can." Or from "Goldilocks," "Who's been eating my porridge?" and "Who's been lying in my bed?"

IV. Musician's Poetry

Choose music that suits the mood of a favorite poem; then read it to children as they listen. Repeat the music and have children create movements while you read the poem again.

V. Letters in the Air

Ask children to write letters in the air using their fingers, toes, knees, elbows, and heads.

VI. Our Own Tape

As children learn songs and poems, record them on tape. Place a tape recorder in its own listening and moving center. Even very young children can learn to turn the player on and off, although rewinding may require assistance for some. Children play "their" music and poems and sing or dance as they like.

Mathematics Activities

VII. Hearing One-to-One
Play a brief rhythmic pattern on the drum, counting each beat clearly. Have children repeat by pounding on the floor and counting. They can also step or march in time. (It is good at first to make the beats an even rhythm.)

VIII. Making Shapes
Suggest a familiar shape and ask children to make it any way they choose with their bodies. The shapes can be carried on the wind and then fall to the ground. (Don't be afraid to introduce new shapes, even those not usually associated with preschool, such as trapezoid, rhombus, and parallelogram.)

IX. High and Low
On the piano or other melodic instrument, play high notes or chords and contrasting low notes or chords. Have children make corresponding high and low shapes and movements.

X. Short and Tall
Have children imitate animals that are short and those that are tall. Older children can make this a guessing game as the others try to guess what animals they are.

XI. Being Numbers
Have children use their bodies, or any part of their bodies, to create numbers. Challenging them to move their numbers through space adds a further dimension and can be done to recorded music.

XII. Shape Doors
Use large cardboard boxes for children to crawl in and out of. In the sides, cut holes of varying geometric shapes to be used as doors. Outline the shapes with a bright, wide line of tempera paint. Let children move boxes around and play with them as they like. (A large bread knife makes an excellent saw for cutting the doors.)

Science Activities

XIII. The Seasons

As the seasons change, children can act out what is happening. Some can be falling leaves while others are the wind gently pushing them to the ground. Everyone can be snow, first falling, then spreading over the ground, and finally melting. There can even be a truck coming through spattering mud. In the spring, new leaves grow, flowers come up, and rain falls gently. Using recorded music as background will enrich the mood. Before kindergarten it is preferable to concentrate only on the season at hand.

XIV. The Weather

Use recorded music that evokes images of weather and let children move as they interpret it. Choices of music can be made that coincide with the current weather, or, if a particular type of weather has been absent for a noticeably long time, it can be remembered through music and movement. (One good source is Grofe's *Grand Canyon Suite*.)

XV. Growing Plants

Before planting seeds, have children describe through movement what will happen to them over time. Explain that the actual process will take much longer. Each day role-play the process as it has been achieved so far.

XVI. Animal Comparisons

Do this after learning the characteristics of several animals. Ask children to name an animal that moves very slowly; then have everyone demonstrate the movement. Continue with quick movements—pouncing, slithering, crawling, swimming, climbing, and so on. Be sure to increase vocabulary by using the different verbs.

XVII. Animal Environments

As children learn about animals, have them classify the animals into those that fly, move on the ground, swim, or are amphibious. They can be challenged to name representatives from each group and then role-play their movements. Or they can make chalk drawings of a body of water outside on the concrete. Have "animals" choose their proper environment and show their appropriate movements. Flying animals can light on bushes, steps, and so on.

XVIII. Animal Habitat

Once children have some experience with the preceding activity (Animal Environments), create a center that allows them to experiment and play freely. Cut pieces of green, blue, brown, or tan carpeting to delineate the grass, water, dirt, and so on. Or use plastic tape in those colors to make outlines. Make trees on butcher paper and tape them to the wall. Use whatever materials you have to make an environment complex enough for animal play. Place large scarflike pieces of fabric in animal colors in a box to be draped around the shoulders as a costume.

Social Studies Activities

XIX. Holiday Time
Before beginning classroom holiday activities, pretest children by having them describe in movement whatever they associate with the holiday. As you observe, question them about their understandings.

XX. Holiday Music
During free-play and work times, play traditional and folk songs as background music. Through repeated listenings, and informal singing by the teacher, children will pick up the melodies and words of seasonal songs that otherwise are too difficult for them.

XXI. Class Rules
Children are more likely to obey rules when they have created them themselves. And children are more likely to understand the rules if they have acted them out. As children create rules, present hypothetical situations; then give them the opportunity to act out following the rules in the situations.

XXII. Safety Rules
Safety rules are particularly appropriate when introducing rules for playing on outdoor equipment. Ask children to tell a rule they know for playing on the equipment. Then have children describe through movement what might happen if they disobey the rule. Follow up with a description through movement of what will happen if they obey the rule. (Always end on a positive note.)

XXIII. Classroom Courtesy
At the beginning of the school year or anytime that manners and consideration for each other are lagging, role-play correct behavior. There is usually no need to lecture or to discuss recent bad behavior; role-playing the correct behavior and praising it will change things around. Playing music in the background at snack time or during free work can help set the stage for better behavior, also.

Art Activities

XXIV. Remembered Motion

Have children move to recorded music; then, while the music plays again, have them draw their experience. (Tell them to draw what they felt, not what they saw. There may be swirls to represent turns and pounded dots for marching.)

XXV. Mood Music

Have children listen to music and then choose one crayon or marking pen. While they continue to listen, tell them to draw the way the music makes them feel. For older children, play a contrasting piece of music and repeat it. Then have children dance as the two contrasting pieces are played once again. (Do not expect all children to interpret the moods of the music as you would.)

XXVI. Shadow Shapes

Early in the morning while shadows will be long, take children outside to a large, preferably concrete area. Challenge them to make long and short shadows as well as curved, twisted, narrow, and wide ones, and so on. If you are against the side of a building, experiment with making the shapes go up and down the wall.

XXVII. Learning Colors (adapted from Werner & Burton, 1979)

Pile bean bags or yarn balls, each a different color, in the center of a circle of children. Roll or toss a ball to a child, and tell him to call out its color while catching it. Then have the child pass it around the circle with each child saying its color name when receiving the ball. Variation: When the child catches the ball, everyone calls out the color. Then the group walks around in a circle chanting the name of the color.

XXVIII. What's a Line? (adapted from Werner & Burton, 1979)

Direct children to make different types of lines:

- Stand up straight with arms raised toward the ceiling.
- Bend backward to make a curved line.
- Hold a finger straight, and then curved to compare lines.
- Lie on the floor, making the body into a straight line; then curve the line.

Practice making line drawings on paper afterward. Or, while some children make body lines, have others draw on the chalkboard what they see.

XXIX. Move and Paint

Outside place cans of water and paintbrushes of varying sizes. Place a tape player nearby and select rhythmic music. Permit children to paint anything they choose, their only instruction being to listen to the music as they do so, painting in the way the music makes them feel.

The Teacher's Role

These ideas can be expanded on indefinitely. Whenever you have a theme for study, find songs to learn and recorded music that is suitable for listening. On a daily basis, think about what activities and concepts can be learned better through involvement with the whole body. Music and movement are truly two subjects that can, by pervading the entire day, expand children's understandings and enjoyment of learning. They can be taught through various methods, depending on what they require of the children.

Facilitating   Describing Words, Songs for Stories, Musician's Poetry, Short and Tall, Remembered Motion, Mood Music, Class Rules, Classroom Courtesy, The Seasons, The Weather, and Animal Environments are all activities that will need a head start from you and/or some occasional intervention. Encourage children to work on their own where possible.

Instructing   Activities that require your direction are What I Did This Weekend, Letters in the Air, Hearing One-to-One, Making Shapes, High and Low, Being Numbers, Shadow Shapes, Learning Colors, What's a Line?, Holiday Time, Safety Rules, Growing Plants, and Animal Comparisons. When you sense that you can move away from direct instruction, do provide children opportunities to freely experiment.

Providing Play   The activities that are specifically designated for play are Our Own Tape, Shape Doors, Move and Paint, Holiday Music, and Animal Habitat.

Managing   Music and movement, by definition, move children away from adult concepts of quiet and decorum. While it is wonderful to see children's enthusiasm, it is also possible to let them get carried away beyond the accepted norms of whatever teaching situation you are in. The situation is usually handled fairly easily by having a few rules that are established before activities are started. It is almost impossible to tell children *how* loud they can be, so set up a signal that tells them that they've gone over the line.

Role-play the use of it as a game before you do any actual activities. Then make your rule: "When you hear (the signal), freeze." Children who have a hard time following this or any other rule can be kept close by your side, earning their independence as they behave correctly.

Observing   Most music and movement activities offer excellent opportunities to observe children's progress and their social interactions. If you choose activities that incorporate other areas of the curriculum, you will be able to see their academic progress also. Make note of these as you have a moment.

Evaluating   As you observe children, note any who do not seem to have the same capabilities as the others. Refer to the stages described in this chapter and in Chapter One. Then compare with the child's records to see if a simple age difference or previous physical problems may be the cause of any seeming problems. In both music and movement, provide all children with positive feedback and encouragement no matter what their level. If your observations and evaluations indicate that there may be a developmental problem, speak to the appropriate person in your school and eventually to the parents.

Reflecting and Planning   Reflect on what you are offering the children. Is there enough variety in types of movement and kinds of music? Are they given sufficient movement and music throughout the day? Be sure to provide for enjoyable challenges and growth on a continuing basis.

PRIMARY UNIT: THE FRIENDLY FOREST

In the preprimary years children learn music and movement most successfully if the experiences are informal and naturally integrated into the events of the school day. To some extent this remains true in the primary grades, but at this stage children who have had the informal experiences have a strong base for something more structured and complex. By now they should feel comfortable and competent about taking on the requirements of a dramatic performance. This performance need not be a high-pressure one with a large stage, lighting, and anonymous adult faces staring them down. That's possible, of course, if you and they feel that they are ready for such an experience. However, performances can happily and comfortably be done for other classes, usually younger ones at first to promote self-confidence. Specific roles can be played by different children for different performances so that everyone who wants to can feel like a star. There should also be minor roles for those who want to join in but feel shy about being too visible.

The centerpiece of this unit is a play that contains both music and movement components. This play is one that my own second-grade class (at the Benjamin Franklin International School in Barcelona, Spain) helped write. It was created when the children felt a need to be better friends with each other. In discussing what they might do to make things better, one of the girls suggested a play. The class then suggested the characters, the setting, and the essential plot. They refused my suggestion that they "write" the actual play themselves by acting it out spontaneously, and instead they "commissioned" me to write it more formally. You might have a very different experience with a class that prefers to improvise on its own. The resulting play is included here as an example of what is possible as a product and to demonstrate the ways in which this kind of experience can also cut across the curriculum. The preparation and production of this play provided the children with a broad curricular experience, one with opportunities for learning in four subject areas.

- *Language:* This is a play to be read and memorized. Children can take turns playing different roles, thus expanding their reading experience.
- *Art:* The scenery for the play is simple. Just a couple of trees will do. The children can cooperate to design and paint them. They can also create other props if they choose. Costumes need not be elaborate. They can consist of sandwich boards made from poster board and decorated as desired.
- *Social studies:* The theme of the play is friendship, conflict, and cooperation. Production of the play, including decisions about who will play which parts, requires the kind of cooperation and friendship espoused by the plot.
- *Movement and Music:* Within the play's plot are opportunities for creative movement, and the movement episodes are created with musical background. Songs are sung as part of the production.

In addition to these several subjects, related mathematics problems are possible (see Additional Activities, page 308). When children's thoughts are focused on the excitement of planning for and producing a play, it may be difficult to keep them focused on other classroom learning. Giving them math to do that is related to the same theme makes the day's work more meaningful and enjoyable.

Anticipated Outcomes

I *Student behavior:* As a result of this unit students will be able to:

    A Perform a play for people outside their own class

    B Plan the production of a play from beginning to performance

    C Demonstrate cooperative behavior during all stages

    D Make group decisions based on logical outcomes

II *Student understanding:* As a result of this unit students will understand that:

    A A group production succeeds best if done cooperatively

    B Fairness may mean giving some people turns at what they want to do while others will need to do other things

    C A group production succeeds best if everyone puts forth his or her best effort

The play is written here in its entirety. Suggestions for a successful production effort follow. Ideas for related math papers are included as additional activities. Keep in mind that the anticipated outcomes are based on the children's willingness to do everything except actually improvise or write the play. We might classify the unit as one that is more *facilitative* rather than *play* oriented or based on *direct instruction.* To make a similar project of your own as successful as possible, encourage the children to create as much of it on their own as they feel confident in doing.

"The Friendly Forest"

Characters:

Buddy (or Betty) Bear	Mr. (or Mrs.) Mean
Jaguar	Rabbit
Lion	Giraffe
Monkey	Alligator
Bees (2 or 3)	Woodpecker

Setting: Friendly Forest. Two fairly large trees are placed at far left and far right.

All the animals are dancing happily. As they do, they sing "The More We Get Together" (see Figure 9-2). Teacher may accompany them on the piano or other instrument. Buddy Bear walks in and smiles at them. As he begins to talk, the animals lower their voices but continue to sing.

Buddy Bear: Hello. I'm Buddy Bear and these are the animals of Friendly Forest. As you can see, they all like each other and they all play nicely together. That makes me very happy!

Buddy Bear leaves. The animals keep singing and dancing informally. Mr. Mean enters.

Mr. Mean: Hello. I'm Mr. Mean and I feel just like my name. I also feel very unhappy because I have no friends. I wonder why I

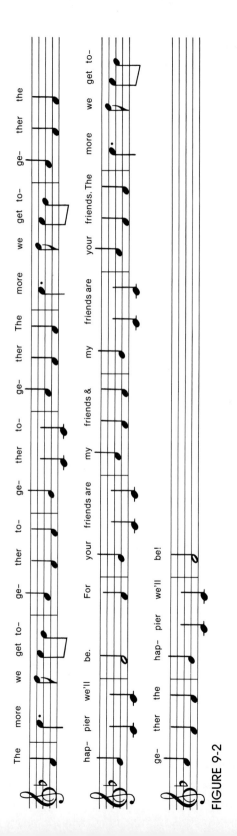

FIGURE 9-2

303

don't. Anyway, I don't like it when the animals are playing nicely. I especially don't like it when they're happy. I'd better think of something to change what's happening here. I know! I'll hit one of them and he won't know who did it. That should start a nice fight. Heh, heh!

Mr. Mean sneaks over and hits Jaguar on top of the head.

Jaguar: Hey! Who did that?
Everyone: Not me!
Jaguar: Somebody is lying! Hey, Rabbit. You did it, didn't you?
Rabbit: I did not. That's a lie.
Jaguar: I'm not lying. You are. And I'm going to hit you back.

Jaguar starts to hit Rabbit. Buddy Bear runs in.

Buddy Bear: Stop! Stop! This is Friendly Forest, not Enemy Forest. Jaguar, did you *see* Rabbit hit you?
Jaguar: Well, no, I guess I didn't.
Buddy Bear: Did you do it, Rabbit?
Rabbit: Of course not. Jaguar is my friend.
Jaguar: I'm sorry, Rabbit. I'm your friend too.

The other animals begin singing "The More We Get Together" as Rabbit and Jaguar improvise a dance.

Buddy Bear: I'm glad they're happy again. But it's very strange. I wonder who did that.

Buddy Bear leaves, and Mr. Mean reenters. Animals pantomime playing.

Mr. Mean: Can you believe that? Buddy Bear ruined my fun! Well, I've thought of another mean trick. I'm going to hide some mud in somebody's snack. That will surely start a fight!

Mr. Mean sneaks some mud into a dinner roll. Then he tiptoes out.

Lion: Time to stop playing, everybody. I'm going to bring you the snacks.

Lion starts to pass a tray of rolls. The animals all sit down nicely.

Giraffe: Yuck! There's something wrong with mine. Hey, there's mud in it. Lion, you played a mean trick on me. You just wait! I'm going to play a horrible, horrible trick on *you*.
Lion: Giraffe, I didn't do that. You're my friend.

Giraffe: Well, if you didn't do it, who did?

Everyone starts to point at everyone else. They argue loudly. A fight between two or three of the animals may be choreographed. Buddy Bear runs in.

Buddy Bear: What is going on here?

The animals get quiet right away.

Giraffe: Somebody put mud in my roll. Lion gave it to me. So I think Lion did it.
Lion: But I didn't do it. Giraffe is my friend.

All the animals say, "I didn't do it."

Buddy Bear: Well, maybe you two could shake hands and be friends again.

They shake hands. Everyone begins to play nicely again.

Buddy Bear: Something very strange is going on. I think I'll hide behind this tree and watch for a while.

Buddy Bear hides behind a tree. Mr. Mean enters.

Mr. Mean: Wow! A person can't even do a mean trick around here. Look at those animals. Doesn't it make you sick to see them so nice and happy? I'll have to think of something else.
Buddy Bear: *(very quietly)* So that's the answer. I'd better watch and see what he does next.
Mr. Mean: I know! I know! When they go to sleep I'll put a bee's nest in one of the trees. Then the bees will sting them. Won't they be mad then!

Mr. Mean leaves.

Monkey: Hey, everybody. It's getting dark. We'd better go to sleep.
Alligator: Yes, I'm tired after all that fighting today.
Monkey: That's a good idea.
Everybody: Yes, yes. A good idea.

The animals put away any toys. Then they all lie down to sleep. Mr. Mean comes in wearing gloves and a beekeeper's hat. He has a bee's nest in his hands. He puts it in the tree where Buddy Bear is watching.

Mr. Mean: Now, this trick had better work. It was really hard getting this bee's nest without getting stung. Okay, bees. Go to work!

Mr. Mean sneaks behind the second tree.

Mr. Mean: This time I'm going to watch to be sure nothing goes wrong.
Buddy Bear: Bears know just how to talk to bees. This should be easy—I hope! Hey, bees! I need to talk to you.
Bees: Bzz, bzz.
Buddy Bear: The man who carried you here is very mean. He wants you to sting the animals and make them mad. Do you like that idea?
Bees: *(shaking heads)* Bzz, bzz.
Buddy Bear: I didn't think you would. Will you just stay in there and go to sleep, please?
Bees: Bzz, bzz.
Buddy Bear: Thank you. And I'll do something nice for you too. I won't eat any of your honey for at least a week.
Bees: Bzz, bzz.
Buddy Bear: You're welcome.
Mr. Mean: What's going on? Why aren't those bees stinging the animals? *(He walks over to the other tree.)* Hey, you bees. Get to work! I said, get to work. Start stinging those animals.

The noise wakes up Woodpecker. Woodpecker flies over to Mr. Mean.

Woodpecker: Who are you and what are you doing?
Mr. Mean: Uh oh. I think I'm in trouble.
Woodpecker: I said, who are you and what are you doing?

All the other animals start to wake up and look at·what's happening. They are very quiet.

Mr. Mean: All right, I'll tell you, Needleface. I'm Mr. Mean and I'm here to cause trouble. Yes, I'm the one who started the fight about hitting. Yes, I'm the one who put mud in the snack. And I'm the one who's trying to get these stupid bees to sting. Hey, stupid bees come out of there.
Bees: Bzz, bzz.
Everybody: Sting him, bees sting him!

Buddy Bear jumps out from behind the tree.

Buddy Bear: No, don't do it. Let's help Mr. Mean stop being mean.

Mr. Mean: Look, Fuzzface. If I want to be mean you can't stop me.

Bees: Bzz, bzz.

Buddy Bear: Mr. Mean, the bees say you can have some of their honey.

Bees hand honey to Buddy Bear, who hands it to Mr. Mean.

Buddy Bear: *(to himself)* Mmm, that looks good.

Mr. Mean: Well, honey is just about my favorite food. Now if I just had a roll to put it on....

Monkey: I think we have one left over. Here, you can have it.

Mr. Mean: Why, thank you—Oh no, did I just say thank you?

Mr. Mean snatches the roll from the Monkey.

Mr. Mean: Give it to me, Snaketail.

Alligator: Hey, you be careful what you call my friend. Monkey, take the roll back.

Mr. Mean: Take it back? Uh, I'm sorry, Monkey. Thank you very much—Oh no, did I just say sorry? What's happening to me?

Buddy Bear: You're in Friendly Forest. After you're here for a while, you start feeling very friendly. You just can't help it.

Jaguar: That's why Rabbit is my good friend. In another forest I would eat her.

Lion: And that's why Giraffe is *my* good friend. Usually lions try to kill giraffes!

Alligator: And alligators kill monkeys.

Rabbit, Giraffe, Monkey: We're very glad you're our friends!

Mr. Mean: Well, who's going to be *my* friend if I stay here?

Everybody: We all are!

Mr. Mean: Could I have a new name? Mr. Mean just doesn't sound right anymore.

Buddy Bear: What name would you like?

Mr. Mean: How about Mr. Nice? Because that's what I want to try being.

Everybody: Yes! Sure! A good idea! *(etc., informally)*

Animals shake his hand, pat him on the back, etc. Then they dance and sing "The More We Get Together." Mr. Mean joins them after a bit.

Suggested Procedures

1. Make sure every child has a copy of the play and tentatively assign them parts to read. Have the children read through the play once.

2. Ask children to list their first, second, and third choices of parts to play. Assign the roles according to student preferences. A third-grade (or even perhaps a second-grade) class might appoint a small group of children to analyze the preference list and make assignments. There may be two or three groups of actors in a large class. In a small class, some students may have to play more than one part.

3. Have children with small parts memorize their lines. Buddy Bear and Mr. Mean may read their lines several times; other children may volunteer to help these two memorize their parts.

4. Have the class discuss what part of the room is best for the play and make a drawing of the scenery. This can be done as a whole class with one or two people given directions by the others, or a small group can volunteer for this task. Discussion may yield extra ideas for props.

5. Have the class divide into groups to paint the scenery. Draw the trees on long pieces of butcher paper and string them from ceiling lights. Add birds, sky, clouds, flowers, and so on, as desired. Use a large ball of brown yarn for the beehive and an old pith helmet for the beekeeper's hat. A honeycomb is good, but a jar of honey makes an acceptable and charming alternative.

6. Have the class practice the song and possible dance movements with your help. If some of the children don't already know this familiar song, volunteers can help teach it during recess time. Two or three children may choreograph a fight for the fight scene. If the teacher stresses in advance the need not to hurt each other, minimal supervision should be needed.

7. When the children feel comfortable that the props are right and that they know their parts, have them invite other classes in for performances. The class should vote on whether one cast of characters should do all the performances of if the second or third groups will also be used.

8. Hold a debriefing session to focus on the following topics:
   - What did we learn about working together?
   - What did we learn about making props?
   - What did we learn about acting?
   - If we did this again, what would we change? What would we want to do just the same?
   - What did we learn about friendship?

Additional Activities

The primary focus of this unit is on the play and its production. However, when a class is wrapped up in this kind of activity it may help them keep on an academic track to provide problems in other areas of the curriculum that relate to their current interest. The children who created this play did several related mathematics papers and projects. The following selections are simply examples of the kinds of problems you might write for children to do. You will need to create problems of your own that relate to math currently being learned and that are at the most comfortable level of reading for the majority of the class. The names used in the problems should be those of students in the class.

1. Adam and Brent packed their lunches and sleeping bags and went to find Friendly Forest. The first day they traveled 20 kilometers. The second day they went 18 kilometers, and the third day they went 12. How many kilometers did they travel in 3 days?

2. Which day were they the most tired? Why do you think so?

3. How many kilometers do you think they went on the fourth day? You decide.

4. Now that you know how far they went the first 3 days and how far they went the fourth day, tell how far they went in all 4 days.

5. After traveling many days, Adam and Brent discovered Friendly Forest. It was such a nice place, they decided to invite the other children. Carolyn, Darcy, Freddy, Ian, and Lana said they wanted to join them. The children brought many things to the forest. Carolyn brought 20 sandwiches. Darcy brought 10 apples. Freddy brought 5 cookies and Ian brought 5 cookies. Lana brought a bag with 200 potato chips in it. How many things did they bring to eat? (Count the chips, not the bag.)

6. Make a list of all the children's names in question 5. Adam is first, so make him number 1. Then do all the others in the order you see them listed.

1. _____
2. _____
3. _____
4. _____
5. _____
6. _____
7. _____

There is a secret that tells why the names are in that order. Can you tell what it is?

In question 6 a language problem is presented. In all problems reading is required along with mathematical thinking. It is possible to introduce other areas of the curriculum into math problems. For example, other possibilities for this paper might be to ask the children to draw a picture of the Friendly Forest or to carry on the plot but give it an open ending that the children get to write themselves. Or there could be an argument that each child would be asked to solve in a satisfactory way, telling why the solution is a good one.

TO DO

1 If you are teaching, make a list of activities you expect to do on your next day in the classroom. Plan as many ways as possible to include movement and music as a part of them. Carry through on as many of these as feasible. Write a journal entry when you are finished to share with the class.

2 If you are teaching reading, plan at least one movement activity for your next story. Children might dramatize the whole story. Or they could act out a new ending. Or you could ask them to demonstrate the feelings of individual characters at turns in the plot.

3 Sing old favorite songs with the children. Note which one seems the most familiar and easily sung. Try making up new words to the melody that are related to something happening in the classroom and/or to the children.

BIBLIOGRAPHY

Andress, B. (1980) *Music experiences in early childhood.* New York: Holt, Rinehart & Winston.

Andress, B., Heimann, H., Rinehart, C., & Talbert, E. (1973) *Music in early childhood.* Washington, D.C.: Music Educators National Conference.

Bayless, K., & Ramsey, M. (1978) *Music: A way of life for the young child.* St. Louis: Mosby.

Beaty, J. (1986) *Observing development of the young child.* Columbus, OH: Merrill.

Brown, A. (1987) pp. 184–193. Approaches to teaching classroom music for children. In J. Peery, et al. (Eds.), *Music and child development.* New York: Springer-Verlag.

Burton, E. (1980) *Physical activities for the developing child.* Springfield, IL: Charles C. Thomas.

DeOreo, K., & Krogh, J. (1980) pp. 76–91. Performance of fundamental motor tasks. In C. Corbin (Ed.), *A textbook of motor development.* Dubuque: Wm. C. Brown.

Gallahue, D. (1982) *Understanding motor development in children.* New York: Wiley.

Hackett, L., & Jensen, R. (1979) *A guide to movement exploration.* Palo Alto: Peek Publications.

Haines, B., & Gerber, L. (1984) *Leading young children to music*. Columbus, OH: Merrill.

Humphrey, J. (1980) *Child development through physical education*. Springfield, IL: Charles C. Thomas.

Keene, J. (1982) *A history of music education in the United States*. Hanover, NH: University Press of New England.

Kirchner, G. (1978) *Introduction to movement education*. Dubuque, Iowa: W.C. Brown.

McDonald, D. (1979) *Music in our lives: The early years*. Washington, D.C.: The National Association for the Education of Young Children.

MENC (Music Educators National Conference) (1986) *The school music program: Description and standards*. Reston, VA: MENC.

Nelson, M. (1955) Music in early childhood. In *Music for children's living*. Washington, D.C.: Association for Childhood Education International.

Pangrazi, R., & Dauer, V. (1981) *Movement in early childhood and primary education*. Minneapolis: Burgess.

Peery, J., & Peery, I. (1987) The role of music in child development. In Peery, J., et al. *Music and child development*. New York: Springer-Verlag.

Riggs, M., Dodds, P., & Zuccalo, D. (1981) *Early Childhood*. Reston, VA: American Alliance for Health, Physical Education, Recreation and Dance.

Shephard, R. (1982) *Physical activity and growth*. Chicago: Year Book Medical Publishers.

Skinner, L. (1979) *Motor development in the preschool years*. Springfield, IL: Charles C. Thomas.

Stinson, S. (1988) Creative dance for preschool children. *JOPERD*, September: 52–56.

Werner, P., & Burton, E. (1979) *Learning through movement*. St. Louis: Mosby.

Zaichkowsky, L. D., Zaichkowsky, L. B., & Martinek, T. (1980) *Growth and development: The child and physical activity*. St. Louis: Mosby.

part 3

MAKING IT WORK

The integrated curriculum, facilitative teaching, and learning through play were not commonly seen in schools a generation ago. Your students' parents may view these unfamiliarities with some alarm unless you communicate your ideas well. Additionally, these parents were your students' first teachers and they continue to teach them in many ways. Thus, it is important that you come to know and understand the parents' views, hopes, fears, and expectations for their children. Parents can be a valuable asset to your teaching in many ways as well as a window to your understanding of the boys and girls they entrust to you. To this end, Chapter Ten provides you with an overview of parenting and some practical tips for working with parents.

Another important element in achieving success is the environment in which the integrated curriculum is taught and learned. As a teacher you can structure the environment in such a way that teaching and management become much easier. The environment becomes your ally. It is important to see the environment from the children's point of view as well, because this is their world for an important part of their lives. In Chapter Eleven the environment is discussed from the points of view of all concerned.

It is one thing to study educational philosophies and to read about classroom ideas. It is quite another to put philosophies and ideas into everyday practice. It is also one thing to try out ideas in the relative safety of a supervised student teaching experience and another to find yourself face-to-face with your own first classroom. To help you on your way, the final two chapters are devoted to suggestions for getting started.

Although Chapter Twelve focuses on the preschool, if you are teaching in the primary grades you should find that many of the ideas are adaptable. However, this chapter assumes quite a bit of independence on the part of the teacher to create a curriculum, which is less likely to be the case in the primary grades.

For teachers working in the primary grades, Chapter Thirteen offers suggestions for using mandated texts in ways that are in keeping with the philosophy of an integrated curriculum. There are occasional schools in which little freedom of choice and decision making are permitted the teacher, but with even a minimal amount of freedom, many ideas from this chapter should be possible. To demonstrate this point, a description of one morning in a school with a difficult schedule is provided.

In previous chapters we have given much consideration to subject matter. As we now discuss implementation of the curriculum, it is time to realize and keep in mind that it is not subjects you teach, but children.

chapter ten

Parents

Train up a child in the way he should go and when he is old,
he will not depart from it.

(Proverbs 22:6)

Advice to parents telling them how to raise more perfect children is as new as last week's addition to the local bookstore and as old as the most ancient written words. Sometimes, as in this well-known proverb, the instructions have religious or moral implications. At other times, the advice is more concerned with intellectual endeavors or health issues. Although parents have historically had little or no access to formal training in child rearing, there have almost always been advice givers to help them along. Other skills are passed on within a family from one generation to the next. A family's time and its place in a culture further determine the parenting strategies that are used.

In the United States today there is no singular view of what is right in child rearing, partly because there is no commonly accepted goal for adulthood or for carrying on a single culture. We are a proudly multifaceted culture with a continually changing influx of races, family types, and life goals. While there are certainly advantages to such diversity, it definitely does not make the job of parenting any easier.

Making the task even more complex is the fact that there are today such diverging and conflicting views of psychological development and of educational methods. Most, if not all, of these fight for the parent's attention in a time when mass communication is at its historically greatest quantity. Bookstores, newsstands, and supermarkets compete with each other to bring the printed word of advice to parents. Television is an omnipresent and insistent voice, again with competing views.

Add to all this a sampling of the problems that have the trademark of the 1990s: parents with drug addictions; single-parent families; mobility, sometimes to the point of homelessness. It has never been easy to be a parent, of course, but these are some of the realities with which parents have to cope today.

Underlying the varying problems, the ever-changing influx of cultures, and the conflicting views of child rearing and education, there is some continuity and stability in the historical patterns of child raising. In this chapter we first look at what these are to get a better feel for where we are coming from today. Then we will discuss briefly the implications for today's culture, finally focusing on our role as teachers dealing with today's parents.

PARENTING IN THE UNITED STATES

Our opening proverb reflects the eternal hope that parental training will have some long-term payoff. What it doesn't do is define "the way he should go." This has changed drastically over the centuries, reflecting the differences in each culture's concepts of what the finished product should look like, based on the vision of what parts of a culture are desirable to hand down to succeeding generations.

Although in the United States today there are people from a world of cultures, the historical roots for present-day parenting took hold in the Renaissance centuries in Europe. Historians (deMause, 1974; Aries, 1962) disagree as to how European parents treated their children during the Middle Ages, but it is certain that Martin Luther's sixteenth-century stand against the Roman Catholic Church wrought some changes. Once the traditional influence of the church was lessened, fathers were expected to step in and fill the gap. In upper-class families, fathers began to tutor their children at home, particularly during the early years. (Mothers could not always be relied on since they were often only semiliterate.) Home schooling for the youngest children would probably include basic grammar and beginning reading. More important perhaps, in the absence of church influence, was the growing awareness that at-home moral training was important.

The colonists who first settled the North American continent were carriers of the European Renaissance tradition. Times were changing in their homelands, particularly in England where the repressive and regressive Restoration was under way. But the Puritans retained the Renaissance views with which they arrived, and it was these views that shaped our country's early attitudes toward child-rearing practices. Later, when many different cultures began to flood the new nation, it was, in part, these ideals that early childhood educators turned to when they looked for ways to bring new immigrants into the mainstream.

The Puritan Contribution

Whether your own heritage includes these early settlers or not, their influence on the course of parenting was great enough to have affected us all in some way. They set the standard by which succeeding generations of parents were measured, and they created the child-rearing philosophies to which the next generations would have to respond.

The nuclear family was the model of that time, although with eight or nine children as the common number, there was less distinction between childhood and adulthood than we see in nuclear families today. Advice to parents existed even then, often reflecting the Calvinist religious tradition that viewed children as inherently evil and in need of redemption. The youngest children were perhaps considered the greatest problems because they possessed that devil-inspired quality: a will of their own. One contemporary writer said to parents, "Children should not know if it could be kept from them, that they have a will in their own, but in the parents' keeping; neither should these words be heard from them, save by way of consent, 'I will' or 'I will not'" (Demos, 1970, p. 135). The "beating down" of willfulness was important in any God-fearing family.

As might be expected at a time when mere survival was a major issue, small children were required to pull their own weight as soon as possible. Yet parents also wanted their children to attain literacy in order to read the scriptures. The apparent conflict between one necessity and another desire was frequently resolved by "putting out," or apprenticing children at an early age—perhaps 6 or 7. Part of the contract between parents and masters might well be that the child must be taught to read.

As has happened throughout history, the Puritan society was aware, in a practical sort of way, of the change in children that takes place around the age of 6 years. In the Piagetian framework, we now call this concrete operations, and parents even then viewed it as the proper time to begin new learning. And then, as now, they were just as likely to ignore these timely stages in favor of pushing too quickly. One case record is that of 5-year-old Joseph Billington, who in 1643 tried to run away from his "master's service" in order to be home with his parents. The master took the child to court and it was decided that he was too young to punish. The parents, however, were ordered not to receive him if he returned home or they would be put in the stocks (Demos, 1970, p. 113).

Actually about two-thirds of all children remained at home with their families. There they learned practical life skills from their same-sex parents. Small boys might work with their father at planting or fence mending. Little girls could help their mother with cooking, spinning, or candle making.

Then as now there was no guarantee that keeping children at home would provide them with suitable educational experiences, even if scriptural literacy was a cultural value. Thus, the first Massachusetts educational law was passed in 1642 in which parents and masters were chastised and required to provide practical education in the survival skills. This was superceded in 1647 with the "ould deluder, Satan" law, which suggested that it was, indeed, Satan who kept people from learning to read the scriptures. This law provided that each town of 100 families or more should set up a "grammar schoole" to help prepare youth "as they may be fitted" for the university. Soon New York, Pennsylvania, and Connecticut followed suit, but to little avail. The frontier was expanding westward and to the south. People who preferred not to pay the taxes necessary to support a school could—and sometimes did—simply move on.

We have no record of the methodology used by families and masters who taught children to read. But based on our knowledge of what happened in schools and of the strict perspective on religion, it is probably safe to guess that the teaching approach was direct, didactic, strict, and dependent on negative reinforcement.

The Nineteenth Century

While the traditional Calvinist outlook of the Puritans was not the only parental viewpoint in the colonies and later in the nation, it was certainly an influential one. By the nineteenth century, the Calvinist view of the infant as born into depravity, to be saved only if predestined for it, gave way to the Evangelical view in which children were born into original sin but were salvageable through individual effort. The Calvinist parent would have wanted to educate and train the child in the eventuality that he or she was predestined for redemption; the Evangelical parent hoped to save the child by providing effective parenting.

Coinciding with this change of view was the increasing industrialization of the work force. This meant that fathers more and more frequently left home during their work hours, leaving child-raising duties to mothers. So it was mothers who were left to determine much of the new methodology of successful parenting. There was a growing acceptance of the idea that children could actually learn through manipulating objects, and it was inevitable that some of these objects would be toys. This was in direct opposition to the old Calvinist idea that play and toys encouraged depravity. But the more positive Evangelical view had taken root, and before the middle of the century had arrived, even this was being replaced by the view of children as born innocent.

A new and positive emphasis on the early years soon developed in new quarters. Physicians began to see that there was a stage of mental development that "...corresponded with the preschool years...early childhood was a time of delight in natural objects, animals, pictures, amusements, and recreation; early education should be a time of freedom of action in which the child was a free agent" (Shapiro, 1983, p. 12). The way was opening for the coming concept of the kindergarten as parents began to see the early years as a time for children to leave home for the more professional guidance of a school setting.

Before the century was out, another major change was in store for parents. The increasing influence of Darwinism meant that the basis of early learning became less religious and more scientific. It became necessary for parents to grapple with this major change both in their acceptance of what was happening to their children in school and in their own child-rearing efforts.

The nineteenth century is not necessarily past history. Many of the problems that children face today are the heritage of the upheaval of those times. We have discussed some of the change that was brought on by evolving religious and philosophical views. Moreover, throughout much of the last century many children were born into slavery, adding another dimension to the upheaval. Today the devastating impact of that cultural imbalance remains a problem. By the mid-nineteenth century when the issue of slavery became a prime instigator of the Civil War, Afro-American families had somehow managed to survive 200 years of mistreatment, including physical cruelty and enforced separations. The traditional African definition of family, however, was somewhat different from the one brought by the Puritans from England. Although varying tribes had different practices, a few broad statements can be made. A marriage was not just between husband and wife, but included all members of the family. Traditionally, this extended family was a strong, cohesive device and qualities such as unity, cooperative effort, mutual responsibility, reconciliation, and so on were valued (Nobles, 1978). In some tribes, the entire tribe itself was considered as one family; in others, the group was not as large but was still more complex than that of the European tradition.

During the years of slavery, parents were separated from their children and husbands from their wives, depending on the needs of the market. The tradition of extending the family to include all those around may have helped slaves support each other during the horrors of their experience. Further adding to the slave families' misery were prohibitions against speaking their native languages, engaging in their own religious customs, or (once they had mastered English) learning to read. "They were completely cut off from their past with no hope for the future. It can be stated without much debate that no other immigrant ethnic group faced such treatment upon arrival in America" (Greathouse & Miller, 1981, p. 72).

Despite the Emancipation Proclamation of 1863 and the ensuing passage of the Fourteenth Amendment to the Constitution, more repression awaited Afro-Americans. The sharecropping system ensured that they remained in economic bondage. In most aspects of life, second-class citizenship was the norm and education was poor. During this time mothers learned to be the underlying strength of the family as their husbands looked for elusive jobs. Husbands learned to help with child rearing. "Role flexibility enabled the family to survive incredible odds" (Greathouse & Miller, 1981, p. 73).

In addition to the African and Puritan heritages, there were numerous others as immigrants arrived from various European, Latin American, and Asian countries. The latter part of the nineteenth century was a period of much immigration, and it was a time when early childhood education was viewed by many as a way to help children and their parents assimilate the traditional cultural norms as begun by the Puritans. Philanthropic kindergartens sprang up in many cities just for this purpose and, like the Head Start programs of today, they included a parent component as an effort to involve the whole family in the child's education.

The Twentieth Century

The upheaval continues, because no totally satisfying answers have been found to the issues raised in the last century. No single philosophy of child rearing has emerged to replace the old unifying views of Calvinism, and it is unlikely that this will happen. Yet it might be said that there has been since the beginning of the century, a central theme for parenting: science. Whether parents have been told that they should use a behavioral approach to manipulate their children or to accept them as they are, to provide affection or to remain cool and distant, to teach academics at home from infancy or to allow children to develop naturally—the advice given parents has almost always been based on scientific research and observations. For parents as for educators, it has been a time of transition and expanding views, sometimes confusing as well as unsettled.

In the 1920s parents looking for answers founded the Society for the Study of Child Nature (later the Child Study Association of America), established a monthly magazine (*Child Study*), and held, in 1925, the first nationwide conference on parenthood. The psychological views that parents were presented for study often conflicted with each other in the extreme. There were the child-centered views of John Dewey and Arnold Gesell with their almost Rousseau-like approach to home care and education. And there was the behaviorism of psychologists such as John Watson and Edward Thorndike, offering a no-nonsense antisentimentalism. Watson's book, *The Psychological Care of Infant and Child* (1928), led to parents who, in obedience to his instructions, keep outside their crying infants' rooms, waiting until the appointed time to offer a minimum amount of care and affection.

There was yet another way for parents to approach their children's development, based on the work of Sigmund Freud. Although Freud's work had been permeating the field of psychology for some time, there had been some reluctance on the part of parents to accept their babies and children as sexual beings. With the post-World War II publication of Benjamin Spock's *The Common Sense Book of Baby and Child Care* (1946), parents were presented with a diluted Freudianism. Now they were to concern themselves with both "emotional depth and a keen intelligence." Despite the enormous popularity of Spock's book, the conflict between the varying scientific views only increased the confusion.

Four decades later the confusion has not yet resolved itself. Throughout the 1950s increasing economic prosperity (despite one short recession) and new developments in home technology (dishwashers, clothes dryers, and so on), made it possible for mothers to cater more to their children's intellectual and emotional needs. By the 1960s parents developed an interest in applying primitive child care to the modern world. Parents began to carry babies on their backs or snuggled to their bosoms. Letting babies join their parents in bed became fashionable as did prolonged breast-feeding. One writer described the transition from Rousseau to behaviorism to primitive caring quite vividly: "The parent, once gardener, later animal trainer, has reached the status of anthropologist... Children are no longer plants or puppies but small savages..." (Hardyment, 1983, p. 227). It is interesting to keep in mind that these babies of the 1950s and 1960s are, by and large, the parents of the children in our early childhood classrooms.

In the following decades, much of the conflict in parenting approaches has been related to educational styles and goals. Parents looking for straightforward cognitive stimulation have had access to Glen Doman's *How to Teach Your Baby to Read* (1964) since the early 1960s. The continuing popularity of this flash-card approach to infant reading gives some indication of the pressures that have been put on children to learn to the best of their capacity and, these parents hope, to a greater capacity than other children with whom their parents put them in competition. As publications from parenting magazines to newsmagazines began to take note of the growing pressures put on very young children, concerns were raised here and there that parents were expecting too much. The best-known backlash book has been David Elkind's *The Hurried Child* (1981). And, if self-recognition is one avenue to humor appreciation, it is no accident that a popular radio show of the last several years ("Prairie Home Companion") has included the on going description of a mythical town where "all the children are above average."

Home Schooling   As the debate between those who would stimulate children to the utmost and those who would let them relax continues, a new twist in child rearing has occurred with the re-emergence of interest in home schooling. Although home schooling can apply to children at any age, it is frequently the younger children that parents wish to keep at home. A number of home-schooling texts and manuals have been published, usually citing the advantages of this form of education. Some of these might include the following.

• Parents can teach children according to their own religious convictions.
• Children can learn in a noncompetitive atmosphere.
• Children can learn to be more independent and to direct their own learning.
• Learning at home is preferable for children with physical or emotional handicaps.
• Parents have a great sense of satisfaction in seeing their children progress.
• Children get more personal attention from the teacher.
• Families can be together.
• Families can create the curriculum together.
• Families can make their own flexible schedule and work at varying paces.

Styles of teaching recommended by the home-schooling manuals can vary widely. There are the direct, didactic, straightforward methods espoused in early Head Start programs (Kendall, 1982). The computer might be the most important tool for other families (Pagnoni, 1984). One manual, just for preschool education, tends more toward warmth and sentimentality (Kuzma, 1980).

Home schooling as an alternative to public or private schools has been and probably will remain controversial for the foreseeable future. The increasing number of laws, regulations, and certification requirements demonstrate a governmental suspicion of education at home. The use of home schooling by some to provide a primarily religious education or to escape the immorality (real or perceived) of the schools may or may not be enduring issues. Surely others will arise.

As long as public school is the norm, however, home schooling will remain an alternative rather than a natural expectation as it was in earlier centuries. This will be true even for the youngest children if the current trend toward public schooling for 4-year-olds becomes widespread. Meanwhile, those who want to educate at home have plenty of support. Not only are there a growing number of self-help books available, but one manual has listed more than 70 organizations devoted to the issue of home schooling (Wade, 1984).

The Place of Today's Parent in History   Whether parents choose to keep their children at home or to send them to school from the earliest years, they must make choices as to how child rearing will best take place. There are fewer universally accepted societal guidelines or long-standing cultural norms today than there were in previous centuries. While child-rearing decisions may be difficult in our fast-moving, fast-changing culture, parents are, on the whole, better educated than they ever have been before. When decisions are made, they are undertaken with something more than blind acceptance of society's expectations.

At the same time, there is a negative side to much of today's parenting. Many parents of young children are increasingly part of a growing drug culture, or they are a part of the growing numbers of the homeless, the divorced, the never married. All these problems put different pressures on young children. The upheaval of the nineteenth century may have a new face, but it is still with us. Teachers of young children can expect to see some manifestation of today's problems in their classrooms every day.

TODAY'S PARENTS: SOME PRACTICAL CONCERNS FOR TEACHERS

Our review of parenting over the centuries is meant to provide more than passing historical interest. The interactions that teachers today have with parents and the views of the parents will often be influenced by some of the historical factors we described. For example, the attitudes of Afro-American parents and their parenting styles may well be influenced by the survival techniques of the centuries of slavery or even by the African traditions that came before. And the attitudes and parenting styles of Anglo-American parents may well have their roots in the movement of scientific child rearing or in Puritan traditions. Parents from various ethnic groups may retain some of the cultural attitudes toward child raising that came with their immigrant ancestors, particularly if the generations are not too far removed. Then there will be parents who take an active part in the trend toward pushing their children's development, while still others may be equally as enthusiastic about avoiding the push. Coping with and making use of today's broadly varying group of parents is the topic of the final section of this chapter.

Involving parents in their children's schooling can and should be a positive experience. It is important for teachers to remember that parents are their children's first teachers, both in terms of chronology and importance. While teachers will probably be responsible for a child's education for a year or two, the parents will have that responsibility for years to come. And, while teachers are expected to provide an academic and social education, the parents must impart the whole of their family's culture and values. Thus, whether a teacher is in complete agreement with a particular family's approach to child rearing or not, it is important that the parents be met with an attitude of respect and cooperation.

The ideas that follow are focused on specific instances when interactions with parents will occur. They are arranged roughly in the order that interactions will probably take place throughout a school year.

Home Visits

Ideally your school or district will allow time at the beginning of the school year for you to visit each child. Although this practice is not widespread, it is highly recommended because so much can be learned in a very short time and because it puts the child in the powerful position of meeting you for the first time on his or her own turf. What can be learned from experience will, of course, vary with the home and the conditions of the visit. Often, questions raised by a child's behavior during the school year can be answered by simply recalling the home visit at the beginning of the year. For the child, much of the fear of beginning a school year and of meeting a new teacher is dissipated by having that teacher in familiar surroundings for a short time. For the parents, the visit provides an opportunity to get to know you informally without needing to interact with other parents—a threatening experience for some. Additionally, they will feel reassured about their child's welfare as the two of you enjoy getting to know each other.

Try to visit every child before school starts. A few minutes will be sufficient. Learn from the parents what they feel they have enjoyed doing most with their children. Let them tell of any of their own educational efforts. Allow the child to show off any knowledge he or she wants to share. Bring the child a small gift: something that will be useful in the classroom, such as a special pencil or a typical toy. The child can then bring it to school on the first day with full confidence that it is an appropriate thing to do.

As you begin preparing the classroom for the children's arrival, schedule some times when individual children can be invited to come "help" you with your work. Advise parents that this visit should last a short time, perhaps 20 minutes. Whatever each child does during this visit will be remembered when school starts. You will see them glancing around the room on the first day to locate the fruits of their labors. Suggestions for helping activities might be such things as moving chairs and tables, cleaning the chalkboard, dusting and scrubbing small areas or toys, arranging flowers or watering plants, or placing toys on shelves.

While home visits at different times throughout the year will have some utility, particularly when a school's philosophy includes working cooperatively with parents, it is this initial visit that will help you get off on the right footing, both with parents and with children.

The Open House Talk

Whether this experience is part of something called Open House, Parent Night, or Back to School, it provides an opportunity for you to lay out your philosophy and then open the session for discussion. For a new teacher, in particular, the prospect of taking this kind of leadership can be somewhat frightening. Chances of survival are greatly enhanced by careful preparation. You should:

1. Know your audience. If your parents are largely middle-class and well-read, you will need to back up your ideas with at least minimal research. If the parents are less-educated and possibly intimidated by you, be more straightforward in your presentation. In any case, show your self-confidence by not condescending, not being defensive, and not being argumentative.

2. State your goals for the year. Let the parents know what they can expect in the total picture. Point out your room arrangement and explain its utility. Describe what they can expect to see happening if they drop by: how much or how little noise, the style of learning going on, and so on.

3. Be sure to allow time for discussion, although this period should take less than your talk in order to be able to share as much information as possible and, perhaps, to enhance your feeling of being in control of the situation. If an issue arises that can't be answered, you might suggest it for a further meeting. If there is friction, try to see the parents' concerns and let them know you really are listening to their ideas.

Of course, not all the parents will show up. Perhaps a minority of them will. A good follow-up is to write a one-page summary of the points you made and the topics that came up for discussion, as well as any resolutions that emerged. Send this home with the children.

Parent Volunteers

Having parents in the classroom can be a mixed blessing. Extra helping hands are almost always welcome. However, there will be parents who think they know more than you do (and that is possible, of course) and others who have no concept of what is appropriate to do or to say. Either extreme and everyone in between will need some training from you, because it is your classroom and your needs that must be met.

The first thing to remember—and it seems so obvious until you're faced with a problem parent—is that this is your classroom. Walk, talk, and act like someone who is in charge. This does not mean you have to be officious or condescending, but that you, yourself, are aware that you are the leader.

You can begin by thanking the parent for coming and then share your needs for the day. Ask that the parent observe for just a short time if that seems to help you keep yourself in charge. Then, be very explicit as to what is needed. If you sense that the parent's philosophy of dealing with children is quite different from yours, it may be wise to put the parent in charge of paperwork or redecorating.

If parents have special skills, interesting jobs, or fascinating hobbies, make use of them. Some parents who work and cannot ordinarily visit the classroom may find it possible to come if they are sharing their work life. Be sure to confer with them in advance so that they understand the needs of young children for concrete experiences rather than lectures.

Many parents who work would like to contribute in some way to their children's classroom life but cannot during school hours. Consider sending them materials to be made or asking them to be part of a telephone committee. Try scheduling some special events during the middle of the day so that those who can manage an extended lunch hour can come.

Parent-Teacher Conferences

Regularly scheduled conferences are usually for the purpose of substituting for or supplementing a report card. Other times it is necessary to call in parents because of some type of problem. A more welcome and rare conference is for the purpose of sharing good news about a child's progress. Whatever the situation, begin by being positive. This may be difficult when you have nothing on your mind but the child's negative performance. But a positive beginning reassures parents that you truly care about their child.

Think of at least one good thing the child does and begin with that. Ask parents for their perceptions about what is happening with the child in the classroom. Ask them what their child has discussed. With children in the preschool and kindergarten years there may be some personal invention of experiences and attitudes—Piaget called this "romancing." Some parents may insist it is lying, or they will take their children's stories quite literally, leaving you a bit surprised at what they think is going on in the classroom. Since this kind of experience is quite common with very young children and their parents, it is a good idea to elicit any concerns from parents during the meeting.

If you do have some negative behavior or lack of achievement to discuss, state your observations clearly, honestly, and without impatience or anger. Ask parents what their perceptions of the situation are. Be sure to have on hand any tangible evidence related to your concerns. Jot down dates and times of problem events. Save papers and projects that demonstrate your point. And then remember to listen!

Let parents know that you wish to work together with them to solve any problems. Be sure the child, at some point, understands that parents and teacher are working together. Try to bring the child in, too, for a three-way meeting when it is necessary to solve a long-term problem. Be sure that everyone understands what is expected and what steps are to be taken. Within the presence of the child, or as soon as possible afterward, write a note summarizing the conclusions. Send the parents a copy and keep one for the child's file.

When a problem has been discussed, be sure to keep in contact with parents, letting them know of progress that has been made. Be sure to let the child know that you have noticed. Young children need frequent reminders that the issue is still an important one, that there are specific things they can do to improve, and that you and they are working continually together with their parents.

Written Correspondence

Actual parent conferences are ordinarily infrequent, but that doesn't mean you can't keep the lines of communication open. Occasional newsletters with upbeat commentaries on what is happening provide parents with openings for discussion with their children. In fact, it may be a good idea to suggest they do this with such opening story lines as, "Be sure to ask your child about...."

If time pressures make a newsletter seem too much of a task to take on, consider doing it as a joint venture with other teachers. You might also issue it only occasionally, rather than regularly.

Notes home now and then are another way to keep communication active. These are especially effective when you have something positive to say. Both parents and child can share in the good feelings that come from a well-deserved note of praise.

Dealing with Problems

Usually, working with parents is rich with the rewards of having goals in common and seeing the progress of the children you share for a while. Occasionally, however, problems do arise. Here are a few with some suggestions for dealing with them.

The Parent Who "Knows" More   Many parents today have theoretical knowledge about education as well as practical experience that is greater than was the case in previous generations. At the same time, no teacher should be concerned that even the most educated parents are more informed about the children he or she teaches or that they are infallible.

One teacher of very young children was totally intimidated by a classroom father who, on the first day, flaunted his advanced degree and announced that he would see to it that his Mary Lee had everything she needed. Daily he checked up on Mary Lee's progress, which he rarely found satisfactory and which he managed to announce in a loud, rather theatrical speech. After a while it became apparent to the teacher, and to some others who frequently overheard, that the father was also intimidating Mary Lee. This gave the teacher new self-confidence, and she began to find ways to respond to the father.

First, she refused to be defensive. This was difficult, because the father entered the room on the offensive. The teacher found that she could greet him with a smile and then quickly offer some bit of progress Mary Lee had made that day. Additionally, the teacher realized that she was pretty intimidated by the man's great height. The level of the classroom floor was two steps up from the outside, so the teacher actually managed most days to meet the father at the door, just about at eye level. This simple, concrete action gave the teacher the needed self-confidence to speak directly, nondefensively, and with assurance.

Some generalizations may be made from this experience. In similar situations it is important to find ways to speak with the parent in a nondefensive way while still respecting the parent's point of view. It is necessary to analyze very specifically what it is that makes it difficult to deal with the parents who think they know more (and maybe do), and then to evolve ways of coping with them. At times it may work out for these parents to help in the classroom, contributing their expertise while learning something about your own.

The Parent Who Thinks You Can't Understand if You Don't Have Children of Your Own   Never mind that you have studied child development for at least 2 years or that you have practiced your teaching skills in a wide variety of classrooms. The argument from some parents will be that you don't and can't understand their children without having some of your own at home.

Dealing with this parent takes at least a minimum of humor. You might or might not care to point out that a lawyer doesn't need to have terminated a bad marriage of his or her own to be able to settle a divorce case and that a doctor doesn't need to have experienced appendicitis to perform successful surgery.

Alternatively, you might begin by pleasantly agreeing that you are, indeed, lacking in this regard. Then remind the parent that each day, all day, you deal in multiples of children. Further, the problems you deal with can be quite different from those at home. As you will have learned during your home visits, children are frequently totally different personalities at home and at school. The child who whines at home and throws temper tantrums may well be the calm class leader. And vice versa. Discuss all this with the parent and extend an invitation to drop by the classroom at any time.

Often this parent is a good candidate for volunteer work. She or he may well have plenty of energy to share as well as helpful ideas. You need to be quite sure of yourself, however: ready to accept ideas with thanks, at the same time keeping the self-confidence to stay in charge.

The Parent Who Wants to Participate But Works   Invite working parents to come during their lunch hours to observe or participate informally in the classroom proceedings. One year a kindergarten teacher discovered that every single father and mother worked full time. Yet most of them wanted to find some way to see their children during school hours. The teacher learned that most of the parents had flexible lunch hours and invited them to visit, observe, or help out as they desired during the times they could come. Somehow, even those with scheduling problems managed to make arrangements, so that by the end of the year every single parent had shown up at least once, to the children's obvious pleasure and delight.

Another teacher with a similar problem tried scheduling special events at different times of the day and evening so that every parent could come once in a while. Her greatest success from the parents' point of view was a 6:30 P.M. holiday party. The room was set up with the usual daytime learning centers, but with special holiday themes. At each center there were instructions for parent and child to read together, and the activities were designed for adult

330 Making It Work

and child to work together. Choices ranged from no-bake cookies to ornament making.

Every child attended this event, and every child was with an adult from home. This was no small accomplishment because a number of the parents in this group had never expressed any interest in attending any school function. However, since this was a special occasion, the teacher felt strongly that every child should attend and that there should be at least one parent or other adult accompanying the child. She stated this in a memo to parents and included a tear-off section on which parents were asked to write the name of the person who would be accompanying the child. If the memo was not returned, the teacher sent home another—and another and another—until the parents finally responded. In two cases phone calls had to be made at the last minute, but the ploy worked.

The Parent Who Avoids School   Some parents do not seem to take an interest in what goes on at school and appear, at least, to go out of their way to avoid visiting at all. The possible explanations for their attitudes and behavior are many and varied. In trying to get to the bottom of them and to attempt a change requires first of all that you try seeing the situation from the parents' point of view. It may be quite different from your own.

Many parents have had bad school experiences of their own. If they achieved little success or if they had unfortunate relationships with teachers, school is probably a place they'd rather not be. They may even be embarrassed about their current lack of knowledge or degree of literacy. Conversely, your interest in becoming a teacher probably stems in part from your own more positive recollections.

Some parents are more concerned about their own problems. It may be that their finances, health, or personal relationships are in a bad enough state that worrying about their child's school is more than they can currently handle. Other parents may be self-concerned due to their own immaturity. They may still be young and childish themselves, resentful of the burdensome responsibility of parenthood.

Still others regard the school as an institution that should do its job and do it well without requiring parental involvement. The division between school and home is natural and should remain. A related attitude that some parents have about teachers is that a distance should be kept. The teacher is actually held a wee bit in awe. (Yes, this is hard to believe in an era when schools are given so little respect, but it does happen.)

Getting through to some of these parents may prove to be difficult, but it's not usually impossible. For the children's sake, it is worth the effort. Extra home visits may help. You might bring something new for the child to play or to work with and then model interactive behavior between child and teacher. Be sure the parent is with you and can also enter in. Informal conversation may lead to a more comfortable relationship, and the modeling may help the parent understand more of what it is a teacher does. The parent will then be free to follow your example and work and play the same way with the child.

When you write notes home, you could have a stated policy that parents initial them and send back the bottom portion. Then you at least know they probably read them. If a note receives no response, send a duplicate with an additional comment as a reminder. Keep your tone positive—and keep trying.

When you need parent volunteers, you might try giving these parents first choice among jobs. Have a variety of things to do and include some that you think will be less threatening and take little time.

EXPLAINING THE INTEGRATED CURRICULUM

Few of you attended schools in which an integrated curriculum was taught and few of your children's parents did, either. In fact, it's possible that none of you will have seen it in action until you institute it in your own classroom. This situation is most likely to be true for the primary grades. When you do introduce it, you will have an advantage that the parents don't: your own background reading, practice experiences, and planning. We are all a little standoffish or concerned about things that are unfamiliar and unexplained, so it should not be surprising if parents react to the integrated curriculum concept with something less than enthusiasm. Positive feelings and support can be attained, however, with a small amount of effort on your part.

If you make home visits before school starts, talk to parents individually. Emphasize that their children will be learning all the skills associated with the 3 R's and that they will be learning much more besides. Then share one or two of the themes or units you are excited about, giving a few specific examples of ways in which skills will be accomplished.

At parent night, take parents on a visual tour of the room if a developing theme is on noticeable display. Share with them some of the activities you are doing and explain the ways in which curriculum coverage is being attained. Make copies of your curriculum web and hand them out. If one or two subject areas aren't well represented in the web, share your plans for other themes that will focus more on the currently neglected ones. Keep parents up-to-date in newsletters home, during conferences, and when you meet them informally before and after school.

Some parents will be expecting lots of ditto work to come home, and you will need to explain to them that although academic learning will take place, it will be done in many different ways. If you are teaching in a school where parents expect and demand that their children will make much academic progress, you will be pressured to assign homework. Often parents will equate homework with workbooks and dittos. If you realize that no peace will be achieved unless homework is assigned, agree to the demand, but emphasize that the homework will actually provide the children with more learning than a simple workbook or ditto sheet would. Then follow through with active homework, perhaps focusing on ideas that involve the parents. When you are studying various aspects of nature, ask children to look for appropriate leaves, buds, soil types, and so on. For math, you can have them count the books in their bedroom or the rooms in the house, for example. Or they might draw pictures of things in the house that are rectangles or circles. Activities of this sort will actually make the ties between home and school closer and make children more self-confident as directors of their own learning.

Also share with parents the ways in which you evaluate progress. Demonstrate the alternatives there are to pencil-and-paper testing. Explain to them that when children are busy working, you are observing them carefully and that you do follow-up activities as necessary. Invite them to visit in order to see all these things in action.

You will no doubt find other ways of your own to communicate to parents what you are doing. What is important is to *do* the communication—to share your ideas and intents. Then be sure to give parents opportunities to respond and ask questions. Once they feel that they are sharing in their children's progress, that they understand what is going on, and that what is happening is good for their children, then you can expect most—maybe even all—of the parents to be your allies.

CONCLUSION

Although you may be a teacher who is just at the beginning of your career, and/or a teacher without any children of your own, you have spent considerable time studying child development and methods of teaching. It is important for you to build the self-confidence that comes with understanding what you are doing. When you have that, it will be easier to interact with parents in such a way that your respect for each other will ordinarily come naturally.

Parents can bring you a wealth of knowledge about their children along with a willingness to help. Whether they know it or not, they themselves supervise an integrated curriculum at home. (Remember the case of Danny and Ben in Chapter One.) Opportunities for learning at home might include helping with cooking, learning a little about household repairs, using bathtime for beginning science understandings, working in the garden, and so on. As you discuss the children you share, you can each become more aware of the learning that goes on in both places: home and school.

Your children's first teachers—their parents—have much to offer and are deserving of your respect and admiration. You are well-trained and should expect to receive the same from them. Learn to listen well, maintain a sense of humor, and remember that you are partners.

TO DO

1 Role-play a parent night in class. Each person is provided the opportunity to act as teacher, giving a 3-minute talk explaining his or her philosophy of teaching young children. Others in the class are assigned to take the roles of various parents. These may be chosen from the descriptions in this chapter: The parent who "knows" more, the working parent, and so on. Other suggestions: The parent who believes his child is a genius, the parent who is a member of the local school board, the parent who is a teacher in another class and disagrees with your philosophy, the parent who believes that teachers should be respected and not questioned. Invent others as needed. Wear self-descriptive labels so that everyone can see them. Help each other learn to speak with courage, conviction, and self-confidence.

2 If you are student teaching, use the opportunity to sit in on a parent-teacher conference. Be sure that the parent feels comfortable with the idea before joining the meeting. Take mental notes (rather than written ones, which may be threatening). Include any questions you have about the way the teacher handled any issues that arose. Be sure to discuss these with the teacher afterward.

BIBLIOGRAPHY

Aries, P. (1962) *Centuries of childhood.* New York: Random House.

Caplan, F. (Ed.) (1978) *The parenting advisor.* Garden City, NY: Anchor Press/ Doubleday.

Cavallo, D. (1976) From perfection to habit: Moral training in the American kindergarten, 1860–1920. *History of Education Quarterly.* Summer:147–161.

deMause, L. (Ed.) (1974) *The history of childhood.* New York: Psychohistory Press.

Demos, J. (1970) *A little commonwealth.* New York: Oxford University Press.

Doman, G. (1964) *How to teach your baby to read: The gentle revolution.* New York: Random House.

Elkind, D. (1981). *The hurried child: Growing up too fast too soon.* Boston: Addison-Wesley.

Greathouse, B., & Miller, V. (1981) The black American. In A. Clark (Ed.), *Culture and child-rearing.* Philadelphia: F. A. Davis.

Hardyment, C. (1983) *Dream babies.* New York: Harper & Row.

Hymes J. (undated) *Living history interviews.* Carmel, CA: Hacienda Press.

Kendall, I. (1982) *School at home.* Laguna Beach, CA: ICER Press.

Kliman, G., & Rosenfeld, A. (1980) *Responsible parenthood.* New York: Holt, Rinehart & Winston.

Kuzma, K. (1980) *Teaching your own preschool children.* Garden City, NY: Doubleday.

Nobles, W. (1978) Africanity: Its role in black families. In R. Staples (Ed.), *The black family: Essays and studies.* Belmont, CA: Wadsworth.

Pagnoni, M. (1984) *The complete home educator.* Burdett, NY: Larson Publications.

Pollock, L. (1983) *Forgotten children.* Cambridge: Cambridge University Press.

Shapiro, M. (1983) *Child's garden.* University Park: Pennsylvania State University Press.

Spock, B. (1946) *The common sense book of baby and child care.* New York: Duell Sloan.

Wade, T. (1984) *The home school manual.* Auburn, CA: Gazelle Publications.

Watson, J. (1928) *The psychological care of infant and child.* New York: Allen & Unwin.

White, B. (1975) *The first three years of life.* New York: Prentice-Hall.

The Environment

Think back, as best you can, to the classrooms and playgrounds you knew as a small child. Can you recall the smell of the chalk, the scent of dust or mud in the play area, or the look of the sun coming through the window? Do you remember how the desks or tables were placed in any of those early classrooms and where you fit into the overall design? Are there any emotions related to these memories?

Just as we remember, however vaguely, the physical environment of our early school experiences, so too will the children that we ourselves teach. And with good reason. The environment provides a strong influence on how children feel about learning, on how well they learn, and on what they learn.

In this chapter we look at the history of experiments with the early childhood learning environment. Modern research will be described, as we then survey the various criteria and considerations for designing environments for learning. It is as important to prepare the environment well as it is to practice a variety of teaching methods or to understand children's development. Therefore, several activities are suggested at the end of this chapter that should make the environmental ideas more real and practical to you.

ENVIRONMENTAL EXTREMES

To begin the chapter let's look first at two examples of what the environment can do to and for children. In the first, a teacher's thoughtlessness deprived children of both enjoyment and learning. In the second, a teacher was well aware of the importance of the environment and continually experimented with it.

Example I The class of twenty-four second-graders spent most of the day seated around three long, rectangular tables. One Friday afternoon their teacher decided to reward the class for a week of good behavior by showing a video of a favorite movie. The children were, as usual, seated at the three large tables. The TV monitor was also in its customary place: about 7 feet above the floor, in a corner, with the screen angled down toward the classroom. Obviously, this meant that the children who were seated with their backs to the TV would have to turn around to see the film. But as the film started, the teacher began to pass around a patterned art project for everyone to do while the movie was on. The children who had their backs to the screen thus had to remain that way in order to use the tables for the art project. The teacher made no comments that would give the children any solution to their dilemma, and the children all stayed the way they were originally seated.

Within a short time, the children facing the screen became involved in the film and lost interest in the art project. The other children finished the project and then began to play games with the leftover paste. Soon the classroom became a combination of two types of behavior: passive movie watching and out-of-control mischief. The teacher loudly reprimanded the more troublesome children, snatching paste away in obvious anger. Quiet was restored. Half the children continued to watch the film and half stared into space, occasionally peering over their shoulders at the movie but without interest in a plot that was, by now, lost on them. The teacher still made no suggestions for turning chairs around.

Example II   The large variety of blocks in the kindergarten block corner made it a popular place. Its popularity was enhanced even further when the teacher combined it with the housekeeping corner. Once the two were intermingled in one large corner, boys became interested in interacting with dolls and costumes while girls participated in constructing airplanes and trucks—as long as they could bring their dolls along.

The teacher still saw room for improvement, for on the opposite side of the room were a dozen drawers filled with assorted manipulatives: Tinkertoys, Cuisenaire rods, dominoes, and so on. The children rarely chose these materials unless coaxed to do so, and free play had become a mass migration to the block/housekeeping area. At first the teacher tried to visualize a way to move the entire cabinet of manipulatives over to this corner, but dismissed the idea as too unwieldy. She then began moving a couple of drawers at a time, placing one with the blocks and one with the housekeeping equipment. She did this for several days, choosing drawers randomly.

The children never questioned the presence of mysteriously placed boxes in their environment; they simply began to use them in their construction and role-play. Before too many days, some boxes began to prove more useful than others, and if those boxes weren't already placed in the center, the children fetched them from the cabinet. At the end of free-play time, without any suggestion from the teacher, the children returned the materials to their rightful cabinet—even when it was the teacher who had removed them.

In reading about these two environments, it is easy to ascertain that the second one is more conducive to children's learning and positive behavior. It is less easy to define a good learning environment or to identify one that has problems when in the midst of trying to work with children. This is particularly true in the beginning years of teaching. For that reason, it is important to enter the classroom with as much understanding as possible of the effects of the environment on children's learning behavior.

Attitude is as important as knowledge. In our first example, the teacher immediately blamed inappropriate behavior on the children even though she had offered them no alternatives to an uncomfortable situation. In the second example, the teacher considered the environment something that was always ripe for improvement. She experimented with it continually throughout the year, hoping always to find more ways to augment her children's learning. Even a beginning teacher can expect a good measure of success when his or her attitude is as open and as observant as the teacher's in Example II.

Of primary importance in planning a successful environment is to keep in mind one's educational goals. In the second example, the teacher apparently wanted to avoid sex stereotyping in the children's choices of materials and she hoped to have them work more with math-based educational materials. It is difficult to try and define the first teacher's goals. She rewarded the children for good behavior by providing them with a movie, and then made it impossible for fully half the class to continue to behave well. In addition, she gave the children a second activity that made it difficult to fully enjoy the first.

SCHOOL ENVIRONMENTS TO DATE

In this section we look at attempts to create and define effective learning environments by several educators of the past three centuries. While the environments differed from each other markedly, they all had one thing in common: The educators who created them had a very clear sense of their educational goals.

Child-Sized Amenities and Outdoor Health

When Friedrich Froebel introduced the concept of kindergarten to Germany in the first half of the nineteenth century, he was fully aware of the influence of the physical environment on children's learning. Although his schools often had to make do with the space available to them, an important part of his philosophy was to make kindergarten a pleasant place to be. The classroom should be sunny, the walls should be brightly painted, and a garden should adjoin the building. There would be plants, animals, and pictures throughout. Froebel has been credited, too, with being the first to design that most logical and humane classroom material: child-sized furniture.

Radically different than any plan seen before or since was the outdoor nursery school designed by Rachel and Margaret McMillan in the early years of this century. Responding to the general ill health of England's children, they were determined to found a school that would not only educate the very young but would nurture their health as well. Thus, the concept of nurturing children led to the name "nursery" school, with the first coming into being in 1913.

Designed by Rachel, the school resembled a lean-to with only three sides enclosed. It was the sisters' belief that fresh air and proper diet would cure most, if not all, of the children's diseases. And, indeed, many successes were reported over a number of years. In 1927, for example, the Open-Air Nursery School reported that just 7 percent of their children were diseased in any way. The national average that year for children entering elementary school was 30 to 40 percent. The school also reported dramatic decreases in cases of rickets, measles, and skin diseases in their children (Nursery School Association, undated).

Clearly, these two designs for preschool learning environments—Froebel's pleasant, child-sized amenities and the McMillan sisters' health-promoting lean-to—reflected their creators' goals for young children's well being. The designs also demonstrated their educational goals. Froebel envisioned children learning through directed but active play and through interaction with carefully designed materials. Thus, the environment contained a combination of open space for games and small tables and chairs for working with the materials he designed.

The McMillans included in their learning materials a number of Froebel- and Montessori-like pieces of equipment but focused more on the importance of outdoor, health-promoting activities. In their case, as in Froebel's, the rooms were designed as places children could move freely in, thus reflecting a view of the teacher as facilitator rather than as authority figure.

Room Arrangement

Over the centuries, the look of the primary classroom has undergone profound change. In medieval Europe, the plan (if it really can be called a plan) generally consisted of a large room broken up in ever-varying designs as different masters spoke on different topics while their students (all ages including primary) gathered around.

During the centuries of the Renaissance, primary education was many things in different places. In the American colonies, for example, space was made available where it could be found, and that often meant storefronts or people's homes. When schools were built purposely, it was usually for older children.

Joseph Lancaster's plan for English children in the early nineteenth century was one of the first to break away from the medieval tradition. The industrial revolution brought with it the need for new kinds of education, including the need for mass literacy. Lancaster designed a room 70 by 32 feet in which 320 children were thus provided 7 square feet each. Long desks and benches ensured a student body devoted to receiving knowledge from the authority figures in front of them (Seaborne, 1971).

In the United States several changes in elementary classroom designs have taken place over the last century. Getzels (1974) suggested that there had been four basic general designs during that time: rectangular, then square, then circular, and finally open.[1] The rectangular room of a century ago contained desks bolted to the floor in orderly rows with the teacher's desk in front. Since learner and teacher at that time were viewed as receptacle and fount of knowledge, respectively, this design made sense. It also had much in common with the earlier Lancaster plan in England.

As research in learning evolved over the first three decades of this century, the view of children as receptacles of knowledge gave way to the concept that they, too, brought something to the teaching-learning experience. Leaders in psychology began to talk about children's affective needs in the learning process. The philosophy of John Dewey—that children learn much from democratic social interaction—began to take hold. These changes in view produced primary classrooms that began to have the freer look of nurseries and kindergartens. Desks were unbolted and the teacher's desk was moved to an out-of-the-way corner. Interaction with materials and with each other became more common as it became physically more possible.

---

[1] Getzels was referring to the placement of furniture, not to the architectural design of the building.

The third classroom shape identified by Getzels was circular. This shape was less important in the primary grades than in upper elementary and secondary classes. Children were encouraged to learn through social interaction by the placement of desks in a large circle shape.

The square and circular classrooms, with remaining vestiges of the rectangular, carried us through World War II and beyond. Once the Piagetian view of children as interactive with their environment, contributing to the creation of their own intelligence, took hold, a new kind of design was needed. Learners were not seen as simply responding to stimuli; they sought them out. This meant that the early rectangular classroom with its rows of bolted desks would be totally inappropriate. Even the square room with its movable desks could be improved upon. Desks might now be removed entirely, to be replaced by tables of varying sizes. Interest centers would beckon the children to come try new activities and topics. Children would naturally seek out new learnings, and it was the teacher's obligation to provide the tools and materials for new learning to open up. To provide optimal interaction with materials and with each other, rooms were made larger or walls were torn down. Teachers were encouraged or required to work in teams.

For the Integrated Curriculum

Since Getzels proposed this history of room shapes (rectangular, square, circular, and open) in the mid-1970s, there has been more change, both in philosophy and in environmental shapes. As he wrote of the progression in designs, a move was already under way to return to an educational focus on "the basics." No longer did free-roaming children fit the educator's vision of what a classroom in action should look like. Walls that had opened were now replaced or sturdy dividers were installed. Teachers who had worked in teams returned to self-contained classrooms.

No doubt there have been times in history when classroom design did not mesh with the goals of that period's education. For the most part, however, the examples we have just seen of preschool and primary environments demonstrate that a consciousness of one's educational goals will generally lead naturally to the appropriate shape and size.

What of the environment for the integrated curriculum espoused by this book? A curriculum based on the view that children take an active part in constructing their intelligence? That interacting with the environment is a vital way of learning?

For this kind of learning, it should be apparent that children need room to move about. Ideally they should be given the opportunity to combine the indoors and outdoors in a natural way.

Thus, the shape of the classroom needs to be an open one. Desks should definitely not be bolted to the floor, and even at the primary level they might best be replaced by tables. In this setting the teacher would be a facilitator rather than an authority figure, so that his or her desk would be of minor size and be well out of the way. (It might even be on-limits to children.) Once furniture was in place it would probably not remain the same throughout a school year but would be altered as needs and interests dictated.

These are generally the ways the classroom might be viewed. For more in-depth ideas and analysis we will look at research findings and theory: first for the classroom; then for the outdoors.

TODAY'S CLASSROOM ENVIRONMENT

The furniture talks. It really does. But then, so do the walls, the halls, the bathroom—the whole school building. The message they deliver is of primary importance for children and has to do with ownership.

Think, for example, of the teacher's desk. If it is large, in the front portion of the classroom, and off-limits to children, the message is that this is an authority-oriented situation. If, on the other hand, the teacher's desk is small, out of the way, and accessible to children, the message is that the classroom belongs to the students as much as to the teacher.

Here are some territories that have been observed and the conclusions reached about each.

Desk: "Probably the most valued and protected space." In traditional classrooms, the child's only personal space; in open classrooms, shared ownership or replaced by tables.

Locker: Shared space.

Assigned seat: Some ownership may be claimed in a special class such as music or art, as well as in homeroom.

Bathroom: Child space. "A private retreat for tears, anger, fights, secrets, mischief and day dreams."

Playground: Shared ownership among children.

Hall: Usually a no-man's land.

Classroom: Depends on teacher's approach: children may feel they own the whole room or only a desk.

School building: Children's feelings of ownership increase with the years they spend in it and will be influenced by such things as the degree of participation in activities (Lewis, 1979, p. 130).

Ownership of the Environment

When the environment talks to children about ownership, they usually understand rapidly what they need to know. In the old, traditional classroom with teacher's desk in front and children's desks in rows (bolted or not), children can see and feel quite immediately whose room this really is. In this design, teachers are allowed to move everywhere and investigate everything, including the students' private property. Nothing is really their own. In this situation, "...children quickly learn to ritualize being in one's seat and can be depended upon to tattle and make judgments on others on the basis of who gets into or out of, or stays put in, seats" (Gehrke, 1979, p. 107).

Children may adjust quickly to this kind of environment, but if they were given the opportunity, is it the one they would design? Lewis (1979) asked young children to design their dream schools. She was struck by the lack of rigidity in their use of space as compared to that provided by adults. She concluded that children's natural freedom is

> boxed in when they come to school—limited by teachers, principals, school boards and society. We should not forget this. Our limits on their freedoms should not be made capriciously, unthinkingly; instead each limit should have validity in their terms, for children are our schools' centers" (p. 150).

A major concern for both Lewis and Gehrke has been that children should be provided with more opportunities to have a sense of ownership of their school space and to let them know that we respect them enough to give them some control over that space. Both of them feel that even very young children should be given more control over their movement and use of space than the traditional school environment provides. As Gehrke says, "...if they never have the opportunity to plan how to use free time and space, how will they ever learn?" (1979, p. 123) Perhaps we could say that if the environment speaks to children they should have an opportunity to answer back.

What kind of physical environment provides children with the most opportunity to feel a sense of comfortable ownership, of at least some power over their surroundings? Obviously, the traditional approach won't be the answer. A new look at space and the way it is arranged is necessary here.

Open and Closed Space

David Day (1983) has argued that large, open rooms can only partially provide children the setting that is best for their well-being and education. If a room is simply large and open, the noise from a woodworking corner can be deafening in the library area. Further, children have little or no opportunity to engage in solitary play or to work without interruption from others. Privacy is virtually impossible although everyone, even a small child, needs it occasionally.

Day does not deny the advantages of openness in children's movement and the kind of teaching that permits children to make choices. He does suggest that this kind of teaching may encourage a room design that leads to the disadvantageous effects of too much open space. He argues for a balance between open and closed space and he gives two suggested solutions for different types of activities: separate rooms or inexpensive barricades.

Day believes that the same considerations can be given for open and closed space whether the classroom is inadequately small or overly large. In either type of room, children can be provided with the open space that gives them freedom to move and the closed space that provides them with a feeling of security or privacy. The following checklist is one that teachers can use to analyze the balance of open and closed spaces whether their room is large or small:

- Has the classroom been arranged so that protected areas exist, or does every activity occur in competition with all other activities?
- Is there any contradiction between activity and type of space?
- Does the arrangement of space lend itself to a variety of groupings—total or large group, small group, individual?
- Is there a place where one or two children can be alone and separated from other areas?
- What is the sound level in the classroom? What is the sound level in each learning area?
- Does the selection of learning areas support the goals of the program?
- Are the children using each area? Are they using each as it was intended to be used? Can children move easily from area to area? Does the arrangement encourage and support combining materials from adjacent areas? Is such use appropriate or disruptive?
- Does the physical setting support, and allow for the full range of child behavior? (Day, 1983, pp. 186–188)

Planning for Integration

Day argues for balance between two types of space, and his reasons have to do with the greatest benefit for the children in the classroom. What would happen if the children were forgotten and space was designed and defined for the convenience of adults and/or ease in housekeeping? This happens all too often, perhaps, and the negative effects on children have been documented.

An interesting study in Canada compared learning outcomes in classes of 4- and 5-year-olds in which the environment had either been prepared for children's learning or, instead, for the convenience of teachers. In all, more than 1000 children were observed in 38 classrooms. It was found that, "Creative productivity and skills, generalisation of number concepts, variety of oral language use and utilisation of listening and pre-reading materials were significantly better for both four-year-old and five-year-old children in the [deliberately arranged for learning] classrooms" (Nash, 1981, p. 144).

An important finding of this study was that when materials were grouped together in subdivisions such as language, number and science, fine-motor development, gross-motor development, and creative skills, children were more able to combine various materials successfully and to solve problems on their own. For example, in a planned classroom various materials for art and construction would all be in one section of the room, inspiring children to combine such materials as rocks, wood, paint, and collage supplies. Children in classrooms where the environment was planned for teacher convenience and/or where no subdivisions were made, knew less about choosing appropriate materials and were less creative.

This large Canadian study demonstrates the great importance of environmental planning in children's learning. But there can be an effect on teachers as well. Weinstein (1981) reported a study of day-care centers in which it was found that when there was a decrease in the quality of physical space, teachers became more restrictive and controlling and they were less sensitive and friendly. Additionally, the children were less interested and involved, and there was more conflict.

Children in the primary grades are no less affected by good spatial planning than are children in day-care centers, nurseries, and kindergartens. One study of second and third grades mirrors the findings of the preschool research on planned subdivisions. It was found that increasing each subdivision's number of related activities encouraged more use of the area (Weinstein, 1981). In other words, given more opportunity to make choices, children will work with more enthusiasm.

Another study of primary grades showed that placing desks in clusters of two or three provided not only a feeling of semiprivacy but also promoted more on-task behavior, longer attention spans, and less conversation. In this nontraditional arrangement, the teacher's desk was most often found in an out-of-the-way corner. This was seen as an advantage because it forced the teacher to move around the room to supervise; simply directing from one authoritarian position was almost impossible.

Based on the findings of these and other related studies, Weinstein has drawn a list of "design principles" that should be useful to teachers as they plan the layout of their preschool or primary classroom. These principles apply to rooms where teachers wish to follow the model of subdivided subject areas and to rooms with interest centers, where they prefer to facilitate rather than direct children's learning.

- Interest areas should be clearly delineated.
- Areas should be located according to type of activity and need for water, light, and so on.
- Incompatible activities should be well-separated (blocks and library, for example).
- All areas should be visually accessible to children.
- Pathways should not go through work areas.
- Large spaces that encourage boisterous behavior should be avoided.
- The teacher's desk should be in a corner.
- Materials should be close to their appropriate areas.
- Places should be provided to be alone, in small groups, or in large groups (Adapted from Weinstein, 1981, pp. 13–18).

The concepts of freedom of movement, of interaction between children, and of environments designed with children's well-being in mind are all a natural part of planning for an integrated, child-centered curriculum. Other criteria that are suggested by this educational point of view include the following:

- All materials should be within children's reach, with a policy of free access for all.
- If materials are frequently abused, they should probably be removed and stored until a later date.
- Experimentation with combining and separating materials should be ongoing. If an integrated unit is being taught, various subject areas involved in it may usefully be grouped in one center.
- In preprimary classrooms, groups of materials should either be isolated enough to avoid diversions of attention or placed close to each other to "seduce" children into cross-usage.
- In primary classrooms, areas that should not be integrated with others can simply be isolated.
- If children have joint ownership of classroom tables or desks, they should be placed close to their related materials.
- The environment should be used to communicate what behavior is expected and appropriate:

Large, open spaces foster running. Arrange furniture to avoid the problem.

Labeling shelved materials not only encourages reading but indicates that everything has its place.

Placing a reading corner on a carpeted area with pillows and a lamp communicates cozy quietness.

A table and chairs on a hard floor with a harsh overhead light promotes discussion and movement.

As teachers plan for an optimal environment, it is tempting to fall back on the traditional plan of the rectangular classroom with its authoritarian teacher directly in front, children in manageable rows neatly filling up the remaining space. After all, it is the design most of us grew up with, and it has been with us for centuries. Before submitting to the siren call of tradition, however, consider the following research findings, which should make one realize that conventional practices based on conventional wisdom need to be rethought:

- Sitting up to pay attention is not always the efficient way to learn. Soft chairs and floor cushions have actually promoted improved test scores.
- Silent libraries and classrooms do not necessarily promote the most learning. In one study 25 percent of the children scored higher on a reading test when there were sounds in the environment.
- Children do not learn best when required to remain in their seats. Achievement scores have been higher when children were allowed to move around while learning.
- Brightly lighted rooms are not best for everyone. Some children become restless or hyperactive and work better in lower light (Dunn & Dunn, 1984, pp. 85–86).

Children's Contributions to the Environment

The various suggestions from the previous lists are all designed to promote children's well-being and effective learning. But they are all suggestions made by observant adults. Earlier we mentioned a study in which children were asked to design their dream classrooms. Certainly, if this daydreaming by children were allowed to become reality, it would empower children in the strongest possible way. Is this necessary, desirable, or even possible in the early years?

Children in the primary grades can begin to design their learning spaces after they have been in the classroom awhile and are comfortable with its physical elements. Presenting a problem for discussion such as, "We need to place the desks in a way that there's room for us to practice our Christmas play and also get our math and reading done" should provoke enthusiastic and creative problem solving. It is the teacher's responsibility to determine his or her own flexibility: Should the experience be a completely democratic one with the final design determined by the will of the majority? Would the teacher rather just take their suggestions under advisement, making adjustments as preferred? While it is important to give children an opportunity to make the classroom really theirs, it is also important that the teacher feel comfortable. Thus, the teacher should make an advance determination about the degree of freedom the children will have and then communicate that to them.

Kindergarten children may be able to participate in the same kind of decision making, possibly to a lesser degree. One activity they will enjoy is creating "box cities" from large boxes such as those that pack refrigerators and other appliances. Even if the classroom is very small, there should be room for at least one box that can be painted, positioned, and provided with windows and furniture—all by the children. It will truly be theirs, even if there is only one.

Even the very youngest children enjoy making their room truly theirs, although they would certainly be overwhelmed by the prospect of redesigning it entirely. Still, they enjoy being in a beautiful environment and can be called on to add to the attractiveness of their surroundings. For example, before determining which artwork should be posted, the teacher might ask the children to make the decisions. Their concept of what is "best" is usually determined by criteria totally at variance with those of adults, so they can be expected to make very different decisions about what should be hung. They will frequently make different decisions about where artwork should be hung, also; teachers almost invariably place pictures far too high for children to see.

Further, children often feel an emotional sense of ownership toward a recently completed piece of artwork and would rather hide it in a cubby or inside a pants pocket for the day than to put it on public display. This may be disappointing to the teacher who sees a picture that will impress adults passing through, but allowing the children to make the decision does make the room more their own.

Another suggestion for the youngest children is to keep on hand a supply of baby food jars, small pitchers of water, and in-season flowers and greens. As a free-choice center this gives children an opportunity to create a spot of beauty, especially when they can place their creation themselves. Again, the decision will likely be quite different from that an adult would make.

No matter what their age, children can help in making decisions about what their environment will be. When they are small, the decisions will probably be moderate. By the primary years the children should be able occasionally to participate more fully in creating the design of their room. In doing so, they are also making strides in a lifelong need to know how to make decisions and live with the consequences. What better time than when they have a knowledgeable adult to guide them!

TODAY'S OUTDOOR ENVIRONMENT

Despite the fact that today's schools are highly unlikely to be as open to the elements as those designed by the McMillan sisters, it is still possible to consider the outdoors as part of the learning environment. Let us look now at theory, research, and some practical possibilities for extending the walls of children's learning environments.

There is a traditional way of looking at the area outside the classroom. In this view, the outdoors is a playground, a place where children can blow off steam—running, shouting, climbing, and swinging—as a break from the rigors of classroom learning. However, if the atmosphere of the classroom is more like those we have just been describing, where children are allowed to move around and talk with each other, then there are fewer times when letting off steam is a critical need. It becomes possible to view the outdoors in much the same way as the classroom is viewed: as a place where there are quiet areas, sections devoted to more movement and more noise, and both closed and open spaces. Depending on the resources available, it is often possible to use the outdoors at the same time the indoors is being used, and for many of the same purposes.

Purposes of Outdoor Use

Turn-of-the-century England is not all that far away in time. The McMillan sisters began their outdoor nursery in great part for the purpose of improving children's health. They didn't have access to the medical technology we do today, but the statistics showing the bettered health of their students gave strength to their argument that exercise and being outdoors was beneficial. Although today we have better medicine and better nutrition, the health-giving properties of exercising and being outdoors remain the same. (Perhaps the overuse of television in the home should be one of today's arguments for providing more outdoor experiences at school.)

A second reason for using the outdoors for learning is that it provides an appropriate setting for those children who learn better through movement. These are the children who become so preoccupied with being cooped up and immobile that they may even refuse to learn. Even if the outdoor area is a relatively confined space, the movement to and from it and the opportunity to do projects that make more use of the muscles can be helpful.

Whether the outdoor learning area is sheltered or open, large or small, children can learn much outdoors just from being a bit closer to the natural environment. The changes of seasons are more obvious outdoors and the variations in weather are more noticeable. Tiny animals can be studied informally; plants will be observed without an assignment being made.

Of course, the traditional purpose of the outdoors—the playground concept—should not be lost sight of either. Even in classrooms where much mobility is permitted, children need the opportunity to engage in active social play; unless, that is, they would rather be inactive or alone for a while. Whichever need a child has, it can be met on a playground that offers play equipment, a bit of landscaping, and room to run. While adults have long observed the physical and emotional release that a playground can bring, they have been more reluctant, perhaps, to consider the possible academic payoff. Yet at least one major study has shown that more use of the playground can actually produce higher academic scores. An in-depth look at this remarkable finding is worthwhile here.

As a society we have become sedentary and more comfortable indoors than out. For some children it is easy to fall into this pattern of life, but for others—probably most—it is frustrating. Some teachers also feel frustrated by sedentary, indoor living and are naturally alert to children's requirements; others have to make a mental leap into their children's shoes to keep alert to their needs. Because sedentary living has become so much a habit, one we pass down to our children, it might be useful to look at the results of a 10-year project that showed definitively the academic, social, and physical benefits of using the outdoors as an integral part of the school day.

In post-World War II France, doctors became concerned for the health of schoolchildren. Programs were universally academic with no more than 5 hours per week spent outdoors (much like the trend in most United States schools today). The town of Vanves was chosen for an experiment in physical education, with some classes assigned to increase their outdoor hours and others to remain with the traditional academic program. Parents were concerned that the children in the experimental classes would fall behind academically or become ill from exposure in all kinds of weather. Nevertheless, the program went on with academics now taught only in the morning for 4 hours and the rest of the day devoted to games, gymnastics, swimming, and recreation. The very late afternoon (when American students would be at home) was devoted to art, music, and supervised study. No extra homework was assigned. Nearly one-third of the daily schedule was given over to physical education in some form.

The results over the entire 10-year period showed that the experimental children, who spent less time on academics, actually did better on the academic tests. Their health, fitness, discipline, and enthusiasm were better. And they were more independent and less aggressive. Similar experiments were done in Belgium and Japan with the same results (Bailey, 1976).

There is something to be learned from this study at a time in the United States' educational history when we are concerned about the academic mediocrity of our schools as compared to those in other countries. It is tempting to think that keeping children at their desks for longer periods of time will accomplish our goal of higher scores. But, as the study in Vanves showed, the opposite results may be produced.

Academic Learning Outdoors

Thus, we see that using the outdoors as a playground and for physical education can have far-reaching academic benefits. Additionally the outdoors, as we have mentioned, can be used as the site of academic learning. It may be a relief to know that something as pleasant as being outdoors can actually provide academic benefits! To demonstrate some ways it can be done, here is a list of academic areas and some activities that are possible either with the entire class or with smaller groups.

1. *Language:* Knowledge of letter shapes can be reinforced by making them with the body. Some letters are more easily made with two or three children working together. Letter shapes can be made mobile; they can dance on the wind.

2. *Mathematics:* Children can count almost anything, but choosing such things as widely separated trees provides needed physical activity. Measuring distances between things can be done with primitive, child-designed implements or with actual tools for older children. Choosing to measure such items as a field for laying out a kickball diamond gives the project meaning.

3. *Science:* Much of what young children learn in science is connected to observation of nature. While much can be brought into the classroom, learnings have more meaning in their original surroundings. A nearby woods is ideal, but a single tree can offer studies of seasonal changes, growth over time, insect life, and the habits of visiting birds and squirrels.

4. *Social Studies:* Beginning map skills are best taught in familiar territory. The outdoor area is usually less complex than the classroom and therefore a better place to start. Maps might be three-dimensional and made with clay or two-dimensional on large chart paper.

5. *Art:* Colored chalk on cement surfaces is a childhood joy that is easily condoned by adults since it washes away completely in

the rain. The whole body can get into making a large mural in a way that's impossible in the more cramped indoors. An idea for the youngest children is to take large paintbrushes and buckets of water and "paint" an available surface.

6. *Movement, drama, and music:* Any kind of movement or dance is, of course, more open and free in the outdoors. Various types of drums that disturb other classes indoors can be played with abandon outside.

These ideas are just a small sampling of the academic variety that can be added to classroom learning by using the outdoors. None of the activities that were suggested require any more than minimal facilities: a single tree or a concrete walkway. More is possible, of course, with a well-planned and outfitted outdoor area, but it's possible to begin with next to nothing.

Planning for Outdoor Academics

Before deciding to make greater use of the outdoors, it is important to analyze the resources available. Taking the whole class outside for an activity is one thing. Allowing children to move in and out freely is another and is only possible with one important amenity: a door. A second important resource, particularly with younger children, is an aide (preferably one who likes being outdoors!). Given the door, and possibly the aide, a lot is possible with a bit of effort and imagination.

First, the area needs to be defined. This should be done physically, and the children should be well aware of the boundaries within which they can move. If there is nothing outdoors but open land, something as simple as garden fencing—the wire kind that is just a few inches high—can serve the purpose. Children are happy enough to be outdoors that they are willing to understand and to agree to this minimal barricade. Nevertheless, it is essential to have adult supervision for safety purposes.

The ideal is to have help from an aide, but if none is available, it is possible to arrange supervision of the class to include the outdoor section by standing close by the door, keeping an eye and ear open. During the free-work time in which children would be in and out, it won't be possible for the teacher to be as mobile in the classroom as ordinarily, but the tradeoff is more mobility for the children.

What work should be moved outdoors? This will depend on the amount of space available, the age of the children, and the degree of maturity a particular group of children has reached. Some activities, such as woodworking and some art projects, lend themselves more readily to the outdoors than to the classroom. Before moving them outside, however, it will be necessary to give very clear and direct instructions as to how the materials are to be treated.

Other, less active and/or noisy centers can also be moved outside, perhaps on a rotating basis. A warm day with a shady corner may be a good opportunity to take the literature corner outdoors. Reluctant math students may be inspired to complete their work if it is placed in a more inviting outdoor setting. A nature research project can be followed up by written stories, and these may be written with more enthusiasm if they are done in the same atmosphere in which the research took place. The principal point is that the outdoor learning area should not be static. To be truly successful, continual reevaluation will be necessary.

While teachers who make use of the outdoors seem to be few and far between, those who have tried it usually find that the benefits outweigh the extra time, effort, and use of resources that are all necessary.

The following descriptions of three teachers demonstrate how it is possible to make use of whatever facilities are at hand. None of the situations could be described as ideal for indoor-outdoor learning.

In a Kindergarten   A concrete, covered porch about 30 feet long by 8 feet wide is bounded by a brick wall with concrete stairs at one end and on the classroom side with windows the entire length of the room. In warm weather this teacher moves a number of tables outside each day and on each one places varying manipulatives, games, and books. In colder weather only active materials such as woodworking are placed there. A ribbon is placed across the top of the steps and only one child, an emotionally disturbed boy, has ever ventured across it. (He briefly lost his outdoor privilege but was later able to recover it with no repeats of the undesirable behavior.) The teacher has no aide but is able to cope because of the large windows.

In a Preschool   A door opens out onto a barren, partly grassed-over strip of ground about 8 feet wide and many yards long. Past the 8-foot width lies a sidewalk that borders a parking lot. The ugliness is relieved slightly by a large, nondescript bush near the door. Although the teacher would prefer to have more active opportunities available, the physical limitations point toward a few, carefully selected possibilities.

She has erected a border of wire garden fencing, like that mentioned earlier, and no child has ever abused the requirement to stay within the area. (She feels that small children are generally more comfortable knowing that they are safely within a confined area.) There is room outside for only two small tables that will seat a total of four children. Choices of activities have included various manipulatives, washing doll clothes, painting on a table or an easel, and self-scheduled snacks. This teacher has one aide, but on several occasions when the aide was absent, she was able to use the outdoors anyway by placing herself just inside the door.

In a Third Grade   The windows along one wall look out on a woodsy playground that has a few pieces of climbing equipment and is surrounded by a high chain link fence. There is no door directly onto the playground, but the windows come down fairly low. The teacher has built a small stile, or staircase, on each side of the window so that children can go in and out easily.

On a formal basis the teacher places no materials outside. Yet the children know they are free to use the outdoors if it fits into their learning plans. They don't seem to take advantage of this, possibly because they already have the freedom of learning centers within the classroom, are provided with two outdoor recreation periods per day, and can take for granted the ability to move in and out.

Some of the children's reasons for moving outdoors have included the following.

• Mathematically calculating the proportional distance from the sun to all the planets (far-distant "Neptune" and "Pluto" had to climb out the window!)
• Comparing trees on the playground with those in an encyclopedia
• Reading under the trees because the classroom became so warm
• Observing snowflake patterns on mittens

All of these were independently decided activities with the teacher as observer. None of them got out of hand, even the snowflake activity, which took place during the season's first snowfall. The children seemed more interested in the quietness that accompanied the snowfall than in greeting it with noisy playing.

These three examples demonstrate that there are many ways to make use of the outdoors, and the most appropriate must be determined by the teacher based on the facilities available and on the children themselves. Not only must their general ages and developmental stages be taken into consideration but also the particular personality of each class. For example, if the kindergarten teacher had more than one emotionally disturbed child, she might not have the freedom to let children in and out as she has done. Or a primary class that took advantage of the window stile and simply played around might need to develop a formal set of behavioral rules. Each physical setting is different and each group of children is different. The conclusions the teacher reaches one year about outdoor use may have to be drastically changed the next. Flexibility on the part of the teacher is quite obviously a positive quality to develop.

Outdoor Learning and the Integrated Curriculum

The wider the environment, the greater the opportunities to integrate curricular areas. Adding the outdoors as part of academic learning provides more possibilities for centers of learning. Furthermore, having the added freedom to make choices in their learning is a developmentally sound, concrete approach to helping children learn responsibility.

Indoors or out, there are certain principles that can be derived from our discussion and applied to the goals of learning suggested in this text. The design of the classroom should be open enough to provide freedom of movement, yet not so cavernous as to promote chaos or insecurity. Materials should be grouped according to interests, themes, or temporary learning purposes. Tables and desks should be placed so that children can choose between working alone or in groups. Tables that are related to materials should be positioned where the materials are within easy reach. Every effort should be made to give children the feeling of ownership of their classroom. This includes decreasing the size of the teacher's territory and increasing the amount of input children have into designing their environment.

In this chapter we have discussed various principles, both current and historic, that underlie the way a learning environment is created. In the next two chapters we will see how learning takes place within the settings that teachers plan. In Chapter Thirteen there is an in-depth description of a school day in which the physical environment is also described.

TO DO

1 Interview a selection of primary-age children to obtain an understanding of their perceptions of classroom ownership. Some questions to ask that may provide food for thought for the interviewer are:

a Why is the teacher's desk in front?

b Why is the teacher's desk so much bigger than yours?

c What would happen if you decided to move some of the desks to a better place in the room?

d Who decides where the furniture in the room should be? Why?

e What do you like best about going outside?

f If you could take any of your schoolwork outside, what would it be? Would you do the work the same way outside, or is there some way it would be different?

g Would you draw a picture of the classroom you would like best? (Decide if you want to give total freedom in this or request that children redesign their own classrooms.)

2 Choose one of the following situations and create a blueprint or design for optimal well-being and learning.

a You have been assigned to teach a class of just ten 3-year-olds. The room is on the second floor of a large house converted into a school. The bathroom (complete with bathtub) adjoins. There is one large window reaching down to waist level of most of the children. The room is a small square measuring 12 feet by 12 feet. The yard of the house is large, and one area, covered in grass, has been assigned for your use as you desire. It also measures 12 feet by 12 feet. You have an aide who works just 2 hours a day with you.

b You are a kindergarten teacher and have been assigned to a large, rectangular room with French doors leading to a yard and garden area. Your twenty-four children have a space that is 15 feet by 25 feet. Your principal has issued you a very large, ugly, old-fashioned teacher's desk with no option to return it. You have no aide.

c You are teaching a combination first- and second-grade class in a room that once provided storage and work space for the teachers. There is plenty of wall space because there are no windows: light comes from several skylights in the ceiling. The only access to the outdoors is at the other end of a long hall. You have twenty-two children, a space measuring 16 feet by 18 feet, and no aide.

(In addition to designing the optimal environments for these rooms you may enjoy listing activities or partial schedules that would enhance the use of the environment.)

3 From the suggested criteria for good environments discussed in this chapter, make your own checklist of those you believe are most important for an effective environment. Observe one or two early childhood settings using your checklist as a guide. Be alert for positive environmental qualities your classroom has that may not have been mentioned in this chapter.

BIBLIOGRAPHY

Albinson, J., & Andrew, G. (Eds.) (1976) *The child in sport and physical activity.* Baltimore: University Press.

Bailey, D. (1976) pp. 81–96. The growing child and the need for physical activity. In J. Albinson & G. Andrew. *The child in sport and physical activity.* Baltimore: University Press.

Day, D. (1983) *Early childhood education: A human ecological approach.* Glenview, IL: Scott, Foresman.

Dunn, R., & Dunn, K. (1984) Ten ways to make the classroom a better place to learn. *The Instructor,* November:84–88.

Gehrke, N. (1979) pp. 103–127. Rituals of the hidden curriculum. In K. Yamamoto (Ed.), *Children in time and space.* New York: Teachers College, Columbia University.

Getzels, J. (1974) pp. 1–14. Images of the classroom and visions of the learner. In T. David & B. Wright (Eds.), *Learning environments.* Chicago: University of Chicago Press.

Lewis, B. (1979) pp. 128–169. Time and space in schools. In K. Yamamoto (Ed.), *Children in time and space.* New York: Teachers College, Columbia University.

Nash, B. (1981) The effects of classroom spatial organisation on four- and five-year-old children's learning. *British Journal of Educational Psychology, 51:*144–155.

Nursery School Association of Great Britain (undated) *To the electors: The open-air nursery school.* Manchester, U.K.: William Morris Press.

Seaborne, M. (1971) *Primary school design.* London: Routledge & Kegan.

Weinsten, C. (1981) Classroom design as an external condition for learning. *Educational Technology, 21(8):*12–19.

_____ chapter twelve

The Preprimary Class

Where to begin? You have just been hired to teach a class of preschool girls and boys and you enter the room that is to be yours. Chances are the environment is in some disarray, with equipment stacked in cupboards and corners. Perhaps painting or other redecorating is going on, causing more disorder. You have a few days (or, if you are lucky, a few weeks) before the children arrive, and you want to turn this chaos into the kind of order that will get you and your class off to the best start. How to do it?

There are several answers, but underlying all of them is good planning. This planning goes on all year, although it is begun before school ever opens. Different teachers have different systems for laying out their yearly plans, and you will eventually develop your own. To help you get started, we will devote this chapter to an overview of an approach you might take when you first begin to teach. Then, as time goes on and you become more experienced, you should adapt and expand on the ideas until the design is your own. The approach we suggest here takes into account each of the chapters in this book. The year's plan is divided into three unequal sections:

August or September to winter vacation

January to mid-March or April

Mid-March or April to the end of school

Although plans of both short-range and long-range nature can be made ahead, it is important to stay flexible. Be sure to take into account the fact that the children themselves may have some ideas about what they want to learn. And what they want to learn one year may differ radically from what another group wants to learn the next. Remembering, then, that flexibility is an important component to planning, let's go back to that chaotic new classroom and see what can be done about it and about the curriculum.

AUGUST/SEPTEMBER TO WINTER VACATION

Before School Starts

Does your school have a prescribed curriculum? A set of goals for the year? General broad guidelines within which you are free to set your own goals and curriculum? These are the critical questions that must be answered before you can begin moving furniture and planning your days. Once you and your supervisors and, perhaps, the other teachers on your school team are in accord with each other, you can begin laying out short-term and long-term curricular goals.

Curriculum Webs and Planning   Until you meet and get to know your children, you will not want to make final plans for learning themes. Nevertheless, you will need to begin organizing ideas and materials, and this is the right time to begin some experimental curriculum webbing. Perhaps the school will have year-long themes that you will want to incorporate into your curriculum. Learning colors is one that preschools frequently use, with a week or two devoted to each color as the year progresses. Another focuses on each individual child with "child of the week." If there are interests of your own that you want to share with children, make tentative plans now for when they might be introduced. For example, if you know a lot about insects, be sure to allow time in the warmer parts of the school year to study them in depth.

Add to these long-range plans the themes you will want to do in the near future. Then start making webs for each one, being sure that curricular areas and skills are covered at the appropriate times. If you have an out-of-the-way bulletin board, one that children won't be distracted by, post the webs there and add to or subtract from the activities as the weeks progress. Otherwise, be sure and designate a safe, permanent place to keep them, perhaps starting a folder for each into which new ideas and materials can be slipped as they emerge. If you have access to an out-of-the-way board, it is also a good idea to post monthly calendars across it. Pencil in themes, holidays, and other scheduling considerations.

Make your first theme or unit a fairly short one, choosing activities that will help you and the children get to know each other. Perhaps no more than 2 weeks should be allowed; although if the children prove very interested, there is, of course, nothing wrong with expanding and developing later. However, with a shorter unit you will not have invested too much energy in curriculum planning for children you don't yet know.

Unless you develop a unit plan that is to specifically introduce children to school, you will probably not want to begin the theme or unit on the very first day. Use the first days to make children (and yourself!) comfortable with their new surroundings and with the rules and requirements of the class.

Creating the Environment   When children enter their classroom for the first time they will be, at the least, nervous and possibly quite fearful. Thus, it is important that the environment be one that welcomes them. Young children respond well to color; be sure that the colors are happy combinations. Young children can also be overwhelmed by too much stimulus; patterns, groupings, and color combinations should be very, very simple. Also, do not put many materials out for the children. Only display those that you want them to feel free to use on the very first day so they will feel less intimidated by many new things.

As you begin to move the furniture, you might want to refer to Chapter Eleven for some general guidelines. Based on the discussion from that chapter, here is a checklist that should prove useful as you are arranging and rearranging.

Environmental Checklist (before school begins)

1. Is there an area large enough for whole-class activities?

2. Are there areas for comfortably seating small groups?

3. Is there at least one private space for children who want to be alone?

4. Have I avoided having an area that is so large and open that children will naturally run noisily through it?

5. Is there a balance of both open and closed space?

6. Are facilities for loud and quiet activities separated?

7. Are activity centers that blend well placed close to each other?

8. Are materials for learning and play located close to the area in which they'll be used?

9. Is access to the outdoors as easy or as difficult as it needs to be for safety and convenience?

10. Is the outdoor environment as safe as it can be?

11. Are materials (indoors and out) in near-perfect condition and working order?

Outlining the curriculum and creating an appealing and appropriate environment are critical to beginning the school year in the best way possible. The human element is the most important to consider, however.

Parents and Children   If a home visit is possible, it may well be the most rewarding aspect of beginning the new year. Seeing children in their own home setting provides a fuller perspective on what they really are than just seeing them in the classroom. (See Chapter Ten for discussion of this.) During the home visit or while parents are visiting the school, learn as much as you can about their employment, hobbies, interests, and abilities. Discuss with them their availability and interest in some of the curriculums you are planning. Add their names and interests to the webs and calendars you have posted or filed.

If possible, have each child come visit the classroom before school starts. (Again, see Chapter Ten for more on this.)

Beginning the School Year

The furniture and materials are set up. You have planned broad curricular ideas and goals. You have established a relationship with the parents. And you have taken the first steps to make the children feel at home in their new setting. Let's see now what the first few days will look like.

So that everything will go smoothly, it is a good idea at first to concentrate your energies on classroom management and on making children feel at home and self-confident. If you take time now to focus on these noncurricular items, it will take less time later to maintain them. First we'll look at points to consider, then see how they fit into the actual schedule.

Establishing Rules   Decide the two or three rules that are most important to the smooth functioning of the classroom; then very clearly communicate them to the children. Soon you will want to have the children help establish rules, and you may even wish to start the process now. Or you may prefer to start with two or three rules of your own and let the children participate later.

Post the rules on a chart that is easily seen by the children. Print the rules and illustrate them with simple drawings. The chart might look like this.

Rules

1. Hugging yes. Hurting no.   [picture]

2. Don't step on work or toys.   [picture]

3. Put toys away when through   [picture]

Establishing Procedures   Make a list of procedures that are important to the smooth functioning of the classroom. Decide exactly—very exactly—how they should be done. (Small children feel most comfortable if they know just how something should be done and are very proud of themselves when they succeed at doing it.) Demonstrate these, and then let the children practice them in the first days. Some procedures to consider establishing are the following.

- Carrying a chair and putting it down carefully
- Laying out mats and rugs (or cots) for naps or to work on; putting them away
- Passing out snacks and cleaning up afterward
- Coming from individual or group work to a whole-class meeting
- Carrying work and toys carefully
- Putting completed work and play away before doing new things
- Using the toilet correctly and washing up afterward

Caring for Others   Young children learn thoughtfulness toward others by establishing their behaviors, and for that reason "Hugging yes. Hurting no." is the first rule suggested above. But, of course, there's more to it than a few rules, and steps can be taken during the first days of school to establish good human relationships. Choose just one or two potential situations or problems and on the first day role-play them. After observing children for a full day, you will probably find that there are other problems in relationships that emerge. Avoid unhappy confrontations by redirecting children to play with others or by themselves for a while. Then, do a whole-class role-play that shows how a similar situation can be handled happily. Do not refer to a previous unpleasant situation unless the children themselves want to discuss it. In any case, keep the role-play brief and to the point. If several children want to participate, repeat as many times as necessary. Some possible situations to role-play include the following.

- Politely asking to join other children at play
- Asking permission to use a toy; politely granting or refusing permission
- Hugging gently
- Touching or not touching classroom pets
- Taking turns by standing in line (e.g., at the water fountain)
- Apologizing after unintentionally hurting someone or knocking someone down
- Offering snacks or chairs to adult visitors

Caring for the Environment   Indirectly we have already discussed this in "Establishing Rules" when we suggested that children not step on work or toys, and in "Procedures" when we discussed ways to carry and use materials. Still, it is important to highlight this aspect of getting the year started well, because if children learn to respect and love their environment on the very first day, there will be fewer problems later with any form of destruction. You will have to decide if blocks must be put away carefully, or if karate-chopping them down doesn't bother you (or the blocks). You will have to decide if some bulk materials such as large stringing beads can just be dumped into one large container, or if they should be sorted gently and carefully. You will have to decide if structures created one day can be left up until the next, and so on. Survey the room very carefully and make decisions about absolutely everything in it. Then, patiently demonstrate or role-play with the children how each material should be handled.

If children are careless at first, don't berate them. Just quietly demonstrate for them again the correct way to do it. For some children it may be necessary to point out, "At home you may do this a different way. This is how we do it at school." Here may also be an opportunity to demonstrate proper handling to the whole class. You can say, "Some of you may be wondering how to carry a chair the best way. Let me show you how to do it so that the chair doesn't get hurt."

The First Day

Underlying the learning for the entire school year is the set of procedures and attitudes that is formed in the first few days. That is why it is so critically important to devote that early time to rules, procedures, caring for others, and care of the environment. Even now in your student teaching you may be observing teachers who seem to have no discipline problems, whose classes run smoothly even on hectic days, who can quietly speak to children and receive consistently pleasant responses. These teachers might possibly have been given the gift of an unusually cooperative and mature class. It is more likely that they took the first days of school to establish guidelines such as those we have just discussed. It would be interesting to ask to see their lesson plans for those days or to talk to them about those early experiences.

Here is one way you might begin your school year. Try it the first time, altering as needed to fit the school's expectations or any other considerations. Adapt and make it your own as you gain experience.

This section will give you a minute-by-minute description of what a first day might look like. The elements that will make it work smoothly and successfully include (1) having all materials ready and easily available and (2) planning transitions as carefully as you plan activities. As the day is described, you will note that activities and transitions both receive their own special subtitles. Overlooking the individual importance of each is often a failing of the beginning teacher. This description is designed to give you added awareness of them both.

Activity   Before children arrive, arrange the room so that there are two or three large tables with sufficient chairs (or stools) for the entire class. On these tables place a few boxes of small manipulatives, or toys, or sheets of paper with crayons. The idea is to choose something that will be instantly understood by the children and will focus their attention for a short while. If you have an aide, this is where she or he will be. If you don't, you will be close enough to supervise if any problems arise (they usually don't).

Transition   As children enter, greet each one individually, showing cubbies, asking a friendly question or two. Direct each child to the waiting tables while you greet others, If one or two children begin crying, it may be a good idea to have the mother sit on the sidelines for a short time while the child gets used to the class. However, this is less likely to happen if you have done home visits and the children have already visited the classroom.

Transition   Once all children have been greeted and have had at least a few minutes at the tables, quietly talk to children at each table, asking them to gently and quietly replace the materials in their boxes. Then call each child individually to place any completed pictures, or other work in his or her cubby and then come to the large-group area.

Activity   Do songs and finger plays that provide some action but keep children in the same area.

Transition   Demonstrate the carrying of a chair from the large tables to the large-group area. Emphasize silence, making a challenge of it. Call on one or two children to try, then three or even four children at a time, until all children have chairs in the group. (Depending on the age of the children and the school's traditions, the chairs may be placed informally or on a line made from tape or on large spots painted on the floor.)

Activity   Read a story.

Activity   If you have an aide, let him or her read a very short story to the girls while you take the boys to the restroom to demonstrate the proper procedures. (Yes, you really will demonstrate.)

The process is then reversed. If you have no aide, take the entire class, but demonstrate to one sex at a time while the others stand quietly at the back. Be sure children understand that they are permitted to use the restroom whenever it's necessary and don't have to wait until someone tells them. Also assure them (especially if they are quite young) that if they don't want to go by themselves at first they can enlist the help of teacher, aide, or older child.

Transition   From this potentially chaotic group scene, release children individually to tiptoe back to their chairs.

Activity   Demonstrate any material from the prepared centers or shelves that requires more than careless handling or informal interaction. Be sure that your behavior removing it from and returning it to its correct place is just as careful as you want the children's behavior to be.

Transition   Demonstrate the proper way to return a chair to its table and then call children individually and in small groups to do the same. Make the challenge similar to that of the previous chair transition. As children complete their mission have them return to the large-group area and sit on the floor.

Activity   Introduce the two or three rules you have chosen. (Or, perhaps with older children, create one or two rules together.)

Activity   Play follow-the-leader by leading children on a tour of the areas in which they will have free play. You may wish to develop body language for moving about the room: hands at side, walking not running, stepping around not over others' projects. Briefly and simply explain any special rules that apply to each area, such as removing and replacing materials. Return to the large-group area.

Transition   Dismiss children one at a time to go quietly to the play area of their choice. If you have an aide, have her or him assist any insecure children. If you don't, call back to the group any children who wander aimlessly. Have them sit near you until they can tell what they want to do or until you are free to help them wander more purposefully.

Free play may last as little as 10 or 15 minutes or as much as 45 minutes. This will depend on the maturity and behavioral abilities of the children. Use as much of this time as possible to observe children's interactions with each other, noting the children who have trouble making friends, those who have a tendency to want to run things, and so on. Gently redirecting some children may make it possible to keep this free time going a little longer. This is the children's first opportunity to be independent and self-sufficient. Help them make the most of it.

Transition   Create a noise the children have never heard before. Ringing a small bell is a good choice. The novelty will direct their attention toward you. Very quietly ask children to put the materials away just as you showed them when they played follow-the-leader. Encourage them to help each other: As you walk, say something like, "I see that the children in the block corner have a lot of work to do, so I'm going to help them." Other children may help, too. If necessary, ring the bell again to bring the noise level down.

As much as possible, time the cleanup so that everyone finishes helping each other at about the same time. Return to the large-group area. The children will follow you without your having to announce it.

Transition   Move to the tables for snacks by dismissing one, two, or three children at a time. If you have an aide, it is easiest the first day to have her or him set everything out while cleanup is going on. If you don't, then have crackers in baskets and juice poured in cups before school begins. Put them at a central location during cleanup; then demonstrate how to carry cup, napkin, and cracker to a place at a table. As children eat, demonstrate how to clean up and return to their seat at the table.

Activity   Snack time. (This will probably be brief. Use it to set up jars of water, small branches, and flowers at each table. These should have been prepared before school started.)

Activity   Demonstrate to children how to arrange flowers, including cleanup of any messes. (Be sure you have cleaning materials handy.) As each child finishes, the completed product is brought to you for your admiration, and then placed wherever the child thinks it will add most to the beauty of the room. (This activity is also described in the unit at the end of Chapter Eight.)

Transition   As children finish, have them carefully carry their chairs back to the large-group area. It should be fairly easy to do any final wiping up as children also help clean and move their chairs. Be sure children understand that earlier rules for carrying chairs are still in effect.

Activity   Demonstrate one idea from the list in "Caring for Others."

Transition   Calling children one at a time, line them up to play outdoors. Do not let this get out of hand in any way. As soon as a child indicates that he or she will misbehave, ask the child to return to the group. Then save that child for last.

Activity Once outside, gather children around you, seated, and explain any necessary safety rules. Then, let children play freely for as long a time as is available to you. This is the best opportunity for children to release the tension of being in a new place. For you it is an opportunity to once again observe social interactions and redirect attention as necessary.

Transition Again using the bell or other sound that carries, call children to you, lining them up in whatever place you have chosen. For young children this will no doubt continue to be a somewhat ragged performance. Perfection is not necessary and it is not worth the time spent on drill. If you simply start leading them toward the door, they will usually fall into line as correctly as they can manage.

At the door itself, it is time to require quiet. Release children one at a time to return to the large-group area. Any child who misbehaves can simply be brought back to the end of the line.

Activity Read a final story, or repeat songs and finger plays from the morning.

Transition Be sure to have worked out the dismissal procedures with your aide and/or the school officials. The procedures should include everything children are expected to do, and this should be communicated to them clearly.

Activity Take three deep breaths, sink into a chair, and treat yourself to a cup of coffee or tea.

The First Weeks

It should be obvious that the preceding description of a first day is long on procedures and short on curricular learning. There is also some repetition, as in the moving of chairs. For the rest of the first week, the style should be similar, although new procedures, rules, and role-plays will be introduced. Old ones should be repeated if they are easily forgotten or ignored. As the days pass, the time allotted for free play can be extended and that given over to demonstrations and procedures can be shortened. Never hesitate to return to something that has been done before. Small children learn through repetition. Without it they may forget entirely that they ever heard or saw something that you want them to remember.

In the weeks that follow, curricular activities, indoor and out-door play, and some nearby field trips should certainly be replac-ing the procedural focus of the first days. If behavior starts to fall apart, spend part of a morning observing the children at play. Tar-get one or two concerns; then demonstrate or have the children role-play proper behavior. Never let classroom behavior really fall apart before you take time from the curriculum to correct it.

As the class begins to develop its own rhythm, it is a good time to take stock of where it is all going. Here is a checklist to use two or three times before the break in late December.

Mid-Point Checklist

1. Are curricular goals being reached? What changes need to be made in long-range goals, current lesson plans, and the goals themselves?

2. Are themes and units still on-target for this group of children? Are major or minor alterations appropriate?

3. Are children enthusiastic about the cognitive aspects of school? What topics and activities are they enjoying most? Least?

4. What materials are being used too little? Should they be re-moved or highlighted in some way instead?

5. Are the cognitive needs of all children being met? Should there be more focus on some individual children or on groups of children?

6. Are all children feeling comfortable socially? Is there anyone who feels unloved or unwanted? Are steps being taken to rec-tify the situation?

7. Are all children making some progress toward independence and self-direction? Do they seem to feel self-confident as they move through the day?

8. Do the daily activities provide opportunities for motor devel-opment? Are there activities that allow children to improve at their own individual levels?

9. Are children getting a good balance between play and more formal learning?

10. Is there a good balance between self-directed and teacher-directed learning?

11. Is the physical layout of the room working well? Could any-thing be altered to make the flow of traffic and usage patterns more efficient?

12. Am I using the aide as effectively as possible?

13. Is parental help turning out as I expected? Can improvements be made?

14. Are my communications with parents as effective as they should be?

After asking yourself the questions on this list, you will understand the need for flexibility! Perhaps only minor changes will need to be made in curriculum, teaching techniques, or relationships. On the other hand, asking basic and, perhaps, difficult questions may turn up the possible need for major adjustments. Informally and in small ways these questions will come up almost daily. The kind of in-depth questioning provided by the checklist needs to take place every few weeks. You can do it collaboratively with your aide if you have a good working relationship. You can confer with another teacher or a supervisor if you dislike the answers the questions bring but don't know how to make corrections.

Whatever conclusions you reach, it is important to keep trying, stay flexible, and stay in tune with the children's needs and interests. At the end of this time period, look backward and forward. Determine what needs have not been met well enough and which have been overemphasized. Think of the children's expressed interests that have had to be put off. Then plan for the term to follow the holiday break.

JANUARY TO MID-MARCH/APRIL

This is a period in the school year when both teacher and students breathe a collective sigh of relief after the special but hectic weeks of fall and early winter. But first it is necessary to settle into the classroom rhythms again. Children have spent 2 or 3 weeks at home, usually with exciting experiences to relate. When they return to school it may be with a bit of rebellion at leaving behind the excitement or with a slightly feverish response to life that comes from having been off-schedule for a while. Yet they will also be glad to see you and each other, so the time should be a happy one. It simply needs some initial direction.

On the first day, do a modified version of the very first day of school. Be more directive than has been your custom in the last few weeks, and give the children less freedom than they have been accustomed to. Structure the day carefully. Have plenty of extra activities in case the free-play time doesn't go smoothly and you need to draw it quickly to a close. At the end of the day, reflect on the experiences of the last few hours and determine how structured you need to remain for the coming days.

Although the children will need a bit of settling down, they will also be eager to begin something new and not feel they are simply going back to the same old thing. Although the first day needs to be carefully structured, it is also a good time to grab their interest with a new theme or unit. This will have been planned, possibly before school started, or it may be one that the children themselves have asked for. In either case, it is important that you will have related it to the curricular goals for this part of the year and to the learning needs of the children at this point.

Since the learning needs of young children include cognitive, affective, and motor development, January is a good time to look back and see if one or two of these developmental areas have been emphasized at the expense of others. As you revise your curriculum plans, include activities that will correct any imbalance.

Balance will also be important in relation to old and new activities, procedures, and materials. Young children need repetition, stability, and familiarity with their surroundings. Making too many changes in scheduling, procedures, and the physical environment can cause insecurity, which may manifest itself in negative behavior. Therefore, redecorate the room for the new season, but (unless there is a compelling reason for change) keep the materials in their accustomed places and keep the basic daily schedule about the same. These familiar landmarks and guideposts will give children the self-assurance to tackle the new challenges about to be presented to them in new curricular themes and in new cognitive, affective, and motor activities.

As the weeks progress, be sure to use the checklist occasionally to see how much progress is being made in all areas. With its shorter days, often inclement weather, and lack of major holidays, this period of the year is a good time to focus on goals and achieving them. Unfortunately, more focusing often tempts teachers to begin teaching skills for their own sake, and both teachers and children may begin to wonder why school is no longer as enjoyable as it once was. It is important to remember the overall goals that include independent, self-directed learning; joy in learning; and time to learn through play. If you continue to focus on cross-curricular themes, the urge to drill on skills will soon be overcome. Winter also will come to a close and, with that change, school almost always will need to be remade yet again.

MARCH/APRIL TO THE END OF SCHOOL

Six or seven months have now passed since the school year began and there will, of course, be changes in the children's size, social maturity, physical capabilities, and cognitive abilities. Some of the progress you should be able to observe now includes the following.

1. When children walk in in the morning, you do not have to have a planned activity ready for them. You can say, "What would you like to do first today?" and each child will be ready with an idea. In other words, free-play time can begin the day. There will be some days when you can extend the free play to last all morning. While this may not achieve the broadest academic goals, it does give children experience in self-direction and decision making, thus making the idea worthwhile on occasion.

2. If you have easy access to the outdoors, children should be able to move freely between their indoor and outdoor play time, choosing for themselves a good balance between the two. If, on occasion, a child chooses to spend the entire morning indoors or outdoors, this should be accommodated. If the preference is continually repeated, some encouragement toward more balance may be necessary. It is possible to join the times of indoor free play and outdoor play to make one large block of time, thus making this indoor-outdoor period feasible. It is also possible to move some of the indoor activities outdoors. (See Chapter Eleven for more discussion.)

3. There will be no question in children's minds about what the correct procedures are, what the important rules are, and what you mean when you give them a meaningful stare. In other words, the management of the classroom will be well under control—allowing, of course, for "off" days.

4. Children who are physically gifted will be looking for new motor challenges, those that regularly belong to the children a year ahead of them. Children who were at first physically timid will now feel at home and comfortable with the motor requirements of the class activities.

5. Power plays will be rare: Leaders and followers will know who they are. As a whole, social interactions are smooth. This does not mean a total absence of conflict. But when conflicts arise, children will know the approved methods for handling them. Even in the heat of battle it will be possible for the teacher to remind them of the rules and procedures for these times and to expect some response.

6. Children are confident when tackling new cognitive challenges. They understand the concept of learning by themes and enjoy delving into new ones.

All these achievements are possible, although there may be years when some of them are difficult to reach. Most years something else will happen, too, particularly with the 5-year-olds and older 4-year-olds. This wonderful time of harmony and progress will be temporary. Just when you think that the rest of the school year will be smooth sailing, a change will introduce itself. It is nothing more than the time-honored and traditional spring fever.

Children who are old enough to have been through a year of school before are aware that there is actually an end to what is going on. Much as they may love school, they also know that there is a more relaxed time ahead. Or perhaps they had a bad experience the previous summer and now are fearful of leaving their current situation. If you live in an area where the climate changes, cabin fever may also set in about now (even if you've resolutely spent the winter zipping up snowsuits and sending children outside). Even in warm climates the temperature changes a bit and the sun travels the sky at a different angle, so that children know something is different and they respond to it. If there is a week off for spring vacation, you are then also faced with somewhat the same need to strive toward normality that you had after the winter break.

The change we are describing in which children go from seeming to be totally with-it to suffering the advanced stages of spring fever may occur at any time, and it may happen quickly or by degrees. You will no doubt feel some of it yourself. Here are some suggestions to help you through the transition and to survive until the end.

1. After spring vacation, begin with more structured directions and activities, just as you did after the winter vacation. This time, expect a higher level and quicker adaptation on the part of children. At the same time, be prepared to accept a less-than-perfect willingness to go along with your plan; the fever may have caught already.

2. Take time, with the children, to rethink the class rules. Are there any that need revising? The children should be feeling very self-confident now. Even the youngest can help with the revision. Their investment in the rules may help all of them get through the coming restless weeks.

3. If the children are beginning to quarrel, try some regrouping. Combine children in new and unaccustomed groups to work with you or to develop projects together.

4. If the children seem bored and generally tired of school, try field trips. These do not need to be major affairs with buses and chaperones. They can even be decided on the spur of the moment. Take a walk to the nearest woods or park, bringing back natural materials for science and art. Talk with nearby merchants and walk to a store that is new to you. Write stories and draw pictures when you get back. Explore your own school and try drawing a map of it.

5. Make outdoor playtime last longer. If you are concerned that not enough learning is going on, take some of the materials and/or centers outside.

6. As you plan activities, think of ways they might be done outdoors rather than inside. Any story may be more pleasant read outdoors this time of year, but it is especially meaningful to have a nature story as spring arrives. Materials for counting and grouping can be carried outdoors, but it will probably be more memorable to count and group objects of nature. And nature is no doubt doing its best to provide you with a multitude of learning experiences on every tree, bush, and plant.

7. It is time to learn new songs, particularly active ones. Include some good walking songs for your neighborhood field trips. Older children will enjoy composing some songs or making up nonsense verses to go with familiar melodies.

8. Find new ways to call the children's attention to you. If you've been ringing a bell all year, now try singing or a musical instrument. Rarely use an old, familiar attention getter as it will begin to fail more frequently.

9. When the weather gets very warm, think water. You might teach a whole unit on water or make water the underlying theme of the school day. Have wading pools, sprinklers, and hoses. Paint water pictures on the sidewalk. Explore puddles after a rainstorm. Take tables and chairs outdoors and wash them in sudsy water. See how many recipes can be followed and created using water. Study how water freezes, turns to vapor, or turns from solid to liquid form again. Focus some activities on water safety in preparation for the summer (and be sure that everything you do that is potentially dangerous is very well supervised).

10. Rehearse being a class ahead. This may be most important for kindergarteners who will enter a whole new world after the summer. Find out from the next teacher(s) what expectations are for incoming children. You should have spent the year resisting their demands. Now, however, the children are excited about moving on and are eager to find out what is expected of them. Now they will see reasons for demands made on them that earlier would have been a struggle. Will they need to sit in desks and in rows? Will they need to raise their hands to use the bathroom? Will they do inactive seatwork? Will they be allowed to move around but need to stay more quiet than in your class? Take a few days to rehearse going to the next class. It will make them so much more confident when they finish their year with you and when, 3 months later, they actually enter their new classrooms. If the children have never eaten in a cafeteria and will be expected to in the fall, arrange for the older children to invite them to school one day. Using a friendly sort of buddy system the younger children will be delighted and happy to learn about this very grown-up activity.

The mood at the end of the school year needs to be warm and positive. It is the children's last possibility to realize that learning is something they love to do, and they will retain the feeling, if not all the memories, of those final weeks during their summer vacation. Whatever calamities, disasters, and bad experiences might have taken place during the year, be sure to do everything possible to have children depart on good terms with the institution that is going to be an integral part of their lives for many years to come.

AFTER SCHOOL IS OUT

Preparing the Room

As you clean the room, store materials according to whatever groupings will make sense to you when the next year begins. If you want to begin with the same centers you began with during this school year, then shelve the materials accordingly. Make one special grouping for materials that need repair. Do not, under any circumstances, pull them out again until they are put back in good condition. If children are presented with materials that are shabby, they will treat them shabbily.

Analyzing the Curriculum

Look through your curriculum, noting the units and themes that worked well and those that didn't. Look at any comments you made when you used the checklists. Now make final notes concerning each, suggesting what needs to stay the same and what would be better if changed. Make a list of materials that you will need to create before they are taught again. Try to find time over the summer so that less time will have to be spent during the school year.

Evaluating Yourself

No doubt, as a new teacher you have been evaluated already by others. It is hoped that you used those opportunities to make improvements and gain self-confidence. Now, have a very personal conversation one-on-one with only you present. Ask yourself:

- Do I enjoy being a teacher?
- What do I like best about the profession?
- What would make this job a better one for me?
- Am I teaching children of the right age? Would I do a better job with older (or younger) boys and girls?
- Do I have any biases against the class, color, or gender of the children I've been teaching? Have I dealt well with them, or do I perhaps need to change where I teach?
- Have I been able to communicate well with the parents? Did anything inhibit my doing well with them? Can things be changed?

• Do I feel comfortable by now with the other faculty members and staff? Could I have done anything differently to make relationships better?

• Have I communicated to my supervisors or principal the positive feelings I have about the school?

Once you have had this conversation with yourself, have left the room in good order, and have said friendly good-byes to all those around you, you can relax and look forward to the next year when you will be—an experienced teacher.

TO DO

1 Interview two preprimary teachers who have very different approaches to teaching. Ask how they plan for the first week of school.
   a What management techniques are used?
   b In what ways is the environment set up differently than later in the year?
   c How are children made to feel comfortable about their new experience?
   d Does the teacher prefer to know a lot about the children before school begins or after having a chance to know them personally first? Why?
   e What contacts are made with the parents before or as school begins?
   f What does the first day look like?
2 Compare your interview results with those of other students in your class. Discuss the difference in approaches. Divide into groups, with each one representing a specific approach. Create a schedule for the first week of school. This should include the tasks you need to undertake as the teacher, the activities you will plan for the children, and the ways in which you will prepare the environment.

_____ chapter thirteen

The Primary Grades

Teacher autonomy—or the lack of it—has been for some time an issue in American education. It is difficult for well-trained teachers to be told that they cannot make decisions about curriculum or teaching styles within their own classrooms. At the same time, legislators and parent groups have strong concerns about the erosion of test scores and general knowledge of schoolchildren. The temptation to make specific demands on the school is difficult to resist. In some counties in some states the trend now is to move back toward trusting teachers to make their own decisions, but in the meantime it is still difficult for most teachers to run their classrooms in just the way they would prefer.

Integrating the curriculum using themes and units is not usually what legislators, parent groups, and county superintendents have in mind when they demand more substance in the curriculum. They are more likely to be thinking of skills attainment, quiet and orderly classrooms, and a book on every subject for every child in every classroom. Still, it is possible for the teacher to make some decisions, create an integrated curriculum, and satisfy the requirement of teaching skills on a schedule.

In Chapter Two we met an English first-grader visiting the United States for a year. His father recalled that in England when he asked Tom what he had learned about that day, Tom replied, "Butterflies" or some other theme. In the United States, however, the answer was more likely to be, "The letter *B*" or some other skill. In deciding to teach an integrated curriculum we are, in a sense, saying that we want our children to go home and tell their parents that they learned about butterflies. The fact that the letter *B* is integral to the study of butterflies is a given. The skill of reading and writing it is not ignored, but it is placed in the context of learning something far more grand, important, and interesting. The need for the teacher who is required to help children do well on tests of skills is to make the children think of butterflies while their scores report that they have accomplished the letter *B*.

A very practical starting place can be to adapt a technique suggested in Chapter Twelve. Use an out-of-the-way bulletin board to mount monthly calendars that cover the entire school year. Before school even opens, begin compiling lists of required skills at the approximate dates they need to be accomplished. Note the weeks that various tests are given and what is expected at those times. Every state and county will have different expectations. As a beginning teacher, you will need to be aware of what those are. Posting them on your calendars will help you confront them, overcome any nervousness, and put them into perspective. That perspective should be that, yes, the skills are important for children to attain, but they are only tools for more complex, exciting, and important learning. Once they are posted, you can begin to fit them into the larger curriculum.

It is then time to take a long, hard look at the basal texts you have been provided. As you compare the books in one subject with those for another, do you see themes and units emerging? Textbook writers hope to engage the attention of their readers with topics that are of interest to their target age group, so you will often find that there are two or three topics that appear in books across the curriculum. Once you find these cross-curriculum topics, you can determine which chapters and stories can be taught out of the sequential order provided by the book. Once you see two or three possible units emerging, you can begin to plan for them in relation to the skills required and posted on your calendars. (It is important to keep in mind that just because a target skill is scheduled for Chapter Two doesn't mean you can't teach it in the context of Chapter Six.)

If you are truly courageous—and it may take some practice in the classroom before you are—you may decide to work with themes that you know will be interesting and beneficial for the children even if they aren't highlighted by the basal texts. Of course, you must still be prepared to test the children when the time comes. Teachers who work with children in this fashion will devote some time to test preparation just before the required date. When most days are filled with the "butterfly" sorts of curriculum and the test preparation is concentrated and timely, children seem to be much less bored and intimidated by the prospect of testing. (And the same generally goes for the teachers.)

Since at first you are more likely to choose to work within the confines of the basals and the skill requirements, we will devote the rest of this chapter to practical ideas for achieving that approach successfully within the context of an integrated curriculum. If you are so fortunate as to work in a setting that provides you great freedom, you may still find the ideas useful in organizing your curriculum.

Each state and school system has its own approach to requiring competencies of its children. Further, there are a number of companies from which to choose when it comes to determining which basal texts will be used. Since it would be impossible to list every state's requirements and to refer to the basals of every company, we will simply use samples of each as a basis for developing some possible curricular units. Marion County, Florida, provides an example of a county that has combined state requirements in some curricular areas with its own requirements for others. These are quite specific and are considered basic to each grade, although they are certainly not the maximum that children should strive toward. For the purposes of demonstrating ways to develop an integrated curriculum, taking into account the required skills, we will use examples from the Marion County listing.[1]

We will also use samples of basal texts to demonstrate ways in which they can be applied to an integrated curriculum. It is important to note that the choice of particular companies in no way constitutes an endorsement of them over others. Further, due to copyright laws, it is not possible to illustrate actual pages from the books. Instead, descriptions of what the books offer should provide an understanding of what is possible to create from whatever materials are provided in your classroom.

Using the Marion County Basic Skills Listing and a small collection of basal texts, we will see how a unit can be developed for each grade level. These units are brief and basic, as you yourself may wish to create some of your units. Other times you may find that you and the children want to study a topic in much more depth and as many as fifty or even sixty activities may emerge as you develop the curriculum. You may also wish to make a topic the overlying theme of the entire school day for a period of time. In addition to focused activities, you might want to decorate the room, invent new words to old songs, use paper for written work that reflects appropriate colors, and so on. You might even choose to adapt and embellish the units presented here.

For each of the units, we follow a five-step process that provides for planning and reflecting on the plan before actual teaching begins. Steps 1 and 2 can be reversed. For some units you may want to begin with step 2 if the basals contain a topic that you think will excite the children; we take this approach in the first- and third-grade examples. Other times you will feel the need to focus first on skills and then attempt to place them in a more meaningful context; this is done in the grade-two unit where the skills are related to learning about money.

---

[1] Selections from the Marion County Basic Skills Listing are printed with the permission and courtesy of the School Board, Marion County, Florida.

Five Steps to Integrating with Basals and Skills

1 List the skills to be highlighted in the unit.
2 Refer to the basal texts to develop a cross-curricular topic.
3 Create a curriculum web of activities drawn from or suggested by the basal texts, coordinating them with the chosen skills.
4 Analyze the web to determine what skills and curricular areas need to be added. Fill in with more activities.
5 Check the web for balance:
  a Is there a balance between teacher-directed, independent, and center-based activities?
  b Is there a balance between focused work and open-ended play or creativity?
  c Does the scheduling and time required of the unit fit into the other elements of the school day?

As you read about the three primary units and see how they are put together, keep in mind that while the letter *B* (the required skills) is always an important part of planning, it is the butterflies (the interesting topics) that provide the real substance. Not the other way around.

GRADE ONE: ANIMALS THEN AND NOW

The choice of subject for this integrated unit reflects the abilities of first-grade children to sort out reality from unreality and to distinguish between extinct, ancient times from living in the present day. For most children these are new-found abilities and thus at just the right level of challenge and interest. Because they are new, it is important not to expect complex understandings, so that it is appropriate to make broad generalizations and comparisons.

Dinosaurs are of great interest to young children, perhaps because of their similarity to the monsters they love to fear. But present-day animals are popular, too, whether they be favorite pets or unusual zoo inhabitants. Capitalizing on these interests and on the children's comparatively new abilities at differentiating (mentioned above), we can create a unit that relates today's animals with those of ancient times. For this "Then and Now" unit we begin with step 2, looking first for the materials available in basal texts.

Basal Resources

Merrill Science (Hacket, Moyer, & Adams, 1989) contains two chapters that can be used: "Animals" and "Life Long Ago." While "Life Long Ago" focuses on dinosaurs and can be used directly as is, "Animals" is devoted to comparing present-day animal groups and learning about habitats. Some adjustments will be necessary to use both chapters at once.

The accompanying *Science: A Big Book of Language Experiences* (Allen, Helenthal, & McLaughlin, 1989) offers ready-made opportunities for integration. Stories, poems, and nonfiction that relate to the two chapters can be used by the teacher with large or small groups of children.

Because young children have an avid interest in animals, most basal readers generally provide possibilities for incorporating this topic into an integrated unit. For our purposes here, we will choose two books that are designed by Macmillan for use at the beginning of the school year: *Close to Home* (Arnold & Smith, 1987a) and *Stepping Out* (Arnold & Smith, 1987b). Between these two paperback books a total of ten stories and poems could be used as part of the unit. Although dinosaurs are not dealt with factually, they are a part of one fantasy story. There are other fantasy stories in the collection as well as those that are reality based, thus providing opportunities for children to compare at three levels: real animals of today, real animals of ancient times, and fantasy animals of any time. The lack of dinosaur stories indicates a need to fill in with other available books.

Although the social studies do not directly include the study of animals, some adaptation of basals can still be made. It is possible to pick and choose portions of the textbook that have application to the unit. For example, Heath's *Homes and Neighborhoods* (Recque, 1987) provides several opportunities. There is a section on globe skills, which could be used to pinpoint the areas where various dinosaurs lived. Another section on hot and cold environments features animals in their habitats. These could be compared to the ranges of the dinosaurs, again using the globe. For discussion purposes, the book provides a number of pictures, some of which include pets and farm animals, as well as a museum reproduction of a dinosaur. All of these lend themselves to comparison and contrast.

Leafing through almost any math book, it is possible to find illustrations that relate to children's interests and current topics of study. One brief example is to be found in the grade-one *Heath Mathematics* (Rucker, Dilley, & Lowry, 1988). One page of addition practice features a humorous picture of a billy goat, and another is decorated with a brontosaurus mother and her baby. These two can easily be tied together with a related project as part of the animal unit.

Focus Skills

Since we are using basal readers that are designed for the first of the school year, we can choose (from the Marion County Listing) skills that are most easily taught at that time.

Language
1. Determine the main idea through pictures.

2. Classify using pictures.

3. Orally describe the sequence of a set of three pictures.

Mathematics
4. Count objects to fifty.

5. Identify the smaller or larger of any two given whole numbers.

6. Add with sums through 9.

Social Studies
7. Recognize and identify that a globe is a model of the earth.

8. Name directional words: "north," "south," "east," and "west."

Science
9. Describe an object based on its color, shape, texture, and size.

10. Identify the sequence of picture problems.

11. Recognize evidence that change has occurred.

12. Identify objects as living or nonliving.

13. Recognize examples of common animals as being fish, birds, or mammals.

The Curriculum Web

We are now ready to see how far the basals have taken us in providing skill coverage and in creating a well-integrated unit. Let's first be more specific about the possibilities provided by the texts, giving each learning activity a name.

I. Now and Then

Photocopy pictures from both chapters in *Merrill Science*. Glue pictures of individual animals on index cards. Have children classify animals into those that lived in prehistoric times and those that live now. (Science, language; skills 1, 2, 9, 11, and 12)

II. Fish, Birds, and Mammals

Use the same cards to divide the entire collection of cards into these three categories. Discuss the attributes of each category. (Science, language; skills 1, 2, 9, and 13)

III. Dinosaur Names

Make two sets of dinosaur cards using the photocopied pictures. To the bottom of one set attach the correct name of each dinosaur. Make a label of the same size for the second picture, but do not attach it. Have children use the labeled picture to find its mate in the book, lay it on the table, and place next to it the matching picture and unattached label. They can learn to read the names, with teacher help, as interested. (Science, language; skills 1, 2, 9, 11, and 13)

IV. Animal Names

A similar set of cards can be made for today's animals. (Science, language; skills 2 and 13)

V. Now and Then Math

Children do the addition pages that are illustrated with a goat and a dinosaur. They can then match them to the appropriate cards in the activity Now and Then. Or attach an extra page so they can write stories with invented spellings and illustrations. (Math, science, language; skills 1, 6, and 11)

VI. Where in the World

Using information from *Merrill Science* and other dinosaur books, indicate on the globe where dinosaur remains have been found. Using the *Homes and Neighborhoods* globe-picture as an example, make (or obtain) globe-shaped maps. With colored pins, indicate areas where remains have been found. With pins of other colors, continue with today's animals as illustrated in the text (some of this information is given along with the illustrations). With illustrations from all basals used in this unit, determine which animals are found in the children's own area and use pins to indicate these. (Social studies, science; skills 7, 8, 11, and 13)

VII. Story Time I

Read the *Science Big Book* to the class and lead a discussion to determine which animals are alive and real now, which were alive and real in prehistoric times, and which have never been alive. A chart in three columns can be made for classification. (Language, science; skills 1, 11, and 13)

VIII. Story Time II

Have children take turns reading to each other from *Merrill Science, Close to Home*, and *Stepping Out*. Observe them informally. (Language, science; skills 11 and 13)

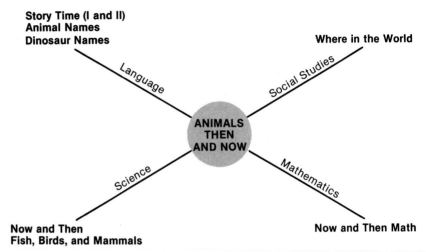

Web I: Grade One

FIGURE 13-1

Web I will now look like Figure 13-1.

Using the basal texts, it has been possible to include language and reading, science, social studies, and math in the unit. Focused skills include numbers 1, 2, 6, 7, 8, 9, 11, 12, and 13. We can now work on the next step: creating a more complete unit with ideas from other sources.

Other Sources

It might be useful to consider the skills that have not yet been included and then find ways in which they can be added creatively to the web of activities. Looking back at our list, we see that skills 3, 4, 5, and 10 have not yet been incorporated. In addition, we have no activities yet that include music and movement or art. It is not always necessary to include every area of the curriculum, and it would be better not to strain to do so. Yet, with some thought and added resources from the library and the toy store, we should be able to complete the web successfully. Some possibilities are as follows.

IX. Dictated Stories

Have large or small groups of children dictate stories about today's animals or about dinosaurs. You (or capable and interested children) write out the story in segments. Have a child illustrate each segment. These can be laminated and used by the children for story sequencing. (Language, art; skills 3 and 10)

X. One Little Dinosaur

With inexpensive plastic dinosaur models, children can sing and count dinosaurs to the tune of "Ten Little Indians." Each verse begins a new set of ten, through the teens, twenties, and so on depending on the supply of models. They can be grouped in tens for counting by tens. They can be regrouped according to colors with discussion focusing on which group contains more dinosaurs. (Music, math; skills 4 and 5)

We can now add these activities to the web (see Figure 13-2).

Checking for Balance

In looking at web II we see that there are four activities that are teacher-directed: Story Time I, One Little Dinosaur, Where in the World, and Dictated Stories. Four activities can be used in centers: Story Time II; Dinosaur Names; Animal Names; and Fish, Birds, and Mammals. Children can work independently at five activities: Now and Then Math; Dinosaur Names; Animal Names; illustrating Dictated Stories; and Fish, Birds, and Mammals. The activities chosen so far that have room for creativity include Dictated Stories and Now and Then Math. There are no activities that offer time for play.

Generally speaking, the activities are appropriate for first-graders who have recently attained an understanding of reality versus fantasy and of broad differences in time. For early readers, there is the possibility of reading the animal names on the card-

FIGURE 13-2

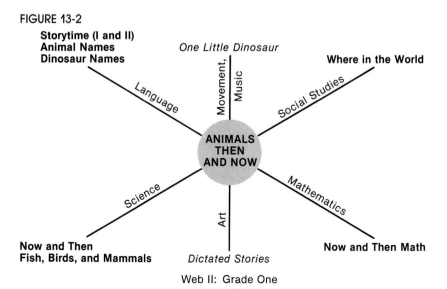

Web II: Grade One

matching sets or of writing rather than dictating stories. Children who are not yet ready to read can match and sequence by looking at the pictures.

At this point we could decide to expand the unit in two ways: by adding activities that cover the curriculum more fully or by including more activities for play. Let's assume that at this time there is no pressing need to include more art, music, movement, or social studies. But we feel the children need more play opportunities. We will define play here as opportunities to choose freely among self-directed, open-ended activities and add some ideas accordingly.

XI. Animal Library
During this unit, make a collection of books about present-day animals and about dinosaurs available for perusing at any time, either by individuals or by small groups. (Language, science; skills 1, 2, 11, 12, and 13)

XII. Animal Models
Augment the collection of dinosaur models with representatives of present-day animals. Make them available for fantasy play, possibly with a backdrop of trees, lakes, rivers, and so on. (Science; skills 9 and 13)

XIII. Clay Modeling
Have clay available for making additions to the model area. There need not be directives to make appropriate animals or scenery, but pictures and posters for "inspiration" can be in the area. (Art, science; skills 9, 12, and 13)

With these more open-ended activities, we can now make our final web (see Figure 13-3).

Our final task is to determine the time needed to complete the unit. This will be up to the individual teacher, but if the activities of "Animals Then and Now" are incorporated into the typical first-grade schedule, 2 weeks will be about right.

GRADE TWO: LEARNING ABOUT MONEY

In our second-grade unit we approach our planning a bit differently. In this case we'll concern ourselves first with the skills that need to be highlighted and then see how the basal texts can help meet these requirements.

Let us assume for this unit that we wish to meet the county mandate, and the children's need, that information about recognizing and using money be taught. The county lists just three specific basic math skills that children must accomplish, but we can use this

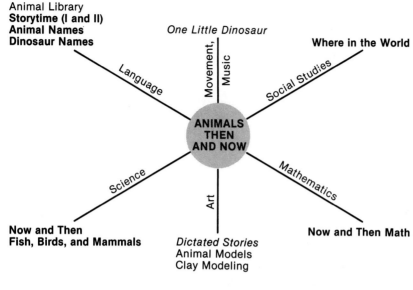

Animal Library
Storytime (I and II)
Animal Names
Dinosaur Names

One Little Dinosaur

Where in the World

Language

Movement, Music

Social Studies

ANIMALS THEN AND NOW

Science

Art

Mathematics

Now and Then
Fish, Birds, and Mammals

Dictated Stories
Animal Models
Clay Modeling

Now and Then Math

Web III: Grade One

FIGURE 13-3

opportunity to focus on skills from other curricular areas concurrently. This will make it possible to create an integrated unit using one set of math skills as the core topic. As we choose skills from areas other than math, we should be aware of what the current capabilities and needs of the children are and of what would work well with the chosen topic.

Focus Skills

We begin with math as the central focus and then branch out to other curricular areas.

Mathematics

1. Read and write, in numerals, 50¢, $1.00, and $5.00. [In first grade children learned 1¢, 5¢, 10¢, and 25¢.]

2. Identify a set of coins equivalent in value to a given set of coins with the value not to exceed 25¢.

3. Use addition, without regrouping, to solve real-world problems involving two purchases totaling no more than 50¢.

Language

4. Determine the main idea stated in a paragraph.

5. Obtain appropriate information from the tables of contents.

6. Spell numbers from one to ten.

Science
   7. Describe an object based on its color, shape, texture, and size.

Social Studies
   8. Define a producer as a maker of goods or a provider of services and a consumer as a user of goods or services. Recognize that people can be producers or consumers.

   9. Recognize that scarcity requires choices (when wants are greater than resources).

   10. Become aware that communities in the past and in the present have both similarities and differences.

Basal Resources

Macmillan's reader, *Bit by Bit* (Arnold & Smith, 1987), contains an entire unit on economics entitled "Pennies and Presents." It includes stories, poems, nonfiction information, and a story requiring mathematical thinking. It is designed to be used in the late fall of second grade.

The Heath Co.'s social studies basal, *Neighborhoods and Communities* (Recque, 1987), contains no specific economics unit, but there are useful segments throughout that can be adapted. These include "United States Money" and "At the Store."

At the second-grade level, mathematics basals typically provide some focus on learning about money. For our purposes we will choose *Heath Mathematics* (Rucker, Dilley, & Lowry, 1988), which devotes more than thirty pages to the topic. These are interspersed throughout the book, but we may choose to cluster them within our unit, depending on which pages integrate most successfully with the other parts of the unit and on which skills children may be required to learn by specific dates.

We included one science goal within our list of skills, but the study of money doesn't typically appear in science basals. We will rely on other sources to meet this skill's requirements.

The Curriculum Web

As we did in the first-grade unit, we'll now be more specific, giving names to the curricular ideas we pull from the basals.

I. How Money Is Made
Neighborhoods and Communities includes a diagram showing the steps in making coins. The steps, however, are unnumbered and may be

unclear to some children. Numbered sequencing cards can be made by photocopying the pictures. Have children order them and write brief descriptions about what is happening in each. Various pages can then be used for reference in *Heath Mathematics*. These provide photographs of coins as part of addition and subtraction pages. Here, children will use them for identification and terminology. (Math, language; skills 1 and 4)

II. Why We Have Money

Neighborhoods and Communities contains a unit about Abe Lincoln, which includes an illustrated description of the general store near Pigeon Creek, Indiana. It is pointed out that the store permitted both buying with money and trading. A much more complex illustrated picture appears in a later unit, showing a present-day department store with a greater number of goods. Have children use the two pictures at one time to discuss the differences in lifestyles, availability of resources, and needs of the two times. (Money may not be as necessary in a less complex time and place. Trading would be clumsy in the more complex setting.) (Social studies, language; skills 4 and 10)

III. How Do We Get Money?

Bit by Bit includes stories that answer this question: "Flags for Sale," which introduces the idea of buying and selling for profit, and "Bit by Bit" and "Amanda's Computer Kingdom," both of which explore different approaches to earning and saving money. To choose the stories they want to read let children have this opportunity to learn to use the table of contents. After reading the stories, have the class discuss materials or items they would like to obtain for the classroom and then brainstorm ways to obtain them. As a starting point for this brainstorming, chart the main ideas or "morals" of each story for later use. (Language, social studies; skills 4, 5, and 9)

IV. Deciding What to Buy

Using the two shopping pictures from *Neighborhoods and Communities* ask children to list needs and wants according to the lifestyles of each century. Do this on two charts or on one chart with color coding according to century. (Language, social studies; skills 1, 4, 9, and 10)

V. How Do We Know How Much Money We Need?

Heath Mathematics contains several pages devoted to combinations of quarters, dimes, nickels, and pennies. These are best accompanied by actual coins for adding. Make cards with a coin (such as a dime) taped to one side followed by the number of cents it equals (ten pennies) taped to the other side. Have children use this as a concrete reference as they add combinations. (Math; skills 1 and 2)

VI. How Do We Know? (II)
Use real money or cardboard money supplied in the basal text. On a sheet of paper write specific amounts of money, e.g., 22¢ or 18¢. Leave a space between each. Have children manipulate coins to see how many ways they can make the same total. Then have them draw pictures of their results under each written quantity. (Math; skills 1 and 2)

VII. How Do We Know? (III)
Using the same supply of coins, have children refer to pages in the basal text that show objects with price tags. For each one, ask them to arrange their coins in as many ways as possible and to draw the pictures next to the objects. (Math; skills 1 and 2)

With these activities we're now ready to make web I (see Figure 13-4).

Other Sources

Our first activities have focused on skills 1, 2, 4, 6, 10, and 11. Further activities can meet the others.

FIGURE 13-4

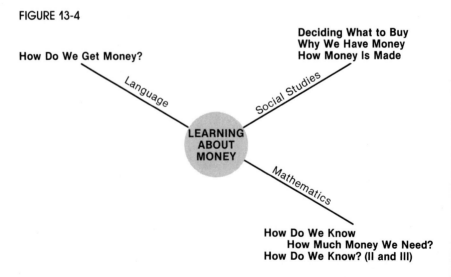

Deciding What to Buy
Why We Have Money
How Money Is Made

How Do We Get Money?

Language

Social Studies

LEARNING ABOUT MONEY

Mathematics

How Do We Know
How Much Money We Need?
How Do We Know? (II and III)

Web I: Grade Two

VIII. School Store

During the time that money is studied, a store may be created as a permanent center. Children can earn "money" to spend there by doing special jobs in the classroom or for other predetermined activities. During center times, children are given designated times as storekeepers. The store's goods can be special school supplies or donated discarded toys from home.

Determining how much money each item is worth can be done by individual storekeepers during their turns, by class discussion and vote, or by teacher decree. The last approach is the most efficient but denies children a (sometimes difficult) learning experience.

The store can be made from discarded appliance boxes and designed and decorated according to the children's interests.

Storekeepers and shoppers all must audibly and visibly count charges and change for accuracy. Storekeepers are in charge of labeling items with their correct prices. (Language, mathematics, art; skills 1, 2, 8, and 10)

IX. Earning Money

It is possible that in How Do We Get Money? the children will have thought of ways to be producers of goods. If that is the case, it is only necessary to describe them as producers and their buyers as consumers in an informal fashion. Permit children to create their own ideas for earning money for the class as well as their marketing strategies. If it is necessary to buy supplies, then they must also learn that the money must come out of their profits. (Social studies, math; skill 9)

X. Multiple Purchases

Depending on pricing practices and money supplies, children may or may not purchase more than one item at a time in the store. In either case, it will be helpful to visit the store in small groups to demonstrate how to write up a "sales slip" placing the prices of purchased items in vertical order, then adding the total. A second paper can be used to enter the amount given by a customer, then subtract the price to obtain the correct change. (Math; skills 1, 3, and 10)

XI. Mystery Money Bag

Place several coins in a drawstring bag. Children can play in pairs with one child blindfolded, the other acting as "judge." The blindfolded child tries to identify a coin by feeling it and then draws it out for the judge to identify correctly. (Science; skill 8)

XII. Spelling Numbers

"Beautify" the school store by making decorative signs with costs of items spelled out as well as written in numerals. Decorate the signs with child-selected designs. (Language, art, math; skill 6)

With the second web we can expand somewhat on the curriculum and cover more skills (see Figure 13-5).

Checking for Balance

Teacher-directed activities include the final part of How Money Is Made, Why We Have Money, How Do We Get Money?, Earning Money, Multiple Purchases, and Spelling Numbers. Centers can be created for How Money Is Made, Deciding What to Buy, How Do We Know How Much Money We Need?, How Do We Know? (II and III), School Store, and Mystery Money Bag. Children can work independently at How Money Is Made and at the reading portions of How Do We Get Money?, How Do We Know How Much Money We Need?, How Do We Know? (II and III), Mystery Money Bag, and Spelling Numbers.

Play experiences are provided by the School Store. If it is popular, it can be kept up and modified according to interests over a long period of time.

Some children will find the use and calculation of money confusing. This unit provides various approaches to defining and un-

FIGURE 13-5

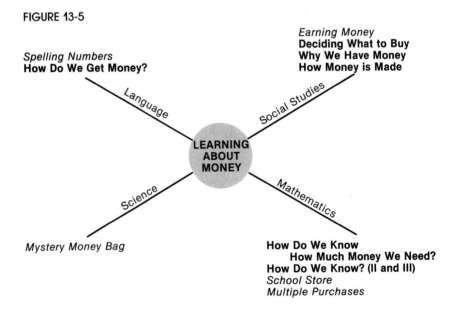

Web II: Grade Two

derstanding the different coins and their values. If taught as centers and over repeated experiences, the definitions, uses, and values should be clarified. Because money can be difficult for children to understand, it may be best not to predetermine the length of time needed for the unit. Reintroduce the centers and keep the store open as long as the learning need exists.

GRADE THREE: A JOURNEY INTO SPACE

Children have a great interest in learning about space, particularly if they can visualize themselves journeying into it. Yet this "last frontier" for human exploration contains concepts that are difficult for primary-age children to grasp. If they do not yet have an understanding of the structure and content of the solar system, they will also lack understanding of what is and is not possible for people to undertake in space exploration. It will be difficult for them to differentiate between science fiction and reality. (This is a new enough area of study that even adults sometimes confuse the two.)

The purpose of this unit is to provide a foundational understanding of and excitement about the solar system. It may be considered a springboard to study of space exploration. As with the first-grade unit, we will look first at the resources provided by selected basals and second at the skills list.

Basal Resources

Many third-grade science books offer some study of space. Laidlaw's *Journeys in Science* (Shymansky, Romance, & Yore, 1988) presents a three-chapter unit with one of them devoted to the solar system. This offers both informational reading and suggested experiments.

The space theme also appears in math books. In *Heath Mathematics* (Rucker, Dilley, & Lowry, 1988), for example, brief stories pertaining to distances between planets and moon landings give children practice in reading large numbers.

In the third-grade reader, *A Soft Pillow for an Armadillo* (Alverman, 1989), there is a unit devoted to space and one feature is a play in which children act the parts of planets in our solar system. A science fiction story describes the experiences of two children, who have lived all their lives on a space station, as they visit earth for the first time. Although this story may be most appropriate for a follow-up unit about space travel, it does focus on earth's attributes as a planet in the larger system.

Focus Skills

In a study of the solar system it is logical to think of science skills, but the topic is rich with opportunities to integrate other curricular areas as well. Some integration can be done through use of the basal texts. In this unit we will not attempt to include the social studies, although it would be appropriate for follow-up study of space travel. For example, the story of the children from the space station could be reread with a different emphasis on interrelationships and the need to establish communities in settings not on earth.

Science
1. Identify relationships among the sun, moon, and earth.
2. Identify the planets, moon, and sun as part of the solar system.
3. Identify the forms of matter as solid, liquid, and gas.

Language
4. Follow four-step written directions.
5. Identify sets of words that are in alphabetical order using the first three letters.
6. Identify the meanings of verbs denoting the past, present, or future.
7. Identify meanings of comparative and superlative forms of adjectives.

Mathematics
8. Determine length, width, or height by measuring objects with centimeters, meters, inches, feet, or yards.
9. Identify solids: cube, cylinder, cone, and sphere.
10. Read and write numerals for any whole number, 101–500.

The Curriculum Web

The basals we have chosen provide a variety of possibilities for activities, although we will also make use of outside sources.

I. Playground Planets
Use *Journeys in Science* to identify the planets, their order from the sun, and the shapes of their orbits. You will then need another source book, such as an encyclopedia or any of several basic books on the solar system, to research the comparative distance between each planet. Ask children to volunteer to represent the sun and the

planets and pace off the relative distances between themselves. Have them walk to orbit the sun, while observers note which planets take the longest to complete an orbit.

Once they are back in place, ask the remaining children to volunteer to be moons for the planets who have them. Moons can then orbit planets as everyone orbits the sun. (Orderliness usually dissolves in a short while and a partial orbit will probably be enough for class purposes.) (Science, math; skills 1 and 2)

II. The Planet Parade

This is the title of a play in *A Soft Pillow for an Armadillo*. It includes ten characters: nine planets and the sun. It is informational in that each planet tells something about itself and they all place themselves in correct order around the sun. Children should all be given an opportunity to play parts, so in a class period the play will no doubt need to be done three times.

The plot of the play centers on the attempts of the sun to find the best planet of all, so that in comparing themselves to each other many comparative and superlative adjectives are used. Pages can be photocopied and children can use magic markers to highlight with one color every adjective they can find. Ask them to circle comparatives in pencil of a second color and superlatives in pencil of a third color. (Language, science; skills 1, 2, 4, and 7)

III. Expanding the Play

Ask children to use information found in *Journeys in Science* to learn more about the planets they portray in the play. They can then add this information to their lines. (Science, language; skills 1, 2, and 9)

IV. Big Spaces/Big Numbers

The *Heath Mathematics* book approaches the reading of large numbers, through three places in the thousands, by using examples from space. Children are given opportunities to read in both words and numerals. Use the two pages in the text either as an introduction to the concept or as a wrap-up activity. During the entire unit, have children keep an ongoing chart of Big Spaces and Big Numbers. On the left, have them write the new, large numbers they encounter in their reading and research. On the right, have them put the numbers in context. For example:

250,000	The moon is 250,000 miles from Earth.
25,000	The Earth is 25,000 miles around.

(Math, language; skill 10)

V. Same and Different
Using information found in *Journeys in Science* and in *A Soft Pillow for an Armadillo,* have children list ways that each planet is the same as or different from Earth. This can be done as a chart or in essay form. (Science, language; skills 1, 2, and 3)

VI. Space Dictionary
Select space-related words from the various readings and provide each child with a list. Using one page for each word have the children illustrate and then place pages in alphabetical order before binding. (Language, art; skill 5)

Our preliminary web is as shown in Figure 13-6.

Other Sources

Thus far we have used the basal texts to create activities in science, language, math, and art. Skills taught in these activities are 1, 2, 3, 4, 5, 7, 9, and 10. For this unit we are fortunate in having a national resource that can provide us with numerous additional curriculum ideas.

Scattered throughout the United States are nine teacher-resource centers sponsored by NASA (the National Aeronautics and Space Administration). Teachers may visit and obtain materials or request them by phone or mail. There are large packets of

FIGURE 13-6

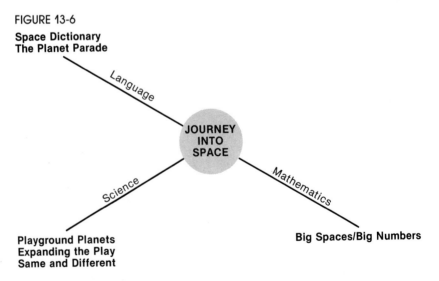

Web I: Grade Three

information appropriate to the learning of third-graders. Teachers have developed lesson plans that can be photocopied. Videotapes, slides, and audiotapes can be copied. All of these materials are available at no charge. In the case of the tapes and slides, it is necessary only to send blank tapes or slide film and they will be mailed back with the requested programs and texts. To locate the Teacher Resource Center nearest you and to receive NASA Educational Mailings, write to

National Aeronautics and Space Administration
Educational Publications Services, LEP
Washington, D.C. 20546

Although most materials concern the space program, there are still good numbers of videotapes and slides on the solar system in general. We will make use of them here.

VII. Solar System Research

Have children split into small groups, each one assigned to study one planet in depth. Videotapes and slides from NASA can be watched, rewatched, discussed, and written about. Library resource books will provide additional information. The final product of the research can take different forms: factual reports, poems, illustrations, short plays, or panel discussions. (Science, language, art; skills 1, 2, 3, and 9)

VIII. Space-Libs

This activity is modeled after the popular "Mad Libs" that can be purchased in bookstores and toy stores. These incomplete stories require at least two people: one to read the story, the other(s) to fill in the blanks. The blank spaces are located in various places, mid-sentence, throughout the story. Beneath each one is a designated part of speech, which the reader identifies to the partner before reading the story out loud. The partner chooses any desired word, usually something preposterous, and the reader writes the word in the space. The final step is for the reader to read the story aloud with the newly added words included.

In this Space-Libs version, you write a story about space leaving blank words that are verbs (past, present, or future) or adjectives (simple, comparative, or superlative). After several practices, some children will be able to write their own, which can then be photocopied for sharing with the entire class.

Here is a sample story beginning so that you can see what the Space-Libs will look like:

Once there was a young boy who wanted to be the first child astro-
naut to_____to the moon. So he_____hard at being the
  verb, present tense   *verb, past tense*
_____student at school.
adjective, superlative

(Language; skills 6 and 7)

IX. Indoor Solar System I

Replicate the playground experience on a smaller scale indoors by
using clay planets made by the children in their appropriate colors. Have children measure distances between the planets and
from the sun to each one in centimeters or in inches. (Art, math;
skills 8 and 9)

X. Indoor Solar System II

Blow balloons up to equal the relative sizes of the planets. Cover
them in papier-mâché and paint in their appropriate colors. Hang
them in order from the ceiling after measuring their circumferences
in inches or in centimeters. (Since you will no doubt have more
than one set of planets, you may wish to hang other sets in display
cases in the school hall. Backdrops can be added.) (Art, math;
skills 8 and 9)

XI. My Planet: Its Story

Have children invent their own planets, giving them whatever
characteristics they desire. They should be able to place them
within the solar system and identify the probable traits their planets would have. (This reinforces the children's factual learning
while permitting them creativity as well.) Tell them to describe
their planets in story form and then illustrate them. These can be
short stories or complex and lengthy and made into bound books.
(Language, art; skills 1 and 2)

XII. My Planet: My Corner of It

Use shoeboxes to create dioramas of the children's own home area
of their invented planets. Use plasticene or clay figures and place
them against a backdrop created with construction paper. Either
cut the top of the box off for full viewing or leave it on and cut
large holes at each end of the box for more private peeking. (Art)

Web II will now show a fuller use of the curriculum (see Figure
13-7).

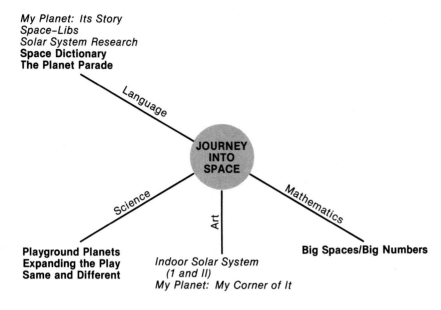

My Planet: Its Story
Space–Libs
Solar System Research
Space Dictionary
The Planet Parade

Language

JOURNEY INTO SPACE

Science

Art

Mathematics

Playground Planets
Expanding the Play
Same and Different

Indoor Solar System
(1 and II)
My Planet: My Corner of It

Big Spaces/Big Numbers

FIGURE 13-7   Web II: Grade Three

Checking for Balance

The activities that are most likely to need teacher direction are Playground Planets, The Planet Parade, and Indoor Solar System I and II. Centers can be created for Big Spaces/Big Numbers, Same and Different, Solar System Research, Space-Libs, My Planet: Its Story, and My Planet: My Corner of It. Only Space Dictionary will probably be best done independently. Children of third-grade age generally prefer to work in groups, so this is not really an unbalanced division of learning methods.

Play and creativity are provided in the My Planet activities and to some extent, in the Indoor Solar System projects. Advanced readers may wish to extend their research reading and will probably be the only ones who can create their own Space-Libs.

Since some of the projects in this unit tend to create artistic messes, it may work best to schedule solar-system study in a concentrated period rather than stretching it out over an extended period. It should probably be expected that children will wish to continue on with further studies of space exploration.

MAKING IT WORK

To see how your classroom might look with one of these units in full swing, let's assume that you are teaching third grade and are well into the unit, "A Journey into Space." Let's also assume the worst in scheduling: School starts at 8:30 and by 9:00 several children go to their special gifted class for 45 minutes, followed 15 minutes later by the departure of two or three others to their 45-minute special education class. Just as this last group returns, and 15 minutes after the gifted children come back, the entire class must leave for their weekly 10:00 music class. They return at 10:45 and at 11:30 the class goes to lunch. Making this difficult schedule even worse are your added responsibilities: By 8:50 you are to have the attendance records and lunch count in the office. In summary, your schedule for the morning looks like this:

8:30	Children enter.
8:50	Attendance and lunch count in office.
9:00	Children to gifted class.
9:15	Children to special education class.
9:45	Children return from gifted class.
10:00	Children return from special education class.
10:00	Class goes to music.
10:45	Class returns from music.
11:30	Class goes to lunch.

While all these elements taken together don't add up to a desirable way to begin planning your morning, the situation is, unfortunately, all too common. But it's not impossible, as we shall see.

The Afternoon Before

Explain and demonstrate the new project that will begin the next day: Space Dictionary. (Children will do this at their own seats.)

In the Morning Just Before School Starts

Put supplies for Space Dictionary in an easily accessible place. Check centers to be sure they are in working order. These might be Space-Libs, Big Space/Big Numbers, Solar System Research, and an art table on which children are creating cardboard planets to use as costumes for the play, "The Planet Parade." All of these centers have been up for 1 day or more and children will not need further direction.

Everything in the room need not be devoted to the topic, and you should have a set of shelves on which are placed math and other games as well as a good collection of books. Books about space can be incorporated into the larger collection, to be discovered by the children, or they can have their own specially designated place. Check these shelves also to be sure that everything is in good condition. Remove anything that is not.

On the chalkboard write special instructions as needed, for example:

> Tina, Drew, Jenny: Finish your costumes before 9:45.
> Alex and Christian: Finish your costumes before 10:00
> All children: You may begin your Space Dictionaries, use the centers, play math games, or read books. Music is at 10:00. When we return we will have a dress rehearsal of our play.

Finally, plan which children you would like to work with individually or in small groups during the morning. You will no doubt have thought about this the previous day as you reflected on the children's academic needs.

As School Begins

Greet each child at the door. Advise the children you'll work with first (individually or in groups) that you will be with them as soon as possible. They are all responsible for signing the class attendance sheet and for signing up for lunch. If money is to be collected, keep it in a container fairly close to you. Since the children are accustomed to having instructions on the board, they will know to look there right away. Because the Space Dictionaries are new, they will probably be quite popular, but there are class rules already in effect for standing in line and/or sharing materials. From your position at the door you can then greet each child in a welcoming, relaxed fashion, setting the tone for the day. You will also be able to handle minor emergencies that arise as children begin their work.

As the Morning Progresses

At 8:45 an assigned child takes the attendance sheet and lunch count to the office. By now everyone should be busy and involved. Take a brief walking tour to assure yourself that this is so. Observe children as they begin work on the Space Dictionaries to see who might be having problems. Give individual assistance as appropriate, or suggest that two or three children work together if it will help them.

As soon as you feel that everything is under control, quietly request that the first individuals or small groups work with you. During this time you will probably engage in language learning or mathematics, whatever is currently needed as part of any ongoing study. As you finish with each child or group, take another observation tour before beginning with someone else. The few children who must go to other programs should be accustomed to the schedule and will probably remember to leave on time, but keep one eye on the clock just in case. The gifted children should be allowed to work up until the minute they leave and then to clean up their projects during the 15 minutes available after they return. Their arrival back in the classroom, in fact, will be the signal that everyone should start cleaning up. The special education children should use whatever time is necessary to clean up before they leave. They will then be ready for music as soon as they return. On this particular day, part of the cleanup will include placing the finished costumes on their owners' desks.

When the children return from music, they will sit at their own desks ready to perform the play for each other. (Of course, they have already been reading and memorizing it and planning for this day.) The time before lunch is then devoted to each of the (probably three) groups taking their turn at performing the play. If there is sufficient time, the class can dictate, as you write on the chalkboard, an invitation to other classes to view their play. If time runs out, make this activity part of your afternoon schedule in which you have already set aside time to write and send the invitations.

This chopped-up morning is certainly not the best way to carry out an integrated curriculum unit any more than keeping tabs on rigidly scheduled skills attainment is. Nevertheless, this is the kind of morning that often faces primary-grade teachers, and the description is provided to show you that integrated learning is still possible. To make this morning work successfully, you will have had to give the children many opportunities to take charge of their own learning, make their own decisions, and help run the classroom. If that has been accomplished, you should have a minimum of management problems.

The plan for this morning calls for free movement among the centers. There will be other times when you might need to be more demanding of children's schedules, but if all is going well, free choice is to be preferred. And if you are fortunate in not having a schedule as complex as the one just described, make every effort to have a large block of time when children can move among centers and you can work with individuals or small groups.

As you progress through the school year, try to have at all times some umbrella theme for your classroom work. You can create math papers with theme pictures and story problems; provide opportunities for writing stories, poems, and plays; role-play events that have been studied; and so on. Once children have been exposed to two or three themes they will come to expect it. If you introduce a story on a new topic or a science lesson that doesn't fit the most recent classroom experiments, you may hear them say, "Oh, is this what we're going to be studying now?" Children enjoy getting wrapped up in the study of a new topic and they look forward to feeling enthusiastic about what they are learning. Simply providing them with drills to increase their skill levels or reading from basal texts round-robin style will not go far toward creating enthusiasm. Putting skill requirements together with the basals and then expanding on them takes a little extra work, but the increased learning and enjoyment for the children makes the effort more than a little worthwhile.

TO DO

1 Collect samples of primary-grade texts for all areas of the curriculum. (The local school district headquarters will usually lend these to you. Another source is a nearby elementary school.) Work with a partner or with a small group to create a thematic unit that uses the basal texts. Create additional activities to round out your unit, following the steps suggested in this chapter.
2 If you are currently working with children in the primary grades, choose one or two of the activities and try them with children.

BIBLIOGRAPHY

Grade One: Animals Then and Now

Allen, K., Helenthal, J., & McLaughlin, L. (Eds.) (1989) *Science: A big book of language experiences*. Columbus, OH: Merrill.
Arnold, V., & Smith, C. (1987a) *Close to home*. New York: Macmillan.
Arnold, V., & Smith, C. (1987b) *Stepping out*. New York: Macmillan.
Hacket, J., Moyer, R., & Adams, D. (1989) *Merrill science*. Toronto: Merrill.
Recque, B. (1987) *Homes and neighborhoods*. Lexington, MA: Heath.
Rucker, W., Dilley, C., & Lowry, D. (1988) *Heath mathematics*. Lexington, MA: Heath.

Grade Two: Learning About Money

Arnold, V., & Smith, B. (1987) *Bit by bit*. New York: Macmillan.
Recque, B. (1987) *Neighborhoods and communities*. Lexington, MA: Heath.
Rucker, W., Dilley, C., & Lowry, D. (1988) *Heath mathematics*. Lexington, MA: Heath.

Grade Three: A Journey into Space

Alverman, D. (1989) *A soft pillow for an armadillo*. Lexington, MA: Heath.
Recque, B. (1989) *Communities large and small*. Lexington, MA: Heath.

Rucker, W., Dilley, C., & Lowry, D. (1988) *Heath mathematics*. Lexington, MA: Heath.

Shymansky, J., Romance, N., & Yore, L. (1988) *Journeys in science*. River Forest, IL: Laidlaw.

Other

Marion County Basic Skills Listing; Science/Health and Social Studies Sequences. Marion County School Board, Ocala, Florida.